# GREEK MYTHOLOGY FOR EVERYONE

## LEGENDS OF THE GODS AND HEROES

## Donald Richardson

AVENEL BOOKS

NEW YORK

TO VERLA JEAN

Originally published as *Great Zeus and All His Children*

This 1989 edition is published by Avenel Books,
distributed by Crown Publishers, Inc., 225 Park Avenue South,
New York, New York 10003, by arrangement with
Prentice Hall Press, a division of Simon and Schuster, Inc.

Printed and Bound in the United States of America

Library of Congress Cataloging-in-Publication Data

Richardson, Donald (Donald P.)
  Greek mythology for everyone.

  Reprint. Originally published: Great Zeus and all
his children. Englewood Cliffs, N.J. : Prentice-Hall,
c1984.
  Includes index.
  1. Mythology, Greek,   I. Title.
[BL782.R5   1989]   292'.13               88-33353
ISBN 0-517-66561-1

h g f e d c

# Table of Contents

The First Gods   1

Gaia and Ouranos, Creation, Castration of Ouranos, War
of the Titans, Provinces of Authority.

Mount Olympos   13

Births of the Younger Olympians, Theft of Apollo's Cattle,
Prometheus, Ares and Aphrodite, Persephone.

The Ways of the Gods
to Men and Women   31

Deucalion Flood, Phaethon, Callisto, Daphne, Echo and
Narcissos, Adonis, Baucis and Philemon.

Heroic Beginnings   51

Rape of Io, Daughters of Danaos,
Rape of Europa, House of Cadmos.

Bellerophon and Perseus   71

Bellerophon, Pegasos, Danae, Medusa, Andromeda.

## Voyage of the Argo 85

Phrixos and Helle, Jason and Pelias, Women of Lemnos,
Cyzicos, Phineus, Clashing Rocks.

## Jason and Medea 101

Reception at Colchis, Medea,
Jason's Ordeals, Seizure of the Fleece.

## Homeward Bound 115

Murder of Apsyrtos, Circe, Murder of Pelias, Revenge.

## Two Other Argonauts 127

Orpheus and Eurydice, Death of Orpheus, Calydonian Boar
Hunt, Death of Meleagros, Atalanta's Race.

## Theseus 137

Aigeus and Aithra, Labors of Theseus, The Minotaur,
Daidalos and Icaros, Death of Minos, Lapiths and Centaurs,
Phaidra, Theseus in the Underworld.

## The House of Laios 159

Delphic oracle, Oidipous, Teiresias,
Seven against Thebes, Antigone.

## Young Heracles 174

Zeus and Alcmene, Infancy, Daughters of Thespios, Erginos,
Marriage and Madness.

## The Labors and Apotheosis of Heracles 185

Twelve Labors, Deianeira, Nessos,
Apotheosis, Battle of the Giants.

## Prelude to the Trojan War 204

Leda and the Swan, Paris, Marriage of Peleus and Thetis, Judgment of Paris, Abduction of Helen, Assemblage at Aulis.

## The Wrath of Achilleus 218

Falling out, Single Combat, War without Achilleus, Night Raid, Counterattack.

## The Wrath Unleashed 234

Death of Patroclos, New Armor, Rampage, Achilleus and Hector, Priam.

## The Fall of Troy 247

Madness of Ajax, Death of Paris, Trojan Horse, Aftermath.

## The Wanderings of Odysseus 261

Calypso, Lotos-eaters, Polyphemos, Circe, Journey to the Underworld, Sirens, Scylla and Charybdis.

## Home to Ithaca 276

Phaiacians, Beggar's Disguise, Test of the Bow, Battle in the Hall, Penelope.

## After Heroes 291

Hero and Leandros, Eros and Psyche.

## Index 307

# Preface

This is a first book in Greek mythology. Its concern is not so much with the representation of authentic folklore as it is with the lively depiction of characters and actions that have become so much the topics of art and the stuff of allusion and metaphor in our own tradition that an ignorance of them is an ignorance of our language itself. In a prose that retains some of the epic and dramatic flavor of the ancient masters, the stories of classical gods and heroes are coherently and chronologically set forth.

One will encounter in these pages the most famous figures of Greek myth, though by no means all of them. The intent here is to acquaint the reader with a manageable number of gods and heroes with the personality and deeds of each portrayed in sufficient detail so as to make him or her seem like an old acquaintance rather than someone bumped into at a parade. The reader will be spared an avalanche of names and terms that will only distract and confuse.

The myths and legends are, for the most part, set in a context of a fabulous history, starting with primal Chaos and ending a generation or so after the Trojan War. From story to story there is a sense of continuity. Events and characters are not presented as though in isolation from one another but, like the fates of men themselves, are interwoven into a common and continuous tapestry. Mankind is seen as passing from age to age, and, more subtly, so also are the gods.

Those versions of the stories have been chosen which seem to come up most frequently in Western art and literature. In no way do we want to suggest that they are the only versions or even that they are the versions most believed by the Greeks of ancient times. Variation is as much an inherent characteristic of mythology as it is of common gossip; strictly speaking, then, there is no such thing as a *true* version of a myth, only more and less celebrated versions, depending largely on the fancies of writers and artists whose first concerns have usually been art rather than myth.

It should be emphasized that this is not another adaptation of Greek mythology for children. In approach and content it is addressed to the adult reader. It includes stories that were often either omitted from popular myth books of the past or were altered to safeguard the minds of the innocent. No matter how crude the detail, however, it is always couched in language the end of which is to communicate rather than offend.

Eventually the reader will go on to other books on myth or Greek literature and will soon discover that Greek proper names are spelled differently from one translation to the next. Older translations have generally favored traditional Latinized spellings. Those are the ones we are most used to. Modern classicists, however, favor transliterated spellings that more closely approximate the original Greek.

The spellings in this book are a compromise between the two. Lest some names be totally unrecognizable, the traditional Latin consonants are retained; diphthongs and endings are, however, rendered as the modern classicists would have them. Thus, "Hephaestus" becomes "Hephaistos," "Oedipus" "Oidipous," and so on. All the names are close enough to what the reader is probably used to so that he or she should have no trouble knowing who is who. There is one exception to the principle: Because "Aias" might not be recognized as "Ajax," the traditional spelling is retained.

*Great Zeus*, then, is comprehensive though not exhaustive; it includes the most famous stories of Greek mythology but not all their variations. It is designed for the person for whom a simple dictionary of mythology is too uninspiring and lifeless but who feels a need for something nevertheless substantial before plunging into the classics without any preparation at all. It is for the serious student as well as the casual reader.

For their help in the preparation of this manuscript, I wish to thank Linda Deutsch for her multiple typings of it, my sons Todd and Scott and Scott's wife, Shirley, for their helpful and authoritative criticisms, and the University of Evansville Alumni Association for a typing grant.

# The First Gods

In the beginning, as was so often the case, the world was without form and void. There was only a single deity back then, it was so very long ago; her name was Gaia, and she, alas, did not have much form or shape either. This was, of course, long, long before Zeus or Apollo or Poseidon or any of the gods we readily recognize came upon the scene. There was neither night nor day then, neither sea nor sky, nor was there earth in any sense we think of it today—only the primal goddess Gaia brooding over a vast expanse of formlessness called Chaos.

Above all else Gaia longed to be a mother. She yearned to bring forth new life. Never has there been a generative urge so complete and absolutely undeniable as Gaia's while she tossed and turned out there at the threshold of Chaos. It was so overpowering, we are told, that eventually all by herself in her sleep she brought forth Ouranos.

It is as impossible to describe Ouranos as it is to describe Gaia; for although we may speak of them in some of the same terms we use to describe men and the Olympian gods, they really were not on the same order at all.

True, Gaia was the original earth goddess; but she was also, in a somewhat bizarre sense, the earth itself. Her name means Mother Earth. Likewise, Ouranos, whose name means Father Sky, was not only the first sky god, but also the sky itself. And so they should never properly be thought of as mother and son, which is a good thing too, for before long they began to cohabit as shamelessly as rabbits and almost as productively.

Their first three children were monstrosities. They were absolutely gigantic, and each one had fifty heads and a hundred hands. Gaia, all mother, was apparently quite satisfied with them; Ouranos, the prototypical father, hated them from the very beginning and wished them out of the way. However, getting rid of something as immortal as himself was no easy task.

Nonetheless, he did manage to do it and in a manner most crude. One at a time he stuffed all three of the Hundred-handed Ones back up into Gaia's womb. Thoroughly intimidated by Ouranos herself, Gaia offered little resistance. Nor did she try to bring her freakish offspring a second time into the world of light—at least not right away. Her figure had a pronouncedly spherical aspect to it from that time on.

Unabashed, Ouranos routinely returned to Gaia's bed and she, although beginning to despise him, received him. Their second venture into parenthood was at best only a slight improvement over the first. Again they produced three perfectly enormous sons, all with a wild and ferocious look about them. Each one had but two hands; however, in the middle of concentric wrinkles making up each of their foreheads was a single, large, round eye. All three turned out to be extraordinarily strong and skilled craftsmen. They were called the Cyclopes.

Ouranos instinctively hated them too and pondered daily how he might remove them permanently from his sight. He viewed them as competitors. Finally, over the protestations of Gaia, he tied them up and packed them off to Tartaros, the lowest and most remote level of existence. So far down is Tartaros that, if you dropped an anvil, it would take a full nine days for it to get there. Anyone or anything in Tartaros was generally regarded as being a fairly comfortable distance away.

This is not to say that the marriage between Gaia and Ouranos was a complete disaster. It was not. Ouranos from his abode on the mountain tops sent soft, fertile rains down to earth. Earth opened her clefts and crannies and valleys and secret places to take them in. Lakes formed, springs began to gush forth, and streams splashed down the hillsides over the rocks in dancing cascades to the broad seas below. Life-bringing water collected into pools underneath the ground, where also coursed rivers hidden to mortal eyes.

Gaia was in her element. Her eyes flashed hither and yon over the whole world, and everywhere she looked new life burst into being. Trees sprang up along the slopes of Parnassos and in the vales of Arcadia: rangy and wind-blown cypresses, cedars, myrtles, and abundant oaks. A thousand varieties of wild flowers popped up along the banks of the brooks and rivulets; lush, dark undergrowth unrolled across the forests' floors.

Fish, millions upon millions of them, fluttered their fins for the first time and set about to explore the mysteries of the wine-dark seas. The great barrenness was being filled with living things, and everywhere Chaos was giving way to a greatly complex but ordered nature. Shapelessness took on form, and form a primordial beauty.

All was bathed in the rich rays of the sun as it made its maiden journey across the heavens. Birds dotted the skies and filled the new creation with their happy airs; beasts of every size and description began to scamper about the woodlands and tall meadows. When the sun had completed its journey, the earth rested, and then it was that the moon and a million stars filled the hitherto vast empty spaces overhead, lighting the way for those creatures that move by night, the owl and the bat and the crafty weasel.

Meanwhile, deep within her womb Gaia could feel the Hundred-handed Ones groping blindly about, and her thoughts once more turned to Ouranos and his hateful tyranny over her and their imprisoned offspring. The more she thought, the more intense her loathing became. Almost as great as her desire for motherhood was now her desire to strike back, somehow to destroy or bring down her brash and brutal mate. She did not, however, turn the lusty Ouranos from her bed, for she knew all too well she could not do what she had to do alone.

Whether she actually conceived her grim plan before the Titans and Titanesses were born or after these dozen young gods and goddesses had all made their advents into the world of light we have no way of knowing. What we do know is that one by one she took them all into her secret counsel in an attempt to enlist their help and that at first she met with little success.

Now the Titans and their sisters were of monstrous size also, but, because each had the regular features of respectable gods and men, their appearances were far less imposing than those of their confined siblings. Perhaps it was for that reason that Ouranos, who hated them every much as he did the Hundred-handed Ones and the Cyclopes, delayed containment action against them.

Gaia by now had her plan worked out to the smallest detail and but needed the assistance of one of her sons to see it through. "Sons of mine," she addressed them one day when they were beyond Ouranos's hearing, "and sons of a father most evil, let us join in vengeance against him for all his atrocities. Help me in this thing. Did not he himself, after all, set the pattern for outrageous deeds?" The Titans sat in silence, we are told, as their mother outlined her scheme. Fear shot through them.

At length, however, the youngest, Cronos, found courage and said,

"I too loathe this my father most damnable. He did indeed set the pattern for outrageous deeds. And so, mother of mine, I join you in what you propose."

Gaia was jubilant. At no time since the dawn of creation had she felt such lightness of heart, such joyful anticipation as she felt now. Wasting no time, she took her youngest son with her to where she had hidden a jagged flint sickle that she had secretly fashioned for the occasion. She gave the sickle to Cronos and next took him to her own bedchamber, where she posted him in a dark corner not far from the entrance. Then she herself went to the marriage bed and stretched out like a young bride famished for love at day's end.

The sun finished its trek across the heavens and dark night began to descend, and so also did Ouranos. As he moved toward the bedchamber, he could hear Gaia within, stroking the bed beside her and sighing erotically as she did so. His whole anatomy responded. Never was a fond lover so magnificently prepared to serve the needs of his beloved. This was, of course, in the days before either men or gods wore so much as fig leaves in the interests of modesty. Thus when Ouranos bounded into Gaia's bedchamber, his features were clearly outlined in the half-light of dying day.

At that moment Cronos lunged forward out of hiding and seized his father's mastodonic member with his left hand and with his right hand brought down the sickle of jagged teeth in gruesome surgery. As a gardener prunes unwanted branches from his leafy magnolias, close to the trunk, even so did Cronos of the Crooked Counsels cleave from the great Ouranos his privy parts and fling them far, far out into the wine-dark sea.

His power gone, his strength ebbing, Ouranos sank slowly to the floor. As he did so, he leaned toward Cronos and, with a death-like rattle in his throat, whispered a prophetic curse that momentarily froze his son's countenance in icy apprehensiveness: "Exult not, for as you have done to me so also shall your son do to you."

Cronos looked long at the sickle in his right hand, still dripping blood, and then over at his mother. Her doleful eyes confirmed what the strengthless Ouranos had spoken. Suddenly then, as though the future years were already upon him, the wily God of the Crooked Counsels heaved the weapon of jagged teeth frantically far out into the sea also. It quickly disappeared beneath the night-black waves.

The genitals of Ouranos, however, tossed about on the sea's surface like a dying whale lathered in its own secreta. Brackish waters beat against them, churning the spent seed into banks of thick, white foam. Out of the foam rose a goddess of incomparable beauty. Never was a female form so perfectly proportioned; never was there to be. From her trim ankles to her smooth, delicate shoulders there was no part of her that the world's greatest connoisseurs of beauty would want more prominent or less prominent, larger or smaller, or shaped any differently from what it was.

Her face and flowing hair were no less perfect. Her flashing eyes and full lips, parted, moist, and ever so slightly upturned at the corners, suggested an inordinate penchant for frivolity and fleshly pleasures. Yet, even in her nakedness, there was a hint of maidenly innocence about her that would have made her absolutely lovely even to those of her own sex. Hers was the kind of beauty that could provoke fiery passion in ordinary men and, at the same time, inspire in eunuchs and philosophers contemplation of the sublime. Her name, Aphrodite, soon became synonymous with rapturous love.

In time the foam began to break up and dissolve into the sea, revealing a huge half-shell upon which the newborn goddess was standing. The waves propelled the shell and Aphrodite toward the nearby island of Cythera and from thence to seagirt Cypros. Attended by Love and Desire, she strolled about the beach of the island that would soon be most sacred to her and then ventured inland. Where her lovely, tender feet touched ground, immediately luxuriant green grass sprang up and patches of bright-colored flowers.

Back in Gaia's quarters an air of celebration prevailed. The Hundred-handed Ones had once again squeezed out into the world beyond their mother's womb, and the Titans, once the threat of danger had clearly passed, had come from their place of hiding. As grandstand enthusiasts burst onto the playing field the moment their champion drives on to sweet victory, even so the Titans and Titanesses descended upon the chamber where Gaia now gloated in triumph over the fallen Ouranos.

Certain of the Titans, prompted by Gaia, set off to dark Tartaros to free the three Cyclopes. The celebration continued in their absence, but Cronos, now grown sullen and edgy, stayed to himself for the most part, only occasionally exchanging cordialities with his brothers and sisters. Gaia, however, was the only one to notice. Even the return of the delegation from Tartaros with the Cyclopes did not perceptibly change the God of the Crooked Counsels' mood.

The Titans, clearly in charge, made Cronos the lordly king of the immortals and gave to him for his queen Rhea, the most stately and lovely of the Titanesses. The dowager queen offered no objection, nor did the Cyclopes or Hundred-handed Ones.

5

Under Cronos's watchful eye and by his wily judgments the world took on yet more form and splendor. The trees reproduced after their kind, and so also did the fish that swam the clear streams and deep seas and the birds of the air and the animals that roamed the forests and broad meadows. Every living creature reproduced after its kind, with each species becoming more and more refined with each new generation.

The gods too were prolific, Titans pairing with Titanesses and bringing forth also after their kind. Not least was Iapetos, brother to Cronos, who was joined to his slim-ankled niece Clymene. Of their union came stout-hearted Atlas, Menoitios of rare glory, farsighted Prometheus, and Epimetheus of the foolish counsels. In the years ahead Prometheus would prove to be humankind's greatest benefactor, Epimetheus its greatest curse.

It was, in fact, Prometheus who made man in the first place. To some of the gods the world already seemed complete, but not to the farsighted Son of Iapetos. He watched the birds stir the air with their wings and the fish glide almost effortlessly along the shoals of the sea. Something seemed missing. Turning his gaze landward, he studied each species of animal that ran four-footed through the woods and grass. He looked upon the creeping things and crawling things too and even the multitudinous insects that buzzed about. It all fit together, this creation; it was harmonious and good.

Still something was lacking. Of all the creatures, there was none that bore the image of heaven; none seemed marked to be earth's master. And so Prometheus gathered some of the clay that had lately been suspended in heaven's atmosphere and mixed it with earth's own life-giving waters. He labored over the clay, shaping it into the figure of a miniature god.

When satisfied that this part of creation was also good, he gave it life and called it man. All the other animals walked the earth with heads down, looking at the ground; this new creation walked erect, his gaze fixed on the clear blue of the sky. Thus was the race of man fashioned by the farsighted Son of Iapetos.

Man's first age, under Cronos's rule, was called the Golden Age. It was a time when his life was in total accord with the world about, beyond, and within. He trusted his fellow men and was rewarded with their trust in return. No hint of green-eyed envy or foul caprice ever intruded into his rustic paradise. There were no laws then nor stone-faced judges nor sentried walls; neither were there troops to answer the bronzed trumpet's clarion blast with uplifted spears and shields. War was unknown.

The earth herself was virginal, knowing neither spade nor ploughshare. She gave of her abundance freely. Cherries, strawberries, plump grapes, and acorns were easier to pick than from a grocer's shelf and always at the perfect stage of ripeness, though the season was forever spring. Wine and milk and honey dripped from the stately oak.

Order prevailed in Cronos's reign, on earth and in the heavenly regions of the gods. The Titans trusted their wily brother even when his counsels seemed perilous and bizarre. Stout-hearted Atlas, mightiest of the Titans, was foremost among his champions. However, even he looked askance when Cronos ordered that both the Hundred-handed Ones and the Cyclopes be bound over to dark Tartaros and that a guard be stationed there lest some further challenger release them to his own purposes. The order was carried out, though, without murmur.

The Titans also charitably withheld judgment when he swallowed his children, apparently feeling that Cronos was doing no more than exercising a legitimate prerogative and that, after all, what he did with his own offspring was no concern of theirs. His wife Rhea, however, unkindly complained. Five times she had labored, and she had nothing to show for it except for a bulge and an occasional movement in her husband's abdomen.

Hestia had been her firstborn. Cronos had insisted on attending the birth. As soon as she was completely outside her mother's body, the wily Son of Ouranos lifted the infant goddess by her tiny ankles, as might a midwife to slap first air into her lungs; and then, while Rhea looked on in horror and disbelief, he swallowed the child whole. Likewise did he later swallow Demeter and Hera fresh from their mother's womb and then Hades and Poseidon.

Order was the rule of Cronos's regime, but mad frenzy reigned within him. He was still haunted by what his father Ouranos had whispered to him, now centuries past, as he slumped sans genitalia to the floor of Gaia's bedchamber. Though in his heart the God of the Crooked Counsels knew the awful prophecy must come to pass, he desperately tried to avert it.

Rhea, however, was not in the least interested in the reasons why; she knew only that Cronos was gulping down her babies as soon as they were born, and she wanted them back. When her sixth confinement drew near, therefore, she excused herself to the island of Crete, home of the Curetes, mountain nymphs sympathetic to her plight.

Finding refuge in a huge, dark cave on one of the darkest nights of the year, Rhea, attended by Curetes, was delivered of her sixth child, a god. Quietly, quickly she hid the baby in a remote recess of the cave, and

7

then she wrapped a rock in a blanket and held it in her lap. And none too soon, for Cronos presently came charging into the cave wanting to know if the blessed event had occurred yet.

"Yes, my lord," Rhea told him quite loudly, for the Curetes were beating their spears against their shields to drown out the infant's crying. She handed Cronos the carefully wrapped rock. "We have a little god. I think we should call him Zeus."

Cronos took the rock, opened wide his mouth, and swallowed it, blanket and all. Then he bid his wife good health and left. Knowing that she soon must follow, Rhea entrusted the baby Zeus to the faithful Curetes to be nurtured into godhood. And so it was that Zeus escaped the fate of his brothers and sisters before him and, nourished on the milk of the great goat Amalthea, grew to rugged adolescence, his existence unknown to his wretched father.

The seasons rolled by, and then one day Rhea approached the Lord of the Gods, her husband, with a suggestion that he take to himself a cupbearer, a young god perhaps who would pour his nectar and bring him his chalice on command as would befit a god of his station. The by now declining Cronos seized upon the suggestion at once. When Rhea told him of a beautiful youth in Crete who would be perfect for the office, he accepted her counsel on that point as well and sent for the youth forthwith. And thus Zeus became his father's cupbearer.

Conspiring with Rhea and Zeus against the wily Cronos was Oceanos's daughter Metis, wisest of all the Titanesses. She it was who one day prepared a concoction of mustard and salt and instructed Zeus to mix it with Cronos's honeyed nectar. The chiefest of the gods, his taste buds impaired by age and anxiety, drained the cup and demanded more. Zeus cheerfully obliged him.

Having drunk deeply, Cronos sank into a stupor. The mustard and salt then began to take effect. The wily god first twitched, then turned in discomfort, and soon his whole digestive system seemed aflame. Still in stupor, he opened his mouth and belched forth the rock he had swallowed years before. Then in successive belches he vomited up Poseidon, Hades, Hera, Demeter, and then Hestia, all very much alive, though somewhat pale from lack of sunshine. In all those years only the receiving blanket, being neither immortal nor mineral, had been digested.

The sons of Cronos developed rapidly. They did not have the proportions of some of their Titan cousins, but in agility and craft they could better than hold their own. Cronos, thoroughly shaken by the threat they posed, persuaded his own brothers and their sons to make war on them;

but the upstart gods were not to be easily vanquished. For ten years they fought the Titans to a standoff.

Of the new gods Zeus was clearly the master strategist. Earlier he had sought the sage counsel of his mother Rhea and keen-witted Metis; now, after ten years, he went also to the great primal Mother Earth goddess herself, Gaia, to discover whereby he might bring the strife to an end. "Release the prisoners of dark Tartaros," she told him, still somewhat piqued that the wily Cronos had betrayed her first sons to that remote and gloomy quarter, "and thine shall be the victory."

Forthwith then did Zeus fly to those dark, dank regions beyond the dusky Night and came unawares upon the napping Campe, stern jaileress set there by Cronos to guard his awesome brothers; and he slew her and took her keys. He then unlocked the gates that held the Cyclopes and Hundred-handed Ones and loosed the fetters that bound them and brought them, enfeebled and drained by their long imprisonment, back into the world of light.

Ambrosia and nectar were food and drink to the deathless gods; these did wise Zeus place in lavish abundance before his father's awesome brothers, who ate and drank most heartily thereof. Fresh strength entered their limbs, and within their breasts their spirits waxed bold.

"Glorious sons of Gaia and Ouranos," said Zeus to them, when at last they put down their cups, "heed my words. War has raged for, lo, these many years between us and the Titans. Daily have we fought but not prevailed. Join, therefore, your strength to ours, you who have lately come from the dark dungeons below. Remember who bound you there and who broke you free."

The noble Cottos, one of the Hundred-handed Ones, spoke for all his brothers: "Oh king, Son of Cronos, wiser are you than all the gods. When we were beyond hope, you brought us out of our bondage beneath the misty darkness. Therefore, our strength we will join to yours against the trustless Titans." Cheers went up from his brothers as he spoke these words and from the sons of Cronos. Fire gleamed in every eye; the veins stood out in every forehead. Each soul yearned for heated battle and for the sweet victory beyond.

Quickly the Cyclopes fired up their forges and began beating out on their anvils weapons for the stalwart sons of Cronos. Deftly, tirelessly they worked, not breaking from their labors until they had fashioned arms appropriate to each. To Zeus they presented the powerful thunderbolt, to Hades a helmet that makes its wearer invisible to all, and to Poseidon the fear-inspiring trident.

On the day of the great battle Hades, donning his helmet of darkness, stole into the Titans' camp and confiscated their arms. But even then they were not to go down easily. Led by stout-hearted Atlas in aged Cronos's stead, the Titans advanced en masse upon their adversaries. The ground quaked under their feet, and the waves of the sea broke with pounding, resounding rolls of thunder; the heavens groaned, and lofty Mount Olympos was shaken from its foundations. So mighty was the advance of the Titans that the shock could be felt even in blackest Tartaros.

Then did Zeus, primed for battle himself, let drive his first thunderbolt. It flashed through the air and instantly found its target with an ear-piercing crash; shafts of fire leaped forth from where it struck. The Titans froze in place.

On their other flank an earth-shaking, shrieking aboriginal cry split the air. They turned, and there stood wild-eyed Poseidon brandishing his terror-striking trident. Like a fierce, untamed beast about to spring, he shifted ever so slightly from side to side, eyes aflame, face flush, hair disheveled, every muscle taut, biceps bulging, and teeth bared to the gums. His well-honed trident glistened in the sun.

With all the Titans' eyes fixed momentarily on Poseidon, mighty Zeus moved in and hurled a barrage of thunderbolts such as has never before or since been seen. The bolts flew everywhere. Thick flames hit the earth, blistering the soil and turning the vast woodlands into broad, scorching bonfires. Cracking, banging, booming, the bolts filled the firmament with such a deafening din one would have thought heaven itself had come crashing down upon the earth in unspeakable vengeance. Crystal springs and rivers began to boil, and the wine-dark seas also and the great Ocean Stream.

Blinded by the flashing bursts, the Titans recoiled, but quickly found their courage once more and resumed their charge. Directing his thunderbolts now at individuals, Zeus, standing tall amid the flames, felled the bold Menoitios and after him others in the Titan vanguard. Never was Zeus stronger or more stately. Still the Titans came.

At that point from elsewhere on the field the Hundred-handed Ones rushed forward and raised a blustering battle cry. Each had a rock in each of his hundred hands. Massive and brutish were the arms they brought back to take aim; savage the aspects of each one's fifty faces. Virulent hatred was in their eyes. Omnidextrously they let fly their first volley of rocks, in velocity like shafts from crossbows, and with quick movement picked up more. Like machines, not living beings, they fired their missiles with such rapidity that at any moment no fewer than a hundred rocks were whizzing through the air to their marks.

The Titans tried to protect themselves but could not. Stunned, a number of them swooned to the ground; others were literally bowled over by the sheer force of the rocks' impact. Meanwhile, Zeus, moving in on them, continued to pound them relentlessly with thunderbolts. Vainly they arched their arms to ward off the barrage and hastily closed their ranks, still more of them falling, some now partially buried under the rocks.

Then, all at once, the Hundred-handed Ones bolted forward and fell upon them. Battered, half-conscious, without spirit, the Titans offered little resistance as their fierce captors, each using all hundred hands simultaneously with the skill of a master weaver, swiftly bound their arms and legs.

By decree of the victorious sons of Cronos, the Titans, save only three of Iapetos's sons, were condemned to misty Tartaros. Farsighted Prometheus was spared because, loath to oppose the sure dictates of Fate, he had reluctantly turned from his brothers' side and had given wise counsel to mighty Zeus; foolish Epimetheus, judged by the sons of Cronos to be of no threat, had likewise absented himself from the Titan ranks.

Broad-backed, stout-hearted Atlas, who had led the Titans in battle, was spared only for a more arduous fate. Him the sons of Cronos placed where the Great Sea joins the Ocean Stream. There with his powerful head and hands was he made to bear the great sky.

To assure themselves that never again would they have to battle the formidable Titans, the sons of Cronos raised a great bronze fence around the dark regions of Tartaros. Poseidon cast for it impenetrable gates of bronze, and they set there the Hundred-handed Ones as faithful watchers.

And aged Cronos of the Crooked Counsels did Zeus also banish forever to those misty, dank confines beneath the earth. Some of the generations to come would remember Cronos as the trickster that was; others, more charitable, would think of him as the lord of heaven and earth during that golden time when primal man walked the land in goodness and true piety.

Recent generations might have forgotten the wily Son of Ouranos entirely except for one thing: His name is almost the same as "chronos," the word which means "time." By a curious confusion, then, he is featured as Father Time. And so even now, as each year comes to a close, his image can be seen throughout the land, jagged sickle and all, though few will tell their children the purpose to which he put the dreadful scythe.

When once the Titans were safely secured in black Tartaros, lots were cast among the sons of Cronos. The sky, the mountains, and the broad surface of land were appointed the habitation and domain of cloud-gathering Zeus. Poseidon's lot was the wine-dark sea and the life-giving streams; he was given the power also to shake violently both land and sea with mighty earthquakes. To Hades was given as his kingdom the region beneath the ground, richest of all, with the countless dead his subjects and the deep earth and all the gems and precious metals contained therein his treasury.

Their sister Demeter became goddess of barley and all other growing things. At her beck the life-sustaining grains sprouted in the fields and grew, with heads heavy and bent, to golden splendor at harvest. Hestia, kindest and sweetest of all the deities, chose the hearth as her portion. So delicate were her sensitivities that, in time, when she was courted by both Poseidon and Apollo, so anguished was she over being the cause of a conflict that she rejected both their suits and vowed to remain a virgin for her whole immortal life. White-armed Hera, who eventually married aegis-bearing Zeus, became the stern protectress of home and marriage.

The abode of the deathless gods was now high atop Mount Olympos. From there cloud-gathering Zeus could look out over the world and survey the affairs of men; from there also the ever-watchful Hera could look out over the world and survey the affairs of Zeus. Over the years, we are given to understand, there was much for both to observe.

# Mount Olympos

In time Zeus would be called the Father of Gods and Men. This was to be a benevolent and respectful epithet and, as far as we know, had nothing to do with his assorted amorous escapades those first centuries of his reign as deity major. There was ample reason, however, to suppose there might have been some connection.

Upon the Titaness Themis the Lord of Olympos sired the Seasons and the three Fates, and upon Mnemosyne the nine Muses. Eurynome, daughter of Atlas, bore him the Graces; and Demeter lay with him to bring forth the maiden Persephone, who later would be the cause of much sorrow for her mother.

All these affairs white-armed Hera could abide, for they occurred well before she and Zeus were married. His brief romance with the slim-ankled Titaness beauty Leto, however, took place almost on the eve of their wedding. This the Queen of Olympos could not overlook. Adding to her humiliation, during the first months of her marriage Hera had to endure the sight of Leto's body beginning to swell with the fruit of Zeus's passion.

Her power now almost equal to her indignation, the wrathful goddess commanded the great serpent Python to pursue and harass Leto wherever she fled. "No land will give you rest," decreed the Daughter of Cronos, "nor shall you be delivered of the god you carry anywhere the eye of heaven shines."

Nowhere that she fled would for long extend its welcome to poor Leto, for the hissing, menacing Python was never far behind. Not until she came to the island of Ortygia did the Titaness find respite—and that but briefly. There she was delivered of the first of the twins she was carrying, a little goddess whom she called Artemis, but so soon did Hera's

13

avenging serpent drive her from the place that the second twin had no chance to be born.

Off it was then to nearby Delos, where palms and olive trees hid her from the sun as well as from the eyes of Python. And there beside a lagoon she brought forth her son into the world of light and named him Apollo. Artemis, who grew up most rapidly, we are told, assisted in her brother's birth. In the meantime, Python pressed his search for Leto elsewhere.

Apollo also grew up quickly. When he was four days old, he learned of his mother's harassment by the serpent and, properly outraged, set out with silver bow and arrows to bring the slithering menace to justice. Off to Mount Parnassos he hied, where last Python was seen.

Spying the great reptile silhouetted against a high crag, the youthful god unloosed two shafts, both biting deep into the serpentine flesh. Python took quick refuge in the oracular cave of Gaia at Delphi. Brashly then Apollo charged into the sacred haunts to finish off the loathsome serpent with more well-aimed arrows from his silver bow.

Gaia was little pleased with this profanation of her holy precincts; the young God of the Silver Bow soon placated her, however, by instituting the Pythian Games at Delphi. Then so ably did he charm the great Earth Mother, it is said, that she bestowed upon him the gift of sure prophecy and gave him charge over the Delphic oracle. Thereafter the region became sacred to him, and he collected to himself a goodly herd of peerless cattle there.

Early in their marriage Hera presented her lord with three children: Hebe, bearer of her father's cup; Eileithyia, friend to women in sore travail; and Ares, handsome lover of strife. Zeus, nonetheless, preferred his children by slim-ankled Leto over his legitimate heirs. When at the age of three (though already a fully matured, beautiful, blooming goddess) Artemis climbed onto his lap and put her arms about his neck, the chief god could but smile and murmur, "Say what you would have, my child. It shall be so."

"First," she said, "I would like to maintain my virginity. Then I would like an array of names like my brother Apollo, a bow and quiver like his, sixty nymphs as maids of honor, twenty more to carry my hunting clothes and feed my hounds, all the mountains in the world, and one good city to call my own."

"A modest suit," said her father. "It shall be as you say."

So furious was Hera when she learned of this that, to spite Zeus, she parthenogenetically conceived Hephaistos. Now it was her husband's turn to become angry, for when she began to show he knew the child she carried was not his. "Faithless wretch!" he fumed. "Betrayer of my bed, whose is the babe that feeds beneath your heart?"

"My own and only mine," she told him.

"Do not mock me! I will have the truth."

Into a specially designed chair he then forced her, the arms of which folded in so as to make the sitter a prisoner. "On the River Styx swear that you speak the truth," he demanded. "Else the child will be old before you are released from where you sit. Not even you, I know, can swear falsely by the River Styx."

"By the River Styx it is as I have told you," said Hera calmly and smugly.

She was not so smug some months later when the child was born. Never had she seen a baby so ugly, so totally bereft of redeeming feature. He was emaciated and grotesque, and one of his legs was deformed. Hera gagged at the sight of him; then, motherly instincts notwithstanding, she heaved him as far as she could from her sight.

Happily for Hephaistos, immortals do not die easily. He landed far out at sea in enough water to break the fall of broad-backed Atlas himself. All this was observed by Eurynome and Thetis, who lived in the area. They fished him out immediately and took him to their own cave quarters and there nurtured him, unknown to gods or men, for nine years.

In no time at all Hephaistos, full grown, was limping about the cavernous apartments of his foster mothers. He was still far from what anyone would call handsome, nor could one exactly say he compensated for his natural comeliness by sparkling wit or polished social graces. Indeed he was rather dull-witted and socially inept.

He was kindhearted, however, and had unquestionably the most talented pair of hands in the whole world. Never was god or man more gifted in making things intricate or beautiful or ingenious. Daily he stood at his anvil, his huge muscles glistening in the light of the forge, bending, twisting, pounding gold and bronze into a vast variety of exquisitely resplendent and useful shapes. Thus did he fashion for his benefactresses lovely cups and brooches and spiral armlets.

When one afternoon Thetis appeared at an Olympian function, Hera was unable to take her eyes off the delicately wrought, glistening jewelry that graced the lovely sea nymph's arms and throat. "My husband's Cyclopes seem to have a rival in craftsmanship," she finally ventured, with affected casualness.

15

Thetis only smiled, but the Queen of Olympos plied her with questions until she got the whole story about Hephaistos and his rare gift. Suddenly Hera was all mother. She desperately wanted her long lost son back. "Come home to me, my child," she went to him and pled. "A handsome smithy will I have built for you, one with twenty bellows in continuous operation. The beautiful Aphrodite, now the adopted daughter of Zeus, will I arrange to be your bride."

As magnanimous of heart as he was slow of wit, the bandy-legged god quickly complied. Before his advent Mount Olympos had been palatial but plain. Now every room, every patio soon became a show place for the exquisitely styled chairs and tables, chalices, lamp stands, and finely wrought gold and brass curios from the forges and great anvil of the parthenogenetic Son of Hera. For each god he fashioned a magnificent bed, Zeus and Hera's the most magnificent of all.

For himself he designed the world's very first robots. They were made of gold and looked and functioned like serving girls. One would have been hard put to tell them from the real thing. They were programmed both to talk and to reason and could hostess an Olympian nectar party with a grace and efficiency never seen in mortal mansions. Hephaistos would have traded the lot of them, though, for that one living, breathing, warm-blooded creature his mother had promised him for wife.

At about the time Hephaistos returned to Olympos, Zeus started to experience strange twinges inside his head. He said nothing to Hera because he suspected the probable cause. Many years earlier, it seems, he had been married ever so briefly to the Titaness Metis, whose brilliant counsel had been crucial in his triumph over Cronos. Metis had conceived immediately and before long began to show evidence thereof.

When Gaia (who by now had great powers of prophecy) noticed, she congratulated Zeus, but added this warning: "This child shall be a daughter; the next a son, who shall be lord of gods and men, of exceedingly great wisdom and overweening heart."

Zeus, who profoundly feared that he might suffer his father's fate and his father's father's before him, paled at Gaia's words. He soberly took his leave and went back to his chambers to ponder his dilemma.

It did occur to him that he could avert certain disaster by never again making sweet love to Metis. He knew his own weaknesses, however, and elected not to take so great a risk. There had to be a more sure way, and only when it finally occurred to him did his color return and he rest easily.

16

That next evening he dined Metis sumptuously and then suggested they go to his bed to taste once more the delights of paradise. She went most willingly. The bedroom door closed, he made as if to kiss her but opened his mouth incredibly wide and then yet wider and wider until, as unbelievable as it may seem, he took her whole head into his mouth and proceeded to swallow her. Resistance on her part was to no avail.

The physiological details of what happened over the next several years are still vague, but somehow, we are told, Metis's fetus became detached from her system and entered Zeus's system directly. It then began to rise and eventually settled in the great god's head, where it resumed its normal fetal development. The strange twinges Zeus felt now were, of course, caused by Metis's fetus as it began to stretch and genuflect inside his head. His cranium began literally to swell. The kicking, sometimes stabbing pain was almost too much for him.

Retreating to the Triton River, Zeus screamed in great agony as his head finally went into labor. His thunderous cries for help brought the kindhearted Hephaistos to his side, ax in hand. Zeus stooped down and between contractions begged the bandy-legged Son of Hera to split his head open. Hephaistos dutifully brought down his ax and made an incision straight across Zeus's enlarged head. The head immediately opened up, and out leaped a spritely new goddess, full grown and (accounting for some of Zeus's agony) fully armed with crescent helmet, breastplate, shield, and spear.

The new goddess was named Athene, and thereafter she of all the Olympians was most privy to the mind and counsels of the Father of Gods and Men. Her name was synonymous with wisdom; when she spoke, more often than not she was speaking for Zeus himself. To her alone he entrusted his aegis, a panic-inducing goatskin which by now had become the chief symbol of his authority and power. When, later on, men sought to protect their gates from barbarous invaders, it was to this bright-eyed daughter of Zeus they directed their supplications, seldom in vain.

Zeus, now more kindly disposed toward Hephaistos than ever, was ready to negotiate with him for the incomparably beautiful Aphrodite's hand. It was an exorbitant bride-price of cups and jewelry and finely made gold work that Zeus insisted upon; but the lame god, no less a deity of passion than Zeus himself, happily agreed, and so the wedding was arranged.

Now Maia was the lovely-haired and bashful daughter of stouthearted Atlas. She lived in a deep cavern at Mount Cyllene in rustic

Arcadia. In the dead of the night, when sweet sleep had claimed the white-armed Hera, Zeus would steal away to Maia's cave. Their love was hidden to men and the deathless gods, but not for long.

After ten moons had run their course, all was brought into the open, their doings made manifest when Maia gave birth to the infant Hermes, active and precocious from the first day. Born in the morning, at midday he found a large tortoise outside the cave and from its shell invented the celestial-sounding lyre.

At nightfall the son of Zeus's stealth, tired of his toy, slipped out of the cave and ventured forth to the pastures where far-shooting Apollo kept his cattle. He singled out fifty of the best and drove them to a high-ceilinged cave near the meadows of the Alpheios River. Craftily he confused the trail, first by forcing the cattle this way and that over sandy ground and then by making them step briskly backwards; for himself he made sandals of brushwood to make tracks unlike any god or man or beast. He was seen but once, by an ancient man in Boiotia whom he charged to keep silent.

Two of the cows he slaughtered and offered them in sweet-smelling sacrifice to the twelve Olympian gods. He then threw his makeshift sandals into the river and burned the heads and hooves and all other evidence of his theft. The two hides he took with him back to Mount Cyllene and stretched them out over rocks.

As carefully as he had left the cave, the infant god sneaked back into it, just as rosy-fingered Dawn appeared from beyond the mountains. He found his cradle, donned his swaddling clothes and pulled up his blankets around his chin, playing with the fringes of them like a simple-witted babe. With his left hand he reached down to touch the lyre beneath the cradle.

"My, my, aren't we clever," came his mother's voice from across the cave. "In you come brazen as can be. Out you'll go—just wait—dragged by Apollo in shackles. Trouble you're going to be to the gods and men."

"Treat me not as a helpless baby, mother of mine," Hermes told her. "I'll look out for you. Of all the immortal gods we will not be stuck here without sacrifice and without prayers. Oh no, mother of mine. We shall be revered even as Apollo. Mark my word."

At that very moment at the pastures of Pieria, golden-haired Apollo was just discovering the theft of his cattle. With silver bow in hand he quickly set out to find them. From Onchestos to Pylos he searched but without success. In soft ground the tracks went every which way, in places

18

leading the very directions from which the cattle must surely have come. Always puzzling too were the strange, huge imprints of freakish feet, the likes of which he was unable to associate with any god, man, or beast he had ever seen. No one along the way could help him either, that is, until he came upon the ancient man in Boiotia.

"Strange things these eyes have seen," said the old man. "Who knows what? Methinks, though, of late I saw a little boy, an infant no less, chasing some cattle. From side to side he drove them and backwards, so it seemed, with their heads facing him."

The Lord of the Silver Bow perceived immediately that a new son must have been born to Zeus. He asked where the child chased the herd. The ancient pointed toward Arcadia. And so it was that the golden-haired god came soon to the cave at Mount Cyllene, where he found Maia and her babe. Hermes was curled into the fetal position beneath his cradle covers and feigned peaceful sleep.

Pythian Apollo first went to one closet in the cave and then to another and then a third and threw open the doors expecting to find his crooked-horned cattle. The closets contained but the nectar and glad ambrosia all the deathless gods have in store and the usual amounts of gold and silver plus Maia's jeweled and purple gowns. Not so much as a coarse lash from one of the cow's eyes did he find.

"Take me to my cattle, child," at last he demanded, standing over Hermes' cradle, "or you'll be doing your thieving in murky Tartaros here-after."

Baby Hermes blinked his eyes and knit his brow as if in disbelief. "How gruff you sound," he finally said. "You're looking for your cattle here? I don't understand. Do I look like a hardened cattle thief? I was born but yesterday. Tender are my tiny feet and rough the earth out yonder. Have your cattle. All I want are clean diapers and warm baths and my dear mother's breast. I'm sorry, but I know nothing of your livestock."

Golden-haired Apollo could not contain his laughter. "Spoken like a true rogue. From now on nothing is going to be safe. The king of thieves has been born. Up with you. Lead me to my cattle."

"I know not of your cattle. I swear before Zeus, our father."

"Which is exactly where you and I are going," said Apollo, who forced the infant from his cradle and speedily escorted him to the knees of aegis-bearing Zeus atop Mount Olympos.

"Quite a prize you have there," the Father of Men and Gods chided the Son of Leto. "Newborn I see, and you dragged him all the way here by yourself."

"He stole my cattle. It was a theft so slick only a god could have done it. He was seen though. I have an eyewitness."

"Let me tell you the truth, my father," said Hermes, holding one of his swaddling bands against his cheek. "I know not of what he speaks. He came to our cave threatening me with Tartaros, but no witnesses did he bring. I was only born yesterday. Do I look like a thief?"

The great Cloud-gatherer laughed till Olympos itself began to shake, so amused was he with the performance and craft of his youngest son. He was joined by the other gods, even by far-shooting Apollo, who marvelled at the newborn babe's sheepishly innocent eyes. When the laughter subsided, Zeus commanded Hermes to show his brother forthwith where he had hidden the cattle.

And so first back to Mount Cyllene, the light-fingered god led the Lord of the Silver Bow. There he took from beneath his cradle the tortoise-shell lyre and began to play music wondrously sweet as he showed golden-haired Apollo the two cowhides he had stretched over the rocks. The older god was more astonished than angry. "Newborn, and you slaughter two cattle," he said. "To what purpose?"

"To offer as sweet-smelling sacrifices to the twelve great gods of Mount Olympos," Hermes told him.

"Twelve?" said Apollo. "Our father Zeus most certainly and white-armed Hera, the earth-shaker Poseidon, Hestia, Demeter, my sister Artemis and I, Ares, gray-eyed Athene, and, oh yes, bandy-legged Hephaistos and laughter-loving Aphrodite. But that's only eleven. Who, pray tell, is the twelfth?"

Glorious Hermes bowed deeply. "Yours truly," he said.

Apollo shook his head in amazement, charmed in part by his new brother's cheekiness and in part by the seven-stringed instrument he was strumming. Then the infant god began to sing. In clear, melodious tones he sang of the love affair between his mother and father and of his own begetting. Apollo laughed and then joined him in song as they made their way to the cave by the River Apheios.

Hermes went into the cave and began to drive the crooked-horned cattle into the light. Apollo's eyes, however, were fixed upon the tortoise lyre his brother held under his arm. "You clever rogue," he said, "music from that is worth fifty cattle and more."

Hermes handed him the lyre. "A gift from me, dear brother. Play well."

"Still I fear you, Son of Maia," said the golden-haired god. "One of these days I might turn my back and then find both my lyre and bow missing."

Grieved, Hermes pledged by the River Styx never to steal from his brother or go near his dwellings. In return Apollo vowed that never would man or god be dearer to him than the Son of Maia. On Mount Olympos Zeus laughed with delight. He made the precocious Hermes lord of flocks and herds; and when he grew up, which he did with astonishing speed, the Father of Gods and Men gave him winged golden sandals and installed him as his personal messenger.

With his Olympian pantheon temporarily complete, great Zeus could now turn his attention to the problem of Prometheus. The Son of Iapetos was blessed with greater foresight than any other god; at the same time he seemed to favor the race of men over the undying gods.

For both these reasons the Lord of Olympos had always secretly feared him. The brash Titan's most recent actions, however, now made some dramatic response on Zeus's part imperative.

Men of the Golden Age, who had flourished under Cronos, had long since disappeared from the earth; in their place had come another race of men, less perfect though still not bad. These had been of the Age of Silver. In time a third race of men had been born. It was these that farsighted Prometheus had taken most to heart. He had taught them astronomy and the art of writing, then how to train animals to share their toils and then how to make tools from bronze. He had also taught them carpentry and after that the skills of navigation so they could sail the wine-dark seas.

When the question of sacrifices had arisen, it had been to Prometheus that these men of the Bronze Age had turned. "Which portion of the sacrificial animals should be burnt to the gods," they had wanted to know, "and which should be eaten by men?"

"Let the gods choose," the farsighted Titan had told them. "Bring me an ox."

They brought him the ox, which he killed and flayed. Skillfully he made of the hide two large sacks. Into one he placed the sirloins and the rounds and all the other meaty parts, and into the other he put the bones and entrails and all such parts as are unappetizing to men and gods. Atop the former he set the stomach of the animal; atop the latter he placed a layer of shining fat.

He then called for the great Cloud-gatherer himself and bid him choose which portion would thereafter be the gods' and which would belong to men. Zeus, looking first to the sack topped with the fat and then to that topped with the indecorous paunch, chose the former, declaring that to be forever the gods' portion and the other men's. When he dumped the intestines and meatless bones from his sack, he glowered in anger at Prometheus. "Eat flesh, if you will," he declared, "but eat it raw!"

Thus aegis-bearing Zeus decreed that mankind should be denied the gift of fire. The Son of Iapetos, however, had not exhausted his ingenuity. Craftily he gained entrance to Mount Olympos and lighted a torch at the fiery chariot of Helios, embers of which he dropped into a large, hollow fennel stalk. So it was he stole fire and brought it to his beloved man after all.

Zeus now fumed as he pondered the farsighted Titan's caprice. To bandy-legged Hephaistos he called out angry commands: "To the craggy cliffs of Caucasos take this defier of my decrees, and there bind him with chains and shackles unbreakable."

Sadly and most reluctantly Hephaistos obeyed. He took the Son of Iapetos to a ledge overlooking the Euxine Sea (later called by men the Black Sea) and fastened tight manacles around his wrists and ankles and a bronze strap across his ribs. Through the eyelets of the strap and manacles chains were run, which in turn were anchored to the rocks. Then Zeus sent a long-winged eagle to devour Prometheus's liver; each day the eagle gorged himself, and each night the liver grew back into place.

The Father of Gods and Men would doubtlessly have rid himself of this champion of men for good were it not for one thing: Prometheus, it was rumored, knew the mystery of his undoing. In vain Zeus dispatched wing-sandaled Hermes to threaten and cajole his one-time counselor; the wise Son of Iapetos defied him most magnificently.

Devious indeed was the evil then hatched by Zeus against men for being Prometheus's accomplices. He had the Lame One mold of clay a svelte, curvacious figure, not too tall, pleasingly proportioned, slender at the waist but full elsewhere, with trim ankles and smooth neck and long, flowing tresses. The face, with the bloom of innocence about it, was delicately shaped with classic nose, sparkling eyes, white skin with a trace of blush, and full, coral-colored lips.

Pallas Athene draped the figure with specially embroidered raiment of finest gossamer; frills and lovely laces and exquisitely ornate needlework decorated the raiment all around. Over this, though by no means covering it in all places, the bright-eyed goddess placed a shining, glittering gown, wondrous to look upon, and then on the figure's head a cunningly fashioned veil. With flowers and garlands she trimmed her hair and her clothes. Then the glorious lame god set a delicate golden diadem on her head. When he stepped back, all the gods and goddesses cheered, Zeus not the least.

Then the four winds blew into the lovely creation the breath of life; her lips parted in a smile and her eyelashes fluttered. Aphrodite, at her father's command, bestowed on the maidenly form an insatiable passion. The wily Hermes put into her breast all manner of lies and cunning words and deceit; it was he also who gave her the gift of endless speech. All this the gods did to punish man for receiving fire from the Son of Iapetos.

They called the maiden Pandora, "gift from us all," and sent Hermes, herald of the deathless gods, to deliver her to Epimetheus, who now in his brother's stead championed the cause of man. From Pandora was to come the race of woman-kind created by Zeus to be the bane of mortal men, warm companions in prosperity but, luxury-loving, no helpmates when hard times come knocking at the door, an evil thing surely.

Epimetheus, remembering his brother's warning never to accept a gift from the Olympians, sent her back, but then he relented and accepted her and soon afterwards learned the meaning of sorrow. With Pandora the gods sent a box, but Epimetheus had been warned by his brother of that also and forbade her to open it. He could not watch her always, however, and one day she found herself with the box alone.

Possessed by an irresistible curiosity, she slowly lifted the great lid, peering, as she did so, under it into the strange box for her first glimpse of its lavish treasures. Suddenly out flew Old Age, followed quickly by Dread Disease, Madness, Bestiality, Drudgery, License, and a thousand other plagues that ever since have plagued mankind.

She slammed the lid shut, but alas too late. Had not Prometheus in his great foresight also placed Blind Hope in the box, the evils released by Pandora would have driven man quite to the brink of despair. Because he cannot see into the future, however, man can still believe all things, endure all things.

Of all the goddesses of Olympos only Aphrodite did no work. She was good for one thing and for one thing only: love. And for that she was very, very good. Hers was the magic girdle that could inspire uncontrollable passion in the most solid and respectable. Zeus was ever at its mercy. It could provoke, some claim, lustful fantasies in even the mutilated Ouranos himself. There was no need for the girdle, however, when she wished to be the object of passion herself. No goddess was more enchantingly lovely, more perfectly made.

Her marriage to the smith-god Hephaistos took place in heaven, but grave doubts soon arose as to whether it was made there; for before long she made war-loving Ares her lover. Afternoons when Hephaistos labored over his forge, Aphrodite would furtively unlatch their doors to the brazen Son of Zeus and Hera, and arm in arm they would repair to Hephaistos's palatial bedroom and to the wondrously wrought four-poster he had fashioned with his own hands. There they would sport themselves in sensual diversions unknown to husband, reserved for lover alone.

The afternoon trysts did not, however, go unobserved. Helios, God of the Sun, looked down from high above Mount Olympos at the shameless comings and goings; and when unable to contain his indignation for Hephaistos's sake any longer, he went to the Smith God and revealed all.

Angry, spirits crushed, Hephaistos shuffled back to his smithy and set his great anvil on the anvil block. Nor did he leave the anvil until he had hammered chains unbreakable and finely wrought and had joined the chains together into a most subtle mesh. Still bristling with anger, he went to his own bedroom and spread the mesh over the posts of his magnificent bed just under the canopy. It hung there, like a thinly spun spider's web, invisible to the naked eye.

Then to the shapely Aphrodite he went. "I must betake myself to Lemnos, of all islands to me most precious," he told her. "Can you manage a few days without me?"

Sweetly she bid him good-bye, and off he hobbled as if to his beloved island. Ares, keeping careful watch, saw him leave and, ravenous for his beauteous paramour, made haste to the lame god's familiar doorsteps. The door was already wide open. The lovers fell into each other's arms. Without delay the war-loving swaggert took the love goddess's soft hand in his own and led her to the bedroom.

Laughingly she went, shedding her clothes en route, and he likewise. When, moments later, they threw themselves onto the broad bed to sate their passions, both were as naked as the day they were born. So absorbed were they in their love play that neither noticed when the fine mesh dropped into place above them and on all four sides. Soon they heard Hephaistos's telltale shuffle on the steps outside.

Throwing wide the bedroom doors, the simple Smith God roared in his anger. Neither Ares nor Aphrodite could move from the bed; prisoners they were in a showcase cell. Hephaistos went to the balcony and, in loud

24

voice both pained and triumphant, called out to Zeus and the other gods to witness his wife's disgrace.

"Come in here, all of you, and see how clever she is now," he shouted. "She dishonored me because I was lame and chose Ares. He's handsome and well built, and I'm a cripple. Well, come in and see what this cripple has done. They're in bed together, and they'll not be moving for a long time, no, not till her father has returned every last thing I gave him for his slut of a daughter."

Out of modesty the goddesses all declined the lame god's invitation, but earth-shaking Poseidon came with quickened pace and so also did Hermes, bringer of luck, and the glorious Apollo. As they stood in the doorway, the two younger gods broke forth with inextinguishable laughter. "I thought Ares was the fastest god on Olympos," said Hermes. "He must not be. A cripple caught up with him."

"Oh, to be in bed with her! Who would worry about the chains," the Far-shooter remarked, pressing his face against the transparent mesh to get a better look.

"If I had a chance at her," Hermes replied, "there could be three times as many chains. I wouldn't notice. And the galleries could be filled with all the gods and goddesses looking on."

The two smacked their lips and let loose another round of laughter. All this time Poseidon, whose eyes had not left the shapely Aphrodite since the moment he entered the room, bore a serious aspect. He did not mask his irritation over the lightheartedness of the other gods. "This is truly outrageous," he said to Hephaistos. "Let him go. He'll pay you for this. I'll see to it myself."

"No," said the Smith God, "From a villain I expect only more villainy. If I free him, what surety do I have? He'll leave his debts behind with his chains."

"If he does that, I'll take his place," promised Poseidon, his eyes still fixed on the lovely goddess.

Hephaistos pondered the proposition while Apollo and Hermes doubled up with new laughter. At length, however, the lame smith relented and loosed the mesh from his violated marriage bed and its prisoners. Off fled Ares immediately to Thrace, one of the few places he was welcome.

Laughter-loving Aphrodite betook herself to Cypros, her favorite island, where the Graces bathed her in her virginity-restoring bath and rubbed oil of ambrosia into her unflawed skin. When she returned to her husband, she radiated the innocence and sweetness of an untouched bride.

Zeus did not return the dowry, nor did war-loving Ares or the earthshaker Poseidon come up with so much as a bronze ring in compensation for Hephaistos's humiliation. Aphrodite simply charmed her way back again into her husband's good graces, no great feat for her; and then, when all was returned to normal, again she played him false and again and again and again.

Hades also was in love. The lovely, trim-ankled maiden Persephone, fruit of Zeus's love for Demeter, had quite turned the dark God of the Underworld's head. He tried to abide his passion in silence at first, then no more. Secretly stealing off to his brother Zeus, he asked for the young goddess's hand.

Although he saw only benefits for his daughter in such a union, the Aegisbearer knew well that golden-tressed Demeter would see only calamity. A bedroom without windows in a world without light was not what mothers dreamed of for their daughters. Also knowing his sister's power over things that grew, Zeus could but respond somewhat cryptically, winking as he spoke, "What you ask I cannot give; neither do I forbid it."

Hades returned jubilantly to his kingdom beneath the earth, confident of Zeus's tacit blessing to court the fair Persephone after the manner of his own ingenuity. When, shortly afterward, it was reported that the fair maiden and her maidenly compeers were in the meadows near Eleusis picking wild flowers, the dread God of the Underworld ordered his chariot to be made ready.

The meadows of Eleusis were broad, broken up by many a grove and hillock, and flowers adorned the landscape everywhere. Persephone skipped about from one patch to the next, first picking long-stemmed irises for her basket, then ruby-tinted roses and lilies and lovely crocuses. Near a wooded glen she spied a bank of dainty violets and airily tripped off in that direction. Already out of sight of her companions, she now moved beyond their hearing as well.

Singing merrily to herself, she knelt to pick the delicate little flowers, careful to break off leaves with them but not too many, and tucked them with care into the hollow between her breasts, her basket already too full. A sudden noise only paces away brought her to her feet. In the direction of the noise the earth had split, and out of the dark seam a chariot was speeding toward her, its driver invisible.

In a moment dread Hades had the terrified maiden in his arms. His hands tore at her clothing; the little violets fell to the ground. Then onto the soft earth, cushioned by thatch, amid the multicolored blooms of the glen, the grim god feared by all men forced the maiden Persephone under him. When they arose, she was a maiden no longer. He carried her, sobbing quietly, offering no resistance, to his chariot and drove back into the world below. The seam closed after them.

When her daughter did not come home, Demeter began to fear for her well being. She inquired of Artemis and Persephone's other friends; but, no, they had not seen her since she strayed from them while picking flowers. Surely she had met someone and must be with her.

The following day, when there was still no word from Persephone, the goddess with tresses the color of ripe grain went forth in agonized search. For nine days and nine nights she wandered throughout the world, too heavy of heart either to eat or drink, calling out for her lost daughter. On the tenth day she went to Helios, great God of the Sun, who sees all.

"If I have any sway with you," she addressed the Light-bringer, "tell me, please, one thing. What do you know of my daughter, the flower of beauty itself? You see all. Did you see her?"

"You, dear goddess, who uses my light to make things grow, do have sway with me," said Helios. "And I pity you for your slim-ankled daughter's sake. She is now mistress of the Underworld, bride of its master, gift from his brother, her father. He took her by force. Grieve not, dear goddess, for the bridegroom is your brother too and rules a third of the world."

Demeter found no consolation in the Sun God's words. She left his palace more anguished than ever. Eschewing the company of gods, by whom she felt betrayed, in disguise she betook herself to the cities of men. So wasted was she that as she approached Eleusis, where last her daughter was seen, she appeared to passers-by as an old woman, her best years far behind her, good now for nothing except maybe as a nurse.

When she stopped at a well under a broad-branched olive tree just outside the city, four girls there, in fact, asked if she would be interested in being nurse to their baby brother. They were, they explained, from the household of Celeus, king of the region. Partly out of maternal curiosity and partly because she still hoped for fresh information about Persephone, Demeter went with them to Celeus's home.

Metaneira, Celeus's good wife, was the soul of hospitality. She offered the disguised goddess her best chair and sent a girl for their finest wine. Her daughter clowned to make the guest smile and then laugh. When the wine arrived, Demeter declined, saying she was not permitted to drink red wine but wondered if perchance they might have a pitcher of good barley water handy. She was quite thirsty.

A large pitcher of barley water was brought in, spiced with tender leaves of mint. Metaneira poured her a cup. Not having drunk anything in almost two weeks, though, Demeter lifted the pitcher to her lips and did not set it down until she had drained every drop. It made the girls giggle to see such a thirst.

Demeter took to the baby Demophoon, a robust little boy, almost as soon as he was placed in her arms. She stroked him gently with her deathless hands; and when he looked up with eyes sparkling, her mother heart was overjoyed. In becoming the child's nurse, she purposed a great boon to the family by making the boy immortal.

Each day into the baby's creases and folds she rubbed oil of ambrosia and softly breathed upon him her own immortal breath. At night, when sleep held the family in her spell, Demeter would place Demophoon in among the still hot coals of the fireplace to burn away his mortal parts. The family marveled at the baby's progress. Within a week he seemed to have doubled in size and strength and, if they could believe their ears, had spoken his first words. Were it not for Metaneira's suspicious curiosity, the child would no doubt have achieved deathlessness by the end of the month.

One night, though, the mistress of the house thought she heard some small commotion in the kitchen and ventured from her bed to check on it. Without making a sound, she opened the kitchen door but a crack and peered into the room. There in the middle of the fireplace, covered by a bright pink blanket of glowing embers, was little Demophoon, his head barely visible. The nurse was turning him as a cook might turn a suckling pig.

The mother, easily given to hysteria, completely misread the scene and bolted, screaming at the top of her lungs, toward the hearth. Demeter, both surprised and piqued by the clamorous intrusion, turned from her enterprise. She stood tall before the raging Metaneira and, suddenly deciding to end the charade, allowed her divinity to shine forth.

Good King Celeus, roused by the uproar, was now at his wife's side. They stood with gaping mouths as the bent hag was transformed before their eyes into a dazzling goddess with hair the color of ripe grain; the transformation accomplished, they prostrated themselves in awe before her. In the fireplace the unattended Demophoon burned to a crisp.

Not without heart, Demeter compensated the family for the Demophoon disaster by installing the oldest son, Triptolemos, as the first high priest of her mysteries at Eleusis. To him she also gave seed corn and the wooden plough and sent him forth to teach to others the arts of agriculture. Triptolemos, in turn, told the goddess of a strange happening reported to him by his shepherds not a month before. There was a great cleft in the earth near where they watched their flocks, and it seemed a faceless charioteer drove into it with a limp maiden propped against his chariot rail.

A renewed disgust filled the great Grain Goddess as she pondered afresh the duplicity of Zeus, without whose consent the dark God of the Underworld could not have carried out his evil enterprise. "Does he not know that it is I who give life to the barley in the fields? The green shoots, the sap-plump stems are my handiwork. He has grown fond of the race of man, their prayers and sweetly scented sacrifices. Does he not know their life depends upon me?" she indignantly mused. Then it was she determined to withdraw her life-giving magic, enervated already because of her sorrow, and let offended nature take its course.

All over the world the stunted, pale green plants shriveled and died; newly planted seed lay encased in the hard sterile soil like so many little coffins in clay crypts, unable to burst into the light of day. Everywhere the green earth became brown, and once-living things crumbled into the dust from whence they came. Man was, of course, threatened with extinction along with everything else; from all quarters anguished cries went up to Zeus, refuge of suppliants.

Through twelve new moons the earth groaned and living things died. Then it was that the Father of Gods and Men sent for the irate, doleful goddess with hair the color of ripe grain. In their confrontation Demeter spoke first. "She's your child too," she told him. "Show then some decency as a father. Is it fitting that a daughter of yours should be married to a thief and a rapist? Return her to me, and I will forgive all."

"She is the bride of your own brother and mine," he answered. "Hardly a disgrace. No harm has befallen her. Nonetheless, if you so choose, you may have her back—that is, if she has not tasted the food of Hades. If she has, there is nothing anyone can do."

And so, at the golden-tressed goddess's request, aegis-bearing Zeus sent wing-sandaled Hermes forthwith to the dark kingdom beneath the earth. "Release the maiden Persephone," he told the grim, rich Lord of the Dead. "So commands the Father of All. Send her back that her mother might forego her frightful assault against the race of men."

Hades reluctantly hitched his undying steeds to his chariot; and, giving his bride of a year a pomegranate seed to eat, he placed her, eyes at long last aglow with hope, into the vehicle and bid her farewell. Thus was she delivered to the loving arms of her mother. Glad reunion accomplished, Demeter of the ripe grain hair asked anxiously if her daughter had tasted the food of Hades' table.

"Nothing did I eat, dear mother," trim-ankled Persephone assured her, "nothing save a single pomegranate seed." Demeter's heart sank. Forever now would her daughter live in a world devoid of light; forever would the mother's eyes be swollen with tears of sorrow, forever her office neglected.

However, the Father of Gods and Men decreed that his dark brother's bride would be required to spend but four months out of every twelve with her husband in the shady region below. The other eight months would be spent in the world of light with her mother. And so it is even to this day that for two-thirds of each year the goddess with golden tresses is happy and light of heart, and the great green earth reflects her cheery disposition. For one third of the year she bemoans her beloved daughter's absence; then it is that the earth too dons the drab clothes of mourning and refuses to yield its fruit.

# The Ways of the Gods
# to Men and Women

W|ithout Prometheus, Bronze man lost all vision of his own destiny; he was without direction. The influence of blood-stained Ares could be seen everywhere. Men of this age had massive shoulders and huge, heavy arms; they ate flesh with their bread and turned their bronze tools into swords and spears and shields. Each other's blood they shed in endless wars, nor did they give the gods their due.

Then it was that Zeus, thinly disguised, journeyed the earth to test the sorry race of man. Into wooded Arcadia he ventured, into the realm of the tyrant Lycaon. The sheepherders and simple peasants of this rugged Grecian land, not insensitive to the aura cast by the aegis-bearing god, prostrated themselves before him and offered up their fearful prayers. Lycaon and his fifty sons jeered at the worshippers and worshipped alike.

"We'll see who's a god," the impious tyrant snarled, escorting the great Aegis-bearer into his courtyard. A wave of whispers rose from the peasants as they watched the two pass through the gates and then the gates close behind them. Strangers who accepted Lycaon's hospitality were seldom seen in the morning.

Lycaon purposed to make his guest's eyes heavy with food and strong drink and then, in the dead of night, when he was unconscious to the world and without defense, to test his deathlessness with a broad-bladed axe. Nor was it an ordinary table the scornful tyrant prepared. A hostage he ordered brought up from his dungeon; with his own hands he slit the pathetic creature's throat and drew a knife across his abdomen. The warm and dripping viscera were placed in a pot to boil and, seasoned with mint, were served up to Zeus.

The Father of Gods and Men leaped to his feet. He threw the table high into the air, splattering the walls and ceiling with the umble soup. Withdrawing from the house, he hurled a thunderbolt that reduced building and grounds to smoldering cinders. The tyrant ran from field to woods for cover, but he could not escape the sure eyes of Zeus. His cries of terror suddenly became hideous howls; his coat became mangy hair, and his arms and legs like those of a wolf. Beast he was; beast he became.

Zeus's patience quickly became exhausted. From the vantage once more of Mount Olympos he carefully observed the sons of Lycaon and found them more vile, more given to blood-lust than their father; and men elsewhere were, with few exceptions, the same. It was as though the blood of monsters had somehow become mixed with the clay from which this Bronze Race was made. No wayfarer was safe; no child either, even in the house of his father. "Violent their ways. Violent shall be their end," at last pronounced the great Cloud-gatherer. "We would have healed them, if heal we could. Now it is best to cut off this foul, infected part that something of the world might be redeemed." Even as he spoke, he collected clouds from the remotest parts of the sky and set them in great black banks above the earth. So dense were they that, if men had repented of their evils and built huge fires for sacrifice, the gods on Mount Olympos would not have seen so much as a glimmer. Then, of a sudden, Zeus hurled a thunderbolt into the black mass. An ear-splitting crash resounded through all the world; lightning pierced the clouds like a thousand dazzling darts, and the rains began. Day and night the downpour continued, relentlessly, without break, always heavier, never lighter. Ripe barley was beaten to the ground; then, as the waters rose, making swamps of grain fields, it disappeared completely. A season's hard labor was lost and more.

Fountains of water from the earth burst forth as well, and great waves were driven landward from the wine-dark seas. Torrents raced down the mountainsides where rivers had never been; the broad plains were turned into veritable oceans, the valleys their estuaries. Only the tops of trees could now be seen in what days ago had been lush orchards. Mean hovels and plush mansions alike were swept away by the raging waters. Except for a few mountain peaks, all things vanished beneath the flood, and before long they too disappeared.

To the north of Arcadia, across the Gulf of Corinth, in many-flowered Phocis on the slopes of Mount Parnassos a man and his wife lived who, unlike their neighbors, were by all accounts the best of people, god-fearing and without guile. He was the son of Prometheus and she the daughter of Epimetheus, begotten on Pandora. Both were well lessoned in civility. His name was Deucalion, hers Pyrrha.

Before he was thrust into chains, Prometheus had told his son of the great deluge that was to come and bid him build a stout ark against that day and stock it with fruit and dried meats and other such provisions as he and Pyrrha might have need. Deucalion did as his father told him.

And so, when the black rain clouds first appeared, making all the earth dark as midnight, Deucalion and his good wife Pyrrha had no fear. Moments after the downpour began, even before the streams overflowed their banks, both of them were safe in the ark, the door tightly latched. By nightfall they could feel themselves afloat.

For nine days and nights they tossed on the turbulent, flotsam-littered, carrion-strewn waters with not the least hint of land anywhere in sight. On the tenth day the clouds became soft and wispy and then were swept from the sky entirely by a gentle north wind. The wind gradually picked up, driving across the face of the deep, whipping the water into a spray and carrying it off to the distant south. By afternoon the tip of Parnassos broke the surface, and by evening the upper slopes could be seen.

The waters subsided almost as fast as they rose. Cliffs and ravines became once more defined, and then hillsides, river banks, and the shore-lines of lakes. Trees were draped with debris and seaweed, their foliage yellowed and splotched with mud; fields and meadows, still drenched, looked and smelled like stagnant marshlands. Here and there could be seen the wreckage of human habitations. It was a world resurrected from the grave. From the door of their ark Deucalion and Pyrrha looked upon it and wept.

"Most precious wife," said the husband, "of all mankind only we are left. Why did not the gods destroy us too?"

The prospect of a world without people saddened and frightened them both. Deucalion still nursed his father Prometheus's vision of man, a vision that over the years Pyrrha had come to share: man the paragon of mortal creatures, capable of great thoughts and noble actions, beautiful himself and beautifier of all he touched. The death of man to these last two people on earth was the death of what man could have been as well as what he had become.

The two quickly built a crude altar and offered to aegis-bearing Zeus a sacrifice for their deliverance. With the sacrifice they offered up a prayer: "Hear us, oh gods. Be merciful, we pray, to mankind whom in your anger you have destroyed. Is there yet salvation?"

From Mount Olympos the great Aegis-bearer sent wing-sandaled Hermes to their side. So swift was the herald of the gods that by the time the couple had finished their prayer he was standing there with them. "Walk away from here," he told them, "and with heads covered, stripped to the waist, over your shoulders cast your mother's bones." The god then vanished as quickly as he had come.

Deucalion and Pyrrha found his words strange. It was a god who spoke most certainly, but could he possibly have said what they thought they heard? Pyrrha broke into tears. "Profane my mother's bones? Surely the gods mock us."

"Trust the gods," her husband charged her. "What they loathe they will not command."

"Cast our mother's bones?" said Pyrrha. "How can it be?"

Deucalion turned the matter in his mind a moment, then spoke, "Is not the Earth our mother? Yes, and are not the rocks her bones? Surely that must be it."

Broken in spirit, amenable to anything at all that might offer the faintest hope, Pyrrha took her husband's hand and walked to where the floods had left a ridge of mud-spattered rocks in what had once been a roadway. There they stripped to the waist and covered their heads, then bent down and picked up rocks, one each, and cast them over their shoulders.

Afraid to look but more afraid not to, they turned enough to see a most astonishing thing transpire. The rocks multiplied in size and, before their eyes, turned into statues of human beings. Wet mud changed, it seemed, to flesh as it spread over either form. Veins appeared and taut sinews under copper skin. The wind suddenly blew a mighty gust, and the two figures, one the likeness of a man and the other a girl, became living souls.

Their spirits now soaring, Deucalion and Pyrrha quickly bent to pick up more rocks. From each rock they cast over their shoulders the deathless gods created a new human being. Those cast by Deucalion became men, those by Pyrrha girls.

The world was quickly restored. Flowers began blooming again, and the trees once more were clothed in their many shades of green. Everywhere animal life was reborn. Swamps again teemed with creatures that wobbled, crawled, slithered, and glided through their thick glades; foxes, hedgehogs, deer, black bears, wild pigs, and hares by the hundreds skipped and lumbered across the forest floors. Birds swooped and darted high in the blue sky above. And through Deucalion and Pyrrha the gods brought forth on Earth a new race of men, a Second Bronze Race, to be that part of creation closest to themselves.

However, it must be remembered, this was all in the early days before the gods became as aloof and sophisticated as they are now. Doing things right took practice even for Olympian deities; and so, before the first truly stellar figures of the Second Bronze Age emerged on the scene, a number of bizarre and often disastrous episodes took place. Only a few need be mentioned.

One incident involved Helios, who, though busy each day driving his great chariot across the sky and thoroughly exhausted each night, managed to impregnate a maiden who lived in what is now Egypt. The girl soon married an understanding prince, however, who raised her son as his own; and all would have gone well had she not one day told the boy, whose name was Phaethon, that his true father was the God of the Sun. Phaethon went forth to tell his friends.

"If she'd said he was a Nile crocodile, you'd have believed that too," one companion told him.

"Don't worry. All mothers have fantasies," said another.

Phaethon could think of no convincing proof to offer his skeptics. Silent, he endured the gibes, burning within, his face becoming as red as the sun and nearly as hot. Indignantly he turned around and went home to his mother.

"Give me some proof of who I am," he begged her. "By the head of my stepfather, by the candles at my sister's bridal I implore you. If indeed I am the dear son of the great god whose wondrous chariot lights the sky, give me a sure sign."

His mother raised her eyes to the heavens. "I do swear it, my son, by your father the light-bringing Sun. However if you need proof, I know where he lives. I'll take you to him. I've been there before."

Of all the divine palaces none was more grand than that of Helios; it was the crowning achievement of Hephaistian ingenuity and hands. Its ceiling of flawless ivory rested on pillars of brightly burnished gold and bronze, and its great double doors were of silver skillfully rubbed to a mirror finish. Along the broad paneled walls was a panorama of the universe in finely sculpted bas-relief, twelve delightful panels in all, each with a richly colored, intricately carved scene.

So bedazzled was the boy Phaethon upon entering the palace that he almost forgot the mission that had brought him there. Then the humiliating scene with his friends came back to him; and, rage renewed, he wished them there. He would, of course, describe the palace to them. But how could he ever begin to capture its unspeakable splendors?

Helios's own natural brilliance at first almost blinded the boy. Already the god knew what had brought the young man hither, so first was he to speak: "You have come to my celestial hideaway, I understand, to find your true father. Look no further. It would be a foolish father to deny a son such as you."

"It was not my mother's fantasy after all?" Phaethon ventured.

The Sun God shot a mischievous glance at the mother. "No," he said, "most definitely not."

"I need proof, some sign," the boy said, eyeing the great, bright chariot beyond the door. "Doubts still linger. Somehow, I ask, put your stamp upon me."

"Ask what you will," said the god. "By the River Styx I promise to grant it. Ask, my son."

"You say I am your son. If indeed I am, tomorrow morning I would like to drive your magnificent chariot out there across the skies."

Great Helios immediately repented of his rash promise. "What you ask is quite impossible," he said. "Even Zeus himself would be out of his element trying to drive my winged steeds across the sky. It would mean your certain death, my son. Pray, choose another boon."

Phaethon reminded the god that he had sealed his promise by an oath on the River Styx, which no god can violate. The youth had driven his stepfather's chariot and was sure this would be little different. He was not to be dissuaded.

With heavy heart the God of Light led the way to the great chariot, also the product of bandy-legged Hephaistos's skill. Gold were its axles and gold the tongue, the whippletree, and wheels—all polished to high luster. The spokes were bright silver; glistening gems graced the rims, topaz and green chrysolite.

Nearby in their stables the god's four great wild winged horses stroked the marbled floors with their hooves, sending up rich clusters of sparks. It was almost dawn; they had eaten their ambrosia, for they were deathless steeds, and had drunk deeply of their nectar. At that moment the bright stable lackey Lucifer was throwing over them their gold-embossed, diamond-dotted harnesses.

Helios continued to plead with his son to release him from his promise and to abandon the fateful enterprise. When persuasion failed, he instructed the boy in horsemanship, knowing full well the futility of his own words. "Leave off the whip," he said. "Hold firm the reins with your every ounce of strength. The steeds are wild and will run at will. Climb not too swiftly nor dip too fast. Fates more than your own ride with you this day."

Phaethon mounted the chariot and took the reins confidently in hand. The bars were dropped, and the fire-breathing horses bolted suddenly forward and aloft. Faster than the East Wind they flew through the morning mist into the cloudless heavens. Feeling no firm hand on the reins, they shot almost straight up. Effortlessly they jerked the lines from Phaethon's hands; the boy could but clutch the chariot's gold rail and regret his foolish obstinancy.

Flying at will, the horses cut sharply back and forth, now climbing almost out of sight, now swooping to within but a few feet of the ground. As a caged bird, suddenly loosed, first tests the authenticity of his freedom and then gives way to its long pent-up wildness in erratic flight, even so did the Sun God's chargers dart hither and yon about the airy heavens.

Walled cities were scorched to cinders where the chariot dipped too low; barren canyons were cut from lush, green grasslands. At the polar region it climbed so high that the great Ocean Stream froze into rock-solid cakes. Across the broad lake-studded, emerald pastures of Lybia and North Africa, it zoomed at tree level, drying up lakes and reducing the vast expanse into an arid wasteland. The inhabitants of that great land were turned black, we are told, as were those near the wild Ganges where also the Sun God's chariot flew too close to the ground.

All might have been destroyed, the whole of creation brought to naught had not Gaia, suffering these travails as if in her own body, cried out in panic to aegis-bearing Zeus. "Is this your plan?" she shot at him. "Are you going to destroy everything with fire? Do it fast then with a thunderbolt. You, Father of Gods and Men, either save what is left or destroy it utterly."

Moved by the dowager goddess's words, the great Cloud-gatherer posited himself atop the highest pinnacle of Mount Olympos and let fly a slender shaft of lightning at the chariot gone-wild. The bolt caught Phaethon behind the ear, knocking him from the chariot and from the land of the living; the chariot itself was blasted into golden splinters. Helios's fire-breathing horses broke loose, but in time returned to the stables where they were fed and groomed. In time also the lame Smith God fashioned another chariot for all-seeing Helios, more splendid than the first.

Not all the perils from which Zeus was called upon to save people in those days were of others' making. On occasions he turned out to be the source of the difficulties himself. Nonetheless, so adept was he at converting even his own follies into spectacular acts of charity that men began to call him Zeus the Savior. The Arcadian maiden Callisto was one of many who owed both her undoing and her glory to his ingenuity.

The Lord of Olympos, it seems, was strolling one day among the vales of Arcadia near Mount Cyllene when his attention was suddenly diverted by the sound of girlish voices not far from his path. Advancing cautiously in their direction, he saw at once his archeress daughter's entourage, the virgin Artemis in their midst. Close by her a radiant rustic beauty laughed and smiled, looking often to her mistress with fond and worshipful eyes.

Could he have changed places with his daughter at that moment, great Zeus would surely have done so. Until now only goddesses had so stirred the fires of passion within him. This maiden's coarse homespun cloak was more beautiful than any bejeweled gown he had ever seen, the scrap of cloth around her hair grander than any crown. A bow she held in one hand, a bronze spear in the other. They too added to her beauty. In vain did Zeus try to turn his mind again to the great matters he had been pondering. Even when Artemis and her maidens ran into the woods to resume the hunt, the girl's image remained as fresh as life before his mind's eye. He could think of nothing else.

The maiden's name, he quickly discovered, was Callisto, and one afternoon he spied her alone. The band of happy huntresses had chased their quarry vigorously throughout the morning; and Callisto, falling behind the others, had paused to rest in a dark, shady grove. So dense was the foliage Helios could not find the teeniest window there. Her spear and unstrung bow leaned against a tree; the maiden herself lay on the soft grass, her head resting on her brightly painted quiver.

All sense of decorum abandoned great Zeus, all fear of consequence. "Hera will never know," he assured himself. "Even if she does, is not this morsel worth it?" Thereupon, as was his power to do so, he changed himself into an exact duplicate of Artemis. In every detail he looked her twin.

His voice too was identical to his virgin daughter's as he approached the reclining Callisto and said, "Why, here you are, my dearest. Was it a good hunt for you today?"

Callisto stood up. "Greetings, my goddess. How enchanting you look. More enchanting you seem to me than Olympian Zeus himself."

Zeus laughed. Never had he been so favorably compared with himself before. And so charmingly done! The girl laughed to hear him laugh. He moved closer to her so that their bodies touched. "A compliment like that gets a kiss," he said and proceeded to kiss her. But, alas, no virgin ever kissed like that. His tongue teased her lips most strangely, then her tongue. It was not like any sisterly kiss she had ever received.

Still not alarmed, though, she moved her head back and began to describe excitedly the morning's chase. Once more Zeus kissed her, this time putting his arms around her, drawing her close against himself. Suddenly she knew this was not her mistress. Pushing, kicking, twisting, she fought valiantly to keep what could never be regained, but of course to no avail.

She remained on the ground long after the Son of Cronos vanished, quite literally, into thin air. At length she lifted her eyes to the trees that had witnessed her shame, which she had loved but now hated. Rising, though still in a daze, she walked from the grove; then went back to get her quiver, which she almost forgot. Before long she found a pool, a wide place in a mountain stream, where she tried to wash herself clean.

"Callisto, my dear!" came a familiar voice from a nearby path. It was silver-bowed Artemis, followed by the other girls bearing the day's game on long poles. Not knowing whether or not it was the real Artemis, the girl kept her distance, cautiously circling around the party. Finally deciding that not all her friends could be counterfeits, she gradually joined the train.

Eyes cast downward, averting the others' glances, guilt-ridden Callisto tried to act as if nothing had happened. Alas, it was a poor show. Her stride was no longer brisk and confident; no longer did she walk at her mistress's elbow. She said nothing, but her flush face told all; only a true virgin could have mistaken the signs. Artemis could not understand why her girls were suddenly all atwitter.

Nine months passed. Then one late spring afternoon, hot for the time of year, the Archeress and her company came to a large pool at the base of a waterfall. All were grimy and sticky from a particularly vigorous chase. "No one to watch us," said the goddess. "Let us enjoy ourselves." She then kicked free her sandals and loosened the belt at her waist. The others did likewise, save Callisto, whose belt was already far looser than anyone else's.

"You too, my dear," Artemis told her. She started to say something else but stopped in mid-sentence. For the first time the thickness of Callisto's waist struck her suspiciously; it was a painful moment for both of them.

"Help her," the goddess finally ordered the other girls, now stripped. Her voice was suddenly crisp and brittle. The girls quickly obeyed, exposing Zeus's handiwork on Callisto. Artemis ground her teeth in rage. "No," she said in stentorian tones, "no, you shall not make filthy these lovely waters. Away from my presence!"

All this time Hera had known of her husband's amorous episode with the Arcadian nymph and, as usual, blamed the girl completely. With relish she pondered her revenge. When the unfortunate Callisto, abandoned by both her Artemises, went into labor, the Queen of Gods was on hand to assist her. Fresh hatred seized the divine midwife as she lifted her own husband's child, a robust son, into his first light.

"Congratulations, my little adultress. It's a boy," she said, making no effort to mask her emotions. "You must be proud to have compromised a god. Well, don't gloat till you see what can happen to this beautiful body you and he loved so much." With that, she grabbed the poor wretch by the hair and threw her viciously to the ground.

The girl raised her hands to plead with the goddess but was horrified to see on the backs of them heavy, coarse black hair. Her arms, now legs, were covered with the same. At the ends of what had been her fingers long nails, curved inward, grew; and her lips, once kissed by Olympian Zeus, were changed to huge, grotesque jaws. Nor could she speak to beg for mercy. The only sounds she could make were the deep, rasping grunts of a bear.

Within, Arcadian Callisto was still the girl, still the human being; and so at first, unable to grasp what had happened, she preferred the familiar haunts near her old home to the deep glens of the woods. The yelping of hounds and pursuit of hunters, however, brought her quickly to her senses. Farther and farther into the mountains she fled, eschewing the company of beasts as well, always alone.

Callisto's son, named Arcas, was placed in the care of Maia at nearby Mount Cyllene. The Titaness, who had not had a baby to tend since Hermes left the cave now centuries ago, welcomed the opportunity to try her hand once more at motherhood. Early she taught her ward to love the hunt, presenting him with a spear and hounds of his own. He was content as a child to chase ground squirrels and rabbits near the cave; as an adolescent he turned to larger game.

When fifteen summers had come and gone, Arcas followed his hounds deeper into the wilds than he had ever been before. There he set his nets and circled round to chase his quarry toward their hidden coils. Closing in, he saw a large she-bear writhing in the trap. Advancing slowly toward his prey, spear ready, the young huntsman was taken momentarily by the animal's plaintive eyes.

There was no way he could know that at long last he had met his true mother, although she did somehow recognize him. She shrank back in horror as he, avoiding her eyes, raised his spear to strike. At that instant, however, great Zeus chose to act. He stayed the thrust and in a whirlwind caught up both mother and son and flung them far, far into the heavens, there to stay as honored constellations. Callisto still shines brightly as the Great Bear, Arcas as the Little Bear. Thus did the Lord of Olympos bring glory to the Arcadian beauty he once loved.

As fully fateful for another maiden was that day when on the craggy slopes of Mount Parnassos far-shooting Apollo came upon the child Eros stringing his little bow. "Leave the lethal weapons to grownups," he chided. "Other toys would suit you better. Bows and arrows are for gods like me."

Aphrodite's impish son continued stringing his bow without looking up. A smirk crossed the corners of his mouth. His bow ready, he perched himself on a ledge overlooking a blossom-dotted grassy knoll and took from his quiver two arrows: one as sharp as the passion it ignites, the other blunted with leaden tip to dull the natural affections—two arrows but with opposite effect.

Below him Daphne, daughter of Peneus, lusty lord of the river, moved lightly about the meadow picking the multicolored flowers. Eros fixed the leadened dart to his bowstring and let it fly deep into the girl's youthful breast. His second arrow found the heart of Leto's son at the very moment that, from a hillock across the lea, his eyes fell upon the lovely maid.

In an instant all thoughts of marriage, indeed of men, became loathsome to the beautiful, willowy daughter of Peneus. Apollo was smitten with passionate love. He watched the girl pirouette among the columbine and feather-grass, her hair floating across her face like a gossamer veil enhancing the loveliness it partially hid. His eyes moved lovingly from her lips to her shoulders, then to her naked arms and slender hands. What he could not see inflamed him most. "She's all mine," he told himself, sprinting across the meadow to pay her court.

Daphne darted into a nearby woods.

"Don't run. I'm a friend," the lovesick god called after her. "The Lord of Delphi, that's who I am, son of Zeus. Let me play a song for you, oh beautiful nymph. Let me pluck my lyre."

41

The more he talked, the harder the girl ran, he in close pursuit. Down a mountain path she fled, the wind lifting her hair and playing with her loose-fitting shift, giving her a wild aspect that made her even more enchanting to her ardent suitor, now but a few yards away. Hostile branches caught the flowing garment, tearing it from her body. Apollo found his second wind and quickly closed the distance between them.

Daphne could feel his hot breath on the back of her neck. All was lost she thought but then realized the place was familiar. Just below them was the river, her father's home. "Hear me, dear father. If you have power," she cried, "clothe with green this body no longer mine."

All at once her feet seemed rooted in the soil where she stood. Delicate buds tipped the fingers of her outstretched hands. The hands themselves and her slender arms became branches; her white legs and thighs, covered with bark, a single trunk. Her hair was a luxuriant shock of glittering green laurel leaves. Foiled, crushed, her suitor broke a leafy twig from the tree and, bending it into a crown, placed it on his head. In time it would be the crown of those more successful in the race than he.

Apollo quickly recovered from his unrequited love. Such was not the case, however, with either Echo or Narcissos, whose paths crossed but briefly in the foothills of nearby Mount Helicon at about this same time.

By all accounts Narcissos was the most beautiful boy in Greece. Even as a baby he fanned the coals of passion in all the women, young and old alike, who tended him. By his sixteenth birthday he was the object of every female fantasy for miles around and not a few male fantasies as well. Neither girl nor boy, though, interested him in the slightest.

Echo was a mountain nymph who had once served Zeus by engaging Hera in meaningless chatter whenever she came close to where the Thunderer was compromising his marriage vows. Echo's prattle gave Zeus's guests sufficient time to make their exits. When Hera discovered the garrulous goddess's caprice, she flew into a rage: "Henceforth that evil tongue will silent be! Except when spoken to, you shall not speak at all and then but brief noises."

And so when Echo came upon Narcissos one morning as the youth was struggling with a deer he had just netted, she could only gaze and not speak. And gaze is what she did. Even among the deathless gods she had never seen his like. Hot desire coursed through her veins. How she longed to seduce the handsome youth with honeyed words, but she moved her lips in vain.

Narcissos sensed her eyes upon him. "Who's there?" he called out.

"There," answered Echo, who could only repeat what was spoken to her.

"Let me see you," said the boy.

"See you," said Echo.

Momentarily intrigued, Narcissos then shouted, "What are you called?"

"You called," the nymph replied. Then, unable to contain her ardor, she burst from her cover and threw herself, hot and panting, upon the beautiful adolescent. Not unused to such behavior, Narcissos quickly freed himself from her arms and fled posthaste deeper into the forest, leaving his nets behind.

Echo pursued him, trying to call out the words that would assuage his fears, disarm him, but no sounds came. The youth soon disappeared from her sight. For weeks the nymph wandered the forest in search of her beloved, sleeping little, eating nothing. She became so thin that before long there was nothing left of her at all that an eye could discern. To this day she wanders mountains the world over, still looking for Narcissos. The rocky canyons and deep valleys are her home. One can call out to her; and if she is home, she will answer but only with the words first spoken to her. By decree of Hera she can do no other.

One afternoon, within a month of his escape from Echo, in a secluded woods higher up Mount Helicon Narcissos fell to his knees, exhausted from hunting and being hunted. In front of him was a deep, clear pool, the glassy surface of which so caught the light through the trees overhead as to become a perfect mirror. This, of course, was at a time long before mirrors as we know them were invented.

Narcissos had seen his shadow many times but never his reflection. Thus, when he leaned forward on his hands and knees and peered into the pool, he was startled by the image of unsurpassed beauty peering back at him. No face he had ever seen was like the one he now studied. For the first time in his life he fell in love.

He brought his face down closer to kiss the youth and reached into the pool to embrace him. His lips and arms found only water. Although he quickly withdrew, the mirror effect was for a moment destroyed by ripples in the water. Thinking his beloved had fled from him as he himself was wont to do, Narcissos began to weep. Presently, though, the water cleared, and the beautiful face again appeared. "Do not leave me, oh handsome youth," he pled. "Stay, my love."

Again Narcissos reached down to touch the form in the water; again the image blurred when his hand broke the surface. All but positive now his true love was forever lost to him, he tore at his hair and drew his nails slowly down across his throat. When he relented and the waters again cleared, the image of his love reappeared, battered and disheveled. The sight pained him, and he wept.

Helios's chariot finished its trek across the sky, gray night stole over the forest, but Narcissos did not stir. Nothing mattered to him save the elusive youth in the pool. Dawn's first light found him gazing intently into the water's clear depths. The face that slowly appeared was haggard and distraught. He reached his hand into the water to caress that cheek now most dear, and his frustrations of the day before were renewed.

"I love you! I love you!" he shouted a thousand times into the pool. The face, like Echo's, moved its mouth but made no sound. Unwilling, unable to leave the pool's edge, Narcissos at length died there, his once beautiful countenance now twisted and grotesque. Mountain nymphs found him and would have buried him; but as they were preparing for the funeral, his body vanished, and where it lay a flower bloomed with golden petals tinged with white.

Unsurpassed beauty was in those days as now more often a curse than a blessing. Little enough has changed in that respect. Back then, however, beauty's natural drawbacks were not infrequently magnified whenever a deity was inadvertently offended. One, for example, never compared a mortal's comeliness to that of a goddess without incurring the gravest of consequences.

Thus, when the mother of Smyrna, the most lovely princess of all Asia at the time, said one day, "I say, that girl is more beautiful than Aphrodite," she quite irrevocably sealed her daughter's fate. With a malicious swish of her magic girdle, the laughter-loving goddess caused the wretched maiden to fall in love with her own father.

Shamelessly she sought his presence continually, oftentimes using the slimmest of pretexts to give him most undaughterly hugs. His return embraces fueled her passion. Many were the moments when she almost tore the clothes from her body and implored him with hot tears to have mercy on her or kill her. Her mother became her enemy.

One evening she fashioned a noose from her girdle and, but for the last-second intervention of her childhood nurse, would have hanged herself. At first the old woman did not know what the hysterical girl meant by, "I want my father! I want my father!" Slowly she understood and, setting prejudices aside, vowed to give Smyrna the one thing that would make her life bearable.

Opportunity was not long in coming, for a festival soon took the king's wife from his bed for an extended period. The nurse waited several days and then came to him to tell him of a beautiful girl who had recently confessed her love for him. Choosing her words carefully, she praised the maiden's beauty but, of course, did not disclose her name.

Later that night, when it was dark in the palace and the king was filled with wine, the old woman led Smyrna to her father's bedchamber. Her knees trembling, her heart throbbing violently, the girl opened the door and went in. With sweet words and modulated voice, the king guided her to his bed and then to his arms. He called her "my girl."

In return she mumbled quickly, "Father, my love."

Before dawn, objective achieved, she kissed her sleeping lover on the lips and slipped out of his bed. The next night Smyrna came again to her father's bed, and the next and the next. For twelve nights the king found pleasure with a girl who had only been described for him but whose face he had never seen. On the twelfth night, after their love, his curiosity bested him; he lit a lamp and held it near her head.

"My father, my love," said Smyrna, smiling up at him.

He recoiled in horror and reached for his sword beside the bed. On her feet in an instant, Smyrna tried to calm him with gentle words. His first swing of the weapon, missing her, threw him off balance. Smyrna darted out the door and through the courtyard and out the main gate. Her father, sword high above his head, pursued her.

The distance between them closed. Sensing all was lost, Smyrna cried out in prayer, "Save me, dear gods. Have mercy I pray."

And mercy they had on her of a kind most strange. They transformed her in an instant into a beautiful little tree, called the myrrh after her. Thus, when her father brought down his sword, he only scratched the outer bark.

Ten moons shined upon the lovely, lone, scarred little tree; its trunk grew thick. Then one night it split down the middle at the scar, and out rolled a handsome baby boy. Aphrodite, satisfied that her mischief had gone far enough, attended the birth. She named the child Adonis and placed him in a chest and then turned the chest, lid locked, over to Persephone for safe keeping. "No peeking," she said on the way out.

The Queen of the Underworld immediately pried open the lock and was soon holding the baby to her breast. She fell in love with him on the spot. He was, beyond question, the most adorable infant she had ever seen, and under her attentive care he grew up to be the world's handsomest man. What Helen of Sparta would someday be among women, Adonis was among men: one whose physical aspect was so perfect you could not imagine even the slightest alteration for the better, in form a god, every woman's secret dream. Persephone took him for her lover as soon as his body reached full bloom.

It so happened, however, that Aphrodite dropped down one morning to check on the chest that she had put in storage eighteen years earlier. She was not a little taken back to discover that its contents, now incomparably handsome, had his arms around Persephone's bare shoulders. "Oh, I see you peeked," said she.

"I rescued him," said the Underworld Queen. "But for me, he would be in the chest yet."

"Many thanks from both of us. Well, at last I've come for him. You won't have to sweat over him, or under him, anymore. Keep the chest. It's little enough for your troubles."

"The chest is yours. He's mine."

"He's mine," said Aphrodite.

It became abundantly clear that both goddesses had claim to the handsome mortal and equally as clear that neither was going to relinquish her claim to the other. Their verbal sparring went on for weeks, bringing a note of rancor and unpleasantness to the Realm of the Dead. At length Zeus was called down to arbitrate. His judgment seemed both wise and equitable: The goddesses would share Adonis, each having exclusive claim to him for four months out of every year; the remaining four months would be his in which to relax and recover.

Aphrodite, however, played it less than fair. One evening after Adonis had finished his eight months' service to the two goddesses and was pondering what to do with his free months, she stole into his chambers and flashed her magic girdle. A passion more wild and irresistible than anything he had experienced hitherto quite took possession of him. He chose to abide his long vacation in Aphrodite's arms.

A model for lovers whose intrigues offend propriety, the two tried to be discreet, taking their love in remote rustic places; he oftentimes in guise as a shepherd, she as his country maiden. Before long, however, Aphrodite's guile was discovered, and word of it reached her rival in Hades' dark kingdom. Persephone passed along the information to Ares.

That a mere mortal should be preferred to him thoroughly enraged the God of War. Afire with envy, he forthwith went to Mount Lebanon, where the couple were sporting themselves in a woods. Then, when they came into his view, he changed himself into a monstrous curve-tusked boar and charged the unhappy mortal, ripping his body mercilessly, with Aphrodite helplessly looking on.

Death's icy fingers soon closed Adonis's eyes, and his soul returned to the gods beneath the earth. Aphrodite thereupon rushed righteously to Zeus to protest that it was unfair for Persephone to have Adonis now for twelve months a year and her not to have him at all. Made wise by his earlier mistake, the Aegis-bearer split the year in two, giving Aphrodite and Persephone each six months to enjoy the company of Adonis, who, though boar-gored, was still the handsomest man in the world.

With peace the order once more among the undying gods, the Son of Cronos again turned his attentions earthward. Had the unfortunate circumstances to which he himself had sometimes contributed, he wondered, had an adverse effect on his new race of men? Did this Bronze Race, after all, turn out to be any better than the first?

And so a second time he humbled himself and traveled the earth incognito, this time with Hermes at his side. Into distant Phrygia they journeyed. At first their reception, to say the least, was discouraging. On a thousand doors they knocked to beg for shelter, and a thousand doors were barred against them. At last a door was opened, one door only, and that of a humble cottage with a roof of straw and grass. An old man and his wife lived within its meager walls. She answered to Baucis, he to Philemon.

Thinking the strangers but two ordinary wayfarers, the good Philemon bowed and stepped back from the doorway to let them enter. Zeus had to stoop to avoid hitting his head on the low lintel; Hermes likewise. The little table and two benches in the cottage were clean, of course, but the master of the house wiped them with a cloth to make sure and then spread a mat over each bench before bidding his guests sit down. As ancient as the hosts themselves, the benches cracked under the unaccustomed weight.

Lovely old Baucis, the meanwhile, rekindled the fire in the hearth with dry leaves and bark, bending over and blowing on them until they glowed red. Then she took some sticks from the rafters; and, breaking them against her knee, she set them carefully on top of the burning bark and over the fire hung her bronze kettle. With practiced hands she trimmed the cabbage her husband had brought in from the garden just outside the door. Philemon took down a piece of cured meat from a high peg for her, from which she cut a goodly number of strips to put with the cabbage into the seething kettle.

As the two prepared the simple meal, they talked about the weather and the hazards of travel and such, with conversation trying to put their guests at ease. Smiling always and bowing often, they worked as one in preparing the decrepit three-legged table, first putting a mat on it and then the most brightly colored cloth they owned. One leg was shorter than the other two, causing it to tip noticeably, a condition white-haired Baucis routinely corrected by slipping a piece of shard under the worn leg.

First on the menu were brown-ripe olives, Athene's fruit, and after them a bowl of autumn cherries marinated in sweet wine, lettuce from the dooryard garden, radishes, and an egg for each guest. The cabbage soup, hot from the hearth, was brought on in well polished wooden bowls; all else was served on heavy rustic clayware plates.

For each a cup of Philemon's wine and a full flagon on the table to refill them. Nuts, figs, and dates were next set before the strangers and crisp apples and clusters of lush deep-purpled grapes in rush baskets and honey dripping from a honeycomb.

Posting themselves unobtrusively to the side with more fruit and honey close at hand, the elderly pair watched their guests partake of the simple banquet. All at once their old eyes seemed to deceive them. It looked as though the soup bowls, drained to the last drop, were filled again, as if by magic, to their brims.

The hosts rubbed their eyes, and, lo, now the wine cups had miraculously refilled themselves as well. Cold horror seized them both. Throwing themselves before their guests, surely of no mortal stock, the two lifted their hands in fearful prayer. Both shaking, they begged for leave to prepare another meal, a meal more worthy.

Quick glances were exchanged between man and wife. Old Philemon went outside to chase a large goose that served the couple as watch-dog and pet. The crafty bird guessed his ancient master was running after him to no friendly purpose and darted deftly out of reach. Though the goose continued to dodge and outdistance him, gray Philemon hobbled after him in almost comic pursuit. Finally, seeing the open cottage door, the bird charged through it, wings flapping frantically, into the lap of Aegis-bearing Zeus.

"Spare the poor goose," said the god, staying Philemon with his hand. "Gods we are, and ungodly is the land in which you dwell. It's time is brief. So wretched a thing must be destroyed, but not you, dear people. Come quickly."

Moments later the ancient couple and their still ruffled watch-goose were making their way up a high hill, being urged on by Zeus and Hermes ahead of them. Both had need of their walking sticks to negotiate the uneven path. Where it was especially steep, old Philemon first assisted his wife and then followed, using his heavy stick to push himself upward. On a knoll, little more than a bowshot from their home, though it seemed much further, they rested and looked out over the area below. Save for their little cottage alone, water covered everything; as far as their eyes could see, there was nothing but endless flood.

The two fell down and wept. Their neighborhood was not worth their tears, but they wept nonetheless, as much as anything out of seeing what was familiar so suddenly taken away. Lifting their heads, they looked down again at their home. It seemed somehow much larger. They blinked their eyes. How could it be? Great marble columns, not crude timbers, now braced the sloping roof, and the thatched grass roof itself had been transformed into a glistening golden dome. The kitchen garden and farmyard were now a beautiful marbled patio; the weatherworn gate now an ornately sculptured propylaeum.

Zeus spoke. His voice was gentle. "Your dearest wish? It shall be so."

Man and wife conferred but a moment, for they thought as one. White-haired Baucis, voice faltering, answered, "To be your servants in that beautiful temple. That is our dearest wish, and to die together when that time shall come."

"Never do I want to look upon my dear wife's grave," said Philemon, "nor she mine."

For many pleasant years thereafter the old couple tended the lovely temple and were abundantly provided for by the Father of Gods in return. Then one day, when both were very bent and feeble, they stood together outside the temple and witnessed another transformation, this time in each other. They were talking, as so often they did, of their long life together and of the moments most precious to them both, when Philemon saw green leaves in his dear wife's hair and she in his. Little sprigs also began to appear, and the lines in one another's faces seemed as the lines in bark. They understood the meaning and welcomed it.

"Good-bye, my dear, sweet wife," said Philemon.

"And good-bye, sweet husband," said Baucis.

The two were changed by the Son of Cronos into sturdy, graceful trees, she a lime and he a majestic oak, which still flourish in that remote place, now a marshland inhabited mostly by ducks and wild geese. So close are the trees together that one could imagine their intertwined branches growing from a single trunk.

Assured at last that true piety was possible on earth, the great Father of Gods and Men now pondered the possibility of high courage as well, which to him was the cornerstone of all other virtues. Gradually he was seeing in humankind what Prometheus had seen centuries before. How, he debated with himself, could he best make of man the quintessential creature that the far-sighted Son of Iapetos had always intended?

# Heroic Beginnings

W hat made the Second Bronze Age so different from the age that preceded it and the one that followed was the infusion of human blood with divine. The gods, not least the Father of Gods, from time to time favored the sons and daughters of men with their attentions. Though such attention generally proved inconvenient to the mortals involved and not infrequently catastrophic, nonetheless, in due time individuals and families of extraordinary resourcefulness emerged.

Heroic times, one might say then, officially commenced with Zeus's seduction of a pretty Argive maiden named Io. Little did the girl realize, as she gamboled about the meadows near her home picking flowers and watching the wild creatures at play, that the great Cloud-gatherer was in turn watching her.

At night, however, she had every reason to suspect that something unusual was afoot. In a recurrent dream she heard a voice saying, "Maiden most blessed, cling not to your virginity. Zeus, aflame with love, would make you his."

When finally Io summoned up the courage to speak of her strange dream to her father, he immediately consulted the oracles at Delphi and Dodona. The dream was not cryptic, he was told; Zeus did indeed desire the innocent girl. Therefore, lest she bring catastrophe down upon her family, Io left home and sought refuge as a priestess in the temple of Hera. It was a futile move, for no priestly garments could hide from the Lord of Gods what he knew to be there. His lust continued to burn.

One day he could stand it no more. As a thirst-filled wretch abandons all caution when sighting a shaded pool amid the desert wastes, even so the Father of Gods and Men turned deaf ear to his own better counsels when his eyes fell upon the enchantingly lovely maiden some distance from Hera's shrine. A light wind ruffled her hair and played with the fringe of her skirt, lifting it with occasional gusts almost to her knees. The sky was clear, and from Mount Olympos Zeus could see all as plainly as if he were but a pace away.

Reaching about him, he gathered all the puffy little clouds he could find from the north and the west and amassed them into one huge dark cloud, which he floated over the lea where Io stood, himself in the midst of it. He then lowered the cloud, completely enshrouding the girl. Thinking at first that a sudden fog had descended, Io quickly discovered otherwise when Zeus, with artful strokes, caressed hot desire into her body, making her willing partner to what came next.

From one of Mount Olympos's porticoes Hera chanced to look southward. Strange it suddenly seemed to her. The day was clear, the sky a soft blue, except for a single dark cloud near her temple in Argos. Immediately she cast her eyes about for Zeus. He was nowhere to be seen. The mysterious cloud no longer seemed mysterious after all. Hera, who had more than once of late caught her husband ogling Io, sped to the scene and began waving her arms wildly to disperse the cloud.

Zeus sensed the cloud's disappearing overhead and, guessing the cause, changed Io into a beautiful white heifer. When the cloud was completely brushed away, all Hera found was her husband holding the cow by one of her horns. "Why Hera, my dear, if this isn't a coincidence finding you here," he said.

"What have you there?" she asked.

"A gift for you, my dear. I found her just now. How fortunate you should happen by. I'll have her delivered."

"I'm sure she'll be delivered before the year is out," said Hera. "Here, let me take her, since you no doubt already have." With that, Hera led Io away while Zeus looked on helplessly. Tethering the heifer to an olive tree in her grove near Nemea (which, it so happened, was Io's home village), the white-armed goddess set her favorite monstrosity, hundred-eyed Argos, to stand guard.

Poor Io, but a few hundred yards from her own home, where her father and mother and brothers and sisters were at that moment sitting down for their evening meal, stared at the familiar buildings beyond the grove. She could visualize the family about the table, the roasted meats and succulent fruits before them. With the memory of a girl and the digestive system of a cow, she sniffed at the dried grass near her feet and then, looking once more homeward, tugged desperately at her halter. Great tears came to her large brown bovine eyes. Hunger gnawed at her stomachs. Bending her head again, she bit off some stems of grass and began to chew.

Argos was the perfect watchman. His hundred eyes slept in shifts so that at any moment no fewer than twenty pair were focused on Io. Never was she free from his gaze. At times he let her forage in peace; at other times he chased her viciously over hard and rocky ground. Often at night, racked by pain and frightened beyond words, she mooed out in vain to her father and brothers for help.

It so happened that her father did one day venture near where she was tethered and saw her and walked up to her. How frantically then did Io want to talk, but all she could do was press her face against him and lick his hands with her tongue. Then, as if by inspiration, with her hoof she made the letters IO in the dust, directing her father's attention to the ground with her eyes. He saw the letters and slowly understood.

Horrified, he returned home and offered great prayers and sacrifices to the Father of Gods and Men for his daughter's restoration. Io's own desperate prayers also rose heavenward. Nor did the mighty Cloud-gatherer ignore those entreaties. Straightway he charged Maia's son, wing-sandaled Hermes, to go forth and destroy Hera's many-eyed watchman.

Disguising himself as a wandering shepherd, Hermes rounded up an impromptu collection of wild goats and stray sheep as he approached the Nemean grove. Now pushing them into line with his staff, now mesmerizing them with the music of his pipe, he guided his motley flock around the boulder where Argos sat. The monster, enchanted by the music, invited the gods' herald to sit with him and play.

Not only did Hermes play; he sang and talked incessantly as well. Stories he told of gods and men in such detail that his listener could not follow the main plot lines and, like many a schoolboy in stuffy lecture, found his head now and then drooping. Through the afternoon and evening Hermes chattered on and on, his voice soft and monotonous; the eyes of Argos closed, one pair after another.

At dawn's first light the last pair of thick lids were finally tightly closed. Hermes lifted his crooked sword and brought it down across the monster's bent neck. The severed head rolled into a clump of tall grass, spattering the green-brown blades with rich black blood. Then quickly the wing-sandaled god cut the halter from Io's head and bid her flee.

Only moments later Hera made her morning rounds. She had held Argos in a kind of affection, as a hunter might hold an old hound; and so, when she discovered first the headless trunk of her watchman and then in the grass the head itself, all eyes closed, she wept with grief. Then, as a memorial, she carefully took one of the monster's eyes, opened it, and, with the skill of a jeweler, set it in the tail feather of the peacock, where it can be seen to this day.

Vengeance-bent, next she fashioned a gadfly the likes of which no one has ever seen. Twice the size of its cousins that light upon antlered deer in forests' depths or dray horses in their stalls to draw their blood with stinging bites, this gadfly attacked with the fury of a savage, rabid bat just loosed from hell and with an appetite for blood equally as great. Directed by Hera, the insect, if you could call it that, flew after the fleeing heifer, its wings stirring the air with a loud, menacing buzz.

All over the Peloponnese did poor Io bound and from thence to rocky Attica and fertile Boiotia, the gadfly ever in close pursuit, its buzz always terrifying, its bite unbearable. Seldom stopping to graze, she fed on whatever vines or tasteless leaves she could tear loose in flight. At pools she could but drink briefly, never to her fill. Nor did she know any longer what it was to lie down at night and sleep.

Into Thessaly the gadfly drove her and then the wilds of Thrace and distant Scythia, then down to the narrows where the Propontis and Euxine join; she paused there but for a moment, looking at Scythia behind her and, just across the straits, Asia to the south. The gadfly lit; pain suddenly surged through her body. She bolted forward into the water and made for the Asian shore. (From that time on the narrows were called the Bosporus, meaning "cow-crossing," in her honor.)

Eventually, after many months, Io, no longer even beautiful as a cow, but scrawny and sick, her backside swollen, came to rest near the Nile's mouth. Heeding the pleas of Zeus, Hera repented of her vengeance and called off the gadfly. Then, as suddenly as she had become a cow, Io turned back into a girl. A few days later she gave birth to a strikingly charming little baby boy with a divine sparkle in his eyes. She named him Epaphos.

In the course of time Epaphos married a nymph of the Nile named Memphis and by her sired a daughter called Libya. She in turn found favor in the eyes of the earthshaker Poseidon, who fathered on her the twins Belos and Agenor.

Belos also sired twins, Danaos and Aigyptos. Like so many twins in antiquity, these knew very little of brotherly love. Although the former was king of Libya and the latter of the land that bore his name, each feared the designs of the other. Danaos by his many wives had fifty daughters, Aigyptos fifty sons. When the daughters of the one and the sons of the other were grown, Aigyptos proposed a mass marriage. "Our blood mingled," he argued, "would a great empire make."

"For which of us?" asked Danaos.

"For all our children, my brother."

Danaos took the proposal to his daughters, who all agreed that mass death offered a much rosier future. Their cousins, in their minds, were the equals of marauding jackals in appearance and several grades below them in civility. "Would gentle doves seek union with crooked-beaked hawks?" said one of them.

By consulting an oracle, Danaos confirmed what he had secretly suspected: Aigyptos did indeed plan to kill him once the nuptials made their two kingdoms one. Heeding then the counsels of Athene, he and his fifty daughters set about building a sea-going ship, the first one ever, and, when it was finished, quickly boarded it and set sail. Gentle winds brought them to Argos, their ancestral home, where Pelasgos was king. At his feet the Danaids prostrated themselves as suppliants. "Save us," they pled, "from the sons of Aigyptos."

"Argos must not be destroyed for the sake of foreigners," Pelasgos replied.

"Unless you protect us," they said, "we will hang ourselves from the beams of your temples. Better that than the fate you choose for us."

Moved by pity and not a little concerned that he might incur the anger of the undying gods, Pelasgos relented and pledged his protection should the sons of Aigyptos ever pursue their courtship to Argos. Little did he realize how soon he would be called upon to make good his pledge, for at that moment the bestial cousins, having built ships of their own, were on their way.

The sons of Aigyptos brought with them to Argos a most formidable army. When denied their quest, they quickly laid siege to the city. From outside the walls each day Aigyptos's sons would loudly demand their brides, and from within Pelasgos and Danaos would refuse.

This, however, was before there were deep wells within the cities of Argos; all water had to be brought in from springs and streams without. After a week of siege, therefore, the Danaids were shouting back their refusals with voices more than a little dry. At length, to save the city that had befriended them, Danaos gathered his daughters about him.

"Go through with your weddings," he told them, "though not your marriages. Treachery would they deal; with treachery then shall they be dealt."

"How so, dear father?" they asked.

Danaos opened a case and took from it fifty long, thin daggers, all razor-edged and with points sharper than needles. To each of his daughters he handed a dagger. "Hide these in your bridal beds," he said. "When first your masters attempt their violent pleasures, return to them caress for caress, stroke for stroke. Counterfeit delight, make it seem your pleasure too. When their passions are keenest, my daughters, as they slide their arms under you to draw you into oneness with themselves, then take these from hiding and strike. Violate their bodies as they would yours."

The girls took the knives. "We shall do as you say, dear father," they said.

"All of you? If every one of their heads does not fall, we are lost."

"We promise," said all fifty of his daughters.

The sons of Aigyptos were welcomed into the city; then a few days later, when men and maidens were paired to everyone's apparent satisfaction, the wedding took place. Lasting long into the night, the celebration finally ended in each husband's leading his bride to their marriage bed.

Almost simultaneously the couples embraced, the fifty daughters of Danaos feigning pleasure in their bridegroom's arms, at their finger tips the daggers' handles. The men's strong hands pulled their virgin brides' bodies tightly against their own. Passions peaked. None knew when his wife closed her hand about her dagger nor sensed anything amiss when the muscles of her arms suddenly became taut. In each bridal chamber, save one, the heinous deed was accomplished.

Out of fifty sons Aigyptos had sired one who, unbeknownst to the Danaids and probably his own father as well, was a gentle, sensitive, decent human being. A lamb among wolves, in public he could but move with the pack and be reckoned one of them; only in private dared he show his genteel side, his real self. Lynceus was his name, and of his cousins he was paired with Hypermnestra, in every way his counterpart in gentility.

When on their wedding night Lynceus took his bride to their room, unlike his brothers, he did not begin his love play with breath-stifling embraces and groping fingers but rather with a tender squeeze of his maiden's hand. Though she returned the squeeze, he sensed her heart was not in it. They passed their time sitting on the edge of the bed, hands gently clasped, in pleasant conversation. Lynceus's voice was mellow and well modulated, his eyes picking up the soft glow of the lamp.

Several times Hypermnestra's fingers brushed the handle of her hidden dagger but each time withdrew. Respecting her modesty, Lynceus over and over again assured her there was no need to seal their union

56

before both were compelled by mutual love. Her heart was his object, nothing less. He smiled kindly as he spoke; then he leaned over and kissed his bride on the cheek and blew out the lamp and lay down to sleep.

The maiden lay awake until almost dawn. Though she was betraying her family and feared their reprisals, she could not bring herself to raise her hand against the sleeping form beside her, against the sweet, gentle man she had begun to love.

By command of aegis-bearing Zeus, the daughters of Danaos were purified of their bloodguilt by Hermes, and in time Danaos succeeded Pelasgos to the Argive throne. Lynceus and Hypermnestra spent their first years of marriage apart from each other—he in exile, she in a dungeon. When at last Danaos stepped down from his throne, however, it was the recalled Lynceus who took his place. Nor did the gods forever overlook the crime of the Danaids: When they descended into death's kingdom beneath the earth, they were condemned to draw water in vessels full of holes, punched with the points of their own daggers.

All the time Danaos and Aigyptos were trying to outguess and outpurge each other, intrigues of a much different nature were taking place among their cousins in what would some day be called Phoinicia. Agenor, Libya's other son by Poseidon, had become king in that rich Asian land beside the Great Sea. His sons, unlike those of Belos, lived in harmony the one with the other. Bound each to each by strong family pride, they were at one with their parents in adoration of the household's most prized jewel, their lovely sister Europa.

Seldom back then did a mortal girl possess extraordinary beauty of face and figure and not sooner or later attract the prurient gaze of the cloud-gathering Son of Cronos. Europa was no exception. Afternoons when she gamboled with her maidens in grassy meadows or splashed about in the shallow waters of some secluded beach, the eyes of Zeus were fast upon her. Like a little child, a four-year-old darling, watching his mother prepare honeyed confections at the kitchen table, the Father of Gods took in Europa's every move with flashing eyes, his glands anticipating the delectable treat to come.

At length he called to himself Argos-slaying Hermes. "Go down at once to the land men call Sidon," he told him. "There drive from their mountain pastures all of the king's cattle down to the many-flowered meadows by the sea."

The fleet herald of the gods quickly obeyed. Agenor's handsome kine were soon grazing contentedly in the seaside lea where Europa was

57

wont to pass her time in spirited play with her courtly entourage. Then it was that Zeus, at whose faintest beck the heavens flash and the up-gathered clouds crack with ear-piercing thunder, lay down his sceptre and took upon himself the form of a bull and moved among the cattle.

No ordinary bull was he. His sleek, satiny snow-white coat glistened in the afternoon sun; his brightly polished horns too, perfectly curved as if sculpted from pearl by a master craftsman. Great muscles bulged in rolls about his neck, giving way to a silvery dewlap that hung like a silken scarf. Taller than the rest of the herd, more poised, stately he bore himself, but his face was gentle, his deep blue eyes hypnotically inviting.

The daughter of Agenor could not take her eyes off the magnificent bull. She stood at a distance for a while, pondering the propriety of approaching him; fear did not even occur to her. At length, picking a bouquet of tender young daisies, she moved slowly toward the animal, holding out the flowers for him to eat. He took the gift in his snow-white lips, as he did so pressing them generously against her smooth, warm hand. As a gourmet, sipping his aperitif, teases his appetite for the banquet ahead, even so did Zeus tantalize himself first with the girl's hands, then her arms, then her innocent cheeks.

In his exuberance he broke from her a moment and pranced amidst the violets and blushing columbine, then returned to give her his neck to stroke, sniffing her soft, fragrant hair, brushing her forehead with his chin and lower lip. Europa, mesmerized, bewitched, ran to gather more flowers, making of them chains and multi-colored garlands to wrap about the bull's neck and impale, as sweet-scented crowns, upon his majestic horns. Bloom-bedecked and panting, Zeus knelt to the ground and invited the girl onto his back.

With the glee of a child playing at swift current's edge, not grasping the danger, Europa bounced merrily atop the god-bull as he trotted over the rolling meadows, then along the golden sands of the beach. The soft ocean breeze lifted her hair and felt soothing, cool against her sun-flushed face. New, bizarre sensations made her whole body tingle, yearn for ful-fillment she could not understand. Her host ran through the shallows, sending a refreshing briny spray over her legs. She shrieked with delight. Scarcely was she aware that they had headed out to sea, the bull's feet skimming the surface like a water beetle, until the shore was almost out of sight.

Seized suddenly with fear, when she saw the waves below and the fading shoreline behind, Europa leaned forward and clutched the silvery garlanded horns and, her dress fluttering in the wind, too late pondered the outcome of her adventure. More swift than an eagle swooping down upon a defenseless hare did Zeus speed across wine-dark sea waters. At last he came to that land men now call Crete and there trotted ashore.

Shedding his snow-white coat, his shining horns, he took on an aspect more divine, then indulged himself in pleasures much imagined, long sought.

In due time, still on Crete, Agenor's daughter bore to the great Aegis-bearer three healthy sons: Minos, Sarpedon, and Rhadamanthys. All were blessed by their father with extraordinarily long life; some say they were allowed to live for three generations, some say more. When as yet they were infants, Asterios, the ruler of that land, chanced to look upon the still lovely Europa and paid her court. When she married him, amid celebration shared by all, he took into his home her three babes and nurtured them into manhood as his own.

Agenor, in the meantime, had called his sons about him. "Your sister has been taken," he announced, "where she is great Zeus might know. I do not. Go too, my sons. Find her wherever she may be, and return not until you do."

In obedience to his father's command, therefore, Cadmos sailed west and northward into the sea men would some day call the Aigean. Along the Phrygian coast and on up to untamed Thrace he took his search but found no sign of Europa's having been anywhere. Years passed. Afraid to return to his father empty-handed, Cadmos continued to press on. At length in his despair, like so many ancients before him, he sought the sure counsel of Apollo's oracle at Delphi. The oracle's message was brief and poetic:

> In yonder field a milk-white heifer find
> Whose neck has ne'er to crooked yoke inclined.
> Where she leads follow; wheresoe'er she falls
> A city build with high and stately walls.

Cadmos left the temple bewildered. Then in a small meadow where the slopes of Parnassos were less precipitous he spied a milk-white cow. There was no imprint of yoke upon her neck nor halter marks along her face. When Cadmos approached, she bolted and trotted eastward. The travel-weary Sidonian prince followed. Whenever she stopped, he ordered his men to prod her on. Across rolling hills and grassy plains they chased the cow, trailing after, driving her ever before them where she was wont to go. On a modest hill amid other such hills beyond the plains, she stopped and raised her head, then bellowed mightily and collapsed upon the tender grass.

Cadmos lifted his arms in gratitude to the gods, then bent his great frame to the earth and kissed it. "Make haste," he shouted to his men. "Fetch water. With sweet sacrifice must the gods be thanked."

Nearby where the ground sloped downward were dense, thick woods. Into them the men of Cadmos quickly, obediently disappeared in search of dancing stream or clear, deep spring. Spiritedly they groped their way through the heavy underbrush till at last they found a rillet, the merest stream wetting the gravel and rocks over which it flowed. This they followed to its source, a broad, cool, bubbling spring within a dank and sunless cave.

The cave of Ares it was, but how would they know? And the spring also was his. Guarding the sanctum, beyond the pool, was the god's coiled sentry, golden plumed, its sea-blue body thick and scaled, its hideous eyes spitting forth bile and fire. Three rows of teeth lined the monstrous serpent's powerful jaws; from between them its three-forked tongue darted out and lashed at the air like a bullwhip, leaving foul and lethal fumes behind.

Cadmos's men bent to fill their pitchers and jugs. Suddenly out of the darkness the huge serpent struck. Faster than a bent bow, string released, springs back to its original shape did the scaly sentry, uncoiling half its massive length, shoot its hissing head into the Tyrian ranks. The men dropped their vessels; their blood ran cold. Recoiling and striking again, the great snake rent limbs and heads from bodies turned in flight. Strong men, seasoned sailors, were blown in an instant to dark death's distant shores by the serpent's fiery and toxic breath.

On the hilltop Cadmos busied himself arranging stones for the altar, then killing and flaying the fallen cow, careful to put the gods' portion in one place and his men's in another. Swiftly he performed his happy labors, then looked to the woods into which his men had ventured, bewildered as to why fetching water should take so long. Iron-tipped spear in one hand, javelin in the other, he advanced toward the woods. At the cave's mouth he saw the mangled remains of a man, face torn, garments charred, black blood now congealed, yet recognizable, a friend dear and inordinately loyal. Beyond him the serpentine sentinel fed on the entrails of two other comrades.

"Oh, my friends most dear," groaned the Sidonian prince, "was it for this I brought you hither, for this we left our Tyrian shores? Forgive me, sweet comrades. Mine now to avenge, or to join you in death's dark kingdom."

With that, he shrieked a mighty battle cry and hurled with the strength of ten a large rock at the head of the serpent. On a line, as though fired from a sling, the missile whizzed through the air to its blood-wet target. The force of the rock would have shattered a thick wall or stony tower; off the serpent's scaly armor it but bounced like a cube of cork against a plank of bronze.

Next, before Ares' pet could coil to strike, Cadmos let fly his fine-honed javelin, catching the monstrous snake's body midway between tail and head, its iron tip slicing neatly into the sinewy flesh. Writhing, the serpent whipped its head around and, taking the shaft in its mouth, pulled it out, though not all; the iron head remained imbedded in its spine. Jaws open, its triple rows of gore-scummed, blood-streaked teeth bared, the monster then struck again and again at its adversary, but each time Cadmos stepped back, parrying the thrusts with his lion-skin shield.

Gradually the battle moved from cave to woods. Each time the serpent lunged at him, Cadmos drove his spear into its palate. The snake brought down its jaws and tried to snap the weapon in two, but the shaft was iron and would not yield. Bushes and grass were bathed in the beast's black blood. When at one point the serpent stretched its jaws for yet another thrust, the back of its head brushed the trunk of an aged oak. With both hands, finding strength he did not know he had, Cadmos ran his spear through palate and head, pinning his adversary to the tree.

But even as Ares' serpent twitched its scaly tail a final time, the voice of the god himself broke the momentary lull, its source nowhere to be seen. "Gloat not, son of Agenor," boomed the voice. "A serpent have you slain; a serpent shall you be."

Ares' was not, however, the only voice he heard. A softer, feminine voice came next, that of gray-eyed Athene. "Quick, knock loose the monster's teeth," she told him, "and plant them. Seeds they are, seeds of a new race."

Not comprehending the goddess's meaning, Cadmos nevertheless prepared the soil about him as though for barley and sowed it with the serpent's many teeth. Suddenly the ground he had just planted cracked open, and, as if rising out of so many trap doors upon a stage, men, full-grown and full-armored, began to rise. They were huge men; a veritable army of them soon stood upon the ground from which they had sprung. They advanced en masse toward Cadmos.

In frantic move to ward them off, Agenor's son took several large rocks and hurled them into their midst. The men, each thinking someone in their own ranks had cast the rocks, were thrown into confusion and turned on one another.

In their madness and confusion, they cut down each other until only five were left standing. Nor would those five have survived the day had not the bright-eyed Daughter of Zeus shouted, "Stop! Throw down your arms!"

With the help of the five earth-born men, strongest and boldest of whom was Echion, Cadmos built the walls and towers of a city and called it Thebes. To atone for the killing of Ares' serpent, he was made to serve the god eight years, but at the end of that time he was presented by Zeus with Harmonia, the daughter of Aphrodite and Ares, as his bride.

The twelve Olympian gods all came to the wedding. Never before had they graced the wedding of a mortal. There was feasting and dancing and music: meats and wine for the mortals, ambrosia and nectar in abundance for the deathless gods. The Muses played their flutes and sang such airs as made the birds stop in their flight to listen, and Apollo plucked his lyre to everyone's delight. And all the gods gave toasts. Laughter-loving Aphrodite placed about her daughter's neck a finely wrought necklace designed to make the wearer irresistibly beautiful.

The marriage of Cadmos and Harmonia was blessed with several children, all delightful to the eye and uncommonly resourceful. Autonoe was first to open her mother's womb; then came her sisters Ino, Semele, and Agave; and finally a brother Polydoros. Foolish men envied Cadmos his lot, calling him happiest among men; the wise, knowing that no man could be declared finally happy in this uncertain life, withheld their judgments.

It was first through Actaion, Cadmos's grandson by Autonoe, that the idyllic life of Thebes was shattered. Tall, ruggedly handsome, athletic, Actaion more than anything else relished the hunt. With his fifty hounds and numerous companions, most of them adolescents like himself sporting the down of their first beards upon their chins, he scoured the wooded haunts of Mount Cithairon for game. At dawn they would lay their traps and through the morning try to roust the bear and deer and wild pigs from their hiding places.

One particular morning the game was so abundant that by midday they had taken more animals than they had even seen the whole day before. "My friends," the son of Autonoe said, "enough for today. The sun is high in the heavens. We have earned our rest, so let us take it. Until tomorrow, my friends, at dawn."

Deep in that same part of the forest was a glen and in the glen a cave, the rocks of which were draped with a lustrous, thick green moss. Out of a cleft in the rocks a natural fountain spurted water, refreshing and crystalline, which, wetting the moss, causing it to sparkle where shafts of the noon sun penetrated the shade, collected into a beautiful pool just outside the cave, in part defined by it. Grass as rich as emeralds encircling the pool lent its green to the deep, cool water.

The place was sacred to silver-quivered Artemis and her maidens, who had also hunted the game-rich woods that morning. So secluded was the pool that the usually demure huntress, at last upon reaching it after the long morning's strenuous chase, looked neither to the right nor to the left before, dropping her javelin and unstringing her silver bow, she slid the strap of her quiver from her shoulder and, with almost the same motion, the strap of her short-skirted tunic. Her maidens did likewise. In but a moment all were in the pool playing and splashing like young bear cubs.

This was the scene that, after taking leave of his companions, Actaion came upon as he explored the glen in order to plan the next morning's hunt. He was almost at water's edge when he noticed the unclothed female figures at play. Never had he seen a naked girl before, much less a goddess. Artemis, tall and well proportioned, aglow with virgin beauty, quite dazzled him. He pushed aside a branch to see better.

Suddenly all play ceased. The maidens shrieked like squirrels set upon by crooked-clawed hawks, their high-pitched voices reinforced and made the more shrill by the rocky recesses of the cave. Trying to protect their own modesty with hands and arms, they quickly encircled their mistress to shield her from the voyeur's gaze; however, the goddess so towered above them that the heads of the tallest barely came halfway to her breasts. All flesh, a moment before lightly coppered, became as brilliantly red as the sun through morning haze: the maidens' from embarrassment, from rage their mistress's.

Glancing over her shoulder to where Cadmos's grandson was half hidden behind a laurel bush, the virgin goddess shot, like an arrow from her silver quiver, a look that both transfixed and transformed the unhappy youth. The arrow would have been kinder. "Shout it, if shout you can," she taunted. "Tell the world your eyes feasted on my unclothed virgin body. Test your tongue, do. Shout abroad my shame. Try, you vile little animal. Why don't you try?"

Actaion opened his mouth, not to speak the goddess's shame but rather to implore her mercy. No words came, only muted animal noises. He tried to reach out his arms, but they were no longer arms; the long, lean, bony forelegs of a deer they were instead. Hooves he had for hands. In a shallow pool, overflow from the other, he searched momentarily for his image. Large brown eyes, wide with fright, stared back at him; atop the head two great branches of antlers. A more handsome stag he had never seen.

He turned and ran, heading instinctively for the paths that would take him home. In the distance he could hear his dogs, fifty of them, howling and barking as they trailed his companions, trying to divert them into the deep woods again to take up the hunt. For a moment it was a welcome sound. Then, comprehending, seized by sudden terror, Actaion turned but, alas, too late; the hounds had his scent. Over fallen trees they leaped, through thicket openings, down craggy inclines, along stone-strewn gullies, salivating over blood remembered, blood anticipated, their growls and howls rising to deafening crescendo.

Hunter now hunted, stag-killer stag, Cadmos's grandchild flew down the paths, the ravines, hurdled bushes, sought the dense forest's untracked sanctuaries. "It is I, your master!" he tried to call out to his dogs; strident cries of inarticulate cervine anguish were all that passed his lips. Suddenly from behind, as he cut down a stony embankment, the straight course blocked by raging, cascading waters, a dog, his one-time pride, sprang to his back, clamping its fangs into the narrow flesh at the base of his neck. He leaped high, twisting in mid air, to shake the dog, but the fangs, like the teeth of a sprung trap, held fast. New pain shot through him as a second dog dug its teeth into his shoulder. Then came the pack.

All of Cadmos's daughters were exceedingly fair to look upon, but the fairest of the four was Semele. Not least to contemplate her loveliness was Zeus himself. She was to him a beautiful, exotic garden filled with the rarest fruits. At first he was content to imagine their texture and tang, though not for long.

One day, when Hera was preoccupied with a festival in her honor, he slipped down from Mount Olympos, leaving most of his glory behind, and approached his garden. He told Semele who he was and she believed him. She would have believed him too if he had said he was the North Wind. "Ask of me any boon," he promised her. "It shall be yours." The garden gates were thrown open. Fruits tasted, enjoyed, devoured, Zeus departed, his own divine seed now sown in the rich, hot, moist soil.

The seed grew, and so also did Semele. Hera, already steeped in hate for the house of Agenor because of Europa, was not slow to take notice. "Oh, how proud she is, this betrayer of my bed, to swell with Zeus's child, an honor seldom accorded me," the white-armed goddess said. "Smile not, my little adultress. You will soon be caught in the coils of your own vanity."

Speaking thus, the Queen of Olympos mounted a golden cloud and drifted down to Thebes. In Cadmos's palace she found Semele. Not as a goddess, though, did Hera appear; rather as a crone, hair gray-streaked, face scored with deep wrinkles, skin loose, sagging, hanging like wrung rags from abundant jowls. She was the spit and image of Beroe, Semele's one-time nurse; like Beroe's too her faltering voice. "It is said," she ventured, after amenities, "that the child you carry beneath your ribs is Zeus's."

"It is," said Semele.

"Many a rogue, my dear, claims to be Zeus in order to thieve what cannot be restored," Hera told her. "To look like a god means nothing. Have proof. Insist he take you, not as a gallant takes his whore, but as he took to his breast Hera on their wedding night—resplendent in all his glory."

The advice seemed most reasonable to the lean-witted daughter of Cadmos. When next the Father of Gods and Men came to her, therefore, she reminded him of his promise to grant her her dearest wish. "That I promised," said he, "and, by the River Styx, will I be true to my word."

"Take me then as you took Hera on your wedding night. Hold back none of your glory. Be the bridegroom for me you were for her."

Great Zeus was grieved by her words. He besought her to take them back for she did not know what she asked, but she would not. Heart heavy, he made his way back to Mount Olympos. From his wardrobe he took hoary dew and draped himself with it, his movements labored as though he were dressing for a funeral; then he drew clouds about him and storms, next thunder and lightning and, last of all, fire. The least of his thunderbolts he took, specially fashioned for him by the Cyclopes for dress occasions, a mere toy compared to the heavy artillery with which he had pounded the Titans.

Then back to the Cadmean palace he went, back to the familiar bedchamber of the king's beautiful daughter. Too much was his glory for the silly mortal girl when he tried to make good his promise. More easily could Semele's body have taken a burning brand than the blistering thrust of Zeus's full passion. To smoldering cinders was the once voluptuous figure reduced, to soot the lips to which a lesser Zeus had at one time fondly pressed his own.

From the charred remains the god snatched the unborn baby, enough of himself to be alive, intact, unharmed. Quickly then he opened the hollow of his own thigh; and, as a skilled housewife might stuff a cut of meat, he gently placed into it the infant and with gold thread firmly sewed it back together. While three moons waxed and waned in the heavens, the child grew inside his father's thigh until immortality filled its every part. Then it was that Zeus removed the stitches and brought forth his son Dionysos a second time into the world of light.

Because of the fiery wrath of Hera, Hermes, at his father's beck, spirited the infant god away to the nymphs of Nysa in far off Asia. In a cave there he grew to adolescence, his needs meticulously attended to by the mountain nymphs. Neither deathless male nor mortal frequented the cave. In his youth the only voices Dionysos heard were the honeyed voices of girls; theirs too the only mannerisms he chanced to observe. Thus, like other youths raised in exclusively female company, he took on some of the qualities of his models. It was at Nysa too that Dionysos devised the art of making wine from grapes.

In Thebes rumor grew (fed by her own sisters) that Semele's pregnancy had been the fruit of her whoredom with men, nothing more, and that Zeus, furious over her face-saving fabrications, as punishment had slain her with his fiery shafts. When, therefore, at length Dionysos came to his mother's city, great indignation burned in his heart.

Great was his power by then to charm and bewitch, to take from men their natural reserve, to unfetter within them their impulses, their primal instincts, those unuttered, forbidden longings held hostage by custom and civilization, unfulfilled except in dreams. Under his spell men and women became free as babes; their spirits soared like eagles. In their minds they were transported to realms beyond, unearthly, ethereal. Things familiar took on bizarre shapes and aspects: trees seemed as men and men as beasts, shadows as many-headed serpents, patches of fog as raging bulls. The sinews of those intoxicated by the god became as sinews of iron.

Upon Ino and Autonoe and Agave, sisters of Semele, blasphemous scandalmongers, he cast his magic and not a few other women of Thebes as well. These joined his maenads in manic dance. Kicking high, gyrating, their whole bodies responding to pulsating rhythms within as to the pounding of the sea or to the unrelenting beat of savage and distant drums, the Bacchai flocked after their god. Beyond the towers of Thebes they followed him and from thence to Mount Cithairon.

"Surely a new god strides among us," said Cadmos to his grandson Pentheus, now king in his stead. "We must worship him too."

"A magician, no more," replied young Pentheus, "certainly not a god and not the son of Semele who perjured Zeus. He seeks but to defile and debauch. Orgy, not worship, is his object."

"Whatever your doubts, my grandson, treat him as a god anyway. It is the safe course—and to your family's credit as well."

Rejecting his grandfather's counsel, the youthful king forthwith ordered the arrests of Dionysos and his entire entourage. Although his guardsmen set out on their mission with great apprehensiveness, their chore proved astonishingly easy. Dionysos, feigning to be but a devotee and not the god himself, cheerfully held out his hands for the irons, much as a child might for promised sweets, as did also the women. As she-goats at milking time, the Bacchai were happily herded into the royal dungeons. Among them, feeling no pain as if in a world apart, was Agave, the king's own mother.

The royal guardsmen had scarcely left the dungeon, however, when suddenly all the locks turned and, assisted by no mortal hand, the bolts were drawn back. At the same instant the manacles mysteriously loosed from the prisoner's wrists. Doors flew wide open, and the women, like wintered kine let out to spring pasture, ran en masse into the open space, buoyantly, friskily leaping into the air, and sprinted spiritedly back toward the shady haunts of Cithairon as if drawn there by some irresistible force.

To effect his designs against the impious young king, his cousin, Dionysos remained behind in Thebes. Still bound, he was brought before Pentheus. "So sweet a face, such lovely long locks," sneered the beardless monarch. "Are you sure nature meant you to be a man? Your skin's so pale. Too much time in beds perhaps and not enough in the sun. What rites are these your god brings to my kingdom?"

"Perhaps you would like to see them firsthand," suggested the god.

"You mean to spy upon those wanton strumpets in Cithairon's glens, to witness their debaucheries?"

"To see dances man has never seen, to watch them tear asunder wild beasts with their bare hands, their bodies writhing, pulsating with lust, all you imagine."

The young king gradually came under Dionysos's spell. His eyes became wide; his voice higher pitched, though not to him. "One must know whereof he seeks to make reform," he said.

"You can, yourself unseen, watch them from behind trees or beneath heavy-leaved bushes, and so have proof of their lewd and sensuous ways."

"Yes, one must have proof."

"Then be quick about it. Don a disguise," said Dionysos. "Deck yourself in dainty linen robes."

Without argument Pentheus followed the twice-born god through the palace to the residence chambers. There Dionysos fitted him with long tresses and with skirts down to his feet. A prettily embroidered headband he put around his hair. Then about his shoulders the god draped a fawnskin cloak and into his hand placed a cone-tipped thyrsus. By the time the two slipped into the back streets of Thebes, Pentheus, pinched by girdle and sash, streaming with gay ribbons, was springing through the air in ornate heeled sandals. Everything he saw now was in doubles. Nor did he know which Dionysos to follow.

The noises of the Bacchic celebration, the drumbeats and aboriginal screams, could be heard long before they reached Cithairon. "Cries of passion," said the young king excitedly. "I can hear them."

"Soon you will be able to see their revelries as well."

"Women, they say, scream like that when their passion is most unbearable. Listen to them, will you! What kind of love play can they be up to? Let us run faster. I feel I can outrace the swiftest hind."

"Run then, my impious cousin," laughed the god. "Your reward is not far off."

The Bacchai were sporting themselves in a grassy glen guarded on two sides by high cliffs. Near the approach to the glen was a stately pine, taller far than any of the trees around it. This, at the god's suggestion, the bewitched young king rapidly climbed—more to be seen, as it turned out, than to see. When he was perched against the upmost branch, Dionysos cried out, "Look you here, my maidens! Behold the blasphemer!"

As one the women turned and fastened their gazes on the daintily bedecked figure in the tree, but what they saw, their minds also under the god's spell, was not a man but a mountain lion. Like swift-flying hawks they sped to their god, now seated at the tree's base. Agave and her blood sisters in the lead, their feet hardly touched rock or grass so swiftly did they move. Quickly they picked up stones to pelt the pathetic king.

"It is I," called Pentheus to Agave below, "your son, mother, Pentheus your son."

All Agave heard was the challenging snarl of a trapped animal. The women now put their hands against the trunk and, as though it were but a five-year sapling, soon had the tree swaying in a wide arc from side to side. So great was their strength the roots began to tear loose from the

68

ground. In moments Pentheus, dizzy and drained of vitality, lost his purchase and fell to the ground. He cried for mercy once more from his mother, who, with the wide, wild eyes of one possessed, was the first upon him. Froth oozed from her mouth.

She gripped his left arm firmly at the elbow; then, placing her foot against his ribs, with the strength of fifty she tore the arm from its socket. Her sister Ino after the same manner ripped off his other arm. Screaming savagely, the other Bacchai dug their nails into loose flesh and pulled, as if in contest with one another, in several directions at once. Actaion's hounds could not have dismembered a body more thoroughly nor more quickly. Last of all, Agave, casting aside the arm, curled her fingertips around either side of her son's jawbone and wrenched loose the young king's head.

The daughter of Cadmos thereupon impaled the head, as though a rare trophy, on top of her thyrsus and, leaving the company of the other Bacchai, headed jubilantly, triumphantly back to Thebes. "Look upon my prize," she shouted to all she met, "captured by me without snare and without nets."

"Who struck the blow that killed your quarry?" asked a passerby.

"I, with my own hands," said Agave. Even as she spoke, a drop of blood from her son's head fell to her shoulder. "Call me Agave the blessed."

"Agave the blessed," said the passerby.

At the palace she found her aged father, who had by this time already learned of his grandson's fate. "This day, my father, have I done honor to your house," she exclaimed. "These hands, skilled in working the loom, have also proved able in the hunt. Something for your wall, dear father."

"My poor wretched Agave," said Cadmos.

"Why do you weep, great Cadmos? I brought you a prize."

"Look up at your prize, my wretched daughter. Look and weep."

Agave, her mind clearing, lifted her eyes to the mass atop her thyrsus and for the first time saw her son's head for what it was. Horror-stricken, she asked how it came there, and slowly the whole story was told her. Man's peril is never so great as when he ventures to challenge the sovereignty of a god. That the family of Cadmos had done and, in return, had felt the full measure of the god's fury.

In Thebes thereafter was Dionysos most honored as was also his mother Semele. Polydoros, the youngest child of Cadmos, succeeded to the throne. The daughters of Cadmos were banished as well as the now aged founder of the city himself because his homage to the god had been out of expediency rather than faith. Harmonia followed her husband into exile.

Tragedy continued to stalk the house of Cadmos however. Each year brought him and his banished queen yet new reports of disasters to their children and grandchildren. "Maybe it is all because I killed Ares' serpent," he said. "Our woes, my wretched wife, stem from that time."

Harmonia thought awhile. "Yes, that might be," she said.

"If that is why the gods have turned their backs on my house," the frail king prayed, lifting his eyes to the heavens, "then let me be a serpent myself to atone for it, that my house might henceforth be blessed." And what he prayed came to pass. Not he alone, but Harmonia too, became great serpents with impenetrable skin and brilliant, glossy spots. They slithered together into the dense green forest and were never seen again.

# Bellerophon
# and Perseus

T he distant cousins of the Cadmeans in Argos all this time were enjoying comparative tranquility. Lynceus, sole son of Aigyptos to live past his wedding night, became king after Danaos, his father-in-law, and his son Abas succeeded him. Good times reigned with both. When the scepter fell to Proitos and Acrisios, twin sons of Abas, however, peace fled from the kingdom forthwith. The two were ever at emnity the one against the other, even in their mother's womb.

Eventually Acrisios prevailed against his brother and drove him from Greece. In far-off Lycia the bitter and dispossessed Proitos spent his exile, there wooing and winning the exotically beautiful, sensuous Stheneboia, daughter to Iobates, king of that Asian land. It was the armies of Iobates that in time effected Proitos's return to Argos and made him king again over half the land. Rancor still burned in his soul, however, against Acrisios, his brother.

Now Acrisios had a daughter by the name of Danae. While yet an adolescent she was in body the equal of any woman in Argos and, because of a glow of innocence about her, infinitely more lovely. At first when he looked upon the girl, Proitos saw her as a means whereby he could avenge himself against his hated brother. Gradually, however, thoughts of vengeance gave way to other thoughts. He could not be sure, but at moments it almost seemed that Danae was returning his lustful leers.

His designs toward the girl, however, were interrupted by the arrival of a young stranger in Argos begging him for sanctuary and ceremonial cleansing. The man had accidentally killed his own brother. Filled with remorse, driven from his own country, he threw himself now on the mercy of Proitos to restore him to the favor of gods and men. Proitos obliged him and, after sacrifices for his purification, took him into his own house.

71

The young man's name was Bellerophon. Out of gratitude he sought to serve Proitos and return to him loyalty for kindness. Stheneboia, Proitos's wife, however, whose eyes also sometimes wandered, looked upon Bellerophon and found him exceedingly handsome. Wherever he went she chanced to be also. Always standing close to him, her body brushing his, she would often place her hand on his arm or shoulder, as if to emphasize a point in conversation, and let it linger there. Although her advances had no effect on Bellerophon, they nourished in Stheneboia a passion of enormous magnitude.

One day, when Proitos was absent from the palace and the servants were reposing in their quarters, the queen on a pretext brought the young man into her chambers. Closing and bolting the door, she suddenly brushed her gown from her shoulders and let it fall to the floor, then took his hand to lead him to her bed. "Lie with me," she said, "and I will make you feel like a god."

"I will not betray my benefactor," Bellerophon told her and straightway fled the palace.

It was a furious and spiteful Stheneboia who, later that same day, met her husband upon his return and quickly took him aside. "Kill Bellerophon," she said to him. "I demand it, for this day he tried to defile your bed."

Proitos became infuriated himself as he listened to his wife's spurious account of the incident. He was loath, however, to dispatch the young man himself because, after all, Bellerophon was his guest and the sure and awful vengeance of gods against the slayer of a guest, whatever the reason, was not to be taken lightly. He, therefore, sent for the young man and, giving no indication of anything amiss wherein Stheneboia was concerned, asked him if he would serve him as envoy to the court of his father-in-law Iobates in Lycia. Bellerophon welcomed the assignment.

On a tablet Proitos wrote a letter to Iobates in which he recounted Stheneboia's version of the attempted rape and requested Iobates to kill the bearer of the letter without delay and without mercy. He then gave the sealed tablet to Bellerophon, telling him it was a letter of introduction and bid him farewell. Stheneboia was not on hand to see him off.

And so the gods brought the maligned young man safely to the shores of Lycia. The king was immediately taken with him, and for nine days he held feasts in his honor and killed nine heifers and opened nine amphoras of wine. On the tenth day Iobates sent for Bellerophon and sought to know more about his mission. Then it was that the young man remembered the tablet and gave it to the king. Cold dismay seized the heart of Iobates as he read the letter, for, like his son-in-law, he was fearful of shedding anyone's blood who was now his guest.

Now there was in that country an awesome she-monster, fiendish and unnatural, called the Chimera. She had for a head that of a lion and for a body that of a goat and for a tail that of a serpent. From her mouth belched forth terrible blasts of blazing fire. So hot were the flames no man could approach her. She ravished the crops and killed the sheep and cattle of the land. Against this monster Iobates sent his guest Bellerophon, confident the young man would never return.

Bellerophon, again delighted to be of service to someone he supposed his friend and benefactor, set forth to accomplish his assignment. However, before going to where the dreadful Chimera was, like a savage army gone wild, laying waste the countryside, he found a seer and through him sought the counsels of the gods. "Confront not the fiery beast," the seer told him, "except astride Pegasos, great winged steed that now by Corinth's spring drinks and feeds."

Bellerophon had heard of the mighty horse, but as he journeyed to Corinth he knew neither how he would catch him nor how he would control him to ride him. That night bright-eyed Athene appeared to him as if in a dream. "Take this charm to control the horse," she said, "and to the gods sacrifice an unblemished bull." The young man woke with a start and next to him found a shining bridle of purest gold. Forthwith he erected an altar and sacrificed on it an unblemished bull to the deathless gods of Olympos.

The winged horse Pegasos was drinking at the spring when Bellerophon came upon him. Stealthily creeping up to the magnificent animal, he was able to cast the gleaming bridle onto him while his head was yet bent and, as he raised his head, to slide the bit into his mouth. A potion mixed by Hecate herself could not have made the spirited horse more gentle. Bellerophon quickly mounted him, and the two flew off to do battle with the Chimera in the kingdom of Iobates.

Flames came spewing out of the Chimera's mouth like a volcano as Bellerophon hovered over her head, safely beyond her range. Patiently he discharged his arrows one at a time into the she-monster's body. Not one missed the target. But still she opened her lion's mouth and roared mightily and spat forth her terrible fire. Next, making quick passes, he drew thick blood with his spear. The Chimera faltered but did not die. Then it was he fixed to the tip of his spear a lump of lead and, diving in close, thrust it between the monster's open jaws. The heat of the Chimera's own mouth immediately melted the lead so that the molten metal seeped down her throat and, scorching her vital organs, soon killed her.

Off sped Bellerophon to report to Iobates that his mission was accomplished. Iobates, less than thrilled by the young man's return, before long sent him forth again, this time to subdue the mighty Solymi, fierce and wild tribesmen, incorrigible warriors all. Through them, the king was confident, the attempted dishonor upon his daughter would surely be avenged. By dropping huge boulders on the Solymi while circling safely beyond their bow range, Bellerophon, however, was able to prevail over them as well.

Not far beyond the borders of Lycia there lived a race of women called Amazons. It was against these that Iobates next dispatched Bellerophon, who still supposed that he was but being asked again to return kindness for kindness. The mere mention of the word "Amazon" sent cold shock through the bodies of brave men and, say some, caused those safe in their graves to shudder, and not without reason. Men were the Amazons' mortal enemies.

Only girl babies did they deem worthy to be raised; and, it was rumored, in some tribes full citizenship was not conferred until a girl had killed her first man. Savage warfare was their enterprise, these darlings of Ares; the longbow their chief weapon. No army of men ever drew stronger bows than the Amazons. Each girl, as she matured, had to have her one breast removed lest it alter her aim or deflect her bowstring. Skilled also were they with spears and javelins. But all their training and skills were as naught against sky-riding Bellerophon and the winged Pegasos, nor could their shields parry the bombardment of boulders that rained upon them from the heavens.

Wary this time that another miracle might spare the young man, Iobates stationed his own palace guards, huge men all and seasoned cut-throats, to waylay him on his return. These too Bellerophon prevailed against; however, at last his suspicions were aroused. "Why are you trying to kill me?" he demanded to know of his host.

"Have you no idea?" said Iobates, finally showing him Proitos's letter.

Upon reading the letter, Bellerophon told the king the true story, and Iobates believed him and gave to him Philonoe, his daughter, in marriage. Years later, when death closed the eyes of Iobates, Bellerophon ascended to the throne. Were it not for a restlessness and not a little arrogance, he might have spent the rest of his days comfortable and happy.

Though every bit as striking as her sister, Philonoe was mistress over her own passions and so proved a fit and faithful queen. But even she was powerless to stop Bellerophon that day when he once again mounted the great winged horse Pegasos and, following Helios's bright chariot across the sky, set out for what he thought would be his grandest adventure of all, an audience with the gods of Mount Olympos.

On to Olympos's foothills he sped, then up the jagged slopes, the craggy cliffs to those rarefied, cloud-shrouded climes where mortal eyes have never gazed; up, up he rode toward the glistening, glimmering citadel of the deathless Twelve. Nor was great Zeus blind to the brazen mortal's foolish effrontery. Quickly he fashioned a gadfly, in size and sting the twin of that with which jealous Hera punished Io, and directed it to the flying flank of Pegasos. Instant agony shot through the winged steed's great frame. The golden bridle could no longer control him. He bucked and bolted until he threw Bellerophon from his back into the rocks and thistles down the steep embankment.

Torn, crippled, and blind, Bellerophon crawled and stumbled down Olympos's slopes. He wandered among men, thereafter, a bitter and mean-spirited man, until at last icy-fingered death claimed him. Never did he return to Lycia, never to the waiting arms and warm breast of Philonoe, his wife and queen. The magnificent winged horse Pegasos, quickly cor-ralled by Cronos's cloud-gathering son, was stabled in the golden, bejew-eled barns of Olympos and grew strong and sleek there on the ambrosial grains. Zeus, say some, did occasionally use him as a pack horse to carry his lightning bolts.

Meanwhile, back in Argos a persistent and amorous Proitos was able to achieve with Danae that wherein his wife had failed with Bellerophon. Nor was there any indication that the daughter of Acrisios struggled to prevent the bloom of her maidenhood from being plucked.

Ironically, at the time Acrisios himself was consulting an oracle as to whether or not he would have an heir. He found no cause for comfort in the oracle's reply:

*Aye, Danae's son will your line sustain,*
*Though vaunt not: By the same shall you be slain.*

Initial apprehension soon changed to alarm when vulgar palace jokes reached Acrisios's ear hinting at his daughter's indiscretions. He began to wonder if perchance the seed of his destruction had already been sown;

if not, he feared it soon would be, for ground once worked, he knew, turns more easily to the plow than that which has never been broken.

Thus, to forestall further ventures into carnality on Danae's part, Acrisios commissioned his architects to build for him a great, brazen underground dungeon with but a single window in the ceiling to give it light. Into the dungeon, spacious and plushly furnished, he had his daughter cast; then solid bronze bars he ordered to be placed across the ceiling window so that no one could either enter or leave the dungeon. Having done thus, Acrisios sighed deeply and sank securely into his throne.

What he did not reckon on was the errant eye of the Father of Gods and Men himself. From the airy heights of Mount Olympos Zeus could see into the brazen chamber; as clearly as if indeed his cheeks were pressed against the bars could he see the lovely girl in the cell. Danae, unaware any eyes were upon her, was often given to romping about in her scantiest attire and sometimes not even in that. Like many a maiden who has prematurely tasted love's forbidden fruit, she yearned for more. In her movements, in her dreamy eyes her yearning was abundantly manifest to the Father of Gods, in whom it engendered a yearning not dissimilar. One afternoon, when Hera was not about, in guise as golden rain he slipped through the barred window to the girl's couch. Fluid passion, fierce and rapturous, found fluid response; divine seed ungrudging ground.

Nine months later the cloistered princess Danae brought forth her firstborn, a son, and called him Perseus. Cold terror, not joy, seized the infant's grandfather, proud Acrisios. Thinking the child his brother's issue, he ordered mother and baby to be put into a chest and the chest thrown far out into the sea.

In their tiny tomb-womb ark Danae and Perseus tossed long on the surface of the deep but at last were washed ashore on the island of Seriphos. A fisherman named Dictys found them there and forthwith took them to Polydectes, his brother, who was king of the island. Polydectes received the mother and child into his palace. Though Danae was quick to accept the hospitality of her benefactor's table, she was loath to accept the hospitality of his bed when, within the month, it was offered her. Many a time over the years the offer was renewed, each time declined.

The king's ardor was not, however, dulled by the passing of the years. Even when the babe reached young manhood, Polydectes was still pressing his suit with the ever more lovely Danae. The presence of someone now as big as he did, though, affect his manners for the better. Whenever Perseus was about, Polydectes was the personification of decency, the model of gentility, all of which vexed him enormously. He began to lament not forcing Danae when she first arrived on the island.

There was at this time on the mainland a princess whose beauty and fortune were the talk of all Greece. The guileful Polydectes announced one day his plans to court her. "If I am to win her," he told the people of his kingdom, "I must have your help. Great beauties are won only with great gifts." And so the people brought to him horses and gold and all such wealth as they possessed so that he might woo the celebrated princess and bring fame and prosperity to Seriphos.

Perseus, dependent upon the king for even the raiment upon his back, had nothing to bring. "Gold and horses have I none," he told the king, "but such service as I can render that will I surely do."

"There is one thing I would like," said Polydectes.

"Say, and yours shall it be."

"The head of the Gorgon Medusa," Polydectes told him.

Medusa, it seems, with her two Gorgon sisters was easily the ugliest thing in creation. For hair she had hundreds of hissing snakes dangling from her scalp. Her eyes were fierce and bloodshot, her teeth like the twisted tusks of wild boars. So grotesquely distorted was her aspect that anyone who chanced so much as to glimpse at her turned immediately into stone. In sending Perseus for her head, Polydectes was sending the youth to his certain death, his design from the beginning.

Perseus, however, set about to make good his word. Fortunately, as with Bellerophon, bright-eyed Athene was not far off. "Look not directly upon that snake-tressed head," she warned him, giving him a bronze shield polished to mirror finish, "but indirectly with this. From Hermes take this sword, finely honed and curved to suit your purpose. To complete your task you will yet need a special leather pouch, winged sandals, and Hades' helmet of darkness, all in the possession of the Stygian Nymphs." With that, the goddess disappeared.

No one knew where to find the Stygian Nymphs—that is, except the Gray-ones, three sisters so old that they had but a single eye between them, which they passed around as needed. Neither did they know the time of day, nor would they have given it to a stranger if they did, so recluse and uncordial were they. In order to exact the information he needed, Perseus stood behind the ancient trio and waited until the eye was being passed; then, with deft movement, he reached in and grabbed it. Nor did he return it until they told him where the Stygian Nymphs could be found.

The Nymphs themselves, no champions of the Gorgon sisters, were more hospitable. Perseus had but to hint of his mission, and the pouch, sandals, and helmet were all his. And so off he flew to beyond the great Ocean Stream and came to the land of the snake-tressed Gorgons. Wearing the helmet of darkness, he entered unseen into the cave where they lived.

Medusa and her sisters were asleep when Perseus came upon them. Using his shield as a mirror, stealthily he backed into their chamber, his sword poised and ready. Already Athene had shown him how to distinguish Medusa from her immortal sisters. Athene now guided his hand as he reached back and partially encircled Medusa's throat with Hermes' blade. As a farmer lays his sickle to a thick shock of barley, even so did the mighty son of Danae draw the sword across the scaly flesh of the dread Gorgon's throat and with but a single stroke neatly amputate her head. Before the other two awoke, he had stuffed Medusa's head into the leather pouch and was high aloft above the Ocean Stream.

Over the Ocean he sped, past stout-hearted Atlas bearing up the sky, over the wine-dark sea and over the Libyan desert to those regions from which the great Nile flows, even to Ethiopia, where people stood taller and led lives more idyllic than any other people on earth. So fast did he fly that spurts of Gorgon blood splashed free of the pouch and fell as foul rain to the sands below. Where drops landed, forthwith venomous asps sprang into being, their tongues darting betwixt hideous jaws to test the desert air.

At land's edge, in a place where the irregular coastline jutted sharply out to sea then withdrew and jutted out again so as to define a natural harbor, a most strange sight caught his eye. To a rock in the harbor a girl was chained. Or was it but a wondrously sculpted figure of stone? At first he could not tell, but as he swept down closer he could see her hair jostled by the wind and on her cheeks huge tears. He was dazzled both by her plight and her haunting beauty. Naturally shy, he circled the girl a time or two before setting down next to her. "Lovely maiden," he said, fumbling for the right words, "a lover's bed befits you better than this bed of rock, a lover's arms better than these chains. Pray tell me your name and why you are bound."

The girl, also shy, would have covered her eyes with her hands, if she could have, rather than speak with so bold a stranger. She heaved great sobs, and new tears coursed freely down her cheeks. Perseus soothed her with words, his voice as gentle as the rippling of a meadow brook on a still midsummer's eve. At length, through more sobs, the girl spoke: "By Andromeda does my foolish mother call me. My father is Cepheus, king of this place. But think not it is for my own folly I wear these chains. It is for hers, my poor proud mother, who, alas, did praise my beauty overmuch. More beautiful than the Nereids of the sea did she say was this body you now look upon, kind stranger. Thus was the wrath of earth-shaking Poseidon provoked against my house and me. By prophetic command am I bound here, awaiting the god's avenging monster, his leviathan specially fashioned to tear my body asunder. Else will the whole city be destroyed. It was spoken."

Even then the son of Danae could hear the roar of the great sea monster as it rode the white-tipped waves landward into the bay. On the shore King Cepheus and his queen, Cassiopeia, wailed and beat their breasts as though the horror to come had already been accomplished. "What say you," Perseus called out to them, "if I should save your daughter, would you welcome me as your son-in-law? Zeus's son am I, Perseus by name, begotten of golden showers, slayer of the Gorgon Medusa. Speak quickly. Will the girl I save be mine?"

With one voice the parents consented and promised him choice lands for dowry as well. Nor did they reply a moment too soon, for the fierce sea dragon, like hounds at first clear scent of blood, came charging now across the waters, streaking, skimming, diving, vaulting above the surface so that its green-black scales glimmered in the afternoon sun. Straight toward its victim the great serpentine monster sped. On the shore the queen hid her face against the king's shoulder; both shrieked in mortal terror. Perseus fluttered his winged sandals and was quickly aloft. Once more on his brow he pressed Hades' helmet of darkness; then, as almost a part of the same motion, drew his blood-smeared sword.

Instantly invisible, the golden-rain-begotten son of Danae flew swiftly out to meet his scaled adversary. His shadow on the water's surface marked the speed and direction of his flight. The monster came up quickly from under the shadowy form with triple-teeth-lined jaws stretched wide open then snapping suddenly shut. At that same instant Perseus dove unperceived from the sky. As the eagle of Zeus, talons spread, drops suddenly upon the spotted viper in the grass and drives its crooked claws into its scaly throat, thus did Acrisios's grandson descend upon the leviathan and thrust to the hilt his bended blade into the folds below the base of its awful head.

Withdrawing his sword from its fleshy sheath, Perseus, still invisible, quickly pirouetted into the air beyond the monster's lunging, snapping jaws. Again he swooped down from his lofty heights and again buried his blade in the scaly folds. The sea dragon reeled and thrashed. It rolled briefly onto its back, exposing its smooth green-black underbelly. Thrice did Perseus thrust his sword into those vital parts. The monster's massive body contracted as though pierced by Zeus's lightning; great curds of purple vomit shot, as if from a volcano, out of its dreadful mouth. Purplish-black blood befouled the sea for a hundred yards in every direction. From the shore Cepheus and Cassiopeia shouted loud their cries of jubilation as the grim sea monster twice twitched in its own putrescence and then was still.

Perseus took off the magic helmet and quickly came again to the rock where Andromeda was chained. He set down the leather pouch upon a bed of seaweeds and ferns while he unbound the grateful maiden. By the time he picked the pouch up, the vegetation on which he had laid it had turned to rigid coral. To her royal home he led the princess, more beauteous by far now to his eyes than when first he saw her stretched across the rock. Surrounded by the king and queen, ecstatic, weeping unashamed out of relief, and by masses of courtly well-wishers, boisterous in celebration, the couple walked lightly, like the bridegroom and bride they were, to the place of their nuptials.

Quick were the preparations for the wedding. Meats and fruits were readied in the royal kitchen, while the palace attendants polished the lamps and candlesticks of the great hall. Perseus, in the meanwhile, erected three altars on the grassy lawn and offered on the one a young cow to bright-eyed Athene and on the next a steer to Hermes and on the third a handsome bull to the Father of Gods and Men. He then joined his bride, in her dainty gown approaching for beauty Aphrodite herself (though he dared not think it), and her family in the flower-bedecked hall. Flutes and lyres filled the chamber with sweet music; the guests raised their cups in toast to bride and groom; then joined their voices in such strident, happy wedding airs that the very walls rang with joyous sound.

Then, of a sudden, the twin doors of the hall were flung open, and there, flanked by brutish armed men of terrifying aspect, stood Phineus, brother to Cepheus, fiercely brandishing his thick-shafted, bronze-tipped spear. His face was livid with rage. "For my queen have I come," he roared, "my stolen queen! Aside, alien rogue, wife-stealer!" Speaking thus, he advanced on Perseus, his spear poised, the muscles of his powerful arms taut and bulging.

Cepheus quickly stepped into his path. "Your quarrel, my brother, is not with him, but me. I promised you the girl's hand, I and her mother, but that you forfeited when you stood by and let her be offered to the Earth-shaker's dragon. This gallant stranger brought her, as it were, back from the dead. He acted when you would not."

"Aside!" bellowed Phineus, striking the air with his heavy spear. "A wedding gift I have for this rain-begotten bastard of Zeus."

"I know you, brother. Out of envy you act. This youth did what you dared not attempt. It is for that you hate him, not for the girl's sake."

The truth, more painful than the stings of a thousand scorpions, cut to the quick the wild Phineus. For a moment he glared, eyes aflame with hate, at his brother; then, as a cat springs suddenly from its crouch upon the young deer or goat it has been stalking, he cast his thick-shafted spear at Perseus. A slower man would have been pinned to the cedar pillar behind him, but the agile, quick-eyed son of Danae deftly dodged the bronze-tipped shaft. Then, never taking his eyes from his bride's savage uncle, he wrenched loose the spear and thrust it with authority back toward its owner.

Shifty Phineus veered, as if by instinct, from the lethal bronze. Not so nimble was young Rhoitos, a wedding guest, a looker-on, who was standing behind him. The spear caught the youth in the middle of his face, we are told, and so forcefully was it thrown that the tip emerged from the back of his skull. He fell across a table, spattering the candied fruits and white tablecloth with crimson spray.

Some guests at that point joined Phineus's fearsome guard against Perseus; others, including the bride and her parents, withdrew to places of safety behind upturned tables and hastily fashioned barricades of benches and chests and chairs. Only a few stood as allies to Danae's son as, with scimitar drawn and Athene's shield raised, he backed cautiously to the rear of the hall.

A youth, barely sixteen but famed far and near for his accuracy with the javelin, Athis by name, took aim with his unerring weapon at Perseus. With rapid movement the Gorgon-slayer seized a smoldering firebrand from an altar and hurled it into his would-be assailant's face. A friend of the fallen boy screamed wildly and rushed forward but stopped short when the adamantine blade that felled Medusa found his heart. Then, as if on signal, the horde descended.

Two of Phineus's charging guards slipped in the blood of their companion and slid the space of several yards, as though on ice, to Perseus's feet. With but a single swift stroke of his sword the besieged bridegroom clove open both their throats. Another guard, Eurytos by name, rushed upon him swinging his double-bitted battle-ax. Not an instant too soon did Acrisius's grandson duck. Before Eurytos could swing a second time, Perseus seized a wine-filled urn, beautifully crafted with fine reliefs of gold and bronze and silver, and brought it down across his head. Then he quickly dispatched three more youths, one with long, luxuriant hair and on his chin the down of first beard, his aged father's joy, but no more.

Phineus, fearful of close combat with Perseus, flung his javelin with greater force than accuracy and caught a spectator just below the ribs. Drawing the javelin from his midriff with both hands, the man raised the weapon, dripping of his own blood, and said, "Since you, Phineus, force me to fight, count me now as your fiercest foe. I return your javelin." Speaking thus, he took one step in Phineus's direction and fell forward, ghost gone before he hit the floor.

At his side Perseus's comrades acquitted themselves valiantly, inspired by their champion as though they had known him a lifetime rather than but a few hours. Two brothers, neither of whom had ever tasted defeat in the boxing ring, struck down man after man with their bare fists, though, alas, they proved no match for the cold steel of Phineus, who at last found his courage against unarmed antagonists.

Gradually worn down by the sheer numbers of their adversaries, Perseus and his small band were forced backward into a far corner of the hall. With his back against a great marble column, the Gorgon-slayer with his shield, gift of Athene, parried the barrage of spears now hurled at him. As gale-driven hail in winter the spears flew, it seemed, from every quarter. His arm now heavy, Perseus could feel his strength beginning to ebb.

Suddenly he cried out, "You leave me no choice. This horror you call down upon yourselves. If friend you be, turn thither your face from me." He reached then into his leather wallet and pulled from it the Gorgon's head.

At that moment from close range young Thescelos was taking careful aim at Perseus with his javelin. He thrust his arm forward but a span, no more; for in an instant, in a flash, the arm, the man stiffened into solid stone. A swordsman lunging at Perseus's unprotected side was likewise frozen in motion. Forever after would he hold that pose, as if sculpted in granite, on the verge of memorable action, never achieving it.

Friends hid their faces; and Perseus, grasping the hideous head by its serpentine locks, held it out for all the hostile horde to see. Like a wizard or sleight-of-hand artist, he moved the thing in a slow arc, inviting scrutiny. Throughout the great hall men became as statues. Medusa's head, drained of life, retained its awful power; whosoever looked upon it turned to stone. Above two hundred, we are told, thus were doomed, among them two or three of Perseus's allies, good men but alas, progeny of Pandora, cursed by curiosity.

Phineus saw his guardsmen suddenly freeze in place and reached out to touch those nearest him. Not flesh but granite greeted his finger tips, monuments rather than men. "By what magic, oh Perseus, you make of these men statues I know not," he called out, his tone conciliatory, "but I yield. Not in hate did I raise arms against you, but for a bride first promised me. She is yours. Take her. Spare but my life, and all I have is yours."

"From my sword have no fear, my trembling foe," said Perseus. "But look you on the fruit of your zeal, carnage most foul, and, as that you ponder, look upon this!" With that, he pivoted and thrust the Gorgon's head to within inches of Phineus's face.

In the twinkling of an eye the suppliant became as stone, indeed was stone, his outreached hands forever begging mercy; his hair and brows, like the Earth-shaker's, wild and tempestuous; in aspect the jungle beast— a fitting monument, thought Perseus, to remind his bride of her would-be husband.

Despite its stormy beginnings the marriage of Perseus and Andromeda turned out to be the happiest of marriages. Perhaps the statue of Phineus, never moved from the great hall, did have a fortuitous effect after all. Within the year a son was born to the couple, as much the joy of grandparents as parents. When Perseus and Andromeda in due time departed Ethiopia for Seriphos, the boy, named Perses after his father, was left with Cepheus, who little realized that from his loins would someday spring all the kings of Persia.

In the absence of Perseus from Seriphos, Polydectes had pursued his suit to Danae with shameless persistence. All masks were dropped. Courtship reverted into indecent proposals; amorous entreaty into unabashed threat. When even his most vile intimidations proved ineffective, the blackguard king purposed finally to take by force what he could not gain by persuasion. Frustration, rather than extinguishing lust, only fueled its raging fires. Having determined, then, to ravish the helpless Danae, Polydectes called to his court all the rogues and reprobates of Seriphos to celebrate with him his "wedding" feast. Danae and Dictys took refuge in a temple.

It was on the very eve of this feast that Perseus returned to the island. Quick inquiries brought him to the temple, where his mother, trembling as though it were her last day on earth, tearfully clutched him to her breast and, amid sobs and pants, told him of Polydectes' intent. Hot rage tore at Perseus's heart as he listened to his mother's words. "Nor are you, my son, safe in the only land you call home," she sobbed. "He will surely kill you."

Leaving Danae in the good Dictys' charge, Perseus, his leather pouch at his side, carefully worked his way up to the banquet hall. Within the hour he returned to assure his mother that all danger had passed and that Seriphos had need of a new king. Dictys, the brother of Polydectes, he argued, seemed the logical choice. Noting Danae's reactions, he guessed (correctly, as it turned out) that before long the island would also have a queen.

When the domestic servants opened the doors to the banquet hall that next morning to clean up after the nocturnal revelers, they stepped back and rubbed their eyes, for it seemed the bacchanal was still going on. Cups were raised, lips parted to take the wine, fiendish faces contorted in laughter, yet no sound. It was not a real bacchanal at all, but one frozen in stony tableau.

Anxious now to find his grandfather, Perseus made preparations to go to Argos, careful to send word ahead that all was forgiven and his purpose was reconciliation and not revenge. Acrisios, still mindful of the prophecy that he would die at the hands of his grandson, however, found no comfort in the young man's assurances and quickly fled the country. When Perseus arrived in Argos, no one could tell him where his grandfather might be reached.

It was at that same time that the king of nearby Larissa was holding funeral games in honor of his father. To bide his time, Perseus journeyed to Larissa to participate in the games. All went well for him until he hurled his discus in the pentathlon. His throw went wild, and the discus hit a man in the crowd on the foot, causing an injury that proved fatal. The man was Acrisios.

It was Perseus who, after succeeding his grandfather to the throne of Argos, built the city of Mycenai. As a favor to his mortal son, cloud-gathering Zeus commissioned the three single-eyed Cyclopes to put the huge boulders into place that make up the city's impenetrable wall and also the great monoliths that define its gateway, with the twin lions overhead. At Mycenai Andromeda bore Perseus many sons and daughters. When at length, seasoned with years, the son of Danae was gathered to his fathers, his son Electryon reigned over Mycenai in his stead.

# Voyage
# of the Argo

Now the quest for the Golden Fleece came about in this way. Convinced by the machinations of his wife Ino, crafty daughter of ill-fated Cadmos, that a curse lay upon his land, King Athamas of Orchomenos dispatched envoys to Apollo's oracle at Delphi to find out what he should do. Intercepted, bribed and briefed by Ino, however, the envoys brought back the report she gave them.

"Sore displeased are the gods," they lied. "To cleanse the land our two most precious treasures do they require. Yes, oh king, Phrixos and Helle, your own children, must be offered up. Be merciful to bearers of ill tidings."

As Ino heard these words which she herself had rehearsed with the messengers, she tore at her rich gown and counterfeited the shrieks of a true mother wracked by unspeakable grief. (Phrixos and Helle, it should be said, were not her children but rather those of Nephele, Athamas's first wife, who was now living out her days in a dungeon. It was to make way for her own children that Ino devised her evil design.)

With heavy heart Athamas ordered that an altar should be built. In the meantime, from her dungeon cell Nephele, fearing for the children, raised tearful prayers to Hera in their behalf. When the fateful hour drew nigh, the king took Phrixos and Helle by their hands and led them, as though on an evening stroll, to the altar's side. "What lambs will you offer here, father?" said Helle. "I see none."

"My choicest lambs," he replied. "They will be here in time."

Something in their father's voice sent waves of terror through the children. What words were meant to mask tone told. Their attentions shifted, however, when someone shouted, "Look!" And there, flying swiftly toward them from out of the west was a great golden ram. The huge animal swooped down and, landing directly in front of Phrixos and Helle, beckoned them to get on his back. The two children complied, Phrixos helping his sister.

In an instant the golden ram was aloft again, transporting Nephele's children out of harm's way beyond the ramparts of Orchomenos, beyond Aulis and Euboia, out over the wine-dark sea. Their fingers entwined around the glittering strands of wool, the children held on for all they were worth. At the narrows of the Propontis, however, Helle's small fingers relaxed their tight grip. Into the deep channel thereafter to bear her name she plunged and out of the land of the living never to be seen or heard from ever again.

On flew the ram to the regions beyond, even to the farthest shores of the Euxine Sea. Not until he reached Colchis, kingdom of bold Aietes, did the great glittering animal come to rest. Then, at the ram's behest, the boy Phrixos slew his carrier and offered him up as a sacrifice to the undying gods; the fleece he presented to Aietes, who had it stretched upon an oak in Ares' grove and guarded over by a dragon. Eventually Phrixos was given Chalciope to wed, the king's daughter, who in due time presented him with four sons. The days of Phrixos were brief but blessed, for by him the Golden Fleece came to Colchis.

Not least of the families to be touched by what happened at Orchomenos was that of Cretheus, Athamas's own brother, who reigned over Iolcos to the north. Upon Cretheus's death, we are told, his throne was usurped by Pelias, his stepson, said to be bastard of Poseidon. Aison, the rightful king, whom Pelias did not consider a threat, was allowed to move about in the kingdom as he wished. When Alcimede, Aison's wife, was said to be with child, however, the tyrant showed much concern lest his son Acastos someday be challenged for the throne by a legitimate heir. For this reason he had Alcimede watched day and night.

When she finally went into labor, one of Pelias's henchmen waited with Aison outside her door. By this time, though, Aison and Alcimede had already planned what they would do. Presently the door opened, and the midwife, wan and distraught, came to Aison. "It was a boy," she said, "but he died. I did all I could. I'm sorry."

Aison slumped against the door and wept and then gathered himself together and went into the room to his wife, and the two groaned as one in great lamentation. The henchman slipped out to take news of the infant's death to Pelias; by another door the servants took the baby, very much alive, to safety.

It was to the wise and immortal Centaur Cheiron that the infant son of Aison was entrusted. He it was who named the child Jason. In the Centaur's cave on Mount Pelion Jason lived for above twenty years and was there nurtured by the best of all mentors and at his feet learned wisdom. Upon turning twenty-one he bid the good Cheiron farewell and set out to claim his kingdom.

King Pelias had, in the meantime, been warned by an oracle to "beware of a man come out of the mountains with one foot bare." (And it so happened that en route to Iolcos Jason did lose one of his sandals in the miry bed of the flood-swollen Anauros River.)

The son of Aison arrived in his kingdom on a day that Pelias had prepared a festival to Poseidon and other Olympian deities, though not to white-armed Hera. To the banquet tables Jason came, awesome to behold, bearing a spear in either hand. He wore the coarse-woven tunic of the mountain people and over it a leopard's skin. His shining hair, never shorn, fell in great tresses down his back. Though a stranger, he carried himself as one in command. Whispers rose among the throng. "Surely Apollo has chosen to walk in our midst," said some.

"No," said others, "'tis Ares, Aphrodites' lord."

At once Pelias's eyes fell on the stranger's feet, one sandaled, one bare. "What is your country, vagabond?" he demanded to know. "And from what diseased whore's tired womb were you dropped?"

"Cheiron has been my master," spoke Jason, "his daughters my nursemaids. I have come to claim the kingdom of my father Aison, stolen from him, I am told, by the bastard Pelias. My country? This is my country, and these are my people and I their rightful king."

Aison was in the crowd. Tears filled his aged eyes as he looked upon his son, a true prince among men. Pelias withdrew, and a now jubilant family closed in about Jason. Into the houses of Aison's brothers the royal kindred went, and for five days they feasted and reveled and found great delight in one another's company. On the sixth day Jason sprang from the couch and went forthwith to Pelias's palace, and they that were with him went also.

"Son of Poseidon," he said to the tyrant, "I offer to you the lands you took from my father Aison and all the sheep and fatted kine that thereon feed. Live well. It galls me little. But the scepter and throne of Cretheus shall be mine."

"As you say," replied Pelias. "I am old, and on you the bloom of youth still sits. There is one thing, though, you must do. Our cousin

87

Phrixos cries out from his grave for someone to ransom his ghost, to charge into Aietes' halls and bring back to this land the fleece of that ram by which he fled the snares of Ino's treachery."

"Say you this of your own knowledge or someone else's?" asked Jason.

"In a rare dream it came to me, and so I sent to the oracle of Apollo to know its meaning. 'Fit you a ship,' said the oracle, 'and go.' Now this I say to you. Gladly will I fit the ship, but you must go. The years forbid any such adventure for me. This task accomplish, and sole ruler of Iolcos shall you be."

Having only the godlike Cheiron for pattern, it did not occur to Jason that the wily Pelias purposed his death. So it was that he clasped his uncle's hand and pledged his life and honor to the Golden Fleece's return.

Under the eye of Zeus's unwearied daughter Athene was the marvelous *Argo* built. Argos, the son of Arestor, a goodly man and mightily skilled in shipcraft, worked busily at the bright-eyed goddess's direction, and thus was the ship named the *Argo* after her builder. Into the middle of the prow the Daughter of Zeus fitted a magic beam of oak from Zeus's sacred groves of Dodona; the tongue of the ship it was, and it could speak with wondrous voice. Athene brought to Iolcos also Tiphys, gifted son of Hagmias, to be the *Argo's* helmsman.

Not until the Great War to bring back Spartan Helen was ever such an illustrious expedition to be mounted. Not least among the crew was Orpheus, Thracian son of Muse Calliope, whose magic voice, some attest, cast spells upon the unyielding granite crags of his savage homeland and calmed the raging streams. Jason's own uncle Iphiclos also joined the crew and his cousin Admetos, king of Pherai. The great seer Mopsos, skilled above all others in the art of augury from birds, came also on board. Then came Telamon and Peleus, sons of Aiacos, and after them the Spartan brothers Castor and Polydeuces, Meleagros of Calydon, and Zetes and Calais, sons of Boreas. Acastos, son of King Pelias himself, joined them, for not even his father's cunning words or his old mother's tears could dissuade him from taking his place among these mighty men of valor. Nor were bold-hearted Heracles nor Hylas, his squire, ones to be left behind either.

Above fifty men, insatiate seekers of distant glory, boarded the *Argo* in quest of the Golden Fleece. Manhood more than life mattered to them, areté more than the safety of home, the fame of Greece more than the wives and mothers who wept and would not have them go. With one voice they proclaimed Jason their captain; and, though his own choice was Heracles, he happily consented to their judgment.

Tears filled Jason's eyes as his mentor, the godlike Cheiron, waded into the sea to bid them farewell and safe return. Thetis came also to say good-bye to Peleus, bearing in her arms the babe Achilleus. The men slid their oars into the dark sea and, to the time of Orpheus's lyre, began to row, their blades slicing through the rough surf, their strong backs straining. The wet, armored prow glistened more brightly than a thousand gems in the morning sun. Like a path through a field of grain, the *Argo* left a long, frothy wake as it moved into the open sea.

After many days they came to Lemnos, little suspecting the horrors that had transpired there only the year before. Because the women of the island had long neglected themselves, it seems, their husbands eschewed their beds, preferring rather those of the gamy slave girls they had captured in Thrace and brought across the sea. But briefly did the Lemnian women endure this humiliation. In a swift, well calculated move they rose up and slew all the males on the island, boys as well as men, and all the Thracian wenches too. Only aged King Thoas escaped, whom his daughter Hypsipyle put into a chest and cast out to sea.

Sighting the *Argo* as she approached their shores, the women of Lemnos were thrown into great panic. Quickly they donned suits of bronze and took to themselves bronze-tipped spears and long-shafted javelins. When they were gathered together in the assembly place, it was Hypsipyle who first spoke.

"My sisters," she said, "great secrets have we to hide. Supply the strangers bountifully with good food and wine and all they may desire, wrapped and delivered at ship's side, but do not let them get too close to us."

Polyxo rose next, the oldest woman there. Beside her sat four young virgins, their youthful beauty setting off her fullness of years. She spoke with wizened voice: "Let us not be shortsighted. As these men have happened by, so will others in the future—Thracians perhaps. Who will protect us in years to come? You younger women, when you are old and without children, who will care for you? Look to the future. Your salvation has come to you this day. Let these men supply your needs even as you see to theirs. Be kind, my dears; be very kind indeed."

Cheers went up from the women on all sides at Polyxo's suggestion. The four virgins at her side applauded vigorously. Once more Hypsipyle took charge, dispatching a messenger to the ship. "Bring the captain to my house," she told her. "Assure him that he and his men have nothing to fear. They may come and go as dear friends."

The women then quickly adjourned the meeting and repaired to their homes to shed their armor and prepare themselves for their guests. Water was found and soap as well. From hiding places long forgotten some took vials of fragrant ointments and oils; others found brushes for their hair or deftly improvised with wisps of broom straw. As stabled animals soon lose their shaggy, caked coats and nostril-stinging stench in spring pastures, their pelts becoming sleek and glossy, even so did the Lemnian women transform themselves into damsels their husbands would never have recognized had they, by grim Hades' leave, been able to return from the dead.

In the meantime, the messenger found the Argonauts not far from the shore where they had landed. She delivered her message with rehearsed formality: "The lady Hypsipyle bids the captain of your ship to call on her at her home. Your crew may, if they so wish, come into our town as guests and take their ease. Captain, will you please come with me."

Jason in his broad, flowing purple cloak, gift of Pallas Athene, went with the girl. As he came closer to town, from doorways and garden gates the manless matrons of Lemnos swarmed down to the laneside to gaze upon him. Not a few pressed close enough to touch his eye-stunning cloak. Looking neither right nor left, he followed his young guide to Hypsipyle's sumptuous quarters.

"As you can see, good sir," began Hypsipyle, after seating him in a plush chair, "we are an island without men. Oh yes, men there were not long ago, but, to be frank, they were bewitched by wenches from Thrace. They took their sons and fled, every last one of them, to be with their whores. Last we heard they were sleeping with them still. It is a rich land they left and women better in every respect, believe me, than their seducers. But discover for yourselves. Stay with us, if you will, and take their places."

"We need but a little refreshing," Jason told her. "That is all. Bold adventures beckon us from beyond the Euxine Sea. I'll go to my men, though, and tell them of your kindness."

Dancing girls followed him as far as the city gates. Then, as he told his men what Hypsipyle had told him, scores of women and girls descended upon the Argonauts with gifts and good things to eat. Little persuasion was necessary to get the men to go home with them for further proofs of hospitality.

Aison's stalwart son returned to Hypsipyle. Everywhere on the island torches were raised in honor of Aphrodite, and the sour-sweet scent of burnt offerings saturated the air. To bandy-legged Hephaistos and his shapely wife were the songs and sacrifices chiefly offered. From smouldering embers were new fires kindled the next day, and likewise the day after that and the one after that. Days passed into weeks, and the *Argo* remained at anchor.

Were it not for Heracles the Argonauts might never have sailed beyond Lemnos. He it was who finally called his shipmates to a meeting from which the women were barred. "Comrades of mine," he said, "is it for women we have come thus far? Is this what you want, to plow the soil of Lemnos and no more? There's not much honor in whoring with a tribe of brazen women. No one, I can tell you, will be singing our praises for the likes of that. Aye, our seed will live on, but not our names."

Heracles' sarcasm was not lost on his fellows. Guiltily they avoided his glance and slunk back to their mistresses' quarters to gather their belongings. Perceiving the men's rediscovered sense of destiny, the women gave them warm farewells and offered up prayers for their safe returns. Nor was Hypsipyle one to cling to her beloved Jason. "Go," she said, "get you the Golden Fleece, for such is to be your fate. Months from now, when you're far from here in some distant and savage land, think of me, my Jason, and of the fruit of our love whose heart now beats beneath my own."

A quick embrace, and Jason went down to the ship, his men falling in behind him. Without words they took their places on the benches and thrust their great oars into the untroubled waters. Argos threw off the rope that bound their stern to a nearby weather-worn rock jutting up from the bay, their last line to Lemnos. Striking the waters vigorously with their broad blades, the Argonauts moved quickly out to sea.

Past Samothrace they sailed and on into the treacherous currents of the Hellespont, where years before Helle had fallen to her death, and came at length to the land of the Doliones. There was a natural harbor there, formed by a mountainous island connected to the mainland by a barely visible sandbar. Into it the skillful Tiphys navigated the ship.

The king of the Doliones, the youthful Cyzicos, had been warned by an oracle not to raise arms against the Argonauts. He, therefore, made them presents of his rarest wines and fatted sheep and that evening prepared for them a great banquet. The two leaders sat together, Jason and Cyzicos, and from a distance it would have seemed to a stranger that the two were twins, so alike they were in physique and carriage.

In the morning Jason and his companions, thanking the Doliones once more for their hospitality, drew anchor. A brisk west wind wafted them steadily through the deep waters. At nightfall, however, the wind died, and a contrary wind soon thereafter arose. As dusk gave way to darkest night, the adverse winds picked up in intensity. Before they knew it, the Argonauts were in the midst of a relentless gale, and neither Jason nor Tiphys nor the wise Argos himself could discern what course they were driven.

At last they came to rest in a partially protected bay. Quickly they threw their hawsers about some rocks and went ashore. The land's defenders, supposing a party of Pelasgian raiders had landed there to pillage and loot, soon descended upon the weary, weather-battered Argonauts. Jason and his men responded with quick blades. For half the night, as pitch black as Tartaros itself, the battle continued, with no man seeing more than the most shadowy silhouette of his enemy and then only at dagger closeness. By sound they fought and by smell and body heat. In the end the Argonauts prevailed.

In the first faint light of morning, before rosy-fingered Dawn had yet begun to part the clouds and gray mists, the Argonauts looked upon the dark outline of the landscape about them. It seemed they had been there before. Then it came to them: It was the land of the Doliones. The raging storm had brought them in the blackness of the night, unbeknownst to them, back into the very harbor from which they had embarked.

Great groans went up as they began to recognize among the dead some of their hosts of the day before. Loudly they grieved for friends they themselves had in ignorance killed. Some wept and tore at their hair. Jason too wept when he saw among the fallen his friend, King Cyzicos. No more would his young bride welcome him to her bed.

For three days the Greeks and Doliones mourned together. Three times around the dead king's bier they marched in battle gear, wailing and tearing their hair, and then placed him in his tomb and held funeral games in his honor. The skies themselves, turbulent and shrouded over with thick, black clouds, also seemed to grieve.

For twelve days the hostile weather kept the Greeks in port. Then, in the early morning hours of the thirteenth day, a halcyon fluttered above the *Argo's* high mast and piped sweetly its song. Mopsos, on watch, quickly understood the bird's cheery message and called for his companions to prepare to sail. On flew the halcyon in the direction of Colchis; then forthwith the clouds gave way to blue skies, and soft southerly breezes replaced the savage gales

When Helios was yet at the beginning of his trek across the heavens, the winds died down completely. The only ripples were those created by the oars of the *Argo* and by its wake as it glided through the waters. Heracles pulled his oar with the strength of ten, with each stroke so mighty the timbers of the *Argo* vibrated as though shaken by an earthquake. At length the oar's shaft, of hard wood and as thick as his own forearm, snapped. Half the oar fell into the sea and the other half, with Heracles, into the hull of the ship.

By late afternoon new winds brought the ship safely to the Mysian shore. While some of the seamen prepared a sacrifice to Delian Apollo, god of happy landings, others went into the nearby woods and fields to find sticks and tinder for a fire. Heracles also struck out for the forest, though out of no concern for finding firewood.

Soon he found the tree he was looking for, a young poplar, slender enough for his hands and thick enough so as not to break. Positioning himself with his legs on either side of the tree and his arms wrapped tightly about it, with an earth-jarring heave he tore it from the ground. Happily, with the untrimmed poplar over his shoulder, he headed back to the ship to shape his new oar.

Hylas, his squire, was not at the *Argo* when Heracles returned. He had wandered into another wood by himself to find fresh water for his own and his master's meal. The spring he soon came upon was the favorite of several water nymphs who abode in those parts. One of the nymphs looked up from the waters as Hylas approached and immediately fell in love with him. Suspecting nothing, the boy knelt down and began to fill his pitcher. Suddenly the nymph reached up and threw her arm around his neck and pulled him into the pool. Never would Hylas return to his shipmates, nor would he ever want to.

"Hylas went for water and has not returned," Heracles was told when he rejoined his companions. "It has been a long time. We fear for his safety."

Casting the tree from his shoulders, Heracles stomped frantically, wildly into the forest. Like a bull made mad by a gadfly's sting he raged fiercely through the dark woods. His cry, too, resembled the bellow of a great beast in pain. Relentlessly throughout the night he stormed the forest as fast as he could run. Neither pain nor want of breath stayed him for so much as a moment.

Dawn brought favorable winds, and at Tiphys' urging the Argonauts went aboard the ship. "We must embark at once," he said. "Sail while we have the wind. We may not have it again for many a day." No one raised contrary voice. Quickly they hauled in the anchors and loosed the hawsers, and within the hour the *Argo* was once more on the high seas, lighter by two men than it had been only a day earlier. Jason sat silent in the bow wringing his hands in despair.

"You left him there on purpose," Telamon suddenly accused. "Afraid his glory would overshadow your own? That's it, isn't it? I say we go back and get him."

He then made a sudden rush at Tiphys to compel him to turn the ship around. Fire shot from Telamon's eyes. Surely blood-letting strife would have quickly erupted had not the sea-god Glaucos risen suddenly before them from out of the choppy waters. Waist high he rose and leaned his great bushy head over the gunwale.

"Set not yourselves against the will of Zeus," said the god. "Argos is the country for Heracles, not Colchis. Let him finish his labors and be on with it. As for Hylas, a nymph has fallen in love with him and has taken him to her breast. Fret not for him either." He then sank back into the turbid, wine-dark sea.

It was not long before the Argonauts had reason to lament the absence of their boldest and strongest comrade, for they next put ashore in the land of the Bebryces. Amycos, brutish son of Poseidon, was king over this savage people. No one now among Jason's crew approached him in size.

"Pick a champion," he called out to the Greeks as soon as they had disembarked, "someone to put up his fists against mine. No man is free to leave here until we have fought."

Polydeuces stepped forward. "Shut your mouth, whoever you are, and show me your fists," he said. "I need no threats to take on excrement such as you."

The taunt struck home. One could almost perceive smoke coming from the huge barbarian king's broad nostrils. He quickly shed his heavy worsted mantle, suitable for a rug in any Greek home, and advanced to meet the Spartan prince. The companions of each closing in behind, the two squared off. Amycos towered over his opponent like an ogre giant born of Gaia long ago.

Like a huge bear standing on its hind legs, weaving, lunging, swaggering toward its prey, pounding the air with bone-crushing blows, the barbarian charged. The young man deftly sidestepped, ducked, and twisted his supple frame, like the slender weasel, first one direction then the other, untouched by his adversary's fists. Only after he had carefully gauged the king's style did Polydeuces close in to deliver quick jabs to the brute's jaw.

94

At length Amycos raised his fist high and brought it down hard toward Polydeuces' head. The young Argonaut veered aside not a moment too soon; his foe's fist glanced off his shoulder. He then responded with a powerful, lightning blow to Amycos's temple, shattering the bone within. Blood shot from the huge man's mouth as his spirit left him.

When they saw their king fall, the Bebryces, armed with heavy clubs and spears, descended as one man on Polydeuces. Just as quick were the Argonauts, swords drawn, to defend their champion. Without Amycos the muddled barbarians proved no match for the Greeks. Like a swarm of riled, loathsome insects, they streamed in flight out into the rocky countryside.

"And just think how fast they would have run if Heracles had been here," laughed one of the Greek princes, throwing a stone after them.

Near the coast across from Bithynia there lived an ancient man once blessed by the Lord of Delphi with great prophetic powers. Phineus was he called. Because in his youth he had discerned the secret counsels of aegis-bearing Zeus and spread them abroad for all to know, the great Father had cursed him with old age and took away his sight, nor would he allow him to enjoy the rich foods brought by those seeking to know their destinies. Whenever he tried to eat, the Harpies, bat-like plagues from Zeus, swooped down and tore the food from his hands and mouth, at the same time befouling everything with droppings so potent in stench that no one could bear to come near him. It was to Phineus's shore that the Argonauts next came.

The very moment the aged seer heard their voices he knew who his visitors were and, furthermore, that they would be his salvation as he theirs. Anticipation made him quake as he took his stick and tapped his way to the courtyard. Weak from age and hunger, when he reached the threshold, his knees buckled under him, and he collapsed just as Jason and his company entered from the far side.

The Argonauts rushed quickly across the courtyard and knelt at his side. Presently the old man raised his head and slowly turned it, as if surveying his guests, until at length his sightless gaze fell, as it were, on Jason. "The pride of Greece," he said, "sent hither in search for the Golden Fleece. And you, you must be Jason. Thanks to the Lord of Delphi, though I see nothing, I know all. Behold my misery, Son of Aison, and succor me. Do not pass from this place and leave me as I am."

"Say what you would have us do," said Jason.

Phineus slowly got to his feet and hobbled to his excrement-spattered bench and table nearby. The Greeks recoiled at the incomparable stench, gagging and clutching at their throats, as the old man described how he would raise a piece of candied fruit or honey cake, gift of some grateful seeker, to his lips and then, darting as if from out of nowhere, the Harpies would tear the morsels from his mouth and pick his basket clean and, having done so, return to besmear utensils and furniture with their nose-stinging putrescence. As he finished speaking, he began softly to sob, and some of the Greeks wept to hear him weep, not least among them Zetes and Calais, sons of Boreas, the North Wind.

Zetes grasped the old man's bony hand. "Surely you are cursed by some god," he said. "Will not, therefore, the man who seeks to succor you share in the same curse? Tell me truly, old man, for I would be your champion."

"By the Delian Lord who gave me my gift and by the Stygian powers below do I swear no man shall bring the fury of any god down upon his head for taking pity on me."

The sons of Boreas nodded at each other, and immediately the younger Argonauts began to spread a table for Phineus. Zetes and Calais stood poised on either side of the ancient seer. Suddenly, at the very instant the old man's fingers found a piece of barley cake, a peal of hair-raising screeches split the air, and three Harpies darted out of the low, overhanging clouds. Swooping in and snatching the bread from Phineus's fingers, in a flash they were aloft once more, leaving behind only their odoriferous droppings.

Nor were Zetes and Calais, winged sons of the North Wind, sluggish in their pursuit. Like two hounds, hot on the tail of a many-pointed stag or swift mountain goat, they closed in upon their quarry, brandishing vigorously their well-honed swords. Bits of black feathery tissue suddenly peppered the sky, drifting downward like ebony snowflakes, as the brothers' sword tips found the hindermost parts of the Harpies. Faster the foul sisters flew, but still faster the sons of Boreas. They would have finished the beasts' mischief forever had not fleet-footed Iris, at Zeus's command, intervened.

"Stay your swords, sons of Boreas," said the goddess. "Great Zeus's own hounds the Harpies are and must be spared. You have saved old Phineus. That is enough. Never again will they visit his table."

When Zetes and Calais returned to Phineus's palace, they found the old man, his body scrubbed of all its stench and his table as well, enjoying a piece of roast mutton prepared by the Argonauts. No man, it seemed to them, had ever been more happy. He attacked the tender meat ravenously. Jason and his men laughed to see him eat and then sat down at the table to join him. Into the night they ate and drank while their ancient host unfolded for the Greeks their destiny.

"It is not meet for you to know all your fate," he said. "But these things know. Beyond this place, at the end of the narrows, are the two Cyanean Rocks. Neither is imbedded solidly in the sea's floor, and so they clash intermittently the one against the other, sending great gushes of water into the air and crushing utterly anything that comes between them. When you get to them, release a dove. If the bird fails, so will you. Better then you bow to Heaven's will and return to Iolcos whence you came."

As a seaman, fresh from his voyages, sees in his sleep the waters he has traveled, each shoreline, each island, each promontory jutting into the deep where danger might lurk, each peaceful haven, even so the sightless prophet Phineus, full-bellied and high in spirits, saw with inner sight the course that lay before the bold young men of the *Argo* ere they would come to Colchis, all of which in detail he related to his guests. By the dancing light of their bonfire the Greeks leaned forward lest a single word from the old man's mouth escape them.

On and on Phineus talked, his listeners in rapt attention huddled about him, their fire now faint. No inlet, no stream, no tribe did he fail to describe. At length, not long before the morning's first light, he described the marshy delta of the River Phasis at the farthest corner of the Euxine Sea. "Into that marsh," he told them, "ease the *Argo*. From there you will see the ramparts of Aietes' kingdom and the Grove of Ares also, where stretched is the object of your quest, the Golden Fleece, guarded over by a fierce and mighty dragon that never sleeps."

"Speak on," said Jason. "What of the rest? When we have gone to the ends of the earth, will the Fleece then prove beyond our reach?"

"Once did I offend the undying gods by saying overmuch," said Phineus. "Never again. Only one more thing will I tell you: In Aphrodite's hands your future rests; no kinder friend could you have than she. Pray, ask me no more."

Building altars, one for each of the twelve Olympians, and offering sweetsmelling sacrifices upon them, the Argonauts pressed once more out to sea. Nor did they forget to take on board a dove. It was not long before the narrowest part of the strait, that of which the aged seer had warned them, came menacingly into view. Two high cliffs, one on either side, suddenly before their eyes began to vibrate and then to close, like the jaws of a gigantic vise, against each other.

Spray from the sea shot up into the air in bold fountains, and a great gush of dark water was forced, as though bursting forth from a ruptured dam, into the path of the *Argo*. The rollers' roar and the thunderous crash of the Rocks all but drowned out the voice of Tiphys as he called out quick orders to his oarsmen. Some read his meaning from his lips; others as if by instinct guessed. All responded in an instant, like parts of a common body controlled by a common mind, and so they rode the surge out safely.

When the Rocks began to part, Euphemos, the keeper of the dove, quickly released the bird, which flew without hesitation into the widening break. For a brief moment the Rocks ceased to move, then suddenly began to close. The dove, midway in its flight, continued its course as though in open sky. Like hands clapping in slow motion, the great cliffs pounded resoundingly once more together. The Greeks, maneuvering their ship deftly out of danger, kept their eyes directed toward where last they had seen the bird. Again the Rocks parted, and safely beyond them was the dove; only the very tips of its tail feathers had been nipped by the Clashing Rocks.

With a great cry of triumph, the Argonauts drove their oar blades into the dark, turbid waters and headed the ship into the narrow, high-walled channel. The backwash rolled in behind them and, like a sudden gust of wind hitting the sails, shot them headlong between the cavernous jaws. Strength born of terror quite possessed the men, and they gave their backs to the oars with such power that the beams bent like the shafts of yew-wood bows. Never more swiftly had they rowed.

Deeper into the channel they sped but then were met with the backwash from the other side, which swept them backward and, were it not for Tiphys' skill, would have surely capsized the ship. So strong was the current that their mightiest efforts could but keep the ship from being driven back farther. Suddenly the great Rocks quaked and began to close, now forcing the water outward, and with it the *Argo*, toward open sea. The men, though it scarcely seemed possible, redoubled their efforts at the oars. Had they been able to triple their speed, however, it would, alas, have been too little too late, for the Clashing Rocks were soon almost within arm's reach on either side and the Euxine Sea yet some ways ahead.

None of this, however, had not escaped the watchful eyes of Athene. As a shaft of lightning is first seen high in the sky and then in the blink of an eye cuts through half the heavens, even so the bright-eyed goddess descended from Olympos's heights to the adamantine gates of the Euxine. With her left hand she stayed one face of the giant vise and with her right pushed the ship on through. Like an arrow from Heracles' bow, the

*Argo* split the air as the Rocks slammed behind her. Nothing, save for the figurehead on the stern, was severed. When the cliffs once more spread apart, the Daughter of Zeus touched each with her deathless hands, forever locking them into place, and then sped back to Mount Olympos.

Shaken by the disaster that almost befell them, Jason sat silent in the prow. "The ship's safe, my lord Jason," called Tiphys, "the gods brought us through the Rocks. Why do you brood?"

"We should never have set out," answered the Iolcian prince. "I should have told Pelias no. Then would I have gambled with but mine own life, not yours, my comrades."

Loudly then did the Argonauts raise their voices in support of their captain. Not one held back. Their cheers brought new courage to the heart of Aison's son and to their own hearts as well. Refreshed as if by food and drink, they returned to their benches and once more took up their oars.

So exact had been Phineus's description of all they would encounter that, whenever they passed a river mouth or an island or promontory, they had the sensation of having seen it before. Even the coastal villages seemed familiar. Everything was as the old man had told them. Where he had said for them to take haven and go ashore, they did so; where he had warned them to swing wide and press vigorously ahead, they did so also.

It was not long, however, before dark clouds hung heavy over the Argonaut's spirits, for Idmon, whom Fate had decreed never to finish the voyage, was gored by a vicious white-tusked boar when he went out to explore the marshes of the Mariandyni. He died in his companions' arms. Shortly thereafter Tiphys was taken in a fever.

These two were soon replaced by others; for as the Argonauts closed in on their destination, they came upon a beach where four survivors of a shipwreck had been washed upon the sands. It seems they had put out from Colchis the day before. With nightfall had come a storm. Thunderous waves had loosened the timbers of their ship as pellets of rain battered them relentlessly throughout the night. Daybreak found all four adrift, clinging to one of the ship's beams. Westerly winds had brought them to the beach where the Argonauts discovered them.

None was more astonished than Jason when the spokesman for the four, in response to the Argonauts' inquiries, said, "Of Phrixos you have surely heard and of the great golden ram, dispatched by Hera, that saved him from his father Athamas's uplifted hand. It was to these parts the ram bore him, where he won the hand of Chalciope, daughter to King Aietes. Of that marriage four sons were born. The same, lashed by Zeus's winds yet by his mercy spared, stand before you now."

"You stand before kin," the son of Aison told them. "My father's father was Cretheus, Athamas's brother. Bound we are for Aietes' kingdom."

Altars were quickly built and a goodly number of sheep offered up to Zeus, the savior of all god-fearing men. Then the Argonauts spread their tables and feasted upon the parts of the animals Zeus had designated long ago to be man's portion. As they ate, Jason disclosed his mission to his kinsmen. "Will you not help us," he ended, "to bring back the Golden Fleece to Greece and so atone for the crime intended against your father Phrixos?"

"Gladly would we join you, but you do not know Aietes nor his fierce host of Colchian warriors," answered one of them. "The son of Helios he claims to be. His hordes are without number."

"You sup with gallants and demigods," broke in Peleus, "the likes of which for skill have never before been assembled."

"Neither do you know of the dragon that guards the Fleece," continued the son of Phrixos. Then with words more horrible than those of Phineus, he described the great serpentine sentry, begotten of Gaia herself, that never sleeps. As he spoke, not a few of the gallants and demigods began to pale. In the end, though, the four sons of Phrixos went on board the *Argo* with the Greeks to serve as their pilots.

On they sailed until they came into view of the steep Caucasian crags where Prometheus was yet bound by bronze fetters and Zeus's eagle daily nourished itself on his liver. The air vibrated with the great Titan's cries of agony. Night had fallen by the time they reached the Phasis estuary. Guided by the skilled sons of Phrixos, with silent strokes the Argonauts rowed up one of the broad river's channels into the rush-filled delta marshlands and there waited for dawn.

# Jason and Medea

While Jason and his men bided their time among the rushes, high atop Mount Olympos two goddesses, united by their concern for the Argonauts' success, conferred in soft tones. "By what means shall we empower them to carry the Golden Fleece back to Greece?" said the white-armed Queen of Heaven.

"The question that has been racking my mind exactly," answered Athene.

"With Aphrodite's help we may find an ally for Jason in that bewitching daughter of Aietes, Medea," Hera ventured, after a brief silence. "Yes, let us see Aphrodite at once. Her son's arrows can awaken such passion in a maiden's heart that she will stop at nothing for her beloved."

"Of such things I have no knowledge," said the bright-eyed Daughter of Zeus. "With you will I gladly go, but you must do the talking."

Forthwith then the two hastened to the resplendent palace built by bandy-legged Hephaistos for his laughter-loving wife. They found Aphrodite seated on a golden chair with jeweled inlays, in her hand a golden comb with which she skillfully stroked the luxurious tresses that fell over either shoulder.

"What an honor!" she said. "A visit at last from the greatest goddess of all. We really haven't gotten together much lately, have we?"

"Do spare us the jest, my dear," said Hera. "Jason is in trouble. We're both at our wits' ends. No man is more dear to me. Years ago, to put human compassion to the test, in the form of an old woman I mired myself in the flood-swollen flats of the Anauros River. The young son of Aison plunged into the stream and in his arms carried me safely to high ground. I will not have him fall prey to Pelias's wiles. Most impious of men that one, neglecter of sacrifices. Oh, how I loathe him! You must not permit him to win out over Jason."

"Tell me," said Aphrodite, "what you would have me do. My humble talents are at your disposal.

"Send your boy Eros to work his magic on Medea. Steep her with passion for Jason. A witch herself, she'll find a way to help him get the Golden Fleece back to Iolcos."

"If that's all it'll take," replied the laughter-loving goddess, "never fear, my ladies. Your Jason shall have his Golden Fleece."

Her visitors left, and Aphrodite quickly set out for the orchards of Zeus, where lush fruit always hung at a perfect stage of ripeness. There she found her mischievous son cheating at a game of knuckle-bones with Ganymede. "I have a gift for you, my beautiful boy," she told him. "The ball with which Zeus played as a child, better than Hephaistos himself could make—a perfect sphere, double-stitched, gold with a deep blue band. Throw it up, and it'll leave a blazing trail, like a meteor, across the sky."

Eros threw down the knuckle-bones and wrapped his arms around his peerlessly beautiful mother. "I'll have the ball at once," he said.

"First a little favor," teased Aphrodite. "Medea, Aietes' daughter, must fall in love with Jason. After you have shot an arrow deep into her heart, then you shall have the ball."

The boy's quiver was leaning against a tree, his crooked bow beside it. These he quickly picked up and, throwing the golden strap across his shoulder, flew forthwith from the luxuriant Olympian orchard to the barbarous land of Colchis.

At the very moment that laughter-loving Aphrodite was bribing her son, Jason, after a sleepless night, was addressing his men aboard the *Argo*: "First by persuasion will we seek the Fleece. It is barbarians who storm and slaughter to gain what might freely be given if they would but ask, not Greeks. If Aietes refuses, then will be the time to turn our minds to stealth. I will take two of our men and these four with me into the city. The rest of you wait here."

And so it was that, choosing Telamon and Augeias to go with him, the son of Aison was soon making his way through the rushes to higher, drier ground. In the meantime, in order that her champion might get to Aietes' place undetected, Hera had hung a thick mist over the entire city. Once the Argonauts were safely inside the broad courtyard gates, she lifted it.

There before Jason, as though the curtain had suddenly been raised on an exquisite stage setting, were dazzling marble colonnades with marble cornices atop bronze triglyphs. At the base of the columns lush rose bushes surrounded four elaborately wrought fountains, one of which gushed forth milk, another wine, the third fragrant oil, and the fourth water as cold as ice. Near the fountains were brazen bulls as large as life whose mouths spewed forth unceasing fire.

One of the heavy oaken doors across the courtyard from the men was suddenly swung open; and a stately matron, dark, glowing with a well kept beauty, came running out. It was Chalciope. Her arms in the air and shouts of praise to the gods on her lips, she ran to her sons and embraced them. Tears flooded her cheeks. "You came back!" she managed in her emotion. "The gods turned you from your foolish venture, back to your widowed mother. Folly sent you away, but now you have returned."

From another door came Aietes himself. Then from other doors came others, and soon it was like a marketplace, with several spirited conversations all going on at once. To different audiences the four sons of Phrixos told of their shipwreck, not without some detail, at various points in their discourses pulling their rescuers into their respective circles to introduce them.

The king ordered a choice bull to be slain and fires prepared and baths made ready. Last to join the company was the dark-eyed, exotically beautiful younger sister of Chalciope, Medea, whom Hera had arranged to keep inside the palace until the right moment. She stood on the steps and carefully surveyed the crowd until at last her eyes fell on Jason.

Then it was that mischief-bent Eros, crouching in the shadows of a doorway, gingerly drew the string across his crooked bow and took from his golden quiver a shiny new arrow. Keeping low, he scampered unnoticed along the bases of the fountains and rose bushes to where Jason stood. He then set himself, pulled the bowstring as far back as his child arms could stretch, and let the shaft fly straight at Medea's heart. It struck true and deep. The impish archer thereupon turned and zoomed back to his laughter-loving mother to claim the blue-trimmed golden ball that was his reward.

Medea stood frozen in place. Eros's dart, more hot than fire, melted within her breast. Her eyes were fixed on the prince of Iolcos. No one, nothing existed for her in those moments, nor indeed ever had existed, but he. Her heart, throbbing violently within her bosom, seemed full to bursting with something strangely potent, overpowering. Had she found words, she might have called it agony, but it was not that; she might have called it unbearable sweetness, but it was not that either. It was more like the two at one and the same time, burning, seething, overflowing into her whole being.

Jason and his party were taken at King Aietes' command to the warm baths prepared for their refreshment by the palace servants. After the baths it was on to the banquet hall, where the fragrance of expertly spiced meats permeated the air. The king bid his guests eat their fill. It was to his grandsons that Aietes first addressed himself after the meal: "Misadventure has taught you, it seems, what I could not. So be it. You must amuse us sometime with stories of your exploits abroad. As for now, pray introduce your guests. How and where came you upon them?"

The oldest of the brothers stepped forward, the same who had been their spokesman with the Argonauts. "As you know already, my lord," he said, "our ship ravaged by the fury of Zeus, we were cast adrift at the mercy of the sea, the four of us clinging to a timber until at length we were thrust by kind winds onto the sandy shores of the Island of Ares. There it was we were found by these men and their companions."

"Then it was your enterprise and not your lives, it would appear, the gods sought to cut short," said the king. "And how fortunate to find these strangers in so strange a place."

"Not strangers, but kin. This man is Jason, grandson to Cretheus, my own grandfather Athamas's brother. Of Aiolos both were sons."

"Is not Greece the other side of the world?"

"They were bound for Colchis—to see you, my lord."

"And to what purpose, may I ask?"

"On my father Phrixos's account the House of Aiolos is under curse, nor will it escape the harshest judgment of Zeus until the Golden Fleece is brought back to Greece. Without it Jason cannot take his throne, now held by a despot. For this cause Pallas Athene designed his ship and herself drove home some of the bolts lest rough seas wrench the beams loose and then hand-picked the flower of Greek manhood to go on board—all, like you my grandfather, sons and grandsons of undying gods."

As the young man spoke, the color rose along the barbarian king's throat. His eyes grew wide, then narrowed like those of an angered, fang-baring jackal threatened in his lair. He leaped from his bench and brandished both fists violently at his four grandsons. "Villains!" he shouted. "Out of my sight at once! Not the Fleece but my scepter you seek. Begone!" Then to the Argonauts, "Had you not eaten at my table, I would have your lying tongues ripped out and your hands hacked off. The sons and grandsons of gods? Of mangy curs more likely!"

Telamon would have hurdled the table at that moment to tear the man's head from his shoulders, and so would have lost the day, had not Jason with quick hands restrained him.

"Destiny and that alone drove us to your shores, oh gracious king," said the Greek prince in controlled tones, "destiny and a spiteful tyrant. We have no designs on anything that is yours, save only the Fleece. And for that we are ready to take on your cruelest enemies."

Aietes continued to shake. His face was still crimson, his fists still clenched. "Soft words, my friend," he finally said, "prolong your life. Good. And now to show that this king, unlike your own, can indeed be gracious, you may have the Golden Fleece. I must, of course, have proof that the hands in which I place it are truly worthy of their prize."

"What proof would your majesty have?"

"A test," said Aietes, "though not one beyond my own powers and courage. Two bulls, brazen-hoofed and breathing fire, feed on the Plains of Ares. These I can yoke in the morning and with them plough the fertile meadow beyond the plain. Into the furrows then can I sow, not barley seed, but serpent's teeth, from which spring almost immediately a host of armed earthmen. These with my spear can I cut down, though they attack from every side, and still be back in my palace for an early supper. If you would have the Fleece, good stranger, prove your mettle the equal of mine. We will know if there be a god in your lineage or not."

"You leave me no choice, your majesty," replied Jason. "That same cruel mistress, Necessity, who through another king's caprice drove me here, now compels me to accept your terms. I do so, knowing my death is probably being required."

"Your acquiescence gives me no small pleasure. Had you refused, I would have been forced to make of you an example to discourage future adventurers who might be tempted to come here and badger their betters." With that the king snapped his fingers, and a door was swung quickly open by which Jason and his men were motioned to leave. The eldest son of Phrixos, nodding for his brothers to stay, went with them. Medea looked on, her heart still on fire. Chalciope, not unused to her father's wrath, retired forthwith to her apartments.

As Jason and his companion retraced their steps back to the *Argo*, it was the son of Phrixos who, once they were safely beyond others' hearing, broke the silence. "There is a young woman in these parts," he said, "a priestess to Hecate, who has incredible powers of magic derived from Hades' dark kingdom beneath earth. Could we but win her to our ranks, tomorrow's ordeal might not hold such dread. My mother is close to her. Pray, let me ask her to intercede."

"Desperation makes us do desperate things," moaned Jason. "Go to your mother. We have no recourse but to seek the woman's help. And be persuasive, good friend. The king means to have our lives."

Even as the men on the ship saw their captain, with Telamon and Augeias on either side, come into view still some distance away, they knew the news they bore was not good. Their gaits were like those of refugees who, their homes leveled, weighed down with great bundles on their backs and yet heavier burdens within, wander the land without hope.

With meticulous detail Jason recounted for his men all that had happened and had been spoken at King Aietes' court. He ended by telling them of the impossible task the king had prescribed for him for the next day. "To this I agreed," he said. "There was no escape."

"Do as you have said, lord Jason," Peleus spoke up. "But should you think it wiser to send another champion, look no further. I stand ready."

"And I too," said Telamon. "They cannot more than kill me."

Idas was next to volunteer, and after him Castor, then Polydeuces and Meleagros. These six stepped forward and no more. Never, even in this Age of Bronze when men were straighter and more manly than any in our own time, have there been heroes more brave than these.

"The task was given me," said Jason, "and I must see it through. Help may, though, arise from other quarters." Then it was he told them of the enchantress whom Phrixos's son had returned to the city to try to enlist.

In the sky above them an eagle was pursuing a little dove. As both birds swooped low over the *Argo*, the eagle impaled itself on a jagged splint from the shattered figurehead. The bewildered dove flopped exhausted into Jason's lap.

Mopsos leaped to his feet. "Behold a sign from the gods!" he shouted. "Remember the words of old Phineus: 'Look for help to Aphrodite'? The bird, it's Aphrodite's bird. It means the girl will join us, else I'm no prophet."

"Haul in the anchor stones and man the oars," commanded Jason. "Let us move in as close as we can. There will be no more hiding."

Meanwhile in Chalciope's chamber back in the palace the eldest son of Phrixos conferred with his mother and brothers, taxing his powers of persuasion to get Chalciope to go to her sister Medea and win her to Jason's cause.

"You say, my son, what my own heart has already spoken," his mother responded, grasping his outstretched hands. "Medea does offer some small hope, but whether it is wise to go to her I do not know. If she were to refuse and expose our involvement, our dooms, though now uncertain, would be sealed."

Just then a maiden, distraught, in tears, burst into the room. It was one of Medea's serving girls. "Come quickly to my mistress," she begged Chalciope. "She weeps and throws herself upon her bed, and I know not why."

Chalciope went with the girl and found Medea lying on her bed, heaving, panting, eyes bloodshot from crying. She took her quickly into her arms and stroked her gently as though she were her child rather than her sister. "Now, now, why all these tears?" she said. "Are you ill? Or has Father just told you the fate he means to visit upon me and my sons?"

"Yes, it is for you I fear," said Medea, her words coming in short bursts, "and for your sons . . . and the strangers. In a hideous nightmare . . . I saw it all. Oh, oh, my dear sister!"

"No nightmares have I had nor ominous visions seen," said Chalciope, "but in our father's eyes have read our wretched end. Is there some means, perhaps through your spells or magical herbs, by which we all can yet escape? If so, by the twelve gods of Olympos I implore you, my sister. Do not stand by and let your nightmares come to pass."

"With all of the power that in me lies will I help you," promised Medea, "though I do not know if I can save you or your sons or the gallant strangers."

"At dawn the Greek leader must take on our father's bulls. Our hope is in his success," said Chalciope.

Medea's heart leaped within her at this mention of Jason. A smile worked at the corners of her mouth and spread, as if by the quick strokes of a master painter, over her whole face. "Whatever I can do I will," she cried. "At dawn, when I go to Hecate's temple, I will have with me a remedy for the bulls. Let the stranger know."

Night fell upon the kingdom and throughout the land brought rest to bone-weary farmers and those devotees of Hephaistos who worked the forges. Sweet sleep came at last to mothers in mourning, and then even the dogs gave up their barking and the watchmen on the ramparts ceased to call out. But to Medea sleep never came.

While it was still dark, though shortly before daybreak, she went with her lamp to the chest where she kept her potions and magical herbs and took out a covered jar. This she tucked into the sash she wore about her waist. A plant had sprung up, it seems, from a droplet of Prometheus's ichor which had fallen from the gore-damp talons of Zeus's eagle when first the Titan was bound on the Caucasian crags. Medea had collected the sap of that plant in a shell and from it made a rare ointment. Such were the contents of the jar.

Twelve virgins served as the princess's attendants and stayed in an adjoining chamber. These she now called to ready her carriage. As was customary, two of the maidens got into the carriage with Medea, one on either side, though it was Aietes' daughter who held the reins. Nor did she spare the whip. Down the well-paved streets they raced; early-risers dodged back into doorways or flattened themselves against walls to escape being trampled. Out of the city she drove, across the plain to Hecate's shrine.

"Let us go now into the meadows and pick flowers as we normally do," she instructed the maidens when they got out of the carriage. "A man is going to meet me here. When he arrives, I must see him alone."

Thereupon Medea tried to occupy herself singing and dancing with her maidens as they gamboled over the meadows, snipping off the morning's brightest blooms. Her mind now was fixed singularly on Jason. Had some peasant that morning, bound for market in the city with his cheeses and plump olives, or perhaps a wayfarer on his way to the sea happened by there and chanced to stand and look upon the scene, he would have beheld the Colchian princess stepping as spiritedly as the other two and singing with equal gusto as though nothing extraordinary at all were afoot.

Soon, however, Jason appeared in the distance, and the girl's demeanor changed. Her movements became less rhythmic, less graceful, twitchy, nervous; her dark eyes, though opened wide, seemed clouded over as if by a mist. She continued to sing, but the notes were softer now and nearly the same. Eyes dreamily focused upon her beloved, she made the motions of plucking flowers, though in fact she gathered into her bouquet more stalks of weeds and grass stems than anything else. She then dropped her bouquet altogether and advanced to meet him.

"Fear not, sweet soul," began Jason. "No harm will I ever be to you. I have come to beg what you have already promised your sister you would give. Oh, please do not go back on that promise now. Name your reward, and whatsoever is in my power to give shall be yours."

Though Medea's heart within her swelled as if to burst, she nonetheless found the words to answer: "Listen to me carefully, and do as I say. First, you must bathe in a stream that never runs dry, and then quickly dig a round hole in the ground. Prepare a pyre over the pit, and on it sacrifice a young ewe, pouring on honey from the honeycomb and raising sweet prayers to Hecate."

"As you say. Tell me more."

Medea took the covered jar from her sash. "Then spread this balm over your whole body, careful to miss no part. Daub it also upon your shield and spear. Matchless then will be your courage and strength, and for a full day neither will the bulls' fire nor the earthmen's weapons be able to prevail against you."

"Say what you would have me to do for you in return," said Jason.

"One more thing," said Medea. "When you have sown the serpent's teeth, do not be awed by the men that will rise from the soil. Throw a large rock into their midst, and they will accuse and fall upon one another. The survivors will be no match for your spear."

"And so will the Fleece be mine," Jason pursued, "but what of you? You have yet to name your reward."

"Yes, the Fleece will then be yours. Take it back to Greece or wherever you are wont to go." The girl's emotions at last caught up with her, and at the thought of never seeing her beloved again she turned her head and began to weep.

Jason put his hand on her shoulder. His touch sent waves through every part of her. Taking his hand in her own, she turned slowly toward him and pressed herself against his body. "Promise me something," she said.

"If what you say is in my power to do."

"When you are back in your home, remember the name of Medea; for as long as I live, dear Jason, I shall remember yours."

At that moment fickle love began to work its magic also upon Jason. There was gentleness in his voice as he said, "Neither night nor day will I ever forget you."

"Tell me of your home," said Medea, suddenly made garrulous by love's energy. "Where will you go when you leave here? Are you bound for the splendors of Orchomenos or somewhere else? I know nothing of your land, nothing of you. Talk to me, Jason. I would know everything there is to know about you."

Jason obliged the dark-eyed princess by telling of his confrontation with Pelias and of the building of the *Argo*. He spoke with the animation of one possessed. Each detail was so vivid and dramatic that, had our peasant or wayfarer stayed and then drawn near enough to listen, he would have thought he were hearing a rare and gifted bard reciting lines he had spoken a thousand times before. To Medea each word was as honey to her love's appetite, at the same time feeding and making it grow; and her face, aglow, looking up at Jason with rapt and worshipful attention, inspired greater skill in his speech than could Apollo and all nine of the daughters of Zeus and Mnemosyne combined.

"Suppose sometime in years to come a great gust of wind should pick me up and waft me far across the oceans to your kingdom of Iolcos," Medea playfully mused, "would I find the palace doors there open to me?"

"Were you to come to Iolcos, my lovely princess, all work would cease, and the men and women would frolic in the streets. Paeans would be sung in your praise as to a goddess."

"And you, dear Jason," she pursued, "what could I expect from you?"

"A bridal bed, my lovely," he answered, "one you and I would share until death should at length snuff out our love's last light."

There was nothing now in the whole world that Medea would have shrunk from for the Argonaut captain's sake. "Go quickly," she told him, "and do as I have said. And remember one thing. In Greece kings may do as they have promised. Take for granted no such integrity here."

With that, they took their leaves, though not without a final reassuring embrace. Medea gathered her two maidens to her carriage and sped off to the city; Jason hurried quickly back to where the *Argo* was now at anchor to prepare his sacrifices to Hecate. Just before dawn, prior to setting out for his rendezvous with Medea, he had commissioned Telamon and Aithalides to go to King Aietes to ask for the serpent's teeth. They arrived back at the ship the same time as he.

After propitiating the Queen of the Underworld with the sacrifices of a young ewe, careful to do exactly as Medea had instructed by first building a pyre over a round pit, Jason opened the jar of magic balm. With the ointment he first coated his spear and shield and then gave them to his companions to test. At first cautiously, then with all their might they tried to break the shaft of the spear and smash the shield, but they could not.

Idas ground his teeth in fury as repeatedly, with blows that would have downed a full-grown olive tree, he brought down his huge sword across the spear without so much as scoring it. The men all marveled. Then, doffing his clothes, Jason covered his body with the balm; no part of his body did he fail to cover.

It was off then to the Plain of Ares, where Aietes, surrounded by a vast host of his tribesmen, was waiting in his chariot. Beyond him were the great bronze-hoofed bulls, smoke rising from their nostrils, and close by them a large iron plow. Clad only in his teeth-studded helmet, shield on his left arm, spear in his right hand, otherwise naked, Jason advanced through the Colchian ranks toward the two bulls. How like a god he looked, like Apollo of the Silver Bow or, more nearly, because of the way his handsome, muscular body seemed to gleam in the morning sun, like the God of Battles whose sacred ground he now trod!

All at once the monstrous animals opened their mouths and belched forth thick tongues of fire that curled around the Argonaut's shield. A gasp of terror went up from the Greeks as they watched. The bulls pawed the ground for a moment before lowering their massive heads for the charge.

Like a rocky reef against the raging surge of the sea, Jason braced himself and stood firm. They slammed against his shield with their curved horns again and again but could not budge him, no, not so much as a hair's breadth. Bellowing, snorting, they spewed fire upon him, blasting him with their molten breath, at moments so engulfing him in flames that his men could not see him except in blurry outline. Grasping first one and then the other by the horns, Jason brought the bulls to the iron plow.

On into mid afternoon Jason ploughed the hard ground. The massive animals, responsive to his command, dug their bronze hooves into the granite-like soil and dragged the plow, turning up great caked clods, as handily as a housewife might run a knife through freshly rendered lard. Task finished, Jason unyoked the bulls and sent them, fuming and steaming, back to their pasture. He then opened the pouch of serpent's teeth and scattered them along the furrows.

Like blades of barley through soft soil in early spring, the earthmen began to sprout in the ridges and among the compacted clumps of the new-tilled field. The ground groaned and crackled. Great fissures, as though described in the earth by lightning, opened up along the irregular rows where the earthmen, their huge trunks now above ground, rapidly rose. Each held a crude shield and a two-pronged spear. The slightest was easily half again as heavy as Jason and taller by a head or more. Their faces were like those of snarling, rabid beasts, radiating primal savageness and insensate fury.

Jason, at the edge of the field, chose a large round boulder, four times the size of anything he would ordinarily have been able to budge. He lifted it shoulder high; then, with feet firmly planted, in a single, fluid motion he lofted it high into the air and out over the heads of the earthborn battalion. Even King Aietes gasped in amazement at the feat. The earthmen snarled accusingly among themselves and then, like a pack of ravenous, crazed curs, fell quickly each upon each in murderous free-for-all.

At last, when not one man was standing except to stagger and swoon, Jason entered their lists with a triumphant cry. Like savage animals in their death throes, however, the surviving brutes found great reserves of strength to strike out at their antagonist even as they reeled and sank to their knees. Jason agilely dodged their thrusts and finished with his bronze-tipped spear the slaughter they had begun on each other.

Aietes stormed off the field without a word, glancing back over his shoulder but briefly at the victorious Greek. His men fell into line behind him. That single glance told all; words were not necessary. Skin taut, jaw extended, the veins along his throat and temples purpled and protruding, his eyes ablaze, the king's face literally vibrated with hate and fury. Jason read the message well.

Returning to their camp along the river bank, the Argonauts quietly set about building a bonfire. They then slaughtered two sheep and commenced to prepare themselves a feast, though whether it was to be a victory celebration or a death banquet they did not know. Save for an occasional word spoken in low tones about the meal itself, they ate in silence.

Suddenly from out of the blackness across the river they heard a familiar voice call out. Phrontis, the youngest son of Phrixos, was standing next to Jason; he grabbed the Argonaut captain's arm.

"I know," said Jason, quickly then shouting for his men to take their places on the rowing bench.

Thrice more, while the Argonauts maneuvered their ship swiftly across the still river, the familiar female voice called out, each time answered by Phrontis. The moment they touched the other bank, Jason nimbly vaulted from the deck of the *Argo* into Medea's waiting arms.

Trembling, she fell against him. "Save me, oh my dear one," she cried. "And save yourself. Aietes knows all. We must act immediately before their chariots descend from all sides. Haste, my beloved!"

"Say what you will have me do."

"Man your oars, and I will get you the Golden Fleece," she told him. "But one thing now I ask: Before the undying gods and in the presence of these men, pledge me your love as you did at Hecate's temple. For your sake I betrayed my house."

Jason entwined his arms manfully about the girl's slender body. "I call upon Zeus, the great Father of Gods and Men," he said boldly for all those present to hear, "and upon Hera, Goddess of Marriage, to be my witnesses that once we get back to Greece you will be my beloved bride."

"Row then, you Argonauts, with all your might!" said the jubilant Colchian princess. "To the sacred Grove of Ares! I will tell you the way."

Jason lifted her quickly then to the ship's deck and leaped aboard himself. They pushed out from the land; and smoothly, silently the oarsmen slid their broad pine blades through the rippleless surface of the river. With no more sound than a swan might make or a high-stepping gallinule, the *Argo* moved swiftly upstream. Sensing rather than seeing the landmarks along the banks, Medea served as pilot. In due time, just as the moon disappeared behind a cloud, making it the darkest moment of the night, they entered a shallow cove and there ran the ship onto the grassy shore. Medea and Jason quickly disembarked.

Up a winding path to the sacred grove the twain sped. Ahead of them, visible through the trees, brilliantly illuminating the woods with its amber phosphorescent glow, was the Fleece—stretched across the limbs of a solitary oak in the middle of the grove. Also visible, as they moved into clear view of the Golden Fleece, was the great reptilian sentry of the place. Its thick-plated scales clinked as though forged of bronze as it raised its monstrous head and, swaying cobra-fashion, let out a series of resounding hisses.

In nearby villages babies at their mothers' sides were startled from their sleep by the unearthly sounds, and their mothers, also awakened, forebodingly drew the infants tightly to their breasts. King Aietes, at the river's mouth barking orders to his own squadrons and those of his son Apsyrtos, heard the hisses too and knew their meaning.

Medea cautiously advanced a few paces. Picking up the dragon's rhythm, she began to move her body sensually from side to side. Then she opened her mouth in sweet song, tender song, in lullaby tones calling upon Hecate and gentle Morpheus to work their wondrous spells. Like dancing partners performing an exotic fertility movement, they writhed and gyrated, girl and serpent, to the girl's sweet hypnotic song until at last sleep closed the serpent's eyes and it slumped drowsily to the ground. Medea beckoned then for Jason to take the Fleece.

The son of Aison's face gleamed like a god's as he loosed his prize from the branches of the sacred tree. The size of a yearling bullock's hide or that of a stag, the Fleece touched the ground in front and behind as Jason draped it over his left shoulder. And where it touched, the ground sparkled with glittering golden patches. When Jason and Medea ran back down the twisted wooded path, it seemed to the Argonauts who saw them coming than an amorphous configuration of fire, like a globule of lightning, was erratically descending upon them. They held their oars, though, poised and ready.

Even as Jason and Medea were being lifted aboard, the order to push off was given, and moments later they were out beyond the cove once more in deep waters. Placing the Fleece, now carefully wrapped in his own mantle, beside Medea in the stern, Jason addressed his crew: "The quest is over, the prize is won for which we braved dangers and rode seas unknown to any Greek. Now bend your backs to the oars as never before. For the sake of our aged parents, for the glory of Greece, let us not fail now!"

With a great shout the Argonauts responded to their captain's words. The oarsmen struck the water so vigorously with their pine-wood blades that the ship bolted forward like a jungle cat suddenly springing toward its prey. Jason donned his battle gear and took his place by Ancaios, now helmsman. So powerful were the strokes of the men at the oars and so strong the river's current into which they presently came that the ship virtually shot, as though gray-eyed Athene's hand were once again on the stern, along the black waters' surface down to the open sea.

When they reached the place where Aietes and his hordes lined either bank, so swiftly did they fly that the barbarians, turning their heads like spectators at a chariot race, looked on in disbelief. Few arrows were loosed, and most of those disappeared harmlessly into the *Argo's* wake.

The Colchian king, now more bent on bringing his treasonous daughter to justice than destroying the Greeks, roared for his men to take to their ships. As the armada was being launched, the men of the *Argo* were running up their sail to take advantage of the brisk ocean breeze that greeted them in the bay beyond the river's mouth.

# Homeward Bound

**B**ecause Phineus had said that they should return home by a different route, Jason directed Ancaios to veer northward. There was a river, the sons of Phrixos told him, that had its beginning along the northern coast of the Euxine and flowed through vast plains and between the great snow-capped mountains beyond Scythia and Thrace until at last it emptied into the Ionian Sea. Surely, he concluded, that must have been the route of which the blind seer had spoken. The winds themselves now favored it.

Where the river began was an island, triangular as though it were a huge plug intended by some god ages ago to stop the river but had somehow worked loose; it was positioned so as to give the broad stream the effect of having two mouths. The Argonauts on their third day from Colchis passed the first, the lesser, channel, sailing several hours along the large island's coast before reaching the second, which they entered.

Once they were beyond where the two channels converged, slowly they became aware of a strange tranquility about. The only ripples in the water were those made by their own oars. Nor was there any movement or sound along the banks, no smoke from village fires, no animal calls. All was silent, ominously so, as if the land, the river itself were sitting there quietly waiting for something to happen. Warily the Argonauts rowed on.

In the meantime, Apsyrtos, son to King Aietes, Medea's brother, had also sailed into the river with those ships in his command. Well he knew the region and also the stories of how the river was a quick and easy passage to Greece. Taking the first channel so that he was now ahead of those he pursued, he purposed to ambush the Argonauts where two islands, both sacred to Zeus's daughter Artemis, broke up the stream's broad expanse. So it was that he concealed his ships at both ends of the islands.

When the Greeks were midway between the islands, the first barbarian ship came into view. Quickly it was joined by another and then a third. More than a dozen others then appeared almost at once to block off the river ahead of them. Nor was there any retreat, for behind the Argonauts more Colchian vessels were strung out across the water. Electing to fight on land rather than from their deck, Jason ordered the *Argo* beached on one of the islands. He and his men then leaped ashore and grimly readied themselves for battle.

Only slowly did it dawn on the Argonauts that they had landed upon sacred soil where no man, for fear of the silver-bowed Daughter of Zeus, dared draw blood. Envoys rather than spearmen came from the Colchian ships, now drawn in tightly around the *Argo*.

"The maiden Medea is all we want," said their spokesman to Jason. "The Fleece is yours. You and your men may sail unchallenged back to Greece, but the girl must answer to her father."

"She is in my protection," Jason told them.

"Leave her here in the protection of Artemis, and let some local king, a neutral party, decide her fate—whether she be returned to her home or sent on to Greece."

More was said, but in the end Jason assented to the envoy's proposal that a king from the area be enlisted to decide Medea's disposition. Medea herself took to the arrangement none too kindly. "Is this how the Greeks keep their vows?" she said, once the envoys departed. "I turned my back forever on my home for your sake. Now you will not lift a hand to save me."

"Look about you," Jason told her. "We're surrounded by an army. Faint chance is better than none."

"Think you there's a king anywhere in this region who cares so little for his own people so as not to turn me over to Aietes? Faint chance? I have none. I am doomed! Here, I offer you my throat. Do me the kindness of drawing your sword across it."

"We need time. For that reason and that alone did I make this truce."

"There was a moment," continued Medea, "when I dared hope my love for you had been returned full measure. 'Twas but the Fleece you saw in my face, nothing more."

"Rather would I be your live champion, dear lady, than your dead love," returned Jason. "To fight now would mean all our deaths. Is that

116

your wish? To see us killed and then become their trophy anyway? Time we must have to plan a stratagem to free us all."

"You will fight if need be?"

"As a last, not a first, resort," he answered. "Often, it is said, the sheep will scatter when the shepherd is no more. Your brother's men are as sheep. I doubt they would risk their lives against us if he were somehow removed."

Medea pondered Jason's last words. For several moments she stared, without saying anything, at the ships out in the river. A new look replaced the anger in her eyes, a colder, more resolute look. There was death in her voice when she spoke. "One betrayal begets another," she said. "Plan your stratagem, my lord. I will deliver Apsyrtos into your hands. Call back his envoys to bear him gifts. When they come, arrange to leave them a few moments with me alone."

And so, on pretext of further placating the Colchian prince, the Argonauts quickly gathered together such treasures as a guest might leave his host and beckoned for delegates from the barbarians to come and receive them. There was a splendid silver vase among the items, with the trials of Cadmos depicted in delicate relief along its brim, and also an exquisite purple robe, present to Jason from Hypsipyle, as well as bronze figurines brought with them from Iolcos for just such a purpose, loot plundered from the Behryces, and presents bestowed upon them by the ill-fated Cyzicos. The Colchian messengers looked at the store with wide-eyed amazement.

Drawing aside the leader of the delegation as if on the sly, Medea whispered, "Tell my brother that one more item will I add to this treasure: the Golden Fleece. He shall have that and me and the heads of all these Greek villains to present to our father Aietes, if at nightfall he meets me alone at the shrine of Artemis. I have a plan that will please his ears. Not by my own will, but by the cunning of Phrixos's sons, do I find myself in this detestable company." She affected great desperation in her voice and aspect as she spoke. Wing-shod Hermes himself could not have been more convincing.

At the first hint of dusk Jason and Medea stole off to the shrine of Artemis at the far end of the island, leaving the main body of the Greeks in plain view of the watchful barbarians. Arriving at the sacred place, Jason quickly found a hiding place, while Medea, as though alone, paced anxiously outside the small temple. The day was but briefly extended by the already disappeared sun's reflection off low-hanging clouds, giving a pinkish cast, like the color of a young lamb's flesh, to all about.

As night began to close out all light altogether, Apsyrtos, lured by his sister's perfidious offer, ventured unescorted to where Medea was waiting. He began a greeting but never finished it, for suddenly Jason sprang from hiding with unsheathed sword in hand. Medea turned her head and brought her arms across her brow to cover her eyes. Nothing, though, stopped her ears from hearing the death blow or her brother's final tormented groan as life quickly drained out of him. Sinking to the ground, Apsyrtos bathed his hands with his own dark blood and, pressing them against his sister, smeared a column of crimson the length of her silvery dress.

Jason, at Medea's instructions, hacked off his victim's hands and feet and three times licked up some blood and three times spit it out after the manner of assassins trying to expiate their guilt. This done, he further dismembered the corpse, scattering some parts about the immediate area and others along the beach and in the river. He and Medea then returned, as stealthily and quickly as they had left, to where their companions under cover of darkness had already slipped aboard the *Argo* and in full battle gear were prepared to run the blockade. They silently pushed out into the river once the pair were on deck. The surprised, leaderless Colchians, though greatly outnumbering the Greeks, offered little resistance as the Argonauts rammed and maneuvered their way through them.

All through the night and the next day and then the following night and day the Greek seamen struck the waters of the broad river with their oars, going to the rowing benches in shifts. No words, they knew, could ever be found now to assuage the hateful fury of King Aietes. Their only escape lay in their own strong arms and backs. Not until the third night did they dare pull ashore to take their needed rest.

The Colchian king had, in the meantime, arrived at the Isles of Artemis. He tore at his clothes, put ashes in his hair, beat upon his chest, and cried with loud shrieks to his father above to rain down terror upon his son's slayers. He did not himself, however, take up pursuit of the Greeks right away; for, as Medea had anticipated, it took him beyond a full day to gather together the several parts of Apsyrtos's body to bury them.

Deeper inland the Argonauts sailed, often rowing now against occasional stiff currents as they moved from the flat-lands into regions with mountains and valleys. At times steep precipices came down to the clear blue water's edge on either side. When the stream narrowed and the current became impossible to navigate, they hauled the *Argo* ashore and cut a goodly number of round logs for rollers. Through mountains then they bore the ships that had so long borne them. In time they came upon another stream, one that became ever wider as they followed it until at last it was broad and deep enough to sail. Into great blue mountain lakes the new river took them and then through deep-set valleys and grassy basins where flocks of sheep grazed along the hillsides. Then, after many days, it brought them into the open sea, though what sea they knew not.

As they were raising the sail, a great voice suddenly boomed out. It was the ship herself speaking, or rather that magic beam placed in the prow by Athene herself. "Men of the *Argo*, men of the *Argo*!" it cried. "Blood you have upon your hands. Endlessly must you wander and know the vengeful wrath of Zeus, whose anger is now kindled by a murder most impious. Cursed you are, never to see your families again! Only Circe, daughter of Helios, can purge you of your bloodguilt."

Hera, however, was not about to abandon her darling, the gallant Greek prince who had once plunged into icy waters for her and carried her to safety in his strong young arms, nor was she going to stand by and let the scheming, irreverent tyrant Pelias have his way. No, not in the least! Her friends among humankind she knew well and her enemies, nor was she one to forget either. She it was who now stirred the winds that filled the *Argo*'s sail and set the Greeks on course for Circe's island.

Thus they came to the enchanted home of Helios's daughter, aunt to Medea, though the two had never met. Anchoring the ship in a small inlet, a natural harbor, they ventured cautiously along the beach until they at last came into view of a beautiful woman washing her hair in the sea. She was surrounded by creatures the likes of which the Argonauts had never seen. Neither men nor beasts were these, though both at the same time, with the hands and forearms of the one and the snouts and jowls of the other. Rising, the woman turned toward the seamen. Her facial features and dark eyes told them immediately they had found Aietes' sister.

She smiled seductively and gestured for them to follow as she walked toward her cottage, from whence came the grunts and squeals of swine. Medea motioned the Argonauts back. Only she and Jason went with Circe. Inside the house, declining the bronze armchairs offered by their hostess, Medea led Jason to the hearth. There they sat after the manner of suppliants. Neither spoke; neither looked at Circe.

The dark-eyed enchantress understood then that they were fugitives with unexpiated blood on their hands. Saying nothing, she snatched a suckling pig from a sow still swollen with milk and then, holding the squealing animal above the suppliants' heads, cut its throat so that blood

119

sprayed over them. After that she poured libations and called out to the Father of Gods and Men to hear the murderers' prayers. Then at the hearth she burned cereal offerings and cakes and other wineless gifts to placate the dread Furies as well.

This done, the Daughter of Helios once more offered her guests the brazen armchairs, which this time they accepted. Only then did Medea raise 'her head. By her eyes Circe knew her to be a kinswoman and asked about her homeland and what strange circumstances caused her to leave it. All of her aunt's questions the Colchian princess answered, weeping from time to time, though she did not tell of the murder of Apsyrtos.

"Vengeance yet stalks you, my poor dear, and shall stalk you even to Grecian soil," Circe said. "Grievous is your crime. Wrong you were to choose a stranger above your own illustrious house. I do not approve your actions. Go at once."

Gentle breezes took the Greeks soon beyond the sight of Circe's island and into new danger, for in that same region dwelt the Sirens, man-hating daughters of the Muse Terpsichore, whose hypnotic songs lured sailors into the rock-strewn shoals about their island. Skeletons of men and ships littered their beaches everywhere.

As the Argonauts approached, the sisters, spotting them from afar, began to sing their spellbinding death song. And the Greeks, hearing its first enchanted strains, would surely have headed their ship into the rocks had not golden-voiced Orpheus begun to pluck his peerless lyre and answer with a song of his own. It was a lively song and a boisterous one. Scarcely was there a moment when the Sirens could be heard. Long he sang until the island was far, far behind them.

Among the Wandering Rocks next they sailed, where volcanic fires raged and spewed forth molten granite and where towering geysers crashed upon the jagged reefs, and after that through the treacherous straits between Scylla and Charybdis. Black clouds then gathered overhead. Winds from the north whipped the waters to a frenzy, stirring up gigantic waves which loomed like great shimmering walls in the *Argo*'s path. Like an inflated bladder the waves tossed the ship lightly across their foamy crests, dropping her, picking her up, flinging her anew. One could have imagined a race of titanic sea gods at play. By the time the storm had abated and the sea was calm again, the Argonauts were as far from Iolcos as they had ever been.

Sore, exhausted were they and near collapse from want of water when, after more than a week, they came into view of Crete. Happy shouts went up from all hands at the sighting. Little did they realize that between them and the island's sweet spring waters there towered a massive bronze giant. Talos was his name, and his office it was to repel foreign invaders who might come too close to the Cretan shore. His entire body was of impenetrable bronze, making him invulnerable except for one place on one ankle where his life fluids were covered by a very thin layer of brazen tissue.

When the Argonauts tried to put in at a cove, Talos spotted them and broke off chunks of a nearby cliff with which to pelt them. Terrified, the Greek oarsmen quickly back watered and, despite their desperate straits, began to swing the ship around to flee the island and its brazen guardian. "Stop!" shouted Medea. "Hear me! Unless that bronze body contains immortal life, he can be destroyed. Row only beyond his range, and give me a chance to bring him down."

The rowers did as she told them. Once at a safe distance they drew in their oars and watched as, with Jason's help, Medea mounted the deck. Strange incantations flowed from her lips. The Argonauts shuddered at what they heard. Upon the Spirits of Death she called, Hades' fleet hounds that devour souls and lurk in the lower regions to spring upon living men. Three times she invoked them on bended knees; three times she serenaded them with sweet and eerie song. Then rigidly she rose to her feet and riveted her eyes on the great bronze figure still breaking lumps of stone from the seaside ledge.

While Medea's eyes remained fixed on him, Talos braced himself to hurl a large boulder he had just broken free. As he did so, his foot shuffled back against a sharp, jagged stone, grazing the thin tissue and the delicate vein tenuously protected by it. His life fluids drained from him like molten lead. He dropped the boulder and staggered there high on the cliff for several moments before his great brazen knees finally buckled and he toppled, like a huge pine felled by a woodman's ax, with an earth-jarring crash to the beach below.

The Argonauts spent that night and the following day and night on Crete, refreshing and recreating themselves. On the third day they left the island and sailed without untoward incident all the way to Iolcos. The closer they came to home, the more vigorously they rowed; toward the end their blades flailed at the sea like the wings of giant hummingbirds. One could see the motion, but not the oars. And so it was they returned after four months, though years it seemed to them, to the port from which they had first embarked.

It was nightfall when the *Argo* moved into the harbor. The day's last light had already disappeared beneath the western horizon, and on the beach was but a solitary boatman, much slower, because of age, than his companions to get his traps together and retreat to his home for the night.

"Call out the city!" cried Jason to the boatman. "We have returned with the Golden Fleece. Summon Pelias, my father and mother. Shout it abroad. The young men who went forth have returned!"

"Shout nothing," cautioned the old man, "until you know what has happened here."

"Speak then, old fellow. What mean you?"

"Word we had that you and all hands were lost at sea," said the man. "This made King Pelias bold to demand your father Aison's life, which Aison by the king's leave took himself. Your mother cursed Pelias and hanged herself. The king is ever on his guard lest the rumors of your shipwreck prove false."

New despair came over Jason. "Tell no one of our return," he instructed the boatman. "We must decide what to do."

Thereupon the Argonauts again boarded their ship and took themselves to a haven where they would be safe. Jason was of a mind to storm the royal palace that very night. "Let us return to our own cities," advised others, "and there raise armies. We are too few to assault the palace ourselves."

"Where force fails," intruded Medea, "craft perhaps can win the day. Let me go into the city to find some means whereby to disarm the king. Remain hidden until I signal you with torches from the palace roof."

At morning's first light Medea slipped into the city and slowly, unobtrusively worked her way toward the palace. By evening she had met the three daughters of Pelias and had so insinuated herself into their confidence that she was invited to stay with them. On the following day, when the moment was ripe, she spoke to them of the pathos of old age, lamenting how sad indeed it was to see those we most love grow old and decrepit and finally wither into nothingness, especially when it was all so unnecessary.

"Oh, but it is necessary," put in Alcestis, one of the daughters.

"The young get old, but the old never become young again," said Evadne, another daughter.

"It happens to us all," contributed Amphinome, the third.

"Oh no," said Medea, "it does not have to happen, if one's youth is restored. Let me show you."

With that, she requested that a brass kettle be brought forth and a hot fire built under it. Jars of water were poured into the cauldron; and into the water, as it began to simmer, Medea sprinkled herbs and aromatic dusts. Then she had led in an old ram, indeed a very old ram, its horns hopelessly bent in, its back swayed, its underside nearly touching the ground. With a quick knife she slit the ancient animal's throat and proceeded to dissect its body into thirteen parts, each of which she gently lowered into the now boiling water. Incantations she made from three positions, and thrice she waved her arms across the steaming pot. Then all of a sudden she thrust her hand into the vapor and, behold, pulled out a fleecy white lamb. The daughters of Pelias were dumbfounded.

"Can you do this with people too?" inquired one of them, as if suddenly getting an idea.

"Of course," Medea assured her.

The three princesses held quick counsel together; and, instructing Medea to remain where she was, ecstatically they disappeared in the direction of their father's bedchamber. Moments later, still beside themselves with excitement, they reappeared carrying Pelias, his throat already neatly slit. As they had seen Medea do with the ram, they cut his corpse into thirteen parts and put them into the cauldron. They spoke the same incantations from the same positions around the kettle as Medea and three times waved their arms through the pungent steam. No babe, though, did they draw from the cauldron.

"Quick, to the roof with torches," said Medea. "Implore the moon while there is still time."

The bewildered girls did as they were told, thereby unwittingly signaling the men of the *Argo* to come to the palace. Without Pelias to give commands, the guards offered no resistance. When Medea's ploy was made known to all, however, many of the Argonauts, though themselves intent on killing Pelias, were aghast at what was done. Nor could the Iolchian council abide it. Rather than declare Jason now their rightful king and accept Medea, his wife, as queen, they chose to banish the pair from the kingdom forever.

Accepting his people's judgment, Jason took Medea with him and wandered about Greece, until at last they came to Corinth, where Creon was king. And there, for the first time since he left the charge of the kindly Centaur Cheiron, the forlorn son of Aison was untroubled by pressures and perils from without. In due time a son was born to him and Medea, and later a second son. A peasant would have envied him the life he shared there in the great port city with his beautiful wife and young family. So would a fisherman or a sheepherder, but Jason was a prince and could never forget that fate and foul play had deprived him of his legitimate kingdom.

When, therefore, after several years the aging king of Corinth, himself sonless, let it be known that he was seeking a husband for his daughter Glauce and hence a successor to himself, Jason did not shrink from showing interest. Medea was not invited to the wedding between her husband and the princess of Corinth. She was informed of it by royal messenger.

A terrible transformation then took place in the once life-loving daughter of Aietes. It is said that the impish son of Aphrodite carries two kinds of darts in his brightly colored quiver: one which inspires love and another which engenders hate. That dart driven years ago into Medea's heart had been the first kind; now, as if by the wizardry of Jason's betrayal, it suddenly became the other. A hate, fully as indomitable and all-consuming as the former love, seized the deserted woman; musings of unutterable vengeance filled to overflowing her maniacal mind.

Of her madness dark plans were born; then were suddenly hate-nurtured, full-grown. To her immortal grandfather she made her prayers: "Great Helios, in your stables are many chariots. Send one hither at day's end when my retribution is accomplished, and to that end steel my courage." At that moment the sun above flashed more brightly than normal, or so it seemed to her.

As a farm wife, eager to please, scurries about the kitchen preparing special delicacies, tarts perhaps or candied fruit, for her beloved toiler at harvest time or as a maid with nimble fingers works her loom to fashion a gift for her swain, even so now did Medea busy herself in her chambers. From a chest she took a delicately woven gown, elegantly embroidered, and a dainty golden diadem; then from her case of potions and poisons, her only baggage from Colchis, her most virulent toxins. Like rare spices she mixed the deadly powders, and as a housewife might season her family's dinner meat, a goose perhaps, she brushed the mixture painstakingly over the gown and diadem, careful to leave no spot untreated.

Wrapping then the two items as gifts, she gave them to her two small sons. "Take these to the princess in the palace," she instructed them. "Give them to no one but her. Say they are presents from someone not so lucky as she but who accepts her fate and hopes she will treat her children well. And hurry back. We have more to do."

The children, death's unwitting deliverymen, did as their mother told them. Jason was not about when they came to the princess's chambers at the palace, but Glauce was. She took the packages from their hands and, while they were still there, made much ado about opening them. As soon as they left, she called for her maids to attend her. So taken was she by the exquisite workmanship of both the diadem and gown that she could not wait to try them on.

Quickly she doffed the dress she was wearing and pulled the gift gown over her head and placed the crown in her hair, using a mirror to determine the most advantageous tilt. Never had she felt more lovely than when she stepped lightly back and curtsied approvingly to the image in the looking glass. Then the poison began to take effect. At first she felt prickly sensations where the crown and garment touched her but quickly afterwards sharp, fiery pain. Suddenly horrified, she grasped the gown to tear it off only to discover it was fused to her skin. The diadem likewise could not be ripped from her head without taking her scalp with it.

The women in the room screamed. One ran to get the king, another to get Jason. White froth now oozed from the corners of the girl's mouth; the pupils of her eyes rolled back almost out of sight. Her face became ashen. She reeled and shrieked in her agony and at last collapsed to the floor. By the time the king got there, the princess, but such a short time before the happiest and liveliest of souls, was dead. Her face had been so distorted by agony that a friend would not have recognized her corpse.

Her father dropped to his knees beside her and took the limp form into his arms. Long he held her, groaning and weeping uncontrollably. "Oh, you gods who allowed this," he screamed, "take me too. Let me die with my child!" When he tried to withdraw his arms, he could not, for the poison had begun its work on him as well. His prayer was soon granted.

More horrid, however, than this was the scene taking place at the same time between Medea and her children. Upon their return from the palace, the two little boys were quickly ushered into a room by their mother, who then bolted the door. An ogre from hell could not have done what Medea did next. Only a mad-woman could have taken her husband's sword from its sheath and with it butchered the darlings she once had suckled at her breast, only a woman driven beyond the brink by insatiable and irresistible hate, no longer human, no, nor animal either, less than beast, less than fiend.

Creon's was not the only prayer to be answered that day. So too was Medea's. The great golden God of the Sun, father to her father, had called down commands for one of his chariots to be dispatched for his granddaughter. As the god's great chariot finished its trek for the day, a far less grand vehicle, drawn by glittering winged dragons, came to a rest in front of Medea's house. The demented woman took the bodies of her two children and laid them in the chariot, then stepped up into it herself and seized the silken reins.

Jason came upon her as she was about to crack the whip above the dragons' heads. She held back as he slowly, torturously, in dreadful disbelief surveyed the situation. The moment was as perversely gratifying to her as it was excruciating to him. "Did you dare think you could scorn my love and not pay for it?" she said to him.

"Of all women most unnatural," he gasped, "those hands stained by your brother's blood are now polluted with your own children. You have quite destroyed me."

"And did not you destroy me?"

"Our deeds do not compare," he said.

"Think you that love is so small a thing," she shot back, again raising the whip, "that its pangs are so easily borne? Let your heart now break as you have broken mine." So saying, she snapped the whip and sped off to the distant haunts of Athens, where she had already been promised asylum by King Aigeus.

Bereft of family, of bride, Jason was indeed destroyed. A second kingdom had now eluded him, and in his adoptive country, once so gracious to him, he was suddenly anathema. He had begun his life an outcast, and an outcast he was again. Cursed he was now to wander the earth aimlessly, without destination, forever homeless, unwelcomed, loathed in every country.

When his drifting about brought him, in due time, secretly back to Iolcos where everything began, he went to the beach to look once more upon the *Argo*, still drawn up on shore as they had left it so many years before. He pulled himself onto the deck and for long stood there, in solitude thinking back to earlier days and the fearless stalwarts who had braved with him uncharted seas in the grandest adventure of them all.

Then, with a rope in hand, he crawled out onto the prow. Tying one end of the rope to the ship's foremost timber and the other in a noose around his neck, he bid the world of light farewell and let himself fall. Unsuccessful throughout his life, he was unsuccessful still. The timber, for years subject to damp winds and worms, snapped under the strain, and Jason landed harmlessly on the ground. At that moment, however, a kind god was perhaps looking on from Mount Olympos and saw and had pity, for the broken timber crashed down upon his head, killing him.

# Two Other Argonauts

A part from Jason himself, those of his shipmates whose names lived on were remembered not so much for their roles in the quest for the Golden Fleece but rather for the sons they sired, whose deeds in the Trojan War greatly overshadowed their own. Two Argonauts, however, without sons, went on to achieve lasting fame in their own rights: Orpheus and Meleagros.

It was for the sake of Eurydice, a lovely maiden with soul kindred to his own, that Orpheus went back to Thrace rather than stay on in Greece where men were civilized and could fully appreciate his golden voice. Soon after his return the two were wed, he the gentlest of men and she of women the purest and sweetest. Theirs was not to be a long marriage, however. It so happened that one day, before the blush of early wedlock had left her cheeks, Eurydice chanced to be alone in the Vale of Tempe when the lecherous Aristaios, Apollo's son by the nymph Cyrene, happened by.

At first, it not being her habit to think ill of another, she took his overtures to be no more than friendliness. When he grew bolder in both speech and action, she surmised his intent and turned to run. He caught her briefly, but she broke loose. So frantically did she flee that she did not see a viper, absorbing the afternoon sun, in the path ahead of her. When her foot came down on the snake's tail, it whipped around and sank its curved fangs into her ankle. Aristaios, close behind, saw it as it happened and gave up his pursuit. When Orpheus found her many hours later, she had already been escorted by Hermes into Hades' dark kingdom beneath the earth.

It had been rumored that a huge cave at Tainaron led all the way to Tartaros. The bereaved, undauntable Thracian lord, not knowing whether the allegation was true or purest folk fancy, went there, lyre in hand, and descended into the gaping abyss. Like a mockingbird that has lost its mate, Orpheus sang more sweetly than ever before as he worked his way yet deeper into the cave. He had no plan, even if this did prove an entrance to the land of the dead, only a vague and desperate hope. The spirits that protected the place were spellbound by his sweet, sad song and let him pass.

Charon, the brusque, surly, implacable ferryman whose boat and his alone transports souls across the River Styx, was also charmed by the clear, beautiful notes of Orpheus's death song for his young wife. The deep lines in the old boatman's brow became smooth, and an unaccustomed tear formed in the corner of one eye. He beckoned the grief-stricken bridegroom into his craft, though he saw he had no coin to pay, and took him to the other side. And when that monstrous, snarling three-headed guard dog of the dark kingdom's gates Cerberos heard the mellifluous, plaintive strains, with three appreciative whimpers he let Orpheus through.

At no time has music's magical power ever been more manifest than when Orpheus's great golden voice reverberated down the corridors of the underworld to bring bliss to the cheerless dead and even to make mellow the stern hearts of the three Judges of the Dead so that they gave the damned in Tartaros a day's reprieve from their unceasing ordeals. Tantalos, his thirst assuaged, ceased to reach his hands down toward the ever receding waters. Ixion's wheel slowed to a stop, and the wily Sisyphos broke from rolling his boulder and sat upon it to rest and listen to the Thracian wonder sing for his lost love to the chords of his matchless lyre.

Nor were grim Hades himself and Queen Persephone untouched when Orpheus at last stood in their presence and bared his heart in mournful song. It was a plea as well as a lament, for he sang of his beloved Eurydice and how in the bloom of her youth she was plucked away, the fairest of flowers, the only flower in a thousand gardens that could bring him joy. Too delicate was the thread of her life, too finely spun, severed too soon. In time they would both in death's dark kingdom dwell, so could it not later be for Eurydice as well as him? Could not the thread be unraveled and respun and, longer made, be entwined and thereby strengthened with his own? If not, and thus he ended his song,

> . . . then cleave my thread as well I pray,
> That with my love I might forever stay.

"Your quest is granted," said the rich, grim God of the Underworld, his

128

face betraying its first signs of civility since the battle in which he and his brothers prevailed against the Titans. "Take your bride back with you into the world of light. You have my leave to do so."

Orpheus beamed with delight. Never before had the Lord of the Dead made such a concession to a mere mortal. "Thanks and sacrifices will I render to you, oh Rich One, all the days of my life," he vowed.

"One thing," added Hades. "You must not look behind you. She may follow you into the upper air. If, however, you but once look back to see her ere you both have stepped fully into the light, she will be lost to you forever."

And so, Eurydice was called up from the ranks of the recent dead and bid to follow her husband out beyond the portals where Cerberos maintained his guard, back across the River Styx, and up once more into the world of living men. Orpheus went first and she after. When they came to the dim passage by which he had entered the underworld, where she was likely to be less sure, he played continuously, zestfully upon his lyre that she by sound would know his position if sight should fail. He proceeded slowly, picking his way carefully, choosing where there was choice the easier climb for her sake.

At length above them a hint of light came into view. Each foot of the way now found Orpheus's spirits mounting. He played louder, more exuberantly songs of earlier days, merry songs, sprightly songs. Stepping finally out of the cave himself, he sensed silence behind him and instinctively, unthinkingly looked backward over his shoulder. He glimpsed but briefly his beloved's shadowy form as she slipped away from him deeper and deeper into the dark abyss ever beyond his trembling, outstretched arms.

In vain Orpheus returned again to the Stygian shore and, weeping, begged ancient Charon to let him cross once more, one way only, into the country where his love abode, and each time the dour boatman pushed him away. No soul would he accept before he was due. Then for seven days the bereaved singer sat in slime, made slimier by his tears, and refused all food and drink, filled to the brim with grief and sorrow.

After this he went back up into Thrace and there gave himself over to Apollo as priest in a small, rustic temple. For three years he tended to the needs of the temple and charmed the birds and animals thereabouts with his incomparable lyre and golden voice. Nor did he ever again find pleasure in women.

Even the stones and trees of that untamed place responded to his beautiful airs and on occasions, some claim, joined the beasts and birds and fish in rare, majestic dance. Only the Mainads, frenzied devotees of twice-born Dionysos who years before had dismembered the luckless Pentheus, of all the creatures thereabouts remained unmoved by Orpheus's songs. They in fact hated him, partly because he shunned the company of their sex and partly because he was so much the opposite of themselves. With a great loathing they loathed him, the kind a vixen has for Zeus's high-flying eagle that is ever a threat to her cubs or the kind men of war, primed and ravenous for battle, have for the voice of peace and reason in their camp. Their hate swelled and then all at once, one morning, exploded.

The women stood on a knoll opposite Orpheus as he emerged from the temple after attending to his early chores. Lyre in hand as he went about his duties, as always he was singing. All nature stopped to hear his song, though on the Mainads' nerves it grated like the sound of steel against slate. Savage in aspect, breasts naked except for fillets of fur, unkempt hair caught up in the gusting wind, they hissed like serpents at their hearts' abhorrence.

One then cried out, "No time for us, sweet man, pretty man? Have our bodies, our voices no power to charm you, unnatural man? Know then the fury of what you scorn!" With that, she let drive her spear at his open mouth. Off the mark only slightly, it grazed his cheek. Orpheus continued his song.

Another Mainad tried to stop his lips with a swift, well-aimed stone, but at the last instant the missile, under the sweet song's spell, arched sharply to the ground at the singer's feet. Nature herself against them, the wild women became the more enraged and launched an avalanche of spears down upon the unarmed man. As though scattered by an invisible hand above him, they all fell short or wide, stuck fast in the soil about him like giant quills. Fury fed on frustration, and the singer sang on.

Then, as they grasped new rocks and with inhuman might hurled them high into the sky out toward their target, they screeched like murderous nighthawks swooping in for the kill and beat violently upon their breasts, by their cacophony trying to undo the sweet song's magic and thus guide their projectiles to their desired mark. And, woe to Orpheus, their strategy proved not unsuccessful. The rocks struck home and fell, blood-streaked, all about him. Songbirds that had paused from flight to take their inspiration quickly took to wing once more, and snakes, made civil by the Thracian lord's clear strains, crawled back into their holes.

The Mainads then descended upon the stricken Orpheus. Some plied his flesh with jagged sticks; others reached in with hands, their bony fingers rigid and arched like owls' talons, and tore at his tender skin. Three together wrenched an arm from its socket and threw it into the crimson grass. Others ripped off a leg at the knee, though his body still throbbed with life. The other leg was next, then the other arm, and then it was, as the animals in their hiding places wept and the trees shed their leaves in grief, the spirit of the man left him for kindlier climes. Last of all his head was torn from his body and cast with the hated lyre into the River Hebros.

Miraculously, as it floated downstream, the lyre played of its own accord. A somber death lament it played, and the dead tongue began to sing, at first softly and then in clear, impassioned tones that echoed off the river reeds and both banks until the whole valley rang with the saddest, sweetest song that was ever heard. Down to the sea the river carried the head and lyre of Orpheus; and, when at length they sank into the great deep he had once sailed with his fellow Argonauts, the lovely music could still be heard.

The story of Meleagros, Orpheus's shipmate aboard the *Argo*, is also the story of Atalanta, who would have sailed with them if she had been allowed. The Arcadian princess was the equal of any man of her time, save Heracles, but she was also strikingly beautiful, and so it had been feared that for that reason she would be a source of contention on the ship. Jason, we are told, had gazed long upon her loveliness and then slowly, reluctantly had shaken his head. Meleagros should have been so wise.

That Atalanta turned out to have such skill with her bow and to be so fleet of foot was not all that surprising to those who knew how her father, King Iasos, disappointed that she was not a boy, had ordered that as an infant she be abandoned in the wilderness. A she-bear, her dugs swollen with milk, found and gave suck to her. In time some hunters came upon her and raised her after their own rugged ways. While the boys about her father's palace played at games and were lessoned in courtly manners, how to dress and such, Iasos's discarded daughter was drawing her bow on fang-baring wolves and giving chase to the light-footed hind.

Meleagros, one of the two men with whose destinies Atalanta's was to be intertwined, grew up in the palace at Calydon. The son he was of Oineus, the Calydonian king, and Althaia, his wife. So auspicious was his birth that the three Fates themselves attended the event and lingered for seven days afterward. From them at their parting came the dire prophecy: "When the hearth-log to ashes burns, then too will this child's life be spent." Althaia, upon hearing this, rushed to the fireplace and pulled out the burning log and doused it and locked it in a chest to which only she had a key.

But a youth when he went aboard the *Argo*, Meleagros returned to Calydon every inch a man. It was to him the people of that region looked whenever danger stalked their families or herds; it was of him stories were told to strangers who chanced to stop there en route to other places. Some of the Calydonians did not know the name of their own king, but none was there who did not know his illustrious son. For that reason, when a great wild boar suddenly began to ravage the land, it was to Meleagros they turned and none other.

The boar, it seems, was set loose against the kingdom by silver-quivered Artemis, whose altar alone had been neglected by Oineus when at harvest he raised thank offerings to the gods of heaven and earth. That this was an oversight, nothing more, did not diminish her fury. "Let it never be said that I'm lightly spurned," she stormed and went out to scour the earth for the monstrous pig.

In some distant primeval rain forest she must have found the savage beast, for larger was it than the bulls that fed upon the lush meadows of Epiros or the oxen that pulled the Boiotian plows. Like rows of spears, the bristles stood up along its thick neck. Great curved tusks protruded on either side of its vicious, misshapen jaws. Seething froth lined its lips; and when it opened its mouth to grunt, billows of steam and spurts of hot saliva shot forth.

Fields of ripe barley ready for harvest were devastated by the beast while heartsick husbandmen could but look on. One day a bumper crop would wait the sickle's stroke; the next it would be only so much straw trodden into the dust. Through vineyards and orchards too the great boar rampaged. Nor were flocks and herds safe from its dreadful tusks. Dogs that had stood against wolves and bears and marauding lions cowered and ran from the great boar, and with them ran the shepherds themselves.

Meleagros sent forth messengers into all of Greece to summon young men to his side. First to come were comrades with whom he had sailed to Colchis and back: Castor and Polydeuces, Acastos, Telamon, Peleus, Admetos, and Jason himself. To join them came Nestor from Pylos and Laertes from Ithaca and Athenian Theseus with his companion, the bold Peirithoos, and a host of others.

And lastly came the Arcadian beauty Atalanta, her gaping cloak held loosely together by an ivory brooch, her face aglow with virginal comeliness. When Meleagros's eyes fell upon her, his heart was set afire.

"Lucky the man who fathers a child on the likes of her," he found himself thinking, nor could he banish that thought from his mind. Certain of his fellows winced at taking up the chase with a woman, but he was insistent that she be included.

The young men hastened to set their nets and traps along the edges of the forest where their quarry had made its lair. Then, unleashing their dogs, some raucously charged into the virgin woods to coax the animal out. All at once, like lightning shooting out of a dark raincloud, the boar bolted from the thick undergrowth. Saplings bowed beneath it like spring's first grass; large limbs were snapped, ripped from the trunks of broad myrtles and low-hanging willows. Had Zeus carved a path through the trees with a blustery tornado, it would have looked no different.

Holding their positions, the hunters let drive their bronze-tipped javelins before sidestepping to safety. Suddenly the boar veered in its tracks and dove into the hound pack, goring, rending, sending the yapping creatures into the thickets on either side. Most of the javelins, hurled in haste, went wide of their mark. The two or three that did find their target but glanced off the boar's tough skin like shafts of bamboo against a brazen shield. Again the monstrous animal turned and this time charged the young men.

Two were trampled to the ground but were quickly pulled to their feet by companions. As they ran for cover, however, one of them, weak from fear, proved too slow. The boar, reversing its direction, with a quick jerk of its head drove a tusk into the small of the young man's back and out through his chest. Death might have likewise come quick for Nestor too had he not used his spear to vault into the branches of a handy oak. Castor and Polydeuces rushed in to attack, but the boar retreated into the dense forest. Only Atalanta in this first encounter drew blood, and that with a well-aimed arrow to the base of one of the great beast's ears.

"A weapon at last strikes true!" cried Meleagros. "And from a second-rate bow at that."

The barb was not lost on Ancaios. Raising his huge double-bitted battle-ax, he darted into the deepest part of the forest after the boar. "Follow me, men," he called to his fellows, "if you want to see a man-sized wound instead of a lucky needle prick. I'll hew the beast in twain before our lord's bosomy champion, though she turn out to be Leto's daughter herself, can draw her bow a second time."

He came upon the animal just as it was turning for another charge. Ancaios raised his great ax but misjudged the agility of the beast. First one of the curved tusks ripped into the would-be hero's midsection and then the other. His intestines and manhood spilled to the ground. Theseus, not far behind, pitched a perfect shot at the boar's neck with his bronze spear, but the shaft was deflected by a branch; Jason's spear, not so well aimed, caught a dog that leaped up at the wrong time.

Meleagros, however, fared much better. His javelin penetrated the great wounded animal's back, causing it to thrash about in circles in its attempt to shake the weapon loose. The gallant son of Oineus closed in with his spear. Blood suddenly gushed from around the javelin, sending a soft crimson rain out over bushes and hunter alike. When the boar began to tire, Meleagros leaped high and plunged his spear between its shoulder blades into its savage heart.

After Meleagros had skinned the beast and severed its monstrous head, he presented the head and hide as trophies to Atalanta. "First were you to spill the great boar's blood," he said. "I but dealt the death blow. Yours was the fatal wound."

At this the two sons of Thestios, Meleagros's uncles, his mother's brothers, rushed to the fore, flailing the air with their arms. "The trophies belong to the house of him who slew the boar, none other," they shouted irately. "If he will not take them to his palace, then we, his kinsmen, shall."

"Take them," said Meleagros to the Arcadian princess.

"Unhand them!" ordered Plexippos, one of the brothers, "We see his intent. Let him win you to his bed some other way. These trophies are family property, and we will stand against the one who says they are not."

The rage of Ares seethed in Meleagros's heart. "Stand then, you thieves, and fall!" he shot back at them. Then, sword unsheated, he lunged at Plexippos. By the time he put the weapon back into its scabbard, it was stained with both his uncles' blood.

Calydon at once rejoiced and grieved. The boar had been slain, and for that there was dancing in the streets; and at every god's and goddess's altar, including Artemis's, prayers and sweet-smelling sacrifices were raised. And Althaia, the queen, went also into the temple to offer thanks for her son's success, but when she came out again she saw her brothers' corpses on their biers, and her gratitude gave way to anguish. Casting aside her gold-trimmed mantle, she put on the funereal black and beat her breasts and wept prodigiously.

Returning to the palace, the sister was at war with the mother. Four times she went to the chest in which she kept the charred log, and four times she retreated to the room which had been Meleagros's as a boy. Family honor and the duties of blood-kin drew her one way, the irrational

134

impulses of motherhood the other. In the fireplace hot embers glowed and crackled. Slowly, painfully Althaia went a last time to the chest and removed the half-burnt log. "Into ashes now fall flesh of my flesh and bones of my bones," she said and placed the piece of wood on the fire carefully as a mother might lay her baby in a cradle.

Beyond the city walls Meleagros suddenly felt a sharp burning in his side and, doubling over, fell to the ground. It was as though his whole body had been plunged into a furnace or liquid lime. Writhing and screaming, he called out the names of his aged father and his brothers and sisters and wife. Breath came in short spurts; his pain was beyond endurance. The last name he called was "Mother," and after that he died.

For Atalanta the fame acquired from the great Calydonian boar hunt, at least for the time being, brought better things. Iasos, her father, heard of her feat and recalled her to his court. "The greatest of daughters have you turned out to be," he said to her. "Yet of you one more thing I ask."

"Say, father," she replied. "If it is in my power to give, it shall be yours."

"Marry yourself a husband and get me an heir," said the king.

Atalanta remembered then an oracle that had warned her against marriage and wished she had not been so free with her promises. "Only a man worthy of your house will I wed, dear father," she said. "Let a race be run between me and any who comes to court. Losers shall forfeit their lives. The one who beats me shall be my husband."

"So let it be," Iasos agreed. "Magnificent will be a son born to a match like that."

Because of Atalanta's great beauty suitors came from throughout Greece. Each in turn ran against her and each lost. Young Hippomenes came also to Arcadia and looked upon the lovely princess and was smitten with love for her. Before he saw her, he thought men were stupid to run in races they could not possibly win and then to die for the sake of a woman.

"Oh, how wrong I was," he said, when at last he chanced to set eyes upon her. "The gods look kindly on those in love. Perhaps I too should run for such a prize."

Summoning up his deepest reserves of courage, the young man approached the Arcadian beauty. "Leave off your races with heavy-footed fellows," he said. "Try your luck against me. The great grandson of Poseidon I am. Should you win from me, think how famous you'll become. You will have defeated the unvanquished Hippomenes."

His speech and badly counterfeited swagger delighted the maiden. For the first time in her life she began to experience the tender feelings of love for a man. His face, with the soft down of first beard upon the chin, suddenly seemed to her like the face of a young god. "Go home, sweet youth," she said to him. "It is death you court, not a wife, when you race with me. That you should love me moves me much. Were not Fate opposed to my marriage altogether, you would I surely take to my bed. But you must go, my dearest Hippomenes. For life and love were you born, not an early grave."

Hippomenes was not, however, to be dissuaded. He pressed his suit; and Iasos, now exceedingly impatient and frustrated, appointed a day for the race. At the altar of Aphrodite the reckless young lover raised his prayer: "Oh, great goddess who made light my heart, make also light my feet. Smile upon me now, and cause will I give you to smile hereafter." The prayer was not unheard. Three golden apples were by the laughter-loving goddess given to young Hippomenes and with them careful instructions as to their use.

On the appointed day Hippomenes flew faster down the track than any of the suitors before him, but Atalanta effortlessly kept pace. At the first turn, as she began to move ahead of him, he tossed the first of the golden apples to the edge of the track. Atalanta spied the glittering treasure and, all woman, slowed to pick it up. When on the straightaway Hippomenes sensed her once more at his heels, he threw the second apple into the grass beside the track. Again the fleet-footed daughter of Iasos swung wide to retrieve it.

Now into the second turn, the youth could see the finish line and, with speed he never dreamed possible, drove toward it. The girl, seeing it too, began to sprint in earnest, holding nothing back; faster than the great Achilleus she ran, faster than Poseidon's swiftest steed. Into the tall grass beyond the track young Hippomenes then hurled the last apple. Without breaking stride, Atalanta followed it and then circled quickly back. When the victor crossed the finish line, she was less than a step behind.

Thus it was that, despite the oracle's admonition, Atalanta became Hippomenes' bride. In her he inspired a passion the equal of his own, thereby rendering to the laughter-loving goddess in apt coin a handsome return for the loan of her apples. So torrid indeed was the love between the newlyweds that one afternoon when hunting near a grove sacred to Zeus, both were so overcome by desire they went into the god's little temple there and on the floor of its most holy chamber took their pleasure. For their sacrilege the Father of Gods and Men turned them into a pair of lions.

# Theseus

The reign of Aigeus, king of Athens, was a most tenuous one indeed. Crowned amidst civil strife, when all the men of Attica seemed at swords' points, kinsman against kinsman, brother against brother, he found himself threatened at every turn by his own brother, the ever ambitious Pallas. As the years passed, Aigeus's strength seemed to ebb while his brother's increased. Pallas sired fifty sons, each one said to be a giant of a man; despite taking to himself a second wife, Aigeus had so far produced none.

And so it was that, fearing both for himself and his city, King Aigeus took himself to Delphi to inquire of Apollo's oracle as to what he must do to have a son. Said the oracle,

> Ope not the wineskin's swollen mouth until
> Again you've come to Athen's marbled hill.

Unable to discern the meaning of this cryptic charge, Aigeus left the temple no wiser than when he had arrived. On the chance, however, that his old friend Pittheus might be able to decipher it, he decided to return home by way of Troizen. His evening with the Troizenian king was one of reminiscence and camaraderie Pittheus pondered the words of the oracle and, though he did discern their meaning, for reasons of his own was careful not to tell Aigeus.

After they had gorged themselves at the table with different meats, Pittheus ordered wine brought in. Several times were their goblets filled and drained, and then they opened a skin of strong wine and drank until their senses seemed to float away into the night air. The host took care, however, not to drink as much as his guest.

Pittheus, it seems, also had problems with respect to an heir. His sole child was a girl, Aithra, who at one time had been betrothed to Bellerophon. When Bellerophon was exiled to Lycia, Aithra's heart had been crushed and for some time she had little enthusiasm for being courted by any other man. Now she was rapidly approaching those years beyond which girls seldom marry; and, with no one in sight, Pittheus was beginning to lose hope that he would ever have a grandson to be his successor.

Thus, when Aigeus mentioned "the swollen mouth of the wineskin," an idea took shape in Pittheus's mind. More often than not the Pythian oracles were double-edged. Not only was this a caution against strong wine, he surmised, but "swollen mouth" referred also to the nether mouth of a woman. What the oracle was predicting, therefore, was that if Aigeus lay with any woman before he got back to Athens she would conceive and bear him a child.

It was with this in mind, then, that Pittheus encouraged his old friend, whose house and bloodline were without peer, to drink heartily from the wineskin. He could ask for no better lineage to be joined to his own. After Aigeus was sufficiently addled, he ordered him to be taken to Aithra, his daughter's, bedchamber.

Aithra quickly perceived her father's intent; and, though her assignment was completely new to her, she rose to the occasion nicely. The goddess Aphrodite for all her skill could not have managed the situation an iota better. When at last Aigeus, drained and drunk, fell into a deep slumber at her side, she felt strangely exhilarated. She was wide awake; bizarre sensations coursed through her body. Rising gingerly from the bed, though there was no danger of rousing the now snoring Aigeus, she slipped from the room and ran down to the sandy beach. A voice from within (or perhaps from without) bade her swim to the nearby island of Sphairia. This she did, and it was there the god Poseidon also made love to her.

When Dawn's first light streamed through the window of Aithra's bedchamber that next morning, Aigeus gazed in horror at the figure of his host's daughter in the bed next to him. Soon, however, she stirred and opened her eyes and smiled at him. Only slightly more at ease, he fumblingly asked her, more by gesture than word, if anything had passed between them.

"Yes, some seed I believe," she said coyly. "That was the idea."

"What of your father?" said Aigeus next.

"It was his idea," she told him.

When he heard that, the Athenian king was much relieved and began his preparations to return to his city. Before he took his leave, however, he led Aithra to a spot outside the palace and there dislodged a great boulder from its place. Into the hole he placed his sandals and sword and then rolled the huge rock back on top of them. "If by me you have conceived a son," he instructed her, "when he comes of age he will be able to move this boulder. Send him then with the sandals and sword to Athens. By them I will know he is my issue and will bestow on him the legacy due him."

After nine times the moon had swollen to full circle, Aithra was delivered of her baby, a son, and called him Theseus. The boy grew up in his grandfather's house and early proved himself a youth of singular resourcefulness and character.

One day, we are told, the great Heracles chanced to visit Troizen, and, as he went in to dine with Pittheus, he cast his huge lion-skin cloak onto the floor of an outer room. It landed in such a way that it seemed like a real lion lying there within the palace. At least so it seemed to Theseus, then seven years old, and his playmates as they burst into the room. The other boys scurried for safety, but Theseus, without any trepidation whatsoever, grabbed a nearby ax and attacked the "lion."

When he was fifteen, his mother told him he was the son of Poseidon but that Aigeus, king of Athens, also had reason to claim him as son. She then took him to the boulder where Aigeus had placed his sandals and sword. "Soon will come the day," she told him, "when you will be able to roll this rock from its place and take what it now guards to Athens to gain your appointed lot."

"Soon?" said the youth. "Why not now?" And with strength to spare he moved the boulder.

Both Pittheus and Aithra begged Theseus to take the direct, easy route to Athens across the Saronic Gulf. The longer route, the land route, was infected with villains and cutthroats who made safe passage all but impossible. So wily and devious were their macabre ways that Heracles himself would not have had an easy time getting past them all.

In dramatic, horrifying detail Pittheus described each rogue to the boy and how each in turn went about savagely murdering luckless wayfarers. His blood-curdling descriptions had, however, quite the opposite effect from what he had intended. In the end young Theseus, zealous to emulate Heracles, was more determined than ever to take the path of danger. Shod in Aigeus's sandals, his sword strapped to his side, the boy set out on foot to Athens.

First he came to Epidaurus, where Periphetes blocked his path. Periphetes was known in the region as the Clubber, for he carried a huge bronze club with which he dispatched any and all who passed his way. Theseus, forewarned by Pittheus, was ready for the sweep of Periphetes' club. Nimbly sidestepping the blow, he closed in quickly and wrenched the club from his assailant's grasp. Then he brought down the weapon across the Clubber's skull, meting out to him the same fate he had served up to so many others.

Next he came upon Sinis, called the Pinebender. This gigantic brute flaunted his strength by bending tall pine trees until their tips touched the ground. He would force passers-by to straddle the tops and then would release the trees so as to catapult them high in the air and out into the bay. Sometimes he would bend two trees together and tie his victim securely to each, then guffaw sadistically when the trees, springing upright, rent the poor man in two. Theseus, playing the innocent, cooperated with the ogre in bending two trees to the earth; but, when Sinis moved to bind him to the trees with a rope, he quickly turned tables and lashed Sinis to them instead and sent him divided toward the heavens.

Now Sinis had a daughter who was every bit as lovely and virtuous as her father was brutish and wicked. When Theseus and Sinis began to struggle with each other, the girl, Perigune by name, ran to a nearby thicket to hide. After he prevailed against Sinis, Theseus found her trembling in among the brush and asparagus-thorn and gently called for her to come out.

"I mean you no harm, beautiful maiden," he said. "Love, not violence, draws me to you."

Perigune, who had been treated more as a slave than a daughter by her father, cautiously withdrew from the thicket into the honey-voiced youth's arms. Theseus marveled at the transformation the girl's body brought to his own. He did not force her, for she gave of herself freely.

Along the approach to Megara, where Theseus soon came, a rogue named Sciron lived among the precipitous crags. In a place where the pathway narrowed by a ledge he sat and compelled strangers who passed by to kneel and wash his feet. When they finished their service to him, he would suddenly drive his foot into them, sending them flying over the ledge to become food for a giant sea turtle below.

And so when Theseus ventured by, he commanded him likewise to wash his feet. The youth knelt and began to comply. When he felt Sciron's sinews tighten, however, he grasped his ankles firmly and used the brute's own movement to spin him off balance and over the precipice. On so huge a carcass the great sea turtle was able to gorge itself for days.

Drawing close now to Athens, young Theseus next encountered Cercyon, in terms of size and strength his most formidable antagonist so far. No stranger ever passed that way but that Cercyon forced him into the wrestling ring and then by sheer brawn crushed the life out of the man as thoroughly as would one of the great snakes where the Nile begins its course. Were the contest between Cercyon and Theseus merely one of physical might, the more massive man would surely have prevailed. Theseus, however, was greatly skilled in the art of wrestling and thus gained the edge. As Cercyon slew other men, even so did Theseus slay him.

Then a little further up the road Theseus could see at last the Acropolis of Athens. As he stood gazing at it, he heard a voice near him say, "Come into my house, good stranger, and rest, for weary you must be from traveling." The man who spoke was Procrustes, whose house was close by. "Two beds I have that fit all," he continued, advancing hospitably toward the youth, "as if by magic. Come, let me show you."

The two beds, one large and one small, did indeed fit all, for it was Procrustes' practice to lash his shorter guests to the larger bed and then pummel them mercilessly with a heavy mallet. As a housewife might pound a stubborn piece of meat to flatten it and make it more tender, thus did Procrustes hammer his guests until they fit the bed exactly. His taller guests he lashed to the smaller bed and trimmed off any parts of their bodies that extended beyond its edges.

Theseus went with him into the house but came out of it alone. He looked again at the Acropolis still a ways up the road ahead of him and then, with quicker gait, went on his way. Back in the house the corpse of Procrustes was so perfectly stretched out across the larger of the two beds that no part of the mattress was showing.

Meanwhile in Athens, both because of what Aigeus had told her and because of her own powers of sorcery, Medea, who had not only found refuge in the city but indeed in the royal palace itself, had long anticipated Theseus's arrival. Thus it was that when the youth came into the city, though he disclosed his identity to no one, she knew in a moment who he was and why he had come. Recently, it seems, she herself had borne the king a son and was not about to let him be supplanted by anyone.

"The man's an assassin," she told the ever fearful, now aged Aigeus, "a rogue in Pallas's hire. He means to take you unaware."

"What would you have me do?" asked the king.

"Invite him to a feast, and there strike him down as he would you," she said. Then handing him a vial, "Put but a few drops of this in his wine cup, and you will never have cause to fear him again. It is from the spittle of the hell-hound Cerberos."

King Aigeus did as Medea told him. He invited the young stranger to a banquet that very day and by his own hand put the poison into his wine cup. A huge roast was prepared and brought into the banquet hall just as Aigeus and his guests were about to drink a toast. As a gallant gesture Theseus handed his host his sword to carve the meat. By the emblem on the hilt the aged king recognized his own sword. Quickly he knocked the poisoned cup from the young man's hand and embraced him and repeated many times, "My son, my son!"

While Athens rejoiced, Medea made her exit and, we are told, was thereafter never seen in Greece again. The jubilant, festive mood of the city was, however, short-lived, for in the midst of the celebration envoys arrived from King Minos of Crete to remind the Athenians that their reparation tribute for the murder of Androgeus was again due.

"For what reason do Athenians pay tribute to Minos?" Theseus wanted to know.

"Many years ago Androgeus, Minos's son, came here," his father explained. "My men, thinking he was in league with Pallas, killed him. In reparation Minos demanded that seven youths and seven maidens be sent to Crete every nine years to be served up to the Minotaur monster."

"And you did this?"

"Twice already," said Aigeus. "This will be the third time. It is better to mourn the few than have the whole city destroyed."

"Let the king's son then be among the seven youths," said Theseus. "On the road to Athens many a rogue and monster did I battle. Why not this Minotaur? Perhaps the gods will show me a way."

Now the Minotaur monster came about on this wise. In the early days, when his kingship of Crete was in question, Minos went before the altar of Poseidon and prayed that a bull be given him as a sign that he as Zeus's son was held in special favor by the gods. "What you give will be returned again to you," he vowed.

Then, as much to his astonishment as anyone else's, a magnificent white bull suddenly came charging out of the surf. Never had Minos seen such a grand, sleek animal. In the end he could not bring himself to sacrifice it and, in its stead, offered up to Poseidon another bull. The white bull was turned loose among his breeding stock.

The unruly God of the Sea was not so easily satisfied, however, and designed a devious recompense against Minos. He inspired in Pasiphae, Minos's wife, an ardent and unnatural lust for the beautiful white bull. She went to the pastures each morning to gaze upon the splendid animal as he moved among the king's cattle. Her heart beat fiercely, and at moments, especially when the heifers proved agreeable to the bull's advances, her skin seemed aflame as if she were seized by a sudden and violent fever.

Each day she left the scene weak and panting, drained of every vestige of vitality. Though herself appalled by her strange obsession and not a little ashamed, Pasiphae lost all interest in everything else and let her mind dwell singularly upon the bull. She thought she would go mad if her passion were not sated.

Dwelling in the sprawling palace of King Minos at that time, it so happened, was the master artisan Daidalos. No man was more skilled in making things than Daidalos nor wiser in discerning by what means the impossible could be achieved. To the amusement of the king and his court he made toy animals that appeared in every respect to be real. It was to him that Pasiphae now turned in her desperation. Sympathetically he listened to all she said. At the end, unable to control herself, she clutched his knees and sobbed, "Oh, help me or I die!"

"At your service, dear lady," he replied.

What Daidalos did was to fashion a large, life-sized wooden cow. Over it he stretched a real cow hide; and in every detail, even to the appropriate odors, he made the replica look more real than the cows that grazed in Minos's pastures. At the rear of the artificial creature he devised a trap door that could be manipulated from within. He helped Pasiphae position herself inside the huge, hollow counterfeit animal and showed her how to operate the trap door. Then he wheeled the great toy with Pasiphae inside down to the pasture where the noble white bull watched over his bovine harem.

The bull, as unperceptive as he was handsome, never suspected that the newcomer was anything other than what she appeared to be. He pushed his face up beside hers; and when she did not run away, he assumed, as was his wont, that his courtship was successful and proceeded accordingly. Suffice it to say that by nightfall, when Daidalos came to wheel the replica cow back to the palace, Pasiphae had been both filled and fulfilled beyond her wildest fantasies.

Never able thereafter to find another cow that would return his passion so appreciatively, the bull soon went wild from his frustration and ravaged the countryside of Crete, treading down crops and goring men and animals not a few. This was the bull that Heracles eventually captured and took back to Argos as one of his labors.

Within the year Pasiphae was delivered of her next child. From the shoulders down the baby was like any other baby, except perhaps a little larger, but its head and face were those of a calf. When Minos saw the monstrosity, he quickly fathomed what had happened and knew it to be the vengeance of Poseidon because he did not sacrifice the bull as he had vowed. Nor did he now dare destroy this symbol of his own and his wife's deep guilt for fear of further enraging the god.

And so it was that he sent for Daidalos and commanded that he should make a place for the bull-man, which was called the Minotaur, so that neither could the creature itself nor any person entering to see it find his way out again. Daidalos built then the labyrinth, a maze so intricate and with so many false turns that escape from it was impossible, and the Minotaur was placed in it. It was into this labyrinth that every nine years the seven Athenian virgins and seven youths were forced for the monster's pleasure and were thereafter never seen again.

All this King Aigeus told young Theseus so that he might dissuade him from joining the youths and maidens chosen by lot to go to Crete. "Should ill befall you, my son, now that you have come here to be a joy to me in my last years," he said, "my life too would be over." In the end, however, knowing his arguments to be useless, the old king gave consent.

Because the ship that the victims sailed was a death ship, it was outfitted with a black sail. Aigeus gave them also a white sail. "If you slay the monster and survive, change then the black for the white that I might know from afar off that you live," he made Theseus promise. "If the ship returns under the black sail, I will know you are dead."

Not all seven of the maidens who sailed with Theseus were in fact maidens at all. Two were comely young men who had yet to sport their first beards, though in strength and daring few were their equals. Theseus had recruited these two and, to pass them off as maidens, had told them to bathe much, avoid the sun, rub their bodies with scented ointments, and practice continually girlish gaits and voices. Both were quick to learn, and by the time they arrived at Crete they were, in appearance and affectation, indistinguishable from the actual virgins.

When the ship docked at Crete, Minos himself was on hand to inspect its human cargo. He did not see through the disguises of the counterfeit maidens—in part because one of the real girls, Periboia by name, so caught his eye that he was unable to concentrate on anyone other than her. In fact, he would have taken Periboia to his quarters had not Theseus stepped forward and said, "By my father Poseidon, it is my duty to protect virgins from tyrants."

"Why invoke Poseidon?" sneered Minos. "Little enough respect he had for virgins."

"Desist I say, or answer to me and him."

"If you are the son of Poseidon, prove it," said Minos next.

"First prove that you are the son of Zeus."

King Minos lifted his arms to the heavens, and immediately lightning shot from the clouds and ear-piercing thunder boomed overhead. "And now it's your turn," he said, taking a signet ring from his finger and casting it out into the wine-dark sea. "If you be son to Poseidon, recovery of that ring should be no object."

Theseus dove into the dark, turbulent waters. With the cheerful assistance of Amphitrate and her nymphs, he surfaced moments later not only with Minos's ring but with a glittering golden diadem as well. The ring he returned to the king but kept the crown for himself. After that, Minos abandoned his designs on Periboia.

When Ariadne, one of Minos's daughters, looked upon Theseus, she thought she had never seen so dashingly handsome a young man, and from that first instant she loved him with an irrepressible love. In secret she came to him and said, "Take me with you back to Athens as your wife, and I will give you the help you need."

"By the lord of the seas Poseidon, my father, and by the other gods of Olympos who never die," vowed Theseus, "I shall not leave Crete without you."

Thereupon Ariadne went to Daidalos and plied him until he told her how one could, having once entered the labyrinth, escape it. Returning again to Theseus, she gave him a ball of thread and told him, as Daidalos had instructed her, "Secure the loose end to the lintel. Then, as you penetrate the maze, unwind the ball. When you have killed the Minotaur, you will need but to follow the thread to find the door again."

Theseus followed Ariadne's instructions and came upon the monster in the innermost parts of the labyrinth. With neither club nor sword but with only his bare fists, he battled the huge, vicious freak until at last he killed it. Winding up the thread, he quickly retraced his steps and was soon outside again, joined there by Ariadne.

While his two men disguised as maidens were freeing the Athenian virgins, Theseus went to where the young men were being held and overpowered their guards and released them. With Ariadne showing them the way, the Athenians under cover of night now hastened to the harbor and boarded their ship. To prevent the Cretans from pursuing them, we are told, Theseus gouged holes in the hulls of all their ships so that they sunk in the harbor.

Throughout the rest of the night they sailed and in the morning found a goodly haven at Naxos. Whatever moved Theseus that following morning to rise up early and order his fellow Athenians noiselessly to board the ship while Ariadne still slept no one knows. Some say he was commanded to do so in a dream, others that he feared to take a foreign wife home to Athens, and still others that he meant to come back for her after he had prepared the way. Whatever the reason, when Ariadne awoke, the ship and all of the Athenians were gone. She wept without ceasing through the day, calling upon the deathless gods to witness her betrayal.

It is quite possible that the gods did, in fact, have a hand in what happened, for shortly before the sun finished its course that day and slid beneath the waters to the west, a ship came to the island and in it was the young god Dionysos, more radiant and beautiful than anyone Ariadne had ever seen. And from the moment their eyes fell upon each other, they were in love, the girl and the twice-born god with vine leaves in his hair. When Dionysos left the island, Ariadne was at his side, and there she remained ever after.

Heavy of heart on Ariadne's account, Theseus forgot to replace the black sail with the white one. Each day since the death ship had sailed, King Aigeus had stood upon the cliffs of Sunion and scanned the horizon southward for first sight of the ship's return. And so, when the ship finally approached the mainland, the old king spied it in the distance and, seeing the black sail, concluded that his son was dead. In his despair he hurled himself off the precipice into the sea which was thereafter to bear his name. Thus, exultation gave way to mourning, and under a cloud of guilt and grief Theseus was installed as the next king of Athens.

Meanwhile, when Minos learned of the escape of Theseus and the death of the Minotaur, he was greatly angered and blamed Daidalos for all that happened because he alone understood the secrets of the labyrinth. He ordered, therefore, that Daidalus and Icaros, his son, be imprisoned in the labyrinth until such time as he could decide their fate. With the help of Pasiphae the two temporarily eluded the king's guards and then set about to find some way to flee Crete and Minos altogether.

"How can we escape," said Icaros, "when the tyrant we flee owns the land and commands the waves?"

146

"But the skies are free," Daidalos replied. "His tyrrany does not extend into the heavens."

And so Daidalos turned his mind to an art which seemed in defiance of nature, never before attempted by man. With the boy Icaros he gathered together a store of feathers and arranged them in rows, like Pan's pipes, with first the shorter and then the longer so that they formed triangular designs. Then with wax and cord he fastened the quilled ends in place.

Icaros marveled at his father's skill and ventured often to help him but proved a hindrance instead. Feathered triangles were next joined to other feathered triangles and tightly bound; and then Daidalos, adroitly drawing the cord just so and no more, arched them one way and then another so that in the end they looked like the wings of gigantic eagles. Four wings he thus fashioned, a pair for himself and a slightly smaller pair for his son.

Carefully he drew the large pair of wings over his shoulders and slipped his arms through the corded straps. Then, flapping the wings slowly at first, cautiously, evenly so as to maintain his balance, and then with increased vigor, Daidalos became airborne. In no time at all he was able, after the manner of birds, to climb at will, drift with the currents of the winds, glide, swoop, and suspend himself momentarily in mid-air. Icaros looked up in amazement, wishing his father would come down so he could do the same.

Daidalos then taught the boy the art of flying. "Set your flight neither too high nor too low," he cautioned him. "If you ascend too close to the eye of heaven, it will burn your feathers and melt the wax that holds them. But should you drop too low, the spray of the sea will soak your wings and weigh you down."

Having spoken thus, he helped Icaros on with his wings, continuing to instruct him all the while. Ominous feelings came over Daidalos, like those of doting parents preparing their child for a long and uncertain journey. Then, with both their wings in place, he leaned close and kissed his son and stepped back quickly and turned his head so that Icaros would not see the tears that suddenly flooded his cheeks. After that they took off.

As the eagle glides down from its heights to teach her young, fresh from the nest, how to fly, even so did the father Daidalos work his wings in simple maneuvers to show the boy what to do. Far off on a shore a fisherman looked up from his nets in bewilderment. In another place a farmer followed his plow dumbstruck as he fixed his gaze on what seemed to be two giant birds high overhead, though they looked like men. And

147

from elsewhere Minos's guards, who had drawn close to where the two had been hiding, saw the fugitives out of bowshot above them and, trembling, put down their weapons, thinking the twain might be gods. By now Icaros, quick to learn, was soaring like a falcon.

Over Samos they flew, Daidalos in the lead, and then Delos and Paros. The boy Icaros, finding what runners call second wind, beat the air vigorously. He became, as it were, intoxicated by the freedom birds must have always known instinctively and men could only imagine; he felt unbounded, wild, loose, self-contained. Without intending to do so, he swept beyond his father and found naught but wide, open skies ahead of him.

The impulse to surge ever upward proved irresistible. Higher and higher he climbed, his spirits also mounting, till gradually he felt the sun's heat through the wings on his shoulders. First he smelled, then felt the fragrant molten wax as it ran down his arms and back. Too late he tried to swoop to lower altitudes, for the feathers of his wings were already drifting freely earthward. He soon was thrashing the air with naked arms, calling out desperately for his father. Moments later, still crying out his father's name, he slipped beneath the surface of the wine-dark sea.

Daidalos came swiftly upon the scene, shouting, "Icaros, my son Icaros, where can you be? If somewhere you hide, once more speak my name and spare me my worst of fears, oh Icaros, my son."

Soon, though, he spied the feathers and what was left of the wings being tossed about by the waves and knew their meaning. He stayed in the area until he could recover his son's body and bury it. Then, grieving, he went on to Sicily and there, because of all his wondrous skills, found favor and sanctuary in the court of Cocalos, king of Camicos.

In every country along the Great Sea Minos searched for Daidalos. With him he took a large spiral shell, into the solid end of which he had bored a small hole. "Great treasures await anyone who can run a thread through this shell," he told people wherever he went. (Only Daidalos, he knew, could do it. And thus it was by the shell he purposed to find where his nemesis was in hiding, for he knew no one would tell him freely.)

And so at the court of Cocalos also, when he was come to that place, Minos held up the shell and the thread and described the treasure that awaited whoever could guide the thread through the shell and out the small hole at the end. "Leave them with me," said the king, "and consider the task done. The threaded shell will be served you with breakfast."

When Minos and his entourage had been taken to their quarters, King Cocalos took the shell to Daidalos and told him what the Cretan king had said. Daidalos guessed immediately Minos's purpose but could not resist the challenge. He found an ant and to it tied a fine filament of gossamer and put it into the shell. All around the hole at the end he smeared honey. The ant, drawn to the honey, soon emerged from the hole. It was then but a simple matter to tie the thread to the gossamer and work it through the shell.

As promised, King Cocalos presented the threaded shell to Minos the next morning with his breakfast. The Cretan knew then immediately that Daidalos was in the city, probably in the palace itself, and demanded that he be handed over to him. "As you wish," said Cocalos. "In the meantime enjoy my hospitality." Almost as though on cue, the Camician king's own daughters, both exceedingly fair to look upon, then came bursting into the room, saying they had come to take their father's guest to his bath. One playfully took one of Minos's arms and the other took the other. Nor did the lusty Cretan resist such lovely escorts. He did not know that by the wondrous things he made them Daidalos had already won the hearts of the two maidens. Once they got Minos into the bath, they unloosed great torrents of boiling water on him from a trough designed by Daidalos and thus scalded him to death. When Cocalos sent the king's body back to Crete, he sent also his regrets, saying that Minos had tripped and fallen by accident into the water.

As the reign of Minos, Crete's greatest king, came to a close, that of Theseus, Athens' greatest king, was just beginning. From the first he ruled with an iron hand, meting out quick and stern justice to all the city's enemies. His father's adversaries, save for Pallas and his fifty sons, he either banished or killed.

Up until this time Attica had not been one state but several, each with its own ruler and own government, each at odds and often at war with the next. Theseus went, therefore, to each chieftain in turn and by strength and persuasion won the assent of them all to unite under one government and one king, himself, and to call the name of the whole state Athens. Before long the Athenian state extended all the way to the Isthmos, where Theseus had a pillar erected which said on one side ATHENS and on the other side THE PELOPONNESE.

Into the city strangers were welcomed and took their places in the prosperity alongside the native-born. Theseus then divided the people into three ranks. To the nobility he entrusted all sacred matters and the fair and equitable administration of justice, but the city's wealth rested upon the shoulders of the husbandmen and its industry with those who worked with their hands. Thus Athens became the envy of all other cities, and the fame of Theseus spread to every part of Greece.

In Thessaly Peirithoos, king of the Lapiths, heard also of the deeds and reputation of Theseus and desired to test the Athenian king's mettle. He went, therefore, to Marathon and there seized a herd of cattle belonging to Theseus. When word of the raid came to Theseus, he armed himself and took out after the rustlers in hot pursuit, but Peirithoos ceased to flee when he learned that the king himself was on his heels. Rather he turned and went back to meet him.

As the two regal figures came into view of each other, each was struck by the carriage and stateliness of the other. They advanced, but neither reached for his weapon. When they were close, Peirithoos stretched out his hand to Theseus. "To your judgment, my lord, I yield most willingly," he said.

"A man such as you I would have for friend, not enemy," said the king of Athens. "There is no transgression between us." And that day the two took oaths and pledged one to the other undying and steadfast friendship.

The two joined in the great Calydonian boar hunt together shortly thereafter, though neither distinguished himself. After that they sailed across the sea and for a ways followed the course of the Argonauts into the Propontis and then the Euxine and so came to the land of the Amazons. Contrary to their expectations, the notorious women warriors were naught but the souls of cordiality to them. They brought gifts to them and came aboard their ship. One of the tribal queens was a woman of extraordinary beauty and form. Antiope was her name. She also at Theseus's invitation came aboard and, when the ship set sail to go back to Athens, was still on it.

Antiope was installed in the palace and within the year bore Theseus a son, whom he named Hippolytos. As the boy grew, he showed promise of being every bit as handsome and robust as both his parents. His father taught him the art of wrestling, and his mother the thrill of the hunt. Domestic harmony reigned in the palace, though not for long. Deucalion, Minos's son and successor, desirous of bringing about an alliance between Crete and Athens, offered his sister Phaidra to the Athenian king to take as his wife. For the sake of the city Theseus accepted.

All Athens celebrated the wedding of their king and the Cretan princess. Not since Theseus's advent from Troizen and his reception by old King Aigeus had there been in Athene's city such cause for feasting and merriment. All festivity came to an end, though, when suddenly without warning Antiope and a company of her Amazon sisters, each in full armor and brandishing a spear, appeared on the scene. Vicious combat ensued. At day's end, battle's end, all the Amazons, including Antiope, and not a few of the Greeks lay lifeless upon the blood-slippery floor, their spirits departed.

So that he might not later on be rival to sons Phaidra would bear, Theseus sent Hippolytos to Troizen to grow up in the care of Pittheus, his great grandfather. It was Theseus's intention, since the throne of Troizen would eventually fall to him as Pittheus's only heir, to make Hippolytos the king there and to bequeath the throne of Athens to one of his legitimate sons. In that way he thought to avoid the ugly antagonisms that sometimes occur when a king has two families.

Both Theseus and Phaidra were pleased that when Hippolytos came to Athens, which he often did, he showed no trace of resentment that his someday would be the rule of Troizen and a younger half-brother would succeed to the throne of Athens. His only interests in Athens were the game in the mountains thereabouts and the exercising yard of the gymnasium. As he grew older, he developed impressively in his physique and in the comeliness of his features. Nor was it easy for Phaidra not to take notice.

Too preoccupied was Theseus with the affairs of state and his friendship with Peirithoos to interpret his wife's hospitality toward young Hippolytos in any way as to do her discredit. It was, in fact, a source of no small comfort to him that she should love the youth as if he were her own son. When, therefore, the time came for him to go up into Thessaly to attend the wedding of Peirithoos, he thought little of taking his leave during his son's visit, for he trusted Phaidra to look after the boy's needs.

Peirithoos's wedding, we are told, turned out to be as fully disastrous as Theseus's. Neighbors to the Lapiths, of whom Peirithoos was king, were the Centaurs. With the bodies of horses and the upper torsos and heads of men, the Centaurs were normally a peaceful race; but whenever strong wine entered their bodies, all judgment and self-control vanished. The animal in them then took charge. They became as long-penned bulls or he-goats suddenly let loose upon the herds. Because they were neighbors, however, Peirithoos invited them to his wedding.

Although the wedding wine was withheld from the Centaurs, its fragrance nonetheless permeated the air about them and teased their nostrils and palates. When they could stand it no longer, they descended upon the wine-skins to help themselves. Emboldened by their first cups, they refilled them again and again until they had drained a whole skin. They then went on to the next.

When Peirithoos came to them, as he did all of his guests, to present his bride, one of them, Eurytos by name, jumped up from his bench to kiss her. Nor was a kiss, once grossly bestowed, the end of his inspiration, for suddenly he commenced to tear the gown from the girl's body in order to indulge himself in grander intimacies. His brother Centaurs seized the attending maidens in like manner and, it seems, some of the serving boys also.

"Stop this madness!" shouted Theseus, rushing to the scene. "You make me your enemy, Eurytos, when you offend Peirithoos. Let go that maiden, half-man." He thereupon caught the girl around the waist with one arm and shoved the Centaur loose from her with the other. Eurytos responded with violent blows to the Athenian king's chest and jaw. Theseus then seized a large, partly filled wine urn and brought it down with all his might across the Centaur's face and forehead, shattering Eurytos's skull so that bits of brain spilled out of it.

General pandemonium then broke loose. Centaurs, Lapiths, and Athenians grabbed what was handy, makeshift weapons, both to defend and attack. One Centaur used a lamp stand to smash in the face of a defenseless bystander, but in turn a Lapith drove his spirit from his body with an oaken table leg. Two other Lapiths were trapped when a Centaur turned an altar onto them and would surely have been finished off had not a quick-thinking companion gouged the Centaur to death with some decorative stag antlers. Torches then became deadly weapons on both sides; staves from the fireplaces were used as spears.

As the battle took to the out-of-doors, the Centaurs picked up boulders, and the Lapiths and Athenians countered with heavy branches of oak and pine. Theseus at one point leaped upon the back of a Centaur and straddled him like a horse, while grabbing his shaggy hair with one hand and driving an oak club against his temple with the other.

In the end the Lapiths, who soon got to their spears and javelins, proved the victors. The matter was not over though, for fierce war raged between the Lapiths and their neighbors, the Centaurs, until at last Peirithoos and his allies were able to force the horse-men from the region for good. Through it all Theseus stood by his friend and distinguished himself in battle as though the cause were his own; nor did he nor those who came with him return to Athens until the last Centaur was driven from the country.

All this time, back in Athens, the embers of passion, which had but smoldered before in the heart of Phaidra for the youth Hippolytos, had gradually taken flame. She told herself that hers was only a stepmother's affection, but she knew better. When he was off hunting or at the gymnasium, her heart yearned after him. In the palace she found excuses to touch him and fought continually against her impulses to do more. The boy seemed not to notice the struggle that warred within her.

Sometimes in the morning when Hippolytos was gone to the gymnasium, she would slip out and visit the temple of Aphrodite, which overlooked the yards where the young athletes, stripped of all clothes, did their exercises. From there she would gaze upon the object of her affections until she thought her own sighs would betray her and then would leave, trembling and perspiring, her heart beating violently.

After Theseus came back and Hippolytos soon thereafter returned to Troizen, the fires in Phaidra's heart still burned as hot as ever. She lost all other appetites, though did her best for appearance's sake, lest her secret be guessed, to feign interest when she had none and passion when no feelings existed toward the man with whom she shared her bed. When alone, she wept much and harbored thoughts of death.

Problems of a different nature, however, soon commanded the attention of Theseus. Pallas and his fifty sons had taken advantage of the king's absence to stir up fresh rebellion in the land. When proof of this was given to Theseus, he gave orders that the insurgents should all be killed. The Athenian court, however, judged his response to be too harsh and therefore ordered that he be banished from the city for one year. And so it was that he and Phaidra left Athens and went to Troizen for the period of his exile.

To be once more in the presence of Hippolytos caused the fire in Phaidra's breast to rage out of control. He seemed to have matured since she had last seen him, though but only a few months had intervened. He was more filled out in the shoulders and chest, she thought, more rugged in the face (if it were possible), more handsome. He was no longer a youth but a man. New scenarios played out in Phaidra's nighttime and waking dreams, both to her delight and torment, causing her to lose some of her customary caution.

There was no temple to Aphrodite overlooking the gymnasium walls in Troizen as there had been at Athens, so Phaidra had a shrine built and called it the Temple of Peeping Aphrodite. She would go there when Hippolytos was at the gymnasium to watch without being seen as he wrestled and ran and practiced with his javelin. After he put on his clothes and left, she would linger in the shrine, sometimes for hours, until she felt some of the flush leave her cheeks and her breathing become more measured and normal.

No food satisfied the daughter of Minos. Naught else engaged her interests except the young man Hippolytos, and when he was off pursuing the pastime of Artemis, his patron deity in every way, she lay upon her bed and pined until he returned. His presence, however, was no less torturous to her than his absence, for then, though closer, he seemed the more beyond her reach. Fever began to wrack her body, and her health soon became the concern of the whole household. She ate less and less and then for three days took no nourishment at all.

Through an intermediary, an aged servant who had come with her from Crete, the desperate, love-crazed queen finally elected to entreat the young man's mercy. The old woman wisely swore Hippolytos to secrecy before she divulged her mission. "Great Zeus!" he cried, when she at last told him all. "Mother Earth and great Helios high above! What is this I hear? You ask me to defile my father's bed?"

"I ask but that you pity someone who suffers greatly on your account," said the old woman.

"Pity? Betrayal is what you ask, no less."

"If you will not restore a sick woman to health, at least spare her name," said the servant in parting. "Remember your oath."

Hippolytos fled from the room as though the walls themselves had become befouled by the conversation that had passed within them. Out into the woodlands he ran as if for cleansing, as if the world of his goddess might somehow counteract the evil to which he had now become exposed, exorcise him, restore the innocence he feared forever lost. Only after a great while did he cease from his running and turn back toward home.

In the meantime, resigned to disgrace and rejected, Phaidra hanged herself. Somehow in her mind the youth had suddenly now become her bitterest enemy, one she loathed and feared with an intensity fully equal to that of her earlier passion. As if by magic, the one emotion had been transformed into its exact opposite. Her madness had become complete. On her bed she left a note accusing Hippolytos of having raped her.

By the time Hippolytos returned to the palace, Theseus had already discovered his wife's corpse and the note. And already also he had gone to the window facing the sea and called out for his father Poseidon to destroy his son. "When Helios shall have driven his chariot beyond the most distant waves this day," he cried, "may then that graceless youth be dead."

Nothing Hippolytos could say, when confronted by his father, no oaths, no denials altered Theseus's judgment that the words of the death note had to be true. He ordered the young man's immediate banishment from the kingdom. "If I am guilty," the youth pled, "may Zeus strike me dead, and may the earth and sea deny my body rest."

"The dead accuses you, the best of witnesses," shot back Theseus. "Go now! Return neither here, you base and damnable villain, nor Athens nor any other place where I am king. For the likes of you there is no pardon, no forgiveness."

In all of his protestations of innocence Hippolytos never once alluded to his conversation with the old servant. His vow of secrecy was sacred. Rather than violate it, he chose to accept his banishment however unjust. He went out from his father's presence with that kind of optimism the pure in heart always seem to have, the sure confidence that their names in time will be vindicated and that the bright light of a new day will dissolve the shadowy horrors of the moment.

"Harness my horses," he commanded his servants. "I must be off. This city is no longer mine."

When his chariot was readied, the young prince gave the goad to the horses and sped off along the coastal road to Epidauros. The breeze caught his hair and cooled his flushed face. And then, as he swept across a sandy stretch close to the water, a loud rumbling like that of Zeus's thunder came out of the sea not far ahead of him. The horses pricked up their ears and whinnied.

Out at sea a wave, much larger than any about it, began to roll rapidly into shore, swelling, churning, pounding, mounting as it came. Then suddenly, just as the wave broke, out of it leaped a monstrous bull. Roaring as loud as a hundred peals of thunder, the great animal charged the chariot of Hippolytos. The horses reared and swerved off the road.

An expert horseman, Hippolytos held a tight grip on the reins but was unable, when the bull charged a second time, to keep the chariot from smashing against a large boulder. Axles, splinters, lynch-pins, pieces of railing shot up into the sky; but, entangled in his own reins, the son of Theseus was dragged past the wreckage and across a rock-strewn course into another boulder before being torn loose. Some young men saw what happened and came to him and bore his battered body back to his father.

Others at Troizen broke the silence that Hippolytos had refused to break and told Theseus of Phaidra's maniacal passion and the young prince's innocence. And the story of how his son would not betray his oath to the old woman also reached the king's ears, and he was doubly grieved. For a long time thereafter, we are told, Theseus tended to the affairs of his kingdom with a sober and gloomy spirit. He did what had to be done, and Athens continued to flourish under his reign, though he himself found little pleasure or cause for rejoicing.

When several years had gone by, his friend Peirithoos also lost his wife, and so the two consoled each other. Gradually then mutual consolation gave way to renewed camaraderie between the pair, and they found delight once more, if not in heroic actions, in reminiscences of past deeds and in fantasies of feats never attempted. Good wine they shared and in generous amounts, but a thirst grew in both which wine could never satisfy, a thirst for fresh adventure.

In Sparta at that time in the palace of King Tyndareus there lived a beautiful girl named Helen, rumored by some to be the daughter of Zeus. The maiden was only twelve but her beauty was already legendary. "Let us go down to Sparta and seize the girl," said Peirithoos. "We can decide by lot who gets her."

"And then," said Theseus, in the spirit of things, "we can find another of Zeus's daughters for the loser."

A pact was sworn between the two, and off to Sparta they went. There they found the young maiden Helen dancing in the temple of Artemis, and they took her and fled with her back to Athens. When they cast lots for her, Theseus won. Because Helen was too young then for him to lie with, he put her in the care of his mother Aithra until she should ripen into full maidenhood.

Then, after an interlude in his own city, Theseus went again to visit Peirithoos in Thessaly. "And which of Zeus's daughters shall we kidnap for you?" he asked his friend.

"Persephone, the bride of Hades," said Peirithoos. "Of all his daughters they say she is most fair."

If Theseus could have taken back his oath, he no doubt would have done so. An oath, however, was an oath, even a foolish one; and so, by the same little-known passage the heartbroken Orpheus had used not many years before to seek his beloved Eurydice, Theseus and Peirithoos journeyed down into Hades' kingdom beneath the earth. Much to their relief and delight, the Lord of the Underworld proved more cordial than his reputation had led them to anticipate. "What brings you here before your time?" he wanted to know.

In unaffected speech as though he had every right to say it, Peirithoos answered thus: "It is your wife, great king, the incomparably beauteous Persephone, we seek and nothing else. Of Zeus's daughters we are told she is fairest."

156

Nor did Peirithoos's words cause their host to be any less gracious. "A rare request from so bold a caller," he said good-naturedly. "Won't you please sit, and we will have some refreshment brought in and discuss the matter. You both must be very hungry after so long a journey."

With that, he beckoned for them to sit down in a wide, ornately crafted, jewel-studded chair near the wall. Any king in the world of light would have been proud to have it as his throne. Neither Theseus nor Peirithoos, so pleased with their reception thus far, noticed the malicious sneer on the great, grim god's lips.

The chair, as it turned out, was Hades' infamous chair of forgetfulness, and as soon as the two mortals sat in it they were bound as though instantly cemented to its surfaces. Out of nowhere hissing snakes sprang forth and coiled round their wrists and ankles, serpentine manacles strapping them to the arms and legs of the chair. When this was done (and it all happened in the blink of an eye), for one of the rare times in his immortal life the Lord of the Underworld leaned back and laughed, and then he went on his way.

Four years passed; and had not Heracles gone also into Hades' kingdom beneath the earth to seize three-headed Cerberos as his twelfth and final labor, Theseus would have been forever bound to the dark god's chair of forgetfulness. When Alcmene's son saw the king of Athens and Peirithoos sitting rigidly in the chair like errant children awaiting punishment, he recognized both at once and inquired as to why they were there. Hades explained all.

"Only one, then, is guilty of impious intent," said Heracles, "and the other of but honoring his foolish oath. Let me take the innocent man back into the world above."

"Take him if you can, by all means," answered the god whose name men fear to speak.

Heracles grasped then Theseus by either shoulder and planted his foot against the base of the chair. With a powerful tug he ripped the Athenian king free from where he had been sitting for the past four years. Only two ovals of flesh, until that moment part of Theseus's buttocks, remained stuck fast to the seat next to Peirithoos. Heracles took the wiser, trimmer king, along with the great guard dog Cerberos, back into the world of living men.

In the meantime back in Athens the brothers of Helen, Castor and Polydeuces, had effected her rescue and installed Menestheus, distant kinsman of Theseus's, as the new king of Athene's city. Menestheus's welcome of the returned Theseus was, understandably, none too cordial.

The ex-monarch soon sailed, therefore, to the island of Scyros, where his father Aigeus had owned lands which were now his.

Lycomedes was then king of Scyros. Feigning friendship, he took his famous guest on a tour of the island and before long had brought him to its highest precipice. "See, there is your land," he said. Then, as Theseus drew closer to look, the Scyrian king, for reasons of his own, suddenly shoved him off the edge to his death on the rocks below. And so a second time the man who, more than any other man, brought civility and prosperity to Greece's most civil and prosperous city entered great Hades' nether kingdom, never ever to leave it again.

# The House of Laios

I n time the throne of Thebes fell to Laios, great grandson to ill-fated Cadmos, the city's founder and first king. Because his father and his father's father before him both died young, Laios was fearful that death might overtake him also before he had a son to succeed him. Therefore, when his youthful wife Jocasta failed to conceive in the first year of their marriage, he repaired impatiently to the oracle of Apollo at Delphi to ask if the line of Cadmos were to end with him. The oracle's reply sent him back to Thebes thoroughly shaken, its words haunting him ever after:

> Why, fool, do you your own death desire?
> A son born you in time will slay his sire.

From then on, Laios refused to touch his wife Jocasta lest the prophecy come to pass. One night, however, when strong wine had dulled his judgment and heightened his desire, he made exception to his continency and lay with her. After they discovered that Jocasta had conceived, grim fear overtook them both, and they covenanted each with the other that if the child were a boy he should be slain forthwith and without delay.

The baby, as it turned out, was a boy. When he was three days old, Laios pierced his feet with pins, and the two gave him to a trusted servant and ordered him to slay him in such manner as he should choose. The servant took the infant, pins still through his feet, to a wild and remote spot along the slopes of Mount Cithairon. There he placed him in a thicket and left him to die.

Not far away a herdsman from the royal house of Corinth was driving his king's flocks to their summer pasture. When he heard the infant crying, he drew near to investigate. "Hey there!" he called out to the retreating servant of Laios. "Why did you leave this child here with its feet pinned together like this?"

"To die," said Laios's servant. "I was ordered to do so."

"My master and mistress, King Polybos and Queen Merope, weep for want of an heir," the Corinthian said. "Aye, 'tis a handsome and vigorous baby. Have I your leave to take it to them?"

The Theban servant gave permission but charged the Corinthian never to connect the child to him. Thus it was that the baby was brought to Merope, queen of Corinth, and she received him as if he were the child of her own womb. With balms and wine she treated his feet so that they healed, leaving only scars. She called his name Oidipous, which means "swollen feet," and doted over him continuously. She and Polybos, her husband, never spoke of him except as their own son; nor, as he was growing, did anyone else suggest anything to the contrary.

By the time Oidipous reached first manhood, no one in all Corinth was more honored than he. In no one were strength of body and quickness of mind more perfectly mixed. Not all, however, favored him; some few disreputable persons about the palace envied him greatly. One day at a dinner where much wine had been imbibed, one of these fellows, barely able to stand because of his drunkenness, raised his cup and said, "To Oidipous, a bastard of a prince and the prince of bastards." The rogue's friends laughed uproariously.

That next day Oidipous went to Polybos and Merope to ask them why the man might have said what he did and why the others had laughed. Polybos grew angry and cursed the man, swearing he would see him severely punished for his filthy innuendoes. Then he and his queen assured Oidipous that the man spoke nothing but lies. When, however, not long after that Oidipous was taunted by another in the same way, he became greatly troubled and set out for Delphi to inquire of Apollo's oracle about his birth. Horrible words greeted his hearing:

> Begone! Most cursed of men shall you be known!
> Foredoomed are you to sow where you were sown,
> With cursed seed to foul a mother's bed,
> With cursed hands a father's blood to shed.

In frenzy Oidipous ran from the temple into the open air and then along the winding, stone-paved roadway that led down the mountain. He ran until he ached from his running and still continued to run. By the heavens he fixed the location of Corinth and ran ever in the direction opposite, purposing never to return there as long as Polybos and Merope were still alive.

When, therefore, he came to a place where three roads met, he chose the path that took him away from Corinth. Nor had he been on the path but a moment when a chariot suddenly bore down upon him from the opposite direction. "Out of the way, blackguard!" shouted the horseman. "Let us pass."

"I give no ground to knaves," Oidipous answered him.

More words were exchanged, and then the driver leaped from the chariot to force Oidipous physically out of his way. Oidipous parried the horseman's blow and knocked him to the ground. Then, as he proceeded to squeeze by the chariot, the passenger, a gray-haired man of aristocratic bearing, suddenly brought down a horse-goad across his head. Oidipous returned a blow in kind with his walking staff, toppling the man backward out of the chariot. Fierce battle ensued as the man's servants rushed to his assistance. Only one man escaped the fury of Oidipous's staff, and he by fleeing in the direction whence they had come. All the others, the gray-haired man included, lay bloodied and dead along the disputed path.

Oidipous, bruised but otherwise undamaged, continued on his way and after many days came to Thebes. Twin misfortunes, he soon learned, had recently beset the city. Laios, its king, had just been ruthlessly murdered by highwaymen while traveling abroad, and a great savage monstrosity called the Sphinx was perched on Mount Phicion devouring Theban citizens at will. The city was in turmoil.

A huge beast with the face of a woman, the body of a lion, and the wings of a bird, the Sphinx sported with each of her victims before eating him by asking him a riddle: "What is it that, being one, has four feet, then two, and finally three? Spare your own life by answering true and set your city free." But no man knew the answer to the riddle.

So desperate were the Thebans that Creon, Laios's brother-in-law, proclaimed throughout the land that the throne of Thebes and the widowed Jocasta's hand in marriage would go to any man who solved the Sphinx's riddle. As soon as Oidipous, alone and homeless and haunted by the oracle's words, learned of this, he went forthwith to Mount Phicion to face the monster. He had far more to gain, he thought, than to lose.

In a woman's voice and with kindly smile, the Sphinx asked Oidipous her riddle: "What is it that, being one, has four feet, then two, and finally three?"

Oidipous pondered a moment and then answered. "Man," he said, "for as a babe he walks upon four feet, as an adult on two, and when his years are almost spent he needs a third, a stick, to bear him up."

Stunned that anyone should answer her riddle correctly, the Sphinx reeled from her perch and came crashing down on some jagged rocks many feet below. And so it was, not long afterward, that amid ceremony befitting the city's savior, Oidipous was installed as king of Thebes and given the still young Jocasta, his own mother, for wife.

For a time thereafter the city and its young king prospered together. As a mother hen spreads broad her wings and takes all her chicks under them, even so did Oidipous with expansive heart bring all his fellow citizens under his personal care. He called the people his children (though not from want of children of his own, for Jocasta bore him two sons, Polyneices and Eteocles, and two daughters, Antigone and Ismene) and responded to their plights more as a father than as a regent. At the very time that Theseus was guiding Athens to its greatest glory, Oidipous was doing the same for his adopted, though native city. Everywhere he was called Oidipous the Great.

At length, however, a plague settled upon Thebes so that its soil no longer produced crops nor its cattle young after their kind and the wombs of its women were closed. Oidipous forthwith then sent an envoy to Delphi to discover from the oracle in Apollo's temple for what reason the gods had sent the curse and what they now required.

"The murderer of Laios, king before you, is still at large and dwells among us," the envoy told Oidipous upon his return. "He is the land's pollution. Him must we banish or requite blood for blood, for so the god demands."

"I will spare nothing then until this man is found out and punished," pledged Oidipous to his people. "Though I myself never met Laios, I shall bend all my energies to finding his murderer as though he were my own father."

Now there lived in Thebes at that time a very old man. Teiresias was his name and he was blind, but no truer prophet ever spoke, no, not in all Greece or anywhere before or since. His remarkable gift came about in a curious way. As a young man, it seems, he was a womanizer of rare aptitude. On his way to a rendezvous one day he was walking through some woods and happened to come upon two snakes entwined amorously the one about the other. Prompted by whim, he knocked the reptilian lovers apart with his staff. Suddenly then he experienced a strange transformation in his own body. The god of the place he had surely offended, for in the flash of an eye all his male parts vanished and he became a girl.

His capacity for love, he soon discovered, had not diminished in the least. He was as strikingly lovely as a girl as he had been roguishly handsome as a man, and before long he found he could make a not uncomfortable living at what before had been but a pleasant pastime. For seven years he lived and loved as a girl. Then again, on a similar errand, he passed through the same woods as before and chanced again to come upon two snakes coupling. As before, he drove his staff between them and immediately felt his own body begin to convulse. Deity seemed satisfied. When he left the woods, Teiresias was once more a man.

While the profligate Theban went about confirming his restored manhood, high atop Mount Olympos the Father of Gods and Men was being sharply rebuked by his queen. "Faithless lecher!!" she screamed. "Have you no remorse for your adulteries? What if I behaved like you?"

"Why, Hera my dear," ventured Zeus in his defense, "we all know you females find far greater delight in the act of love than we poor males. We sweat; you tingle. It's only fair, then, that once in a while we make up for our lack of quality with a little more variety. Only fair and natural, my dear."

"Nonsense!" she replied. "Yours is the greater delight."

"No, yours," he said.

The argument went on endlessly until at last they agreed to settle it by calling upon Teiresias, the world's only expert on the matter, to act as judge. Naively he tried to oblige them. "If the pleasures of sex," he said, "were divided into ten parts, one part would be the male's and three times three the female's." Hera, not a good loser, blinded the foolish mortal on the spot. To compensate, Zeus, who had probably coached him in the first place, gave Teiresias the gifts of unerring inner sight and long life.

It was to this same Teiresias that Oidipous first turned in his investigation of Laios's death. The blind prophet was led into his presence by a little boy. By his manner the old man from the start evinced uneasiness, which Oidipous soon interpreted as obstinacy. "Hold back nothing," he said to him sternly. "If your powers be what men say, you can tell us the name of the man we seek."

"Better would it be for both of us," said Teiresias, "if I left and said nothing."

"No, you stay and speak."

"I have no desire to inflict pain on anyone," the prophet told him next. "Therefore, I have nothing to say."

Oidipous, who had begun the interview with businesslike composure, felt his anger now begin to mount. The old man was, to his mind, either intentionally trying to appear mysterious for reputation's sake or was protecting someone. With shouts and then threats he insisted that Teiresias tell all regardless of whom the information might injure. "Only a confederate in the crime itself," he cried, "would hold his tongue and let his city perish."

"All right," said the aged seer, "have it your way. For the cause of the land's pollution, my lord, look no further than yourself." With that, he motioned for the boy to lead him out.

Although Oidipous decided that the old prophet's parting words came more from his spleen than his inner light, he nonetheless continued to ponder them long after Teiresias had left. Others that day he summoned before him, but nothing anyone else could tell him seemed to bring him any closer to the identity of his predecessor's slayer. Only Teiresias had seemed to know anything at all, and only he had been unwilling to help.

"He would only say that I should look no further than myself," Oidipous told Jocasta, his wife, when the two were alone. "Does he mean that I am Laios's murderer, whom I never even met?"

"Do not set too much store by what that old man says," she replied.

"Only once in my life have I ever killed anyone, and I was by myself then, not in company with a pack of highwaymen."

"Prophecies are but guesswork and those that make them merely fumbling old guessers. The wise pay them no heed," said Jocasta to him. Then by way of example for his comfort she went on to tell how she and Laios years before had given the lie to a prophecy by having their only child slain. "So much for prophets and prophecy," she concluded. "The child, feet-pierced, lies decades dead, and he whom he was supposed to kill fell victim to brigands in Phocis where three roads meet."

"Where three roads meet?" he said.

"Yes," she told him, "not far from Delphi."

Quick questions and quick answers ensued. Oidipous, both seeker and sought, equally fearful now of what he did not know and of what he might discover, pressed to know what Laios looked like, how he was accompanied, exactly when his murder took place. With each question came dreadful revelation. His only solace was that Laios had purportedly been killed by a number of villains and he in his crossroads carnage had clearly been alone. He sent for the sole eyewitness forthwith and, fearing what he could not utter, for the household servant as well who was supposed to have killed Laios's infant son.

The two, as it turned out, were the same man. He came wearing the attire of a shepherd. And in manner, as in dress, he seemed a man who wished that people had forgotten him long ago. When Oidipous put to him his first question about the murder of Laios, the old man's face told all. No more was necessary, though the servant, his voice as frail as his frame, did try to make them understand his fear at the time of being thought a coward for fleeing a single man who was merely trying to defend himself. "For that reason I said there were many," he owned. "It made no difference. The king was just as dead."

"And were you not also the one to whom Laios once gave a baby whose feet were pinned together?" asked Oidipous next.

"Stop!" cried Jocasta. "Ask no more, my wretched Oidipous. I beg of you."

"Answer," Oidipous commanded.

But before the old servant could reply, Jocasta ran from the room screaming, her voice shrill with terror as though she were being set upon by some dark and unnatural fiend. Little enough was there now that Oidipous could not guess, indeed in his soul had not guessed already; nevertheless, needing the worst confirmed, perhaps denied, he continued to interrogate the old man until he learned all.

Then like a wild man, or perhaps like a wounded animal racked by unendurable pain, he reeled and half ran, half staggered from the room, his cries penetrating every corner of the palace as he went. He pressed his hands over his eyes as if they had beheld some incredibly ghastly sight which he could not bear to have them gaze upon a second time.

"Where is this wife that is no wife," he stormed, "the soil from which I sprang and where my seed was sown?"

Crying thus, he came to the chamber he and Jocasta shared. The doors were closed and secured from the inside, but he threw his whole weight against them so that bolts bent in their sockets. And there above their cursed bed hung Jocasta, a rope about her neck. Oidipous gave out a great shriek of agony and rushed to her and cut her down and laid her on the bed.

Then, as he moaned incoherently over her corpse, he tore from her robe the two gold brooches pinning it together and, raising them up as if in consecration to some god he must appease, drove them again and again into his own eyeballs, all the while screaming, "See no more, accursed eyes, the horrors of my life! Look no more on those who should never have been born." Blood spurted from his eyes and, as dark rain, wet his beard and clothes.

When, at long last, he was led out of the room, he was a bowed and broken man, exhausted of strength, unsteady, his beard and clothes streaked with black blood. Someone had given him a stick to lean upon. In all aspects of his gait and carriage he seemed an old man, a very old man. His voice too was languid and shaky, like that of a cowering beggar who has been oft taught by cane and boot the tone to rise to with his betters.

"Have me taken back to Cithairon where first I was taken after birth," he implored Creon, his brother-in-law. "It was to be my tomb, you know. Would that it had been. This time perhaps the gods will be kinder and let me perish."

"As you have spoken so shall it be."

"And my two little girls," said Oidipous, "nurture them, I pray you, as your own."

This Creon also consented to do. And so Oidipous, once called Great by men, hobbled out of his brother-in-law's presence, with his stick groping and steadying himself, led by a servant. Himself the man of the Sphinx's riddle, he now walked on three legs instead of two.

And so it was that Creon assumed the role of king until such time as the sons of Oidipous, Polyneices and Eteocles, would be old enough to ascend to the throne. Thebes once more became prosperous. The pollution purged, the fields again sprouted blades of grain—lush, green carpets— and the sheep and goats and cattle brought forth again after their kind and the women were no longer barren.

When the time came, after Polyneices and Eteocles had grown into manhood, for Creon to relinquish the throne, he did so gladly and not grudgingly. Because it was judged that each brother had equal claim, an agreement was reached whereby they would rule on alternate years, first Polyneices and after a year Eteocles and then Polyneices again. All went well at first. Distinguishing himself for neither good nor ill, the older brother reigned a year and stepped down.

Eteocles also reigned for one year, but while he was king he wooed the people and won the whole city to himself so that they preferred him to his brother. When, therefore, Polyneices came to receive the scepter at the end of his brother's first year, Eteocles, knowing the people were behind him, refused to give it up. "When I can reign, why would I be slave to the likes of you?" he said.

"I ask naught but what is due me," replied Polyneices. "We made an agreement and swore by the deathless gods to abide by its terms."

"Power is the greatest god of all, dear brother," said Eteocles. "Having known now its glory, I would go to black Tartaros itself to pay my homage. Now begone, and let me enjoy my reign!"

"I will not abide this treachery," said Polyneices.

"Nor will I abide you," replied Eteocles. "If at first light tomorrow you are found to be anywhere within the borders of my realm, your life will be required of you. Consider this fair warning."

Thus it was that Polyneices was driven from his homeland by his brother Eteocles. Greatly vexed by Eteocles's duplicity, he came eventually to Argos, where Adrastos was then the king. It was evening when Polyneices first approached the Argive gates. He was bone tired from his day's travels and sought but the humblest of beds where he might sleep the night. Just as he discovered a straw pallet near the wall by the gate, however, another man, also an exile and fully as weary, rushed to it from the opposite direction.

The other man was Tydeus, son of Oineus, half-brother to Meleagros, who had been banished by his uncle from Calydon where he likewise had claim to a throne. Polyneices fought with him over the pallet of straw. Such stir they created that one might well have thought that the pallet for each man was his lost kingdom. King Adrastos himself was called to the scene and had to part the two.

Now it seems that shortly before this Adrastos had inquired of one of Apollo's oracles as to the futures of his two daughters and had been told, "Yoke them to a boar and a lion." As he now separated Polyneices from Tydeus and brought them into the light, he saw on the shield of the Calydonian a boar and on that of the Theban a lion. Immediately the oracle's language came to his mind, and he asked the two to be his sons-in-law.

Both men told Adrastos the stories of their respective banishments, and he shared with them their indignation. "Husbands of my daughters, you shall be as sons to me," said the king. "Your causes and mine will be the same, and with both of you will I march to restore what tyrants have seized."

The double wedding took place, and within the year the king began to mobilize his armies to go into Thebes to regain for Polyneices his kingdom. It was his plan to march against Calydon after that. Seven columns of spearmen, ten thousand strong, did the bold Adrastos recruit in his new son-in-law's behalf.

At the head of the first column he placed Tydeus and at the head of the second Capaneus, a giant of a man whose boasts held respect for no one. Commanding the third column was the insolent Eteoclos. The fourth was under Hippomedon's command, also a huge man with a penchant for bloodletting, and the fifth was under the Arcadian Parthenopaios and the sixth under the soldier-seer Amphiareus. Over the seventh column King Adrastos placed Polyneices himself. And in spite of unfavorable omens, the army set out for Thebes by way of the Isthmos and Attica.

When word reached Thebes that the Argives were on their way, Eteocles went to Creon to seek counsel. "Their numbers are vast," he said to him, "ours by comparison so few. Dare we meet them on the battlefield?"

"Let the war be fought at our seven gates," advised Creon. "There strength and courage, not numbers, will win the day. Choose you seven champions and post one, with his men, at each of the city's gates. If all can hold, at day's end Thebes will yet be in Cadmean hands."

Eteocles did as his uncle told him. At the first gate he posted a young nobleman named Melanippos and at the second Polyphontes, a man of volatile nature and a devotee of Artemis; to defend the third gate he placed Megareus, oldest son of Creon; to defend the fourth Hyperbios, on whose shield was the image of a majestic Zeus hurling thunderbolts; to defend the fifth Actor, who would not suffer insolence to go unchallenged; and at the sixth the seer Lasthenes. And at the seventh gate Eteocles himself took command.

None of this was too soon; for by the time each champion had positioned himself and instructed his men what to do, the Argive battalions were upon them. As a great swarm of locusts from the Boiotian meadows they descended upon the city of Cadmos.

Tydeus, Adrastos's son-in-law, shouted the battle cry and ordered his troops against the first of the Theban portals. Hissing like a serpent at noonday, he raised his huge boar-faced shield and stormed the gate at full gallop. Melanippos, however, in command of the defenders, was undaunted. By deed and word he inspired in his Cadmean cohorts heroism none in his common hours would have dreamed possible, and so it was that the Thebans prevailed. Back in Argos, Tydeus's young wife Deipyle felt the first twitches of new life beneath her ribs and smiled, little knowing that the babe she carried was already without a father.

At another gate the Arcadian Parthenopaios bore down upon the defenders, crying out to those behind him, "Light the firebrands! On with the double-bladed axes! Let nothing, no one be left standing!" However, as the bold commander rode near the wall, a Theban atop the rampart heaved a large boulder down onto his unprotected head, shattering his skull. Blood streaked down his pink-flush face, and he fell from his horse.

The impious, loud-roaring Capaneus, when fighting was stalled at the gate he assaulted, brought on ladders to go over the wall. "Great Zeus with all his terrible thunderbolts cannot stop us now from our prize," he boasted as he ascended the ladder, holding his torch-decorated shield over his head for protection. No man among the invaders or defenders was within a head of being as tall as he, so gigantic was he. To the Thebans vainly trying to slow him with spears and rocks from the tower, he seemed the size of three men and bore himself with the strength and ferocity of ten.

However, just as he reached the top of the wall, a bolt of lightning suddenly broke forth and lifted his massive body backward off the ladder. A loud thunder clap rang out at the same instant, drawing all eyes to the Argive commander. His hair flying, his arms and legs outstretched like four spokes, he went spinning, like Ixion, into the air and crashed to the ground suffused in brilliant flames.

When he saw that Zeus too opposed him, Adrastos ordered his spearmen away from the wall to a place beyond a gully. The defenders, taking heart, now threw their gates wide open and gave chase in chariots and on horseback. Driving into the midst of the retreating Argives, with spears and battleaxes they split the army in two so that the invaders no longer had the advantage of mass. Great was the slaughter then that the Thebans visited upon the seven armies of Adrastos. The seer Amphiareus, who had foretold the deaths of all seven commanders, prophesying that only King Adrastos would survive the campaign, failed to avert a gaping crevice in the earth with his chariot and so proved himself a better prophet than horseman.

Then it was that Eteocles mounted a tower and called out to the Argives, "Hear me, men of Argos! Do not die for a cause in which you have nothing to gain. The feud is between my brother and me. Let me join then in battle against him alone. If I prevail, you can go home; if he prevails, yours will be the victors' spoils. Will you make way that we may fight on neutral ground?"

Polyneices leaped up and shouted, "Make way! Pull back, my dear comrades! Gladly will I do battle against this man in single combat so that no more blood is spilled but ours."

When an area was cleared, the two brothers advanced upon each other, both with shields up and spears poised. They moved cautiously in a circle, each at moments darting in and making quick jabs at the other when a foot or a thigh seemed exposed. At one point Eteocles slipped on a rock; and, to the cheers of the Argives, Polyneices drove his spear into his brother's calf before he could pull his leg back behind his shield. Then Eteocles retaliated with his spear to Polyneices' unprotected shoulder, and the Thebans shouted him on.

Swords soon drawn, they closed in on each other. All at once Eteocles leaped back on his left foot, momentarily throwing Polyneices off guard, and then just as suddenly lunged forward on his right foot, thrusting his blade through his brother's navel into his spine. Life, however, did not quickly flee the fallen man; for when Eteocles bent over him to retrieve his sword, Polyneices, with a final burst of energy born of hate, thrust his steel into his brother's liver.

The Argive survivors, now seeing their last hope for victory as well as their reason for being there dead in the blood-muddied grime of no man's land with his brother's corpse slumped over him, turned and fled from the place. Night being close, the Theban defenders chose not to give chase but rather to exult in the bitter-sweet triumph that was theirs. Creon was offered the crown he had worn briefly twice before and reluctantly accepted it.

When that next morning the sun threw its first shafts of light out over the battlefield of the day before and disclosed the hundreds upon hundreds of corpses that lay there, Creon stood before his people and made this proclamation: "Let us gather our noble dead and bury them with all rites due them as heroes. And at the grave of Eteocles, our late fallen king, let us pay special tribute, for nothing did he spare but gave all in his beloved city's defense. As for Polyneices, who brought an army against his own fatherland, him let no one bury but leave rather as carrion for birds and curs to dine upon. Whosoever attempts to bury him shall do so at the cost of his own life. Such is my decree."

Although Antigone heard her uncle's proclamation, come nightfall she slipped out of one of the gates and past the sentries posted by Creon to where Polyneices' body was lying. Working quickly and quietly, she dug a shallow grave and rolled her brother's corpse into it and covered it up with dirt. Then she poured the libations due kin and left.

The sentries, when they discovered that Polyneices had been buried, quickly dug up his corpse to make it once more the fare of dogs and vultures, this time watching it more closely. That evening, as on the previous one, Antigone went out to perform her duty as sister. The sentries thereupon rushed upon her and seized her and dragged her off to Creon.

"Were you apprehended doing as they say?" her uncle asked her.

"I was," she told him calmly.

"And did you know of my decree that under penalty of death no one was to give burial to that traitor?" said Creon next.

Antigone replied that she had heard the decree from his own lips.

"You knew and yet dared defy this law?"

"The law you speak of did not come from Zeus," she said to him. "Nor did eternal Justice hand down such a decree. Therefore, I did not think that your words, those of but a mere mortal, should countermand the unwritten and unfailing laws of heaven. It would take more than the fear of a man to cause me to risk the sure and just retribution of the gods if I had neglected to honor their laws. Do your worst. I repent of nothing I have done, knowing all along it would cost me my life. Had I left my mother's son unburied, then would I have cause for shame as now I do not."

Angered as much by his niece's lecture as by her insolence, Creon stormed back at her, "Though you were for a time like a daughter to me, think not you will escape the penalty of this offense. The law, if it is to be honored, must apply to all alike, even to those of the king's household." He then ordered the guards to take Antigone away.

When she was gone, Creon called one of his aides to his side and instructed him thus: "Find a cave where people are not wont to go. Take her there and encase her in it, leaving only enough food and water as to spare the city the guilt of her death. There let her pray that Death comes for her swiftly."

Even as these orders were being carried out, others came to the king to intercede for the girl's life. Haimon, Creon's own son, came also. He it was who loved Antigone and would have made her his bride. His entreaties, as all the others', were as but peckings against the monolith of Creon's obdurate will. Last of all ancient Teiresias came into the new king's presence.

"The birds I use for augury have gone mad," he said. "My altar fires will not burn. Some dread evil is in the land, and its source is the unburied corpse of a king and the son of a king."

Creon only winced. "So you too, my old friend, have joined the ranks of those who would oppose me."

"You sent a girl alive into a tomb, but to a dead man refuse the same," said the blind seer. "For that you will pay with a life from your own house." So speaking, he left.

Creon sat for several moments pondering the prophet's words. Never had the old man been wrong in anything. "Quick," the king suddenly called out to those about him, "to the cave where the girl was taken! Bring picks and axes, and pray we are not too late."

First, however, Creon and his guards went to the place where Polyneices' body lay, already badly torn and picked at by animals and birds, and burned the remains and buried the ashes under a mound. And from there they went to Antigone's tomb, but as they came near they heard sounds as of someone in lamentation. "The voice of Haimon, my son," gasped Creon. "Run ahead, someone, and see if that is he or if the gods punish me with cruel tricks."

One of the guards pressed ahead and arrived at the cave before the others. The barrier had been broken down, and at the far corner of the cave he could see Antigone hanging by a noose fashioned from her own clothing. Haimon, wailing loudly, was trying to lift her down. He took the noose from her neck and then lowered her body gently, lovingly to the cave floor. When Creon got to the entrance and saw what had happened, he called into him, "I hear you moan, my son. Come out here that I might join you."

Haimon looked up at his father with savage eyes. "I loved her!" he screamed. "And she is dead by her own hand and yours!" Then he ran at Creon and spit in his face.

Creon drew back, but Haimon unsheathed his sword and began to swing wildly like a madman. His father, though wanting desperately to take his son into his arms, backstepped quickly out of harm's way. The boy, crazed and beside himself with rage, put the hilt of his sword against some rocks and fell onto the blade so that it ran half of its length into his side. Spewing blood, he crawled back to Antigone's body and embraced it and then breathed his last.

Creon's grief, however, was not at an end. Nor had he left off bringing down woe upon his city and upon his own head by his stubborn spirit; for when envoys of King Adrastos came to him under truce to beg the corpses of the Argive dead for burial, he steadfastly refused them and sent them away with threats. When the envoys returned to Argos and reported what Creon had said, the mothers of the fallen champions clothed themselves in sack-cloth and went to Aithra, mother of Theseus. She in turn prevailed upon her son to confront Creon, if need be, with the chariots and horsemen of Athens to get the Thebans to give up the bodies.

And so it was that a second army marched against the city of Cadmos, this time a smaller, far more disciplined force, one that by skill and courage handily brought the defenders to their knees. A lesser man than Theseus would have pillaged the city and seized many a handsome trophy to take back home, but the only trophies the king of Athens had come to take were the bodies of six Argive champions and their unlucky men. This he did and then left the Thebans alone to reflect upon their bitter and painful lesson.

# Young Heracles

hrough his own divinations was the great Father of Gods and Men forewarned that the day approached when all the gods of Olympos would be destroyed by the Race of Giants. Huger than Titans, the monstrous beings would prove impervious even to his most awesome thunderbolts. Only the greatest of mortal heroes, according to the prophecy, could save the gods, for only by his blows could the Giants be finally felled.

For that reason Zeus mused much over the hero-producing potential of the lovely Alcmene. The daughter of Electryon, son of Perseus, and therefore the Olympian lord's own great granddaughter, she was for character and mind as well as body without peer among all the maidens of the world. Above all other women she was the one upon whom the greatest of heroes must be begotten—and, of course, by him.

Now it happened one day that distant kinsmen came to Electryon from Taphos and laid claim to the whole kingdom of Mycenai by right of ancient inheritance. When with harsh words the son of Perseus turned them away, they went into the meadows where the king's nine sons watched over his herds and, taking them unawares, killed all the young men and made off with the cattle. Electryon, upon discovering the outrage, put the kingdom in charge of Amphitryon, betrothed of Alcmene, and set out after them.

Men from Elis a few days later came to Mycenai, saying cattle thought to be Electryon's had been sold to them and they would gladly return them if they could recover what they had paid. Out of his own resources, therefore, Amphitryon ransomed the cattle and soon had them back in the meadows. When, after a week, Electryon returned empty-handed, the young man proudly took his prospective father-in-law to where the cattle were grazing and told him of the sum he had paid the Eleans. "Such a small price for such a fine herd," he said. "I knew you would repay me."

"Repay you?" roared Electryon contemptuously. "I pay no man for what is already mine. You were a fool to suppose I would."

Amphitryon, overcome by anger, hurled his club at a nearby cow. The club glanced off the animal's curved horn and struck Electryon in the temple, killing him instantly. For his offense, though but an accident, Amphitryon was banished from Mycenai, and Sthenelos, another of Perseus's sons, reigned in his brother's stead. Alcmene joined her betrothed in exile, purposing to marry him as soon as her nine brothers were finally avenged. Their wandering took them soon to Thebes, where Amphitryon quickly recruited a small force and made preparations to bring the Taphians to justice.

Before the party set out from Thebes, Amphitryon and Alcmene were married, though at the bride's insistence the marriage was not then consummated. "It is not right," said the loveliest of maidens, "for me to find delight in your bed so long as my poor brothers go unavenged. Go then, my sweet husband, and bring swift retribution to those who shed their blood. I will await your return."

No man ever hoped for shorter war than Amphitryon at that moment. The beauty he saw titillated him; that he imagined tortured him. He gave quick commands to his men, and they departed immediately. The campaign did turn out to be a short one, lasting only a matter of days. The Taphians at first fought the force of Amphitryon to a standstill; but when their champion was killed, dispirited and leaderless, they soon floundered and were handily defeated.

Zeus, who had had no small part in arranging these events, was quick to take advantage of the new bridegroom's absence. He let two days pass and on the third changed himself into a perfect likeness of Amphitryon and came to the house where the bride had prepared herself for her new husband. Even in voice and gesture he was identical to Amphitryon. No one could have ever blamed Alcmene for never suspecting a thing.

"And did you bring justice to those murderers?" she asked him, taking his arm and leading him to the bedchamber.

"Justice as would delight the heart of Zeus himself," he answered. Then as he bathed, with her assisting him, he described in careful detail the battle that was still going on at that very moment at Taphos as though it had already been fought. She marveled at his keen memory and thrilled to the descriptions of his own heroic exploits. Also, his narrative strangely fired her passions for him so that when he helped her into bed she was no less ready for the rites of Aphrodite than he.

Knowing that the greatest of heroes could never be sired overnight, Zeus had dispatched wing-sandaled Hermes to the great golden palace of Helios with orders to unharness his immortal steeds and leave his jewel-spangled golden chariot in the chariot house all that next day. "Great deeds must the Father of Gods and Men do in the dark," Hermes added by way of explanation.

Helios, who sees all, knew exactly where Zeus was as well as the nature of his great deeds. "There was a time," he snarled, "when day was day and night night. Cronos reigned in heaven then, and he did not forsake his rightful wife and turn the world topsy-turvy to adulterate with somebody else's bride in Thebes.

"He has his purpose," said Hermes.

"Yes, I've seen his purpose on many an occasion," said the Sun God. "However, I guess I must do as he says."

Next the winged messenger of Olympos sped off to the Moon to tell it to move more leisurely across the skies through that night and the next. Then to Hypnos, the gentle god of sleep, he went with this message: "Make heavy the eyes of mankind, except Alcmene, that all might sleep for three long nights and think them only one. Let not the maiden Alcmene's senses be dulled by so much as a thought of sweet repose."

And so it was that for one full night and the next day and that night also darkness covered the earth, and men slept soundly all the while as though it were but a single night. In Thebes the great Father of Gods and Men toiled tirelessly and ungrudgingly at his labor of love. Alcmene, chaste until then, had only heard stories about bridal nights and so knew little of what to expect. She did, however, marvel a few times at her husband's endurance.

When, at the end of the long night, Dawn's first half-light began to define the outlines of objects in the room, the daughter of Electryon at last found herself beginning to tire. However, as a long distance runner rounds his last turn and sees the finish line clearly ahead and, finding a fresh burst of energy, breaks into a sprint, even so did Zeus, seeing the day about to commence, draw upon his reserves and finished his feat with such a flurry that Alcmene could but gasp in total amazement.

Shortly thereafter Zeus made his exit. Alcmene remained in the bed thoroughly exhausted, desirous only that sweet sleep close her eyes for a time equal to that she had just spent in love's embrace. Just then, however, Amphitryon returned from his successful campaign against the Taphians.

176

Triumphantly he threw open the door and announced his arrival. "Come, let us bathe me," he said, "and I will tell you what your ears long to hear."

Not a little perplexed, Alcmene did as he suggested, careful to turn away whenever she had to yawn. The story he told of the battle and of his role in it was identical to the one she had heard before, word for word, gesture for gesture, pause for pause. Then Amphitryon took his trim-ankled bride by the hand to guide her to the bed. "And now, while our appetites are strong," he said to her, "let us gorge ourselves at Aphrodite's long-awaited banquet."

Alcmene had heard exaggerated tales of men's sexual proclivities but never anything that approached this. "Maybe we can just talk," she suggested. "You can tell me about the battle one more time."

"Coyness becomes you, my sweet, my lovely innocent," said Amphitryon, taking her gently by the waist and lifting her onto the mattress.

"Perhaps we should save ourselves for another day," she said next.

Amphitryon had heard of blushing brides and so set about to savor his banquet slowly, a morsel at a time, with the effect of whetting his appetite rather than diminishing it. His beauteous brown-eyed bride did not reject his advances, but neither did she respond encouragingly to them either. Often a person at meal will, for politeness' sake, go through the motions of relishing foods not particularly appetizing—nibbling, smacking the lips, sighing appreciatively. Such show was neither in Alcmene's character nor, right then, within her human capabilities. Her bridegroom for all intents and purposes dined alone. When his repast was over, he was more than a little disconcerted to discover that she had fallen asleep sometime midway through the main course.

"What's wrong?" he asked, shaking her slightly. "Does not the goddess Aphrodite inspire the same devotion in you as in me?"

"Not when I've been tending her altar all night," she answered drowsily and fell back to sleep.

Greatly troubled, Amphitryon went that next day to the blind old seer Teiresias to ask him why Alcmene had been so unresponsive to him and also what she had meant by her final remark. "No prophet do you need for such mystery as you describe," the old man told him. "Mortal man did not take your form to take your wife. Of that rest assured. 'Tis no disgrace to be cuckolded by the great Zeus."

Regardless of the high purpose for which Zeus had compromised Amphitryon's wife, he found little understanding and applause from his own. Hera was as furious over his infidelities as ever and, as was her habit, directed the full force of her fury toward the one who was already victim.

When, therefore, the time came for Alcmene to deliver, she dispatched her daughter Eileithyia to Thebes. "Make the adulterous wench languish in her throes," she instructed her, "and let not the babe she carries escape the womb."

And so it was that Eileithyia went to the house of Amphitryon and Alcmene in Thebes. Outside the door she sat with her right leg across her left leg, her arms likewise crossed and her fingers interlocked the one around the other. Softly she chanted a magical spell. For seven days and seven nights inside the room Alcmene groaned with unspeakable agony. The burly babe within fought to get out, and she struggled to release him but could not. Her body was lathered in her own sweat.

"Why, great Zeus," she cried out, "have you made me thus and then forsaken me?" Pitifully she begged of her seducer her death. Violent pangs shot throughout her body so that every muscle seemed to tear asunder and every bone break.

One of her attendants was a redheaded peasant girl named Galanthis. The same noticed Eileithyia ever beside the door to her mistress's room and always in the same contorted position with everything about her person crossed that was crossable. Could the strange woman be a witch perhaps, she fell to wondering, or maybe a malevolent goddess casting a spell? With such thoughts in mind, Galanthis returned to Alcmene's bedside and waited a short while. Then she ran to the door and, throwing it open, shouted exuberantly, "Praises to Zeus! Hera be thanked! My mistress is delivered of her son!"

Eileithyia sprang to her feet in utter amazement and held up her arms. "How could it be?" she exclaimed, perplexed as to what went wrong.

At that very instant Heracles bolted from Alcmene's womb and gave his first hearty cry. Outside the delivery room Galanthis studied the look, first of bewilderment and then of understanding, that spread across the goddess's face. Unable to contain her mischievous delight, the young trickster burst out with derisive laughter. Eileithyia, we are told, grabbed her by her rich red locks and, forcing her to the ground, held her there until she became a weasel, her hair retaining its reddish hue, her disposition not changing either—always sly. Back inside the room, the way cleared, Alcmene gave birth to a second son, though not as hale as the first. This second baby, Amphitryon's, was named Iphicles.

The lesson of Galanthis was not lost on Alcmene. Knowing by now that the infant Heracles was the issue of Zeus and that for that reason Hera was her enemy, she lived in mortal dread of what next the goddess might do not only to her but to Amphitryon and the other baby as well.

In a moment of madness, therefore, she placed the baby Heracles in a deserted spot outside the walls of Thebes and left him there.

Athene, at her father's instigation, went strolling in that same place not long afterward with Hera. Soon they came upon the babe. "By Zeus, it's a little baby and an unusually handsome one at that," said Athene, picking the infant Heracles up. "Poor thing, what's he doing here? Why, look. He seems hungry. Such an adorable child. Hera, my dear, take him and let him suck. You have milk and I do not."

All of Hera's motherly instincts surfaced. She suspected nothing. The milk in her bosoms flowed freely, and her nipples swelled to give suck. Taking the baby into her arms, she slid her gown off one shoulder and bared a breast. Heracles clutched the divine breast with both hands and began to nurse most vigorously. He sucked with such force that Hera in pain pushed him away, but so powerful had been his sucking that a great geyser of milk shot up into the sky from Hera's breast when she pushed him off. This men afterward called the Milky Way.

By this ruse Zeus assured his son of immortality, for he now had nursed at the breast of a goddess. Athene then returned the baby to his mother. "Guard him well," she told her, "for this child is a child of destiny." And so Alcmene took Heracles back and laid him beside Iphicles on a shield Amphitryon had made into a crib by covering its hollow side with lambskin.

One night, when the babies were eight months old, Hera, still fuming over being tricked into giving Heracles her milk, sent two huge serpents into the room where the two were asleep on the shield. Hissing loudly, venom dripping from their fangs, the snakes slithered toward the children, both of whom quickly awakened. Iphicles cried and fell off the shield.

This noise quickly brought Alcmene into the room with a lamp. She saw the two serpents rise to strike the baby still in the hollow of the shield. Her repeated screams in turn brought Amphitryon scurrying, drawn sword in hand. Alcmene raised the lamp to guide her husband to the rescue, only to discover that rescue was no longer necessary. There, sitting in the middle of the shield, was the robust infant Heracles with a freshly strangled serpent in either hand.

"What manner of child is this?" Amphitryon asked Teiresias that next morning, after describing the incident.

"One doomed to many labors, tested by evil men and fearsome beasts and denizens of the wine-dark deep," the aged prophet told him. "But all will redound to his glory when on the Plains of Phlegra he stands with the gods against the savage Giants and with his club and arrows strikes the monsters to the dust. Then will he find a place forevermore among the mansions of the blessed."

When Heracles became older, Amphitryon took him in hand and taught him how to drive a chariot. He arranged also with Eurytos, the greatest archer of that time, to make him skilled in the use of the bow and with Autolycos to teach him the art of wrestling. Linos, the brother of Orpheus, was enlisted to instruct him in playing the lyre. In the skills of physical prowess the boy learned quickly and excelled in all he understood.

He proved less adept, however, in matters of music, all very much to the frustration of the ever temperamental Linos. One afternoon, in fact, Linos became so exasperated with Heracles' musical miscues that he cuffed him across the side of his head. Heracles, like a large puppy having no comprehension of his own size and strength, responded by smashing the lyre over the old man's head. Linos did not live to profit from the lesson.

Concerned that there might be another such incident, Amphitryon cut short the boy's education and sent him into a remote area between Mount Cithairon and Mount Helicon to tend cattle. There he continued to practice with the javelin and bow, achieving unerring accuracy with both. Fire seemed to blaze in his eyes, and when men were told he was Zeus's son they quite believed it. He slept under the open skies and ate enough roast beef and barley cakes each evening for supper to make a dozen field hands say, "No more." By the time he reached his eighteenth birthday, he was eight feet tall.

He was not alone, it seems, in his appetite for Amphitryon's beef, for in that region a great rogue lion was ever on the prowl and on a number of occasions raided the herd entrusted to Heracles. When Heracles pursued the beast, it went on to the herds of Thespios, king of Thespiai, on the slopes of Mount Helicon. Panic at the sight of the huge lion drove shepherds from their flocks and cowherds from their cattle to the safety of houses and walled cities. The people were smitten with terror. And so, when Heracles came to Thespiai to destroy the ferocious marauder, he was welcomed as though the deed were already accomplished.

At the sight of him, magnificently tall with broad muscular shoulders and swarthy complexion, fiery eyes and rugged good looks, Thespios sensed immediately that the rumors he had heard about the youth were all true and so asked him to be his guest in the palace. Never did a young man look more like a son of Zeus.

Thespios, it turns out, had more than the Cithairon lion on his kingly mind. He was the father of fifty daughters, and for not one of them had he yet found a suitable husband, for he was most particular about the quality of grandson who should succeed him. And so it was that he said to Heracles, "Leave the hunting of the lion till morning. Tonight I would have you meet my family."

It was then late in the day and Heracles was famished, so, assuming his host's invitation included a hearty meal, he ventured no objection. Nor was he wrong in that assumption. Great quantities of roasted meats were placed before him and his favorite barley cakes as well. Thespios marveled at the young man's capacity for devouring food. When he was finished, the king said, "Now perhaps you would like to lie down. I'll have someone show you to your room."

"Did you not wish for me to meet your family?" asked the son of Alcmene.

"I'll send them to your room," Thespios told him. "You can meet them at your leisure."

Rather than pursue the matter further right then, Heracles decided to wait to see what his host meant, and so he went with the servant to the guest quarters. The room was spacious and splendidly furnished with finely woven tapestries depicting hunts and chases and nymphs at play. In the middle of the room was a huge four-poster bed, skillfully carved, with azure canopy overhead. A delicately stitched covering was spread over the bed. Not used to sleeping inside at all, Heracles stood for long and pondered as to whether he was supposed to sleep on top of the covering or under it.

Before he could decide, however, the door opened and a girl came into the room. She introduced herself as one of the king's daughters. "Then you would know," said Heracles, fumbling for conversation, "whether one should lie on top of this fine spread or under it."

"Why don't we lie on top of it?" said the girl, and they did.

Soon after this girl left the room, the door was opened again and a second of the king's daughters came in and introduced herself to Heracles, indicating an interest in the same kind of hospitality he had shown her sister. Naively good-natured, Heracles proved agreeable. Then, as soon as she left, a third daughter made her appearance, clearly seeking the same favors. Again Heracles chose not to risk offending one of his host's daughters by turning her away. And so it was that each of the fifty daughters of Thespios, save one, found her way that night to Heracles' bedchamber and left it in high spirits. The one who did not was a shy girl and did not feel herself equal to the adventure.

Early the next morning he went up into Mount Helicon and pulled up a wild olive tree by its roots and from its trunk fashioned himself a huge club that thereafter was to be his trademark. Club in hand, he picked up the trail of the lion from its kill of the night before and tracked it and slew it. He returned to Thespiai to show King Thespios his trophy before moving on. When nine months had passed, we are told, the forty-nine daughters of Thespios who had lain with Heracles brought forth sons. The eldest and the youngest each bore twins, so that there were fifty-one robust babies in all.

From Thespiai Heracles set out for Thebes to bring the huge lion's pelt as a gift to Amphitryon. As he came close to the city of his birth, he happened upon a party of Minyans bound from Orchomenos also for Thebes. The leader of the group, personal envoy of King Erginos, was an insolent fellow, quick with his tongue and short on manners.

"And what brings you to the city of Cadmos?" asked Heracles.

"A hundred of the king's finest cattle," snarled the envoy, "the annual tribute for our old king's death. Know you nothing of the villainy of these people, young peasant?"

"I know of their kindness to my family. That is all," Heracles told him.

The man sneered and spat on the ground. "A vile and base lot they are, all of them," he said and then launched into the story of how, a few years earlier, a Theban charioteer had struck Clymenos, then king of Orchomenos, with a stone. The resultant injury proved fatal. In vengeance Erginos, the king's son and successor, then mounted a campaign against the city of Cadmos and brought the Thebans to their knees. He completely disarmed the conquered city and demanded a hundred cattle each year in retribution for his father's death. "Tribute time has come again," said the envoy in conclusion, "and so I am obliged to enter this accursed city."

"All that for one stone from one man?" said Heracles.

"If it were my place to say," said the envoy, "I would demand a hundred ears and noses and hands as well."

Unable to abide the man's impertinence a moment longer, Heracles seized him and, with his own sword, clove off his ears and nose and both his hands. Nor did he stop until he had done the same to every man in the party. Each man's severed parts he afterwards strung together on a piece of rawhide and hung around his neck. "There," he told them, "you now have the tribute you wished. Take it to your monstrous King Erginos and bid him not to plague the Thebans any more with his contemptible envoys."

When Erginos demanded of Creon, who was now king of Thebes, that he turn over the perpetrator of this indignity, Heracles gathered the decorative weapons out of all the temples thereabouts and with them armed a small force of picked men. He then led his army to a narrow pass near Orchomenos and, posting his men on either side of it, there waited for King Erginos to begin his march against Thebes.

At the opportune moment, when the Minyans were in the pass, the Thebans broke from their ambush. The element of surprise helped, but the margin of victory was Heracles himself. In the tight quarters mass attack proved impossible; thus no more than ten Minyans were able to rush him at a time, odds he was able to manage with no great strain. Erginos himself felt the weight of his great club as did also not a few of his officers.

Heracles was given a hero's reception when he returned to Thebes. Among the gifts bestowed upon the young champion by King Creon was his own eldest daughter Megara. The two were married; and in due time, while Heracles continued to make successful sorties against the Cadmeans' enemies, Megara bore him three healthy sons.

None of the successes of Zeus's bastard son, however, escaped the ever hateful eye of Hera. Great malice welled in her heart until all at once she unleashed her pent-up ire by sending raging Madness, unmarried child of blackest Night, loathed by all the gods, upon the object of her relentless hate. At one moment Heracles was the soul of composure, model father and husband; the next a rabid demoniac.

He stood, we are told, before a fire about to burn offerings to his father Zeus, when suddenly he froze in place. Then, as his three little boys watched on, his eyes began to bulge and roll freely in their sockets; his great muscles tightened, his veins protruding like a network of purpled rope; foam oozed from his mouth and, streaked with blood, ran down into his beard. Throwing himself to the ground, he stripped off all his clothes and began to wrestle with phantom adversaries, babbling violent incoherencies all the while. Then leaping up, he demanded a crown, proclaiming himself triumphant in the bout that never happened.

"And now you, my enemies!" he cried, glaring at his sons, his eyes ablaze. Terror-stricken already, the children rushed for cover. One sought shelter behind a marble column and a second, the youngest, in his mother's robes. The third huddled, trembling like a beaten dog, beneath the altar.

Heracles, still foaming at the mouth, still unclothed, grabbed up his bow and arrows; and while all looked on in horror, he outmaneuvered and then sent a deadly shaft through the heart of the little boy behind the column. The child fell backward, drenching the ground about him with blood. Next he spotted his son beneath the altar and raised his bow. The boy broke from cover and, running to his father, clutched his knees and pled, "Oh, dearest Father, I am not your enemy. I am your son. Do not kill me!" But the demented Heracles imagined him a foe on the attack and with his club crushed the child's skull.

Megara tried to shield the flaxen-haired darling wrapped in her robes, but the bulbous eyes of his father spied him, and he too was dropped by an arrow through the heart. The crazed father then gathered up his sons' bodies, as one might the remains of poisoned predators, and cast them into the blazing fire. Two of the sons of Iphicles, his brother, he likewise slew and tossed to the flames before his madness passed and he came slowly once more back to his true senses.

When it was told him what he had done, the great son of Zeus at first protested that it could not have been so. Then, shown proof, he screamed mightily in his agony and wept so violently that there was no comforting him. Were he not restrained, he would have hurled himself into the same fire that consumed his sons. "Let me go from here," he cried. "Into some distant land let me go. My friends, my wife must never again look upon my cursed face. This city must not harbor the guilt of one who murdered flesh of his own flesh. Henceforth must I be banished and, if I live, live elsewhere."

For long he wandered before finally coming once more into the court of King Thespios. The tales of his madness had preceded him; and so Thespios, obliged to Heracles for several favors, was already prepared to offer rites of purification on his behalf if he should come that way. Once purified by his old friend, he next journeyed to Delphi to consult the oracle of Apollo as to where he should live.

In rare response the oracle's pronouncement was clear and unequivocal: "Go down to Argos, and there make Tiryns your home and Eurystheus your master. Ten labors shall he lay upon you. These you must perform. Then will your cleansing be complete and you will be made immortal."

# The Labors
# and Apotheosis
# of Heracles

Heracles went, therefore, into Argos and came to Mycenai, where Eurystheus, son of Sthenelos, was now high king. The man he found on the throne there was, to his mind, less than a man. In voice and body and carriage Eurystheus reminded him of a certain type of irritating woman he had occasionally come across and ever sought to avoid: plumpish about the cheeks and jowls, round-shouldered, yet fastidious and much given to assorted mannerisms and affectations, sniveling, squeaky-voiced, whiny, and inordinately pompous. It galled the mighty Heracles that he should be required to take such a man for his master.

Eurystheus at first approached the whole matter with an eye to his own amusement. As the oracle had prescribed, he installed Heracles as his liegeman over nearby Tiryns and then, for his first labor, sent him out into Nemea to the west of Mycenai to slay a lion that had been marauding the countryside thereabouts. But no ordinary lion was this one. Sired by the great monster Typhon and suckled by Selene, goddess of the moon, it was huge as an ox and had razor-sharp claws that could slice through thick bronze as though it were suet, though its own hide could never be penetrated by spear or blade.

When he came to Nemea, Heracles had no trouble picking up the great beast's trail. The torn bodies of men and animals were strewn about in its wake like debris from a flood. Coming upon a freshly slain shepherd, corpse still warm, blood not yet congealed, Heracles cautiously scanned the landscape until he glimpsed the huge lion near a cave in the distance.

Quickly he moved in and let loose a barrage of arrows, each one straight to the mark, though bouncing off as though it had struck a lion sculpted from granite. Seizing next his club, Heracles rushed the animal; but his blows, sufficient to shatter the skull of an elephant from beyond the Indos, had no more effect than a switch of laurel. The lion snarled and went into the cave.

It was a cave with two openings. With boulders and tree trunks Heracles quickly closed off the way by which the lion had entered and then went in himself through the other mouth. The cornered lion lunged at Heracles, but the hero leaped to the side and just as suddenly onto the great beast's back, locking his arms around its throat. In vain the lion struggled to free itself, while the mighty Heracles closed off its breath forever. With the animal's own claws he skinned it and afterward took the hide with part of the head attached to Eurystheus.

The lion skin so thoroughly frightened the Mycenaian king that he ordered Heracles to take it away and thereafter not to enter the city with the trophies of his labors. To protect himself further he commanded the royal smith to fashion a huge bronze urn and set it into the ground so that he might hide in it if his massive cousin ever ventured to terrorize him again. From then on Heracles wore the Nemean lion's skin as his armor, fitting the head part over his own head for a helmet. The hide was as impenetrable on him as it had been on its original wearer.

In the swamplands of Lerna, near the mouth of the River Inachos, not far to the south of Mycenai there existed a hideously vile creature called the Hydra. Also sired by the arch-monstrosity Typhon, this amphibious beast had nine heads, eight of which were mortal and the other one, in the middle, immortal. Its haunts were the sloughs, but at will it ravaged croplands and raided herds throughout the region. Through his herald Copreus (for Eurystheus no longer wished to give orders in person to Heracles because he frightened him so) the king sent word to Heracles that destroying the Hydra was to be his second labor.

Young Iolaos, the eldest son of Heracles' half-brother Iphicles, arrived in Tiryns at this time, offering himself in service to his uncle. Heracles made him his charioteer and, as a first test, had him drive him to the swamps of Lerna. It did not take them long to locate the Hydra's lair near the Springs of Amymone. Iolaos stayed with the chariot while Heracles shot burning brands into the den to force the monster out.

When the Hydra showed itself, Heracles leaped immediately upon it, grabbing its trunk with one arm and swinging his club with the other. Each blow landed true with awesome force. Nine times he wielded his mighty club, and nine Hydra heads he smashed like so many grotesque gourds growing on a common vine. Then, just as he supposed the task completed, he felt the monster's serpentine body entwine itself around him. At that same instant a huge crab, companion to the Hydra, clamped its needle-sharp pincers onto one of his feet.

In horror he then looked at what remained of the heads he had just destroyed. Out of each stump not one, but two new heads were rapidly emerging, each as large and hideous as the first. Raising his foot suddenly out of the water, he took careful aim at the great crab attached to it and killed it with no injury to himself. The Hydra, however, now had eighteen deadly, venom-spewing heads, each swaying from side to side like a cobra preparing itself to strike. "Iolaos! Iolaos!" he called to his nephew. "Bring fire! This beast cannot be stopped except by fire. Be quick, my lad!"

Iolaos, who had watched the Hydra's new heads sprout into place, quickly surmised his uncle's plan and lighted two torches at the fire Heracles had used earlier for his firebrands. He then rushed into the swamp with a torch in either hand. Once more with deadly accuracy the mighty son of Zeus drove his huge club against the monster's heads, crushing utterly each one in turn. As he did this, Iolaos darted in and seared the ragged stumps before any new heads could form.

The Hydra's immortal head Heracles severed with a sword and afterward buried beside the road to Lerna and placed a boulder over it. Thus with Iolaos's help he slew the Hydra and so completed his second labor. Before he left the scene, however, he ripped open the monster's body and tipped his arrows with its bile, the most potent of all poisons. Little could he have known then that he was preparing the way to his own death.

"My lord does not accept the slaying of the Hydra as one of your labors," Copreus told him upon his return to Mycenai.

"I have proof that it was done," objected Heracles.

"And he has proof that you needed help and did not perform the feat alone," the herald told him. "Another labor will be added in its place. Go now and capture the Cerynitian hind. Do so without shedding a drop of the magnificent animal's blood. This will be your third labor."

Heracles grumbled about the curse of serving one's inferiors and set out to find the famous deer. Though this hind was crowned with a pair of many-pointed golden antlers like a stag, we are told it was actually a doe, especially sacred to the goddess Artemis, with hooves of shiny brass, the swiftest of animals.

For a solid year Heracles chased her, ever behind her, keeping her ever on the move, until at last she showed signs of fatigue. To Mount Artemisios the sleek, dappled deer took him, Heracles slowly closing the distance between them, and then to the River Ladon. As the animal hesitated but the briefest of moments before testing the stream, Heracles loosed an unpoisoned shaft from his bow that pierced both her forelegs through the bloodless tissue between bone and sinew, thereby pinning them together.

Draping the hind across both shoulders, he then proceeded to retrace his steps back through Arcadia to Mycenai. As he made his way along a narrow, winding path down the side of Mount Artemisios, suddenly two figures appeared as if out of nowhere blocking his way. By her costume he quickly surmised the one was the goddess of the mountain, the other doubtless her brother Apollo. "Whose is the mortal hand that deigns to slay this sacred deer?" asked the goddess.

"None of this animal's blood have I spilt and none shall I spill," said Heracles.

"It is one of my free creatures, meant to run and not be carried," she said next.

"Not by my own choice, but by Eurystheus's you see this fine creature bound captive," Heracles told her. "It is a labor which at great Hera's instigation he has laid upon me. He is the master, I but the miserable slave who can do naught but as he commands."

Satisfied with Heracles' guiltlessness in the matter, the two deities stepped aside and let him pass, and so he brought the hind alive back to Mycenai. Presenting the animal to Copreus, he awaited instructions as to his next labor. "Skilled you are at taking animals alive," said the herald to him, after conferring with the king. "There is a vicious boar on Mount Erymanthos we have heard say. Its curved tusks have rent many an ox and made a goodly number of widows in those parts. Bring that beast here alive also."

It was now the dead of winter, and fresh snow at the higher altitudes made the animal easy to track. At length Heracles found the boar in a lair of heavy brush and by his thunderous shouts was able to scare it out. Chasing the huge beast into banks of drifted snow, he soon immobilized it and was able to tie its feet with chains. Then he dragged it all the way back to Mycenai.

Before he reached the twin-lion gate of Perseus's city, however, word came to him of the assembling of the Argonauts in Iolcos. He then lifted the boar to his shoulders and doubled his pace. While Eurystheus, who had been warned of Heracles' approach, peered out of his brass urn from under the barely uplifted lid, the huge bulk of a man lumbered hurriedly into the agora and tossed his twisted-tusked captive to the ground. Without giving Copreus a chance to tell him what to do next, he turned and sped off, a truant escaping drudgery for play, and never slackened his pace till he came to the shore where the *Argo* was just being eased into the water.

In the end, having but traded drudgery for drudgery and not a little heartache as well with none of the anticipated adventure, he returned after several months to Mycenai to inquire about his fifth labor. Irritated at his behavior, Eurystheus wished to humble his already legendary cousin and had had long to ponder the matter. With smug pleasure, then, he sent word through Copreus for Heracles to clean the dung from Augeias's cattle-yards as his next assignment. "And it all must be done in a single day," the herald told him.

Augeias, it seems, was the king of Elis and the owner of the largest herd of cattle in all of Greece. His father Helios had presented him with good breeding stock that were said never to know sickness and never to miscarry. At this time his herd numbered above five hundred bulls and not a few cows and calves watched over by each one of them. In all the years he was building his herd, Augeias did nothing about the huge quantities of manure that built up in the yards where he kept them. When the dung could no longer be turned under with a plow, it simply got deeper and deeper.

When he got to Elis, Heracles did not tell the king that he had been sent there by Eurystheus. Rather he inquired of Augeias about his cattle-yards as though the idea were his own. "Let me clean these yards for you," he said.

"For what price?" asked the king.

"One cow out of every ten," Heracles said to him. "If by the time your father's chariot has finished its trek across the heavens I am not done, my price will be but the pleasure of serving you."

Augeias roared in derision and quickly accepted the terms. Heracles then took himself immediately to the Alpheios and Peneios Rivers and set about digging ditches and building dams to divert the two streams into Augeias's cattle-yards. This done, he next dug ditches below the yards by which the water and refuse would be channeled back into the rivers and taken out to sea. Then he retreated to a high place to watch the torrents do his work.

In the meantime, Augeias found out that Heracles was acting under Eurystheus's orders, and so when the son of Alcmene came by at day's end for his promised wages the king would not give him so much as a stunted calf. "You were in another's hire," he told him, "not mine. And besides, I promised you nothing."

"Some more refuse needs to be cleansed from this land," Heracles replied, "but not now. I promise you I will be back."

Indignity was heaped on injury when he returned to Mycenai, for Eurystheus refused to accept the feat as one of the labors. "My master says you worked for wages. Whether you received them is not of his concern," Copreus told him. "Twelve labors then must you now complete and not ten. Stymphalos in Arcadia, we hear, is plagued by birds. As large as crows are these, more vicious than lions or leopards and far more dangerous to men. Their feathers, let you be warned, are all venomous darts, their beaks like well-honed spears. Your sixth labor is to free the land of these birds."

Because Heracles had to stay his distance from these winged nemeses and could not risk having them over his head, he was perplexed at first as to how to roust them from the heavily wooded, wolf-infested wilds where they took refuge. The bright-eyed Daughter of Zeus, however, came to his assistance with a large brazen rattle, so that he was able to stand upon the point of a mountain overlooking the place and create such clamor that the birds all took to the air. He then had little trouble picking them out of the sky with his unerring arrows. This proved to be his easiest labor so far.

Up to this point all of Heracles' labors took place in the Peloponnese. The next one, though, did not. Into distant Crete it took him, into the kingdom of the great Minos, for Eurystheus ordered him to bring back alive to Mycenai the magnificent white bull presented to Minos by Poseidon with which Pasiphae, Minos's wife, had later had intercourse. After siring the Minotaur monster on Pasiphae, the bull, no longer satisfied with the ordinary heifers of his herd, had gone on a mad rampage throughout the island, and none of Minos's hunting parties had yet been able to kill it, much less capture it alive. When Heracles told Minos his mission, the king was delighted. "I will give you my every assistance," he promised him.

Heracles, twice burned already, quickly declined. "It is something I must do alone," he said.

Though the great bull by this time was said to have belched fire, Heracles eventually tracked it down and, in a struggle that tested his every ounce of strength, prevailed over it. He took it securely fettered back to Eurystheus in Mycenai. From the turret of his urn the king peered out trembling at the monstrous white animal, then in his squeaky voice gave commands.

"The beast shall be Hera's," he said. "In her honor let it go free."

His order was obeyed without question, and the bull broke for the open countryside, goring not a few hapless Mycenaians en route. Thereafter it wreaked havoc in all parts of Argos and as far away as Marathon until Theseus finally captured it and sacrificed it to Apollo in Athens.

By this time Eurystheus was as thoroughly terrorized by his great, seemingly invincible kinsman as he was by the awesome trophies Heracles returned with from his labors. He was anxious to get him as far away and for as long as he possibly could. When, therefore, he was told of a stable of man-eating mares in Thrace, he immediately dispatched Heracles to raid the stables and return with the mares to Mycenai.

There were four mares in all, as it turned out, and they belonged to Diomedes, king of the Bistones, of the warlike Thracians one of the most savage tribes. The mares were held in check by heavy iron chains and ate from huge bronze mangers. And they did devour human flesh, unsuspecting strangers tossed to them by their master. Each had the teeth of a crooked-jawed wolf rather than those of an ordinary horse. The walls of their stalls were caked with human blood.

When he came into the land of the Bistones, Heracles had little trouble locating the stables where the flesh-eating horses were kept. What he found there was much as it had been described to him. Gore and blood indeed coated the walls, and in the hard-to-get-at corners of the bronze mangers were shreds of rotten human flesh. Careful not to get too close to the mares' heads, Heracles loosed them and started to drive them away.

At that moment, however, Diomedes and his guardsmen rushed in upon him. In the battle that ensued Heracles knocked the barbarian king unconscious with his club and set him before his own horses, which tore at his flesh until he was dead and then devoured him. Leaderless and horrified, his men were quick to retreat, nor did any of them pursue Heracles as he drove the savage animals before him all the way to Mycenai. The mares, their hunger satisfied for the time being, gave him no trouble either.

When Heracles was spotted by the Mycenaian watchmen while he was yet a great distance away, word was sent to Eurystheus, who immediately leaped into his protective urn. Heracles stopped a ways in front of the urn and, knowing the king was inside, called out, "Your horses, my lord."

"Free them," piped Eurystheus, too afraid this time even to lift the lid and peek out.

"They're man-eaters," warned Heracles.

"Free them," ordered the king again.

And so Heracles clapped his hands and sent the mares on their way. Fortunately they soon worked their way up into the wilds near Mount Olympos where beasts as savage as they preyed upon them and killed them.

Anxious to put yet more distance between himself and Heracles, Eurystheus next commanded him, through Copreus, to bring him the belt of Hippolyte, queen of the Amazons, who lived beyond Phrygia near the River Thermodon. Though he had promised the legendary belt to his daughter Admete as a gift, the cowardly king dared hope that at last he had come up with a labor from which his great cousin would not return. The Amazons, he had heard, were the most savage race on earth and by far the best warriors.

Heracles took with him on this labor his companion Iolaos and also a crew of able men, including Telamon of Aigina and Telamon's brother Peleus. Both had sailed with Jason on the *Argo* and knew the waters and lands into which they would be going. When, after many weeks, they arrived in the country of the Amazons, Hippolyte herself came down to the harbor to welcome them. Word of Heracles' exploits had preceded him, and she was most desirous of meeting him in person.

"And what famous quest takes you this time so far from Mycenai?" she asked Heracles, eyeing him approvingly.

Heracles glanced down at the belt with which she was girded. "A very small thing," he replied.

"How small a thing?" she asked.

"Small enough to fit around your waist," he told her. "Indeed it was for your belt Eurystheus sent me."

The Amazon queen laughed until all about her, including Heracles and his companions, also broke into laughter. "If you came all this way for my belt, then you certainly shall have it," she said, quickly unfastening the belt and handing it to him. "You sure there isn't something else?" she added coyly.

Hera, from her vantage point high atop Mount Olympos, looked on the scene aghast. What had been intended a most hazardous labor was turning out to be no labor at all. In the twinkling of an eye, in no time at all, she swept down to the harbor of the Amazons and disguised herself as one of the women. Mingling with the crowd that was looking on, she spread panic by saying, "The foreigners are after our queen. See, they're trying to get her into their ship. To arms, to arms! Stop the foreigners! Save our queen!"

And thus she stirred the Amazons to arm themselves with spears and bows and take to their horses. The Greeks saw them getting into attack formation. "It's a trick," cried one of them. "They mean to kill us." Then they too readied themselves for battle. A scuffle broke out between the men and women near the ship, and the horsewomen began their charge. Accusing her of treachery, Heracles himself slew the statuesque Amazon queen. Then, belt in hand, he ordered his men aboard the ship, and they rowed rapidly out of bowshot. Nor did they, though their hands began to blister, leave off their rowing until they were safely once more in familiar waters.

Upon his return to Mycenai Heracles gave Hippolyte's belt to Copreus, who in turn presented it to Eurystheus, who, as he had promised, made a gift of it to his daughter Admete. Word was then passed back down through the chain for Heracles to go next to Erytheia, an island in the Ocean Stream, farther from Mycenai to the west than the land of the Amazons to the east, where few men had ever gone and none had ever returned. There lived a man there named Geryon, the grandson of Oceanos himself, whose body had three trunks joined at the waist, each with its own set of arms and a separate head. In his possession was a herd of magnificently beautiful red cattle. Heracles' tenth labor was to bring these cattle back to Mycenai.

It took Heracles several months, traveling across Europe and encountering many strange and fearsome beasts on the way, to reach the strait where the Great Sea joins the Ocean Stream. There, we are told, he set up two pillars, one on either side of the strait, to mark the boundaries between Europe and Africa. He had no ship, however, to take him to Erytheia. As he sat on the rocks pondering what next to do, the hot afternoon sun threw down its rays relentlessly upon him. In anger and frustration he took aim at that great, bright, jewel-spangled, golden chariot and let loose a mighty shaft in futile gesture.

Helios glanced down over the chariot rail and saw him do it. "Great heart like that must be rewarded," he said and at the day's end presented the bold son of Zeus with a huge golden basin by which he could cross over to the island.

Upon disembarking, he lost little time finding the cattle. As he began to drive them down to the beach, however, Geryon came upon him, brandishing three spears at once. Heracles evaded his charge and, dodging about in a zigzag pattern, finally maneuvered himself into a flank position to the triple-bodied ogre. With a single swift arrow he then transfixed all three trunks, transporting Geryon almost instantly from the world of living men.

Upon reaching the mainland with Geryon's cattle, Heracles gave back to Helios the golden basin and proceeded to drive his booty cross country all the way to Mycenai. By then eight full years had passed since he first began his labors. Had not Eurystheus disallowed two of the ten labors, he would have then brought to an end his servitude to the whiny, much affrighted king. As it was, he had yet to perform two more feats.

Nothing did Eurystheus fear as much now as the day his renowned cousin would return from the last of his impossible errands. The most distant place of which Eurystheus had ever heard was the Garden of the Hesperides, where the Hesperides, the four daughters of Atlas, were said to be watching over the golden apples presented by Gaia to Zeus and Hera on their wedding day. "Go," he, therefore, commanded Heracles through Copreus, "to the garden of the Hesperides and bring me Hera's golden apples."

Not sure exactly where the Hesperides lived, Heracles set out first to find Nereus, the Old Man of the Sea, who could be made to divulge such information if one could only hold him in one of the many shapes he was wont to change into. The daughters of Zeus and Themis told Heracles where the aged sea god could be found, and so he went there and seized him while he slept. Nor would he release him till he told him what he needed to know. "Find the Garden of the Hesperides in the Land Beyond the North Wind," Nereus said to him.

Before proceeding to the Land Beyond the North Wind, however, Heracles, at his father's behest, went to the Caucasos Mountains where Prometheus was still chained to the rocks and the eagle still feasted daily upon his liver. Zeus had finally reached a concord with the Son of Iapetos and thus sent his son to release him. In exchange for his freedom Prometheus agreed at last to reveal to the Father of Gods and Men the terrible secret which could involve Zeus's downfall. With great pleasure Heracles tore the manacles from the arms and legs of man's greatest benefactor.

When Prometheus thanked the son of Alcmene and asked him where next he was bound, Heracles answered, "To the Garden of the Hesperides, to get the golden apples of Hera. Such is my last labor save one."

"Send rather my brother Atlas to fetch them for you," advised the wise Son of Iapetos. "His daughters are the apples' guardians, and so none can get them more easily than he."

Heracles remembered Prometheus's words when he came to the ends of the earth where great Atlas, damned by Zeus centuries before, was holding up the sky. "A boon I would ask of you, great, kind Titan," Heracles said. "At Eurystheus's command I must bring to him the golden apples presented by Gaia to Zeus and Hera on their wedding day. Your daughters, the Hesperides, I am told, have charge over them. Would you go to them and beg the apples in my behalf."

"Not with this blasted sky on my head," said Atlas. "One does not wander far with a burden like that."

"My neck is strong, my arms like steel," Heracles said. "I will relieve you while you are gone."

And so it was, as gingerly as two would pass a bowl brimful of rarest wine, Atlas transferred the firmament from his head and hands to Heracles'. Then he sped off to the Land Beyond the North Wind to the garden kept by his four lovely daughters, in the midst of which were Hera's three golden apples. His fatherly persuasion prevailed, and that very evening he was back at Heracles' side with the incomparable treasures. "This exchange suits me well," the Titan said. "Your task for mine—let us continue thus. You hold up the sky from now on, and I'll see what I can do for your Eurystheus."

"A marvelous suggestion," agreed Heracles. "Mine is the better end of the bargain you'll see. Never have I felt so rested in, lo, these nine years than right now. One thing I would ask, however, before you take upon you Eurystheus's miserable yoke."

"A parting favor I could hardly deny," said Atlas.

"The sky sits a little uncomfortably on my pate. Pray, hold it a moment while I get a piece of my lion's pelt with which to pad it," said Heracles.

Atlas gullibly set the apples on the ground and helped Heracles shift the sky back onto himself. The task accomplished, Alcmene's son gathered up the apples and, thanking his ally profusely, went on his way. Because the apples belonged to Hera, Eurystheus was afraid to receive them when Heracles, after more than a year, returned to Mycenai. Heracles, therefore, gave them to Athene, who took them back to Atlas's daughters and bade them watch them more carefully thereafter. Thus, nothing was changed by the year except that Heracles was one labor closer to being finished with his servitude.

There was no place left now on the face of the earth that the panicky Eurystheus could send his thrall and have any hope of his not coming back a more honored and seasoned champion than when he left. Therefore, he pondered long before sending Copreus to Heracles with his twelfth and final labor, doubtlessly inspired by Hera. "Send him into the kingdom of dark Hades where the sun never shines," he told his herald, "and bid him bring back the monstrous gate guardian Cerberos." Now Cerberos was a snake-tailed, three-headed brute of a dog, larger than any ox and, like the Nemean lion and the Hydra, was the offspring of the arch-monster Typhon and Echidne. No more vicious beast ever existed.

Hermes, who normally guided only dead men into the black regions below, was sent by Zeus to perform his office for Heracles, though much alive. Through the cavern at Tainaron, the portal of Orpheus and Theseus and Peirithoos earlier, the caduceus-carrying god led his father's prize mortal progeny into the dark confines of Hades' rich kingdom. At the River Styx the huge son of Alcmene glowered at Charon from beneath his lion's skin cowl, thereby terrifying the usually stolid, dour ferryman into giving him passage across to the other side with neither protest nor insistence on pay.

When Heracles stepped off the boat, most of the dead along the shore ran for cover at the sight of him. Only Meleagros and the Gorgon Medusa stood their ground. Medusa began to move toward him, and instinctively Heracles drew his sword to defend himself. "My silly half-brother," laughed Hermes, "do you think you're going to slay the dead?"

Embarrassed, Heracles sheathed his sword and proceeded down the broad, dank corridors until he came to where Theseus and Peirithoos sat in Hades' chair of forgetfulness. It was then, with the Lord of the Dead's permission, that he wrenched the king of Athens free. When Peirithoos stretched out his arms to be saved also, the foundations of the underworld shook as if from an earthquake, causing Heracles to think better of any temptation to effect a double rescue just then.

"What else brings my brother's son to this hateful clime?" then asked Hades.

"The great hell-hound Cerberos," replied Heracles, "for such has Eurystheus made my twelfth and final labor."

"If with neither spear nor sword nor heavily-knotted club you can take him," Hades said, "then the dog you may carry back to your master. At the gates of Acheron you will find him."

Wrapping the Nemean lion's skin around himself, Heracles then advanced toward those gates through which only the most courageous may pass. From the start he took the battle to the monstrous dog; and, presenting the animal's knifelike fangs with only the impenetrable pelt to bite down upon, soon he gained a stranglehold on that thick neck from which the three heads protruded. The beast's serpentine tail lashed out wildly to divert him but likewise wound up striking naught but the protective hide.

As a wild horse, its spirits broken by a master horseman, at day's end becomes obedient and gentle, even so did the monstrous Cerberos become docile in the grip of the mighty Heracles. He nonetheless so frightened Eurystheus when Heracles brought him back to Mycenai that on the third day afterward the shrill-voiced king was still trembling.

Though most anxious to pick up the threads of his life after twelve years of servitude to Eurystheus, Heracles was not comfortable about facing his wife Megara again, whose three sons by him he had slain in madness. He, therefore, gave her to Iolaos, his nephew and faithful charioteer with whom he had shared so much already. "Might your marriage to her be luckier than mine was," he told his young companion and then set about to look for a fresher, more fortuitous bride for himself.

And so it was he came to Calydon, where once the cream of Greek manhood hunted the boar that was as big as an elephant. Oineus was still king there as in the days when Meleagros, his son, slew the boar and soon thereafter died himself because of strife over the hunt's trophies. There was also a daughter in the family, named Deianeira, who, but a tot at the time of the great boar hunt, had by now blossomed into beauteous womanhood.

All other suitors quickly withdrew from their courtship when the famous son of Alcmene entered the scene—all, that is, save one. Acheloos, a powerful shape-changing river god of the region, was not so easily discouraged and did not shy from provoking his foreign rival.

"Make me your son-in-law, good Oineus," entreated the huge river deity, "for then your grandsons will have divine blood flow through their veins."

"Nay," said Heracles, "choose me. Better that the divine blood have some part of Zeus than an overgrown water sprite. By the great Father of Gods and Men was I begot and by his white-armed wife made to endure my labors."

"Zeus, he claims, begot him. If so, that makes his mother an adultress," said the river god, "and himself a common bastard. If it isn't so, he's an impious liar. Either way, a sorry choice for son-in-law."

"My hands speak better answers than my tongue," was all that Heracles then responded as he lowered his shoulder and lunged at the huge glib god. By reason of bulk alone Acheloos withstood the charge. Again and again Heracles threw himself against the massive form, but, as a limestone cliff bears the relentless pounding of the surf, even so did the river god stand immovable against the tree-bending thrusts of Heracles.

Then, rather than charge head-on, Heracles slipped to Acheloos's side and leaped upon his back quickly wrapping his mighty arms around his adversary's throat. Acheloos struggled to break the hold but could not. Thereupon, he reverted to his shape-changing magic and, turning himself into a slender serpent, slithered successfully free of Heracles' grasp. Then he coiled and, with split tongue darting out between his fangs, prepared to strike.

Heracles roared at once with laughter. "In my crib," he said, "I throttled two the likes of you. Compared with the great Hydra, with nine coils more fierce than your one, you are no serpent at all, only a paltry imitation of one."

With that, faster than a flash of his father's lightning, he grabbed the weaving serpentine shape just below the head with one hand and quickly brought the other around it as well, boring his fingers like powerful talons into the supple, scaly throat. Acheloos changed himself then into a raging bull.

Again the great Heracles jeered. "Mean you to frighten me?" he said. "A sickly, new-sprung calf you are, compared to the majestic Cretan beast I delivered to Eurystheus."

Acheloos snorted and charged. Heracles leaped to the left, barely avoiding one of the handsomely curved horns, then threw himself full-weight onto the god-animal's back. Seizing one horn in both hands and using it as a lever against Acheloos, he turned his neck so that he fell sideways to the ground. The horn stuck fast into the earth like a bronze-tipped javelin; then for a trophy Heracles ripped its mate from the god's bovine head. Acheloos thereupon yielded and went back to his river.

Thus it was that Heracles won the lovely Deianeira to be his wife—and with her father's heartiest blessings, for with the mighty son of Zeus in his family Oineus dared assert himself against all his enemies. And cheerfully Heracles obliged his new father-in-law. It was not long, though, before fate forced the luckless champion from that land also; for when at dinner one evening the serving boy chanced to spill some water on him, Heracles in reprimand rapped the boy on the side of the head with his knuckles. Unfortunately he misgauged his strength and crushed the poor cupbearer's skull. Although the boy's father accepted his son's death as an accident, under the law Heracles had to go into exile. He chose to make his home next in Trachis.

It was flood-time when Heracles and Deianeira set out from Calydon to Trachis. Winter rains had converted the narrowest mountain rills into raging torrents and low-lying meadows into marshes. The Euenos River, when the two came upon it, was a full mile wide. Swift, dark waters created rises and troughs midway between the banks and sped uprooted trees and other debris downstream. While Heracles, confident of his own powers to negotiate the river, pondered how best to get Deianeira safely across, the Centaur Nessos galloped up to them.

"Let me be of service," he volunteered. "You swim to the far bank yourself, and I will bear your lady there upon my back. For this purpose have the gods stationed me here."

His manner was disarming, and so Heracles thanked him. Then throwing his weapons clear across the swollen river, he said, "See you on the other side," and dove into the raging waters. With powerful strokes he mastered the current and in a brief span pulled himself up on the distant bank.

"Help! Rape!" he then heard his wife's voice scream. He turned, and there, still on the opposite bank, the lusty Nessos was beginning to mount Deianeira, struggling, screaming, her clothes torn away.

"Gloat not, wanton freak!" he yelled over the waters. "Your prize, so close, is not yet won, nor will it be. My arrow will see to that." He then quickly drew his bow and sent an arrow across the river deep into the middle of Nessos's back.

As Heracles swam cross-current back to his wife, the Centaur, feeling the burning, biting Hydra's venom shoot through his veins, knew his time was brief. Bent on vengeance, he turned to his victim. "It is right that I die," he said to her. "Your beauty bewitched me, and passion overruled my better nature. So that you remember me kindly, let me bestow a favor on you." He then caught in a small bronze urn some of his blood, already as deadly as the gall that infected it, and mixed with it an equal portion of his spent seed.

"If ever the great Heracles grows weary of your love, make a solution of this potion and soak in it one of his garments, something worn close to the skin," he instructed her. "When he puts it on, he will be consumed with an ardor that will burn the rest of your lives." Deianeira took the potion and put it with her belongings, saying nothing of it to her husband when he got back to where she was.

Heracles and Deianeira were heartily welcomed at Trachis. As at Calydon, the son of Alcmene gladly took on all the enemies of the realm and prevailed against them. Almost single-handedly he conquered the Dryopes and then the Lapiths, led in Peirithoos's absence by the haughty Coronos. He also fought hand to hand against the mighty Cycnos, son of Ares, whom he killed. Then he battled to the death Amyntor, king of Ormenion, who sought to keep him from returning triumphant back to Trachis. After that into the Peloponnese he went in his own behalf to avenge himself against Augeias, king of Elis, whose cattle-yards he had cleansed and who would not give him his promised due.

His last campaign after many years, was against the Oichalians. This too was a mission of vengeance, for Eurytos, king of Oichalia, had also in the past played him false. "When I return to Trachis," he told Deianeira as he bade her farewell, "it will be never to leave the city nor you ever again. My ventures as well as my labors will finally be over." The two by this time had four sons and a daughter, and the prospect of spending his middle years with his family was not in the least an unpleasant one.

Fifteen months passed between the time Heracles and his small army set out for Oichalia and the time they once more came into view of Trachis. Though lengthy, the campaign had been successful. Sending a messenger on ahead into the city, Heracles himself went down to the beach to prepare a thank offering to his father Zeus for their safe return. "Tell Deianeira I am on my way," he told the herald, "and to send me my tunic so that I may offer up the oxen in proper dress."

No longer the ravishing beauty that she was when first she caught Heracles' eye, Deianeira had for some time now harbored misgivings as to whether she could continue to hold her husband's interests. Her great fear was that he might find a captive maiden who would please him more than she. Nor had their months apart diminished her anxieties in this regard. And so for that reason, when the herald came to her announcing Heracles' return and requesting that she send along his tunic, she did not give the garment to him right away. First she went to where she had hidden the small bronze urn containing Nessos's blood and semen. From that potion she made a solution in which she saturated her husband's tunic. And only after it had dried did she give it to the messenger to take to Heracles.

By the time the tunic finally arrived, Heracles had already slaughtered twelve bulls and enough other cattle to bring the number to an even hundred. He had also prepared a huge altar and upon it placed heaps of dried, pitch-saturated pine. Donning now his tunic, he made prayers to his father Zeus and the eleven other undying Olympians. Then he laid the torch to the wood upon the altar. Bright red and orange flames leaped up to consume that part of the offering appointed by Zeus as the gods' portion.

The light and heat of the fire also activated the poison in Heracles' tunic. Quickly it attacked his skin, at the same time bonding the tunic to his body as though anointed with a powerful resin. Great droplets of sweat gathered on his forehead. Suddenly he shrieked as shocks of pain shot to his bones. He grabbed at the garment to rip it free, but it was as a sculpted cloak upon a sculpted figure, of one substance with the burning, pain-ridden flesh from which he tried to loose it.

"With which of my enemies did you consort to do this?" he demanded of the herald, seizing him at the ankle.

"From Deianeira I received the cloak, none other," said the luckless man.

"She then has murdered me!" he cried out. "May she be forever cursed!" Impulsively, angrily, crazed by his agony, he hurled the herald into a huge, storm-worn rock that jutted in from the sea.

The onlookers gasped in horror and pulled back. As his pain became more intense, more profuse, Heracles threw himself to the ground and then into the air, screeching, bellowing, crying so that the cliffs on either side of the strait echoed and reechoed with his screams of torment.

When word came to Deianeira that Heracles was slowly dying because of the poisoned tunic, she understood too late the foul Centaur's caprice. Into their bedchamber she ran and spread fresh sheets upon their marriage bed, hot tears coursing down her face all the while. "Never again, dear husband, will I know your love between these sheets," she cried. "Farewell, bed of joy, now of sorrow!" Her weeping now beyond control, she tore off her robe and, holding a short, double-edged sword to her breast, with both hands drove it swiftly into her lungs and heart.

Heracles, in the meantime, writhed in unendurable agony. His screams, at once terrifying and pathetic, were now louder than ever as the poison penetrated his every part. He was a man on fire though not yet consumed. No one stood near him. "My son, my son," he called out to Hyllos, his oldest. "Have pity. Draw your sword and in mercy cut short your father's torment." Then he blared forth again in his pain so that the very trees for miles around, already bereft of birds, quavered as if in terror.

"I cannot be your slayer, dear father," said the boy. "Do not ask that I pollute my hands with your blood."

"Build then for me a pyre," commanded Heracles. "Make a mountain of logs and limbs and scattered branches, and atop it lay this tortured mass of flesh."

"As you say," said the boy, "but do not ask me to light the fire."

Another spasm of pain at that moment shot through the great body of Heracles. He quivered as if in convulsions, stiffened suddenly, and then shrieked so loudly that his children back in the city, who had just discovered their mother's corpse, looked up in alarm from the bloodied spectacle before them. When the spasm passed, he said to Hyllos, "Be quick, my son. Some kind soul other than you can lay the torch."

Hyllos quickly set about doing as his father commanded. When with the help of those about he had finished building the pyre, he and some others lifted Heracles onto it. "Now bring on the torches!" cried the pain-ridden son of Alcmene.

But no one would do it. All alike shared Hyllos's reluctance to kill, even in mercy, their dear friend and oft-times benefactor, the greatest man to have ever lived. It so happened, however, that a shepherd by the name of Poias, together with Philoctetes, his young son, had been keeping watch over their flocks in the area and came near to the pyre.

"Good stranger, have pity!" Heracles cried out. "Light this fire, which my friends are loath to do. My bow, my quiver of arrows will I bequeath to you."

Poias then beckoned to his son. "In mercy do as he says," he told the boy. And so it was that the lad Philoctetes lit the great pile of tinder on which the great Heracles lay. Tall flames soon leaped about the hero's body, all but obscuring him from those who groaned and wept with remorse around the pyre. While they watched, we are told, a dark cloud descended from heaven, enveloping both Heracles and the pyre itself. Then suddenly a brilliant shaft of lightning ripped into the midst of the cloud, accompanied by an ear-rending blast of thunder. When the cloud lifted, all that remained were a few scattered ashes.

His mortal parts now burned free, Heracles was spirited quickly to Mount Olympos to join the company of the undying gods. Hera, throughout his life his most unrelenting enemy, was among the first to welcome him—and not without good reason; for, it seems, the Giants, generated by Gaia to wreak vengeance on Zeus and his brothers for their treatment of the Titans, had now after all these years acquired the size and audacity to march against the Olympians.

"Harken to me," said the Queen of the Gods, rising up to prophesy. "The Giants approach, and against them will our weapons prove little better than useless. Only by one of mortal roots in awesome lion's skin clad can these be slain, though not even by him in the countries of their births."

Even as she spoke, the Giants came into view. They were far more massive than the Titans. Like primeval beings, their heads and necks were covered with long, thick hair, and their feet had scales like those on the feet of lizards. Pinnacles of mountains and rocky cliffs they broke off and hurled before them. Also, uprooting broad oak trees, they ignited them and tossed them as fiery brands into the Olympian ranks. More formidable were the Giants than anything Heracles had ever seen, indeed more formidable than anything Zeus had ever seen either.

Heracles drew his bow against their leader. The Giant fell but quickly stirred again once he was sprawled out upon the ground. "This must be the country of his birth," shouted Athene. "Drag him beyond its borders." Heracles did so before the Giant quite recovered, and, sure enough, beyond the border the huge frame went limp and died.

In the meantime another of the monstrous beings had moved in on Hera. Eros, seeing him charge, let go a shaft at the Giant's heart. It struck true but had the effect of inflicting passion rather than mortal injury, and so the Giant quickened his pace and commenced to tear the robe from Hera's back. As he grabbed her to force her, she screamed. Heracles, just returning, heard the scream and sent an arrow into the Giant's throat in the nick of time to spare the Olympian queen's honor.

Zeus elsewhere, using his heaviest thunderbolts, slowed the advance of the main force of Gaia's sons. The Giants, when struck by the cliff-shattering blows, staggered and dropped; soon, however, shaking off the effects, they drew themselves unsteadily to their feet once more to resume their assault. Apollo stood beside his father, sending his slender silver shafts unerringly into the Giant's eyes and broad nostrils, while Poseidon and Dionysos helped hold them at bay with trident and thyrsus. Athene hurled a handy mountain at one, and Hephaistos poured a crucible of molten iron onto another. With bronze clubs and blazing torches the other Olympians entered the fray to stave off the attacking latter-day Sons of Gaia.

"Come here!" the gods shouted to Heracles whenever they toppled one of the Giants, and quickly would he hasten to the place to loose the fatal arrow or crush the monstrous skull with his many-knotted olivewood club, just as another divine voice would ring out, "Quick! Over here!" Some, like the first, he had to drag into adjacent countries before they would die. At day's end, though, all twenty-four of the super-beings lay dead.

And thus it was that Heracles, greatest of men, earned the undying gratitude of the gods as well and was given Hebe, the daughter of Zeus and Hera, to be his eternal bride. Hera, because he had saved her from ravishment, took him to her heart and counted him thereafter the dearest of all to her save Zeus himself. He had indeed become, as his name indicated, the glory of Hera.

# Prelude to
# the Trojan War

T here was a wide spot on the Eurotas River where the waters ran calm and the bank was carpeted with thick, tender grass. It was a secluded area, and on hot Spartan summer afternoons Leda, incomparably beautiful wife of King Tyndareus, would come there with her attendants to bathe. For fear of the king no man ever dared come near the place. After enjoying the refreshing water, Leda would sit or lie on the bank and let the sun perform its duty of drying her perfect skin.

The fact that no man ever ventured into this area does not mean, however, that the lovely Leda went unobserved by male eyes; for far away, atop Mount Olympos, the eagle-eyed Son of Cronos turned his gaze southward on those sultry afternoons and seldom left off looking until Leda had dressed and was heading home.

One day, when his desire for what he saw became overwhelming, Zeus took himself down to that wide spot on the Eurotas. In an instant he did this, faster than one of his eagles can dive from the sky to fasten its talons into an unsuspecting hare or a fox cub that has strayed too far from its den. As soon as he touched the water, upstream a ways from the bathers, the great cloud-gathering god transformed himself into a large, handsome, majestic swan.

Casually crisscrossing the pool from one side to the other, Zeus made his way unmenacingly ever and ever closer to Leda and her maidens, who were now lounging on the grassy bank. All eyes were soon upon him, for never for grace and beauty had they seen such a swan. Leda in particular was rapidly coming under his magic, desiring to run her hands over the inviting snow-white feathers, to feel the soft downy breast against her bosom; her breathing became pronounced and quick. Had she been asked, she could not have described the strange power the swan had over her, and surely she would have blushed if she had tried.

When the enchantingly lovely creature came up to her, she reached out her hand to touch his extended neck, then let her hand fall slowly, caressingly to his back. The swan, drawing closer, indeed almost on top of her, brushed her cheek with his bill, to which she responded by stroking the feathers along his back with both hands, virtually embracing the magnificent white bird. In return he quite enveloped her in his huge, soft wings, his head now pressed firmly against hers.

Thus in guise as a swan the lusty Zeus accomplished his purpose upon the beautiful wife of Tyndareus. By the time she first sensed his intent, she was so drawn into his spell that neither could she resist him nor did she wish to, but let him have his way. Nine months later, we are told, she gave birth to a very large egg.

The egg was cracked open, and out rolled two babies, a girl and a boy. Tyndareus, owning the children as his own (though the circumstances gave him cause to wonder), named the little girl Helen and the boy Polydeuces. Later on that same day, because she had lain also with her husband the same night after Zeus had taken her, Leda brought forth two other babies, another girl and another boy. The one Tyndareus called Clytaimestra and the other he called Castor.

Even as an infant Helen possessed a beauty worthy of both her parents. The years only added to it. As a delicate flower manifests promised splendor at first bud and at each stage of bloom dazzles the eye even more than at the stage before until every perfect petal unfolds in full blossom, even so did the child Helen pass from beauty into beauty. Before the flower had scarce begun to open, her fame had spread to all parts of Greece.

When she was twelve years old, Theseus came with his boon companion Peirithoos to catch the Spartans unawares and seized the pulchritudinous princess and carried her off to Athens. There he entrusted her to his mother Aithra for two years, and in that time he did not violate her because she was still a child and he was fifty. Rumor was, however, that before her brothers Castor and Polydeuces rescued her, Helen had bloomed sufficiently so that Theseus thought it not unseemly to bear the blossom away.

Tyndareus, with the girl (more bewitchingly beautiful than ever before) once more under his roof, was not a little alarmed at what the future years might bring. Already her beauty had brought much danger and grief to his kingdom. When the gallants of Greece came courting her, as surely they would, how would he keep them, he wondered, from each other's throats as well as his own?

His resolution to the dilemma seemed inspired. As the suitors showed up, he required that each one swear to this oath: "Regardless of whom Tyndareus's daughter takes for husband, him will I defend. Should ever anyone lay hands upon her and spirit her away, I vow hereby to march against that man with all my forces and lay his city, be it Greek or foreign, in utter ruin."

Odysseus, prince of Ithaca, came to pay court, as did also Diomedes, whose formidable father Tydeus had fallen in the assault of the Argives against the seven gates of Thebes. Antilochos, son of Nestor, arrived from Pylos and Idomeneus from Crete and Philoctetes, who possessed the bow and arrows of Heracles, from Thessaly. Ajax and Teucros, sons of the great Telamon, came also as well as Ajax, son of Oileus, and Patroclos, son of Menoitios, and scores of others, all hoping desperately to win the now legendary beauty. Not least to come to Sparta to vie for Helen's hand was Menelaos, whose brother Agamemnon, king of Mycenai, was already married to Clytaimestra, Helen's sister.

All alike were required to put their signatures to the oath of Tyndareus and swear to it with libations and solemn clasps of hands and also to honor the choice made by the girl and her father. In the end Tyndareus chose Menelaos, the son of Atreus, and after the wedding installed his new son-in-law as king of Sparta in his own stead.

At about the same time that Leda was carrying the egg from which Helen and Polydeuces were hatched, far across the Aigean Sea in the city of Troy, near the narrows where the Aigean and Propontis are joined and where the Scamandros and the Simois Rivers run down to the sea, another queen also carried a child within her womb. She was Hecabe, wife to Priam, king of that thriving and wealthy land.

One night shortly before her confinement, Hecabe beheld a terrible vision in a dream. The issue of her womb, it seemed, turned out not to be a child but a flaming firebrand which tore madly through the city setting all the buildings ablaze. Fires shot to the sky in every sector until at last Troy itself seemed one massive inferno. She woke from the dream trembling and screaming. Priam, her husband, asked to know what was wrong, and she related the nightmare to him in detail.

That next morning Priam went to the seer Aisacos to discover the meaning of the ominous dream. With visible alarm Aisacos listened to the king's account of the nightmare, which at every point was just what

Hecabe had told him. "The child will bring down the city!" said the seer, when Priam had finished. "Kill him! Should the babe in Hecabe's womb live to be a man, I tell you, Troy will surely burn as in the dream."

And so it was that when the baby, a robust boy, was born, King Priam gave him to his herdsman Agelaos. "To the slopes of Mount Ida take the infant and leave him," he instructed him. "It is better that my son should die than that the whole city should be destroyed."

The shepherd did as he was told; but when he returned after five days to the barren place where he had exposed the child, he was amazed to find him alive and in the pink of health. A she-bear, it seems, had found him and given him suck. Too kindhearted was Agelaos now to take further measures to kill the baby. "And what," he wondered, "if the gods for some reason have thus spared his life?" Therefore, he took him to his hut and raised him as his own son and called him Paris.

As he grew older, Paris stood taller than the other shepherd boys who sported themselves among the vales and pastures of Mount Ida. Nor was any as comely or strong as he. When he became a man, he took as his wife Oinone, a water nymph upon whom the god Apollo had bestowed wondrous powers of healing; and until the day he was visited by the three goddesses, Paris lived as Nature's own prince, at one with beast, earth, stream, the very air itself. His life was joyous, idyllic, innocent as were the lives of men in the Golden Age when Cronos still ruled the heavens and war was yet unknown.

The event that precipitated the eventual coming together of the handsome, stalwart shepherd prince and the most beautiful woman in the world occurred far away from both, in Thessaly on Mount Pelion, before either had yet been weaned. This event was the wedding of Jason's un-dauntable shipmate Peleus and the sea nymph Thetis.

Prometheus's long-kept secret involving Zeus's undoing, it seems, was simply that Thetis would one day bear a son greater than his father. Upon his release by Heracles, the far-sighted Titan at last revealed this to the Father of Gods and Men, who for centuries now had, it so happened, been eyeing the lovely nymph, fully intending at the opportune time to compromise her. Divine sweat, we are told, suddenly stood out on Zeus's forehead as he pondered Prometheus's words. It was then, lest in a moment of weakness he succumb to temptation, that the Lord of Olympos decided to find Thetis a mortal husband whose son by her would be of no threat to the gods. His choice was Peleus.

The wedding of Thetis and Peleus was like no other. A much relieved Zeus saw to that. Not since the marriage of Cadmos and Harmonia had all the gods and goddesses gathered to celebrate the wedding of a mortal, and never would they do so again. It was held in a lush valley on Mount Pelion, a natural paradise, and even the minor deities, save for Eris, the Goddess of Discord, were invited and came, bearing the happy couple gifts such as only gods can come by.

Ganymede, it is said, poured the wine. Flutes and lutes and pipes were played. The hills and woods echoed each perfect note orchestrated by the Muses themselves in live performance; their hair shimmered in the sun, their golden slippers glistened as the greatest of greats all listened, spellbound, to the bridal song. So sweet was the melody that mermaids danced in circles out at sea.

There was laughter and merriment and more song, and then toasts were offered to the here and hereafter, the grandest by Cheiron. "To a noble couple," said the Centaur, "and to their more noble son. The pride of Thessaly will he someday be. In time to come his legend will be told, written, painted, sung by everyone the whole world over."

Spirited cheers went up from the gods and goddesses when Cheiron finished his toast, and cups were raised in gay approval. Then, all of a sudden, a great hush fell over the festive, jubilant throng, for into their midst, with mischief in her eyes, strode the slighted, uninvited Eris. With underhand motion she sent a glittering, shiny orb spinning, rolling along the ground to where the bride and groom, flanked on either side by the twelve great Olympians, were seated. Just as suddenly then she left.

The shiny object was a golden apple. Upon signal from Zeus, Hermes picked it up and read the inscription on it: "To the fairest of all." In an instant every goddess within earshot rushed to the table to claim the prize. No one after that, we are told, gave any more thought to Thetis and Peleus.

Of the many and beautiful goddesses who laid claim to the golden apple, only three were powerful enough to remain for long in contention for it: Hera, Athene, and Aphrodite. Weeks went by, and none of the three yielded to either of the other two. Nor was Zeus nor any of the other gods so foolish as to take sides in the matter.

Weeks passed into months and months into years, and after twenty years the three beautiful, vain goddesses still strove the one against the others for possession of the apple. "Enough of this!" said finally the Father of Gods and Men. "Go, the three of you, with Hermes into Phrygia and find there on the Gargaron Peaks of Mount Ida a young herdsman named Paris. Let him judge whose the apple will be. Since I love you all equally, I must defer the decision to him. For my part I wish you all could win."

And so it was that one morning, accompanied by wing-sandaled Hermes, Hera and Athene and Aphrodite came to where Paris kept watch over his flocks. In order not to frighten the handsome mortal, they approached him on foot. Hermes spoke first. "Good day, young man," he said.

"Good day," returned Paris. "Who, pray tell, are you, my good man? And these lovely maidens? They seem far too stately and fair to be hiking in these mountains."

"Permit me to introduce the lovely maidens, good Paris," said Hermes next. "This is Hera, this Athene, and this Aphrodite. Oh, do not tremble, sir. Zeus has appointed you to choose which of the three is the most beautiful. Please note the inscription on this apple. Then judge whose it will be."

Paris took the golden apple and examined the inscription. "How shall I, a mere mortal and a lowly shepherd at that, presume to judge such peerless beauty? You will find better judges among those who are city bred. Bring me two goats and I can judge the better beast, or two heifers, but to judge the unending beauty I now gaze upon—that, my fellow, is quite beyond me."

"Well spoken, good Paris," replied Hermes, "but you must judge nonetheless—by command of Zeus. You have no choice but to obey."

"Then let not the losers avenge themselves against me or my people," said the son of Priam.

"Agreed," Hermes said, and the three goddesses assented with nods.

"Very well," said Paris. "Now must I judge on the basis of what I see, or am I permitted to see more? It is, after all, the beauty of their bodies you wish me to judge and not the beauty of their clothes."

"You may see all you desire."

"In that case," said the shepherd prince, warming up to his office, "I must see all. If you would have me judge which of you deserves this golden apple, my lovely goddesses, I must ask you to take off all your clothes so that I might the more fairly take into account that beauty which is now hidden."

Hermes at this point prudently turned his back to the others. Hera, who had never in her immortal life disrobed in front of anyone except her husband Zeus, began to take the brooches out of her gown. "You shall see," she said, as she brushed the gown from her shoulders, "that more than my arms and eyes are fair to look upon. Every inch of me is beautiful. See."

"And you next, fair Aphrodite," said Paris.

Athene quickly interposed herself between Paris and the laughter-loving goddess. "Have her take off her magic girdle first," she insisted. "If she does not, she will bewitch you with its spell. The contest must be fair. And look, if you will, at the way she's painted herself up like a whore. She should remove some of that stuff too."

"Why, of course, we must be fair," said Aphrodite, undoing her wondrous girdle. "So while we are at it, why don't you take off that helmet of yours and treat us to your hairdo rather than that gaudy plume."

Helmet and girdle fell to the ground at the same instant, followed quickly by Aphrodite's thin shift on top of her girdle. Athene, less practiced, was slower shedding her clothes, but in the end managed quite well. Her fumbling with her various straps only added to the pleasure Paris was finding in his assignment. When the three goddesses were all stripped in front of him, each standing erect and posing to show her perfect body to best advantage, Paris could but cast his eyes rapidly from one to the other to the other and then back again, trying to take them all in together but unable to do so.

Decisions of such a nature are never made in haste. Throughout the day the handsome rustic prince labored at his chore, at times standing far back from the three, cocking his head now this way and now that, trying to determine if there was any angle or distance from which any of the divine figures seemed less than perfect, and at times inspecting each up very close, as a jeweler might examine a rare gem, so as to give proper value to complexion, coloring, subtle curvatures, pores, and the likes as well. "So much beauty I cannot take in all at once," he finally said. "I must see each of you apart from the others. Hera, heaven's queen, let you be first."

Athene and Aphrodite withdrew to a nearby grove, leaving Paris alone with Hera. The young shepherd resumed his thoughtful inspection, which, though now more focused, he undertook with no less care and thoroughness than earlier. "When you have finished scrutinizing me, my good man," Hera said to him, "you may give some thought as to your reward should you happen to bestow the apple upon me. Do take your time though. I'm in no hurry."

"Rewards are out of the question," Paris told her.

"You called me heaven's queen, and so I am. Every kingdom under heaven is at my disposal. Choose me, and I will make you the lord of all Asia."

"No rewards," he told her again. "I must judge on beauty alone."

Next to be viewed individually by Paris was bright-eyed Athene.

"Wisdom and warfare are my specialties," she mentioned casually as he conscientiously went about his duties. "If you chance to award the golden apple to me—and most justly, I might add—I would make you of all men the wisest and give you such prowess in battle that you should always be the victor."

"Neither king nor warrior am I," Paris replied. "Your gifts would be of little use to a shepherd's son. It matters little anyway. I must judge as I think right. For beauty and only that will I bestow the golden apple."

Aphrodite was last to be inspected alone. Paris gave her the same meticulous attention he had given the other two—if anything, perhaps a little more. "Look closely. Miss nothing," she encouraged him. "Which pose pleases you more. This or this? There's no need to hurry, my beautiful young fellow. I've plenty of time. Oh yes, I've certainly noticed how handsome you are—the handsomest man without a doubt in all of Asia. Too bad to waste it all on cows and sheep, when you'd make even Helen's head spin. You have heard of Helen, have you not?"

Paris told her he had not.

"The most beautiful woman in the world—very much the image of me, in fact. Oh, she would be most susceptible to your charms, my gorgeous fellow. Look upon me. Would you not like to lie down each night with the likes of what you now feast your eyes upon? Yes, examine me closer. Don't be shy. That's right. Look very, very carefully."

"Is this Helen married?" Paris wanted to know.

"To Menelaos, king of Sparta, a rather dull fellow," she told him. "For you she would drop him in an instant and sail off with you to be your wife. I can assure it. Such things are in my control."

"I fear I love this Helen already," said Paris.

"Then she shall be your present from me. The love of the world's most beautiful woman and a blissful marriage to her—such are my gifts to you in exchange for one small apple."

"Swear to it."

"By the River Styx, it shall be as I have said."

"Here then, take the apple," said Paris. "It is yours."

Not long after this incident, some servants from Priam's house came to Agelaos to fetch a bull to be the winner's trophy at the annual funeral games for the king's son, now long dead (or assumed to be). They chose the finest bull of the herd, one Paris particularly prized. Reluctant to give up the animal, Paris decided to enter the games in hopes of winning the bull himself. "We have plenty of other bulls in our herd," said Agelaos, trying to dissuade him.

"But only one like that," countered Paris. "Besides, this will give me a chance to test my skills against others."

In the end Paris went to Troy, and the now aged Agelaos went with him. First he entered the boxing lists and by sheer strength prevailed over those far more skilled in the sport than he himself. After that, in contention with some of the king's own sons, notably Hector and Deiphobos, he won the footrace. Another race was called for, and he won that one as well. So humiliated was Deiphobos to be beaten by a commoner, and a mere oaf from the country at that, that he drew his sword to kill Paris, who leaped immediately to the altar of Zeus for sanctuary.

"Stop him!" cried Agelaos, running to Priam. "For the one he seeks to kill, great king, is also your son, though long thought dead."

Cassandra, Priam and Hecabe's prophetic daughter, confirmed the fact that Paris was indeed the long-lost son of the royal couple. (In matters of fact Cassandra was sometimes believed; in matters of prophecy never.) Joyous celebration marked every sector of Troy for days afterward. A magnificent banquet was ordered by Priam, and hecatombs were offered up in thanksgiving upon the altars of the gods as when a war is won and the city's spearmen return triumphantly home.

The jubilant king and queen quite forgot Hecabe's terrifying dream and the prophecy attending it. When reminded, Priam could but say, "What is Troy that it should stand at the expense of this, my glorious son?" Soon after he was installed in the palace, Paris began his preparations to go to Sparta.

Cassandra, when she heard of her brother's plans, begged him not to go. "Doom shall you bring down upon yourself and all of Troy," she said, "I can see it now." Then caught up in prophetic vision, she began to scream hysterically, pathetically:

> The Greeks are coming, coming here.
> I see their mastheads, galleys, sails, and oars;
> I see their fierce, relentless crew!
> They're bringing grief to Troy; they're bringing rue.
> Woe to Troy! Woe to Troy! Alas, alas!
> Its glory's over, its grandeur's past.
> I see our battlements; I see our walls;
> I see the streets the dogs have fled;
> On the plains of Troy I see the Trojan dead.

Paris did not believe his sister. Nor, for that matter, as she ran frantically through the streets of the city proclaiming her dire prophecy, did anyone else. No one, in fact, ever believed what Cassandra prophesied, although what she said always came to pass. Apollo, it seems, had given her the gift of unerring prophecy in exchange for her virtue; when, however, the gift once bestowed, she would not lie with him, he added the proviso that she never be believed.

No one, therefore, raised hand or voice to stay Paris from sailing to Greece. Oinone, his wife, bade him good voyage and, not knowing the nature of his mission, said to him, "If in your ventures abroad, you are wounded, fond husband, return to me. I will heal you."

When he came to Sparta, Paris was received into the house of Menelaos with ceremony befitting him as a foreign prince, both he and his entourage with him. Helen, we are told, was immediately struck by the young man's beauty, as Aphrodite had predicted, and he by hers. Neither said much, but to each other eyes told all. He seemed to her the most handsome man she had ever seen. She gazed long upon his dazzling robes of Asian silk, stitched with gold, and tried to imagine the splendor of his barbaric palace and the fabled Phrygian city from which he had come.

In her dreams that night Helen saw visions of a city of glimmering gold and peerless snow-white marble. The people were all garbed in multicolored silks, all swarthy, refined, at one with a world of unending luxury and taste. Amidst the opulence and glamor she saw the beautiful prince, the focus of it all, and herself at his side.

For nine days Paris was entertained as a guest in the royal house of Sparta. In that time both he and Helen stole glances at each other and both indulged in fancy, but neither betrayed in any way their mounting mutual infatuation. On the tenth day Menelaos came to his wife and said, "Catreus, my grandfather, has died. For my mother's sake I must go to Crete to bury him. In my absence please see to the pleasures of our guest."

Helen took too much to heart her husband's words. By the time he returned from Crete, she had abandoned nine-year-old Hermione, their only child, but had hastily packed all else that was hers and was comfortably seated next to Paris in a ship just then coming into view of Troy. In her mind she was already married to the handsome Asian prince and so withheld nothing of herself from him.

As soon as Menelaos discovered that Paris had taken Helen with him back to Troy, he went to Tyndareus, his father-in-law, to get the names of all those who, a decade before, had sworn most solemn oaths to retrieve Helen should anyone lay hands upon her to take her away and to destroy utterly the culprit and his city. Then into all the parts of Greece he sent messengers to call up those men, many of whom were now kings, and all the forces in their command.

Kings and princes he also appealed to who had not pledged the oath, among them Agamemnon, his brother, high king of Mycenai. "If this crime goes unpunished," he had his heralds say, "then look out for your own wives next. Foreigners will perceive that we are fainthearted and soon will come to carry them off too. Greek honor is at issue, not a woman, not a sacred oath. Greece has been offended, and Greece must be avenged."

Odysseus, now king of Ithaca in his father Laertes' stead, felt little compulsion to raise an army to go after a woman he had briefly paid court to in his youth. He was happily married himself now to the lovely and faithful Penelope, who had recently borne him a healthy son. Therefore, when the envoys of Menelaos came to Ithaca to demand his compliance with the oath, Odysseus feigned madness. Wearing a peasant skullcap, he had yoked together an ox and an ass and was found plowing the seashore, merrily sowing salt in the furrows as he did so.

"Let us go find Achilleus," said one of the men, after they had watched him for a time. "We have no need for madmen."

"Perhaps he counterfeits madness," suggested another. "We will see." With that, he moved over toward Penelope, who was standing nearby, and snatched the baby Telemachos from her arms. Then, running over to where Odysseus was plowing, he set the infant in the furrow in front of the unusual team. In the nick of time Odysseus steered the ox and ass wide of his son, thereby ending any illusion he was crazy. It was Odysseus along with Diomedes that Menelaos then sent to Scyros where Achilleus was rumored to be.

Achilleus, it should be mentioned, was the son of Peleus and Thetis, who it was prophesied would someday be greater than his father. So intent was Thetis, in fact, that the prophecy be fulfilled that she dipped him as a baby in the River Styx to make his flesh invulnerable. (The heel by which she held him, however, was not submerged.) Then to singe off Achilleus's mortal parts, the goddess turned her babe each night in the fire and during the day rubbed into the creases of his skin oil of ambrosia. Peleus was astonished at the infant's progress.

One night, however, he came upon Thetis when she was holding the infant over the embers in the hearth. "Stop it! Are you mad?" he screamed.

In pique Thetis turned and handed the child to her husband. "Bring him up yourself then!" she said and then stormed from the house, never again to return.

Peleus took his infant son to the wise and good Centaur Cheiron and entrusted the child's upbringing to him. Cheiron instructed young Achilleus in the arts of horsemanship and hunting. He trained him also in footracing by having him run through the untracked vales of Mount Pelion after the wild deer. To make him strong the wise Centaur fed the lad on the meat of lions and wild pigs and, for treats, the bone marrow of bears, and to make him noble he schooled him in what was right and courageous.

When Achilleus was nine years old, his mother Thetis, knowing even then that joining the Greek expedition would mean his early death, whisked him off to the remote island kingdom of Scyros. Disguising him as a girl, she presented him to King Lycomedes as her daughter. "Please raise her as one of your own until she is ready for marriage," she said to him. Achilleus himself little cared for this masquerade—he would rather have been off hunting with his companion Patroclos—until he met the king's daughter Deidamia, with whom he fell in love and whom, when barely into his teens, he impregnated.

And so it was that when Odysseus and Diomedes arrived at Scyros, all they found on the island, apart from the servants and commoners, were Lycomedes and his daughter and their friends, all girls. In vain they searched the palace for Achilleus, with Lycomedes trailing after them insisting that if the son of Peleus were there he would surely have known about it.

Diomedes was ready to leave, assuming their information to have been in error, but Odysseus said, "We have gifts for these lovely girls we've inconvenienced so."

With that, he laid out bracelets and necklaces, gold brooches, finely embroidered dresses, and colored girdles. Also he placed on the table a shield and a spear. "Choose, my girls, each of you, whatever pleases you," he said to them. The girls stood around the table, wide-eyed and smily, fingering the various items, one finally selecting one thing and one another.

Achilleus was drawn to the weapons; and when, on signal from Odysseus, an attendant blasted forth the call-to-arms on a trumpet, he immediately snatched up the spear and shield. "Come with us, son of Peleus," Odysseus said to him in a whisper. Achilleus let the gown he was wearing fall to the floor, revealing himself to be no girl at all, and went with them. Lycomedes' jaw dropped in amazement; but Deidamia, his daughter, took it all in stride, for she had long had proof of the noble youth's manhood.

At the port of Aulis, across the straits from Euboia, the Greek kings and their ships and armies assembled. Never had so many men gathered for anything ever before. Ajax, son of Oileus, brought forty ships of expert spearmen with him from Locris, and Elephenor came with another forty from Euboia.

Menestheus came with fifty Athenian ships; Ajax, the son of Telamon, with twelve from Salamis; Diomedes with eighty from Argos; and Agamemnon from Mycenai with one hundred ships fully outfitted and filled from gunwale to gunwale with mighty men of war. Menelaos himself brought sixty ships with him and Odysseus twelve and Achilleus fifty.

Besides these, the Cretans under Idomeneus arrived with forty ships of armed warriors and the Pylians under Nestor with forty more. Philoctetes, who owned the bow and arrows of Heracles, came with seven ships. And these were not all; for from Boiotia came another forty and from Orchomenos thirty, from Phocis forty, from Arcadia seven, from Elis forty, from Culichion forty and from Magnesia forty.

Each day increased the number of ships and fighting men. They came also from Rhodes and Aitolia, Cos, Syme, Phylace, Pherai, Cyphos, Ormenios, Tricca, and Gyrtone. The total number of ships that came to Aulis to sail against Troy was one thousand and thirteen. Thirty armies of dauntless spearmen were there in all, and forty-three commanders.

It seemed wise to the Greeks, when they were all assembled, to choose from among themselves one to be commander-in-chief over all. The reasonable choice was Agamemnon, king of Mycenai, who had brought two times as many ships and men with him as any other king and besides was brother to the injured Menelaos. Another choice might have been more fortunate; for while the armies were still being assembled at Aulis, Agamemnon shot a stag and chanced to boast that Artemis herself could not have aimed the arrow better, thereby incurring the goddess's wrath not only upon himself but also upon all he now commanded.

When it came time for them to depart from Aulis, there was no wind to fill their sails and speed them off to Troy. Nor was there wind the next day either nor the day after that. Upon the glassy waters of the strait a thousand ships, loaded down with arms and supplies, lay at anchor motionless as though set in ice, their anchor ropes slack, no wavelets lapping their sleek hulls.

The men, their spirits beginning to ebb, milled about in groups, usually by region, grumbling and complaining; here and there quarrels broke out. Some bided their time playing quoits. Achilleus, we are told, happily occupied himself racing against horses along the seashore. Day followed day, and still not the faintest breeze stirred anywhere. Some of the commanders began to talk of abandoning the enterprise and going home. Their troops were becoming too unruly.

To the seer Calchas now the lordly Agamemnon turned. "What god deigns to keep my army and me from our destined glory?" he sought to know. "By auguries discover why we are held and what sacrifices are required for our release."

Apprehensively, after examining the entrails of birds and consulting his other sources of divination, the prophet made his reply: "By your own boasts, my lord, have you angered the chaste Daughter of Leto. It is she who stays the winds."

"And by what will her fury be satisfied?" asked Agamemnon.

"Only by the sacrifice of Iphigeneia, your most beautiful and beloved daughter," Calchas told him.

And thus it was that Agamemnon commanded a messenger to go down to Mycenai and, on pretext that she was to become the bride of Achilleus, bring Iphigeneia forthwith back to Aulis. Determined that her daughter was not to be married without her, Clytaimestra, Agamemnon's wife, came with the girl to the Grecian encampment and so was present there when Iphigeneia, like a lamb, was slain upon the altar of Artemis. She thereafter hated her husband with an unquenchable hatred.

Before the coals of the altar had cooled, winds began to stir on the strait and the men quickly boarded their ships. Their voyage all the way to Troy was marked by steady winds, which the men took for a good omen. The only untoward incident en route involved Philoctetes, who was bitten on the foot by a viper. So mightily did he bellow night and day in his agony that Agamemnon left him alone on the Island of Lemnos to die.

# The Wrath
# of Achilleus

or nine summers the searing sun, heaven's eye, gazed with relentless, fiery glare down upon a sea of Grecian helmets which,
like glistening crests of waves at flood tide, undulated inward
toward the city, even up to the base of its lofty wall, and then, as if in
obedience to the distant command of heavenly powers, receded with
weakened luster back toward the sea. Winter's fury nine times buffeted
the Grecian host, as though in league with Priam, driving them to cover
with its savage arctic blasts, pelting them from above with its icy missiles.
And so the seasons turned, and the vast army of Agamemnon was frustrated
in its dream of quick conquest.

It was not, however, Trojan resistance alone—no, nor even the
intrusions of those gods who took up the Trojans' cause as their own—
that robbed the Greeks of their goal. Their own commanders were partly
responsible, for hardly had the Greeks landed before some of the armies
diverted their attentions to the coastal towns and islands thereabouts.
Imitating barbarians, they descended upon ofttimes unoffending peoples
and looted their temples and carried off their cattle and young women.
And for that reason seldom in the nine years they were encamped on the
Trojan shore did the armies of Agamemnon take on the cohorts of Hector
in full strength.

In the tenth year of the war, we are told, a party of Greeks staged
a piratical raid on the island of Chryse, where Chryses was high priest to
Apollo. They sacked the island and, among other things, carried back
Chryseis, the priest's comely daughter, as a trophy of war and presented
her to Agamemnon to be his concubine. Gladly he received her into his
bed.

Chryses then came to the Grecian camp, bearing with him a goodly treasure to ransom his daughter. In his hand he held the scepter of Apollo entwined with the wreath of a suppliant. To Agamemnon and Menelaos he made his plea. "May the undying gods grant you success in your ventures here," he said, "and safe return to your own homes. But I ask you, sons of Atreus, in the name of the god I serve, to free my daughter and accept this ransom for her."

But Agamemnon sent him away. "Your scepter and wreath mean nothing to me, you old relic," he sneered. "Be off with you! The girl will go back to Argos with me and ripen in my bed."

And so Chryses went back to his island home and raised his arms in the temple of Apollo, whom fair Leto bore, and there called down the god's curses upon the Greeks in vengeance for his tears. Nor was the far-shooting Son of Leto deaf to his priest's entreaties. For nine days from the lofty heights of Mount Olympos he rained down plague, like an unrelenting barrage of arrows from his peerless silver bow, upon the Grecian hosts. Mules and hounds first writhed in mortal agony, and not long afterward the men themselves. Pyres were soon blazing all day and all night with the dead slain by Apollo in outrage over the treatment of his servant Chryses.

On the tenth day of the plague Achilleus called his fellow chieftains together into council and proposed that they inquire of the gods as to the reason for the curses now cast upon them and what might be done to abate them. It was to them that Calchas, wisest of the soothsayers, when he had been assured protection by Achilleus from King Agamemnon, spoke. "It is Apollo who sends these evils among us," he said, "for the sake of his priest whom Agamemnon has dishonored. More will follow. Nothing will stay the god's fury save for the safe return of the girl Chryseis to her father and a hecatomb in reparation."

Agamemnon, who was present, rose in anger. "The girl is dearer to me," he said, "than my wife Clytaimestra and more gifted in ways to my liking. However, if I must give her up for my army, I will do so. But know this one thing: I shall not sleep without some beauty at my side."

"There are no girls here except those already awarded as trophies to others," said Achilleus. "Pray, do not wait until another shows up before you return Chryseis to her father. Men are dying."

"Find me another, or I shall come to your tents looking for one," said the commander-in-chief. "Perhaps to your tent, outspoken son of Peleus."

"Your insolence is rivaled only by your ambition, my lord," shot back Achilleus.

"The daughter of Chryses shall be returned forthwith," said then Agamemnon to the son of Peleus. "My men will come to your tent this evening for your prize, Briseis. She will be a fair substitute. Have her ready."

Achilleus thereupon, his mighty heart swollen with rage, drew his incomparable sword from its scabbard and advanced on the brazen king. Surely he would have slain him, had not the bright-eyed Daughter of Zeus, invisible except to him, grabbed him by his flaxen hair. With words for him alone she prevailed upon him to forego immediate satisfaction in favor of far greater future rewards. Out of deference to her and the great Aegis-bearer who had sent her, the pious Achilleus reluctantly slid the silver-hilted sword back into its sheath.

"Know you this, oft-drunken wretch with the face of a dog and the heart of a deer," he said then to the kingly son of Atreus, "robber of other men's prizes, I shall not by force of arms try to prevent you from taking Briseis out of my tent. But if you should, I swear by the guardians of the decrees of heaven, hereafter you shall look desperately for Achilleus and shall not find him. Your men may fall by the murderous hand of Hector, even at their burning ships' sides, and you will be unable to help them. In that day shall you and the Greeks rue the hour when you gave insult to your bravest warrior."

That evening, in the final moments of day's fading light, we are told, the heralds of Agamemnon came to Achilleus's tent to get Briseis and take her away. Patroclos, his dear comrade, brought her from the tent and handed her over to them. Alone, Achilleus walked the shore beyond where the ships were anchored. As he did so, from the great wrath that surged within him he wept.

"Oh, dearest mother, who bore me to live but a short season in the world of light," he said, his arms outstretched to the sea, "let not this dishonor by haughty Agamemnon go unpunished. Clasp the knees of great Cronos's son and draw from him a pledge of retribution for the indignity I now suffer."

After that he returned to his ships and stewed in his anger. Neither did he join his fellows in assembly nor stand beside them when they ventured forth to do battle against Hector's Trojans, though his heart yearned to be in the thick of the strife.

In the meantime Thetis, his mother, threw herself down before the mighty Son of Cronos and clutched his knees after the manner of a suppliant and would not let him go. "Father Zeus," she said, "if ever you found me dear, grant my plea. My son has been dishonored by Agamemnon, who stole his prize and took her to himself. Favor, I ask, therefore, the Trojans until the son of Atreus rues his actions and gives my son his due, the girl and handsome treasures in retribution. Nod your head if you assent to my petition."

"What you ask will set me at odds with Hera, so say nothing of it," he replied. Then, even as he spoke, great Zeus nodded his thick brows so that the ambrosial locks shimmered upon his undying head and vast Olympos quaked.

And so that night Agamemnon had a dream in which the figure of aged Nestor, king of Pylos, appeared to him and urged him to take the battle to the Trojan walls because the gods had all finally been won to the Greek cause. Zeus, said the dream figure, was ready to let them take the city. As he woke from the dream, Agamemnon pondered his nocturnal vision and concluded that it had indeed been a sign to him that what was spoken should be accomplished, never for a moment suspecting that Zeus had sent the lying dream to hasten his comeuppance for having dishonored Achilleus.

When Dawn with her rosy fingers had drawn aside the misty clouds of night, Agamemnon sent heralds throughout the camp to call the commanders into assembly. After they had come together at the ship of Nestor, he teased them with talk of curtailing their campaign and embarking that day for their homes. This he did to test their resolution. Some did not see through his cunning and so cheered what he said and started for their ships. Brave Odysseus ran after them, however, to upbraid them for their cowardice and rally them into battle readiness.

Only then did Agamemnon leave off his ruse and make the men privy to his plans for the day. With bold speech he fired up their hearts and whetted their appetites for sweet victory's fare. Peals of applause went up from the men. As the surf surges high in advance of the south wind's blast and breaks upon some rock-bound headland, crashing against it and pounding it without ceasing, as gusts from every quarter stir its fury, even so did the Grecian spearmen, when the son of Atreus had finished his exhortation, leap up and dash every which way to their ships.

Prayers were made and sacrifices all along the shore. Then each army fell in behind its own commander, and en masse they advanced on the gates of Troy. Not since the early weeks of the war had the Greeks moved in to attack in such force. Only Achilleus and his Myrmidons were absent from their number. With no less haste, from out of the gates rushed the Trojans. As south winds drape the mountain tops with thick mist so that a man cannot see a stone's throw away, thus did the dust rise from under the feet of the two hosts as they sped across the plain each toward the other.

While the armies were yet some distance apart, great Hector lowered his spear across the path of his fellows to stay their advance. Then with thunderous voice he cried out to the Greeks. "Hear me!" he shouted. "Trojans and Greeks, hear what I have to say!"

Agamemnon signaled for his men to stop. "We will hear, Trojan," he said.

"I speak for Paris, my brother, who alone is responsible for the strife between us," the son of Priam began. "Let this be a battle only between him and Menelaos. In no man's land between us let them fight singly for Helen and all her charms. Who wins can have her, and the rest of us can go to our homes and live under a covenant of peace."

Menelaos called out then from the ranks of the Greeks, "So be it. Let us slay two lambs, one for the Earth and one for the Sun—nay, three, one for Zeus as well—and over them swear a binding oath."

Loud shouts of approval went up from both sides. Men got down from their chariots and began to shed their armor. Hector ordered two heralds to go into the city to bring back two unblemished lambs. Agamemnon sent Talthybios for the third from their ships. As preparations were being made for the sacrifice that would seal the covenant, a gallery of spectators began to line up along the tops of the city walls, some attended women but old men mostly, too old to fight.

To one of the towers came also Helen, flanked by handmaids on either side. Her white mantle over her head, she strode erect and stately, as lovely as ever. The old men followed her with their eyes. In whispers among themselves they said, "Such a magnificent beauty, so marvelously and divinely formed. Who can blame them for fighting so long and hard for the likes of her?"

King Priam returned with the heralds to where the two armies waited. In addition to the lambs they brought a goatskin of wine and a mixing bowl and cups of gold. The Greeks too brought oath offerings, which were mixed in the mixing bowls with those of the Trojans. Water was poured over both kings' hands, and then to Zeus they lifted their arms in sacred oath, pledging to abide by the outcome of the single combat and thereafter live on terms of peace the one with the other. Even as they spoke, knives were drawn across the throats of the lambs, sealing their oath with blood.

Decked in full armor, the two principals now stepped from their respective ranks and moved into the neutral ground. Each, spear poised and shield raised, took the measure of the other. With a sudden thrust the Trojan prince hurled his spear, but Menelaos's round bronzed shield blocked its path and turned its point. Raising a prayer to Zeus, the son of Atreus then let fly his weapon. Into the shield of his antagonist the spear lodged, penetrating also his breastplate, though no deeper. Menelaos closed quickly with his drawn sword, aiming a shattering death blow at Paris's head but catching only his helmet's projected crest.

Undaunted, the son of Atreus seized his adversary by his helmet and began dragging him toward the Grecian ranks. Invisibly Aphrodite reached out her hand to break the strap, and Menelaos went flying, with only an empty helmet in his hands. He picked up a spear and rushed at the prone, shaken Paris and would surely have run him through had not the laughter-loving goddess again intervened. Snatching up the son of Priam in a flash, she hid him in a cloud and spirited him off to his own bedchamber, to which before long the beauteous Helen also came.

Menelaos, hungry for the kill, searched in vain for his vanished adversary. Nowhere could he be found. The Trojans as well as the Greeks joined him in looking for Paris. Gladly would they have turned him over had they found him, for by then they all hated him as much as death itself. While the two armies hunted for him, leaving no stone unturned, Paris, his passions kindled by his brush with death, led Helen by her peerless hand to their marriage couch.

When the search for Paris was finally abandoned, Agamemnon called out to both sides, "Greeks and Trojans, hear me now. The victory here belongs to Menelaos. Thus to him Helen must be returned and all her wealth with her, as we swore by our oath."

The Greeks shouted their approval to what he said; the Trojans by silence seemed also to give assent. And so nine years of strife might at that moment have come to an end had not Pandaros, goaded on by Hera, arched his bow into a half circle and let fly an arrow above the heads of his fellows to Menelaos's mid-section. It pierced his belt and breastplate and grazed his skin so that blood flowed forth, though the wound itself was not deep.

Agamemnon ran to his fallen brother's side, cursing himself for accepting the Trojan's truce and at the same time calling upon his spearmen to attack the falsehearted foe. The Greeks hastily donned their armor. Fierce was the strife that now erupted. As a giant wave rears its head and comes crashing in upon the shore, its arching crest towering over the jagged rocks and its frothy brackish waters spewed in every direction, even so the indignant Grecian host swept across the strip of unoccupied ground to inundate the Trojan ranks. Nor were the cohorts of Hector caught entirely off guard, though great confusion reigned. Like ravenous wolves they fell upon one another, Greeks and Trojans, man against man in savage death struggle.

The bright-eyed Daughter of Zeus darted invisibly among the Greeks to shore up their spirits wherever she found them lagging. In Achilleus's stead she inspired valor in great Diomedes, son of Tydeus, so that he might excel all other Greeks and cloak himself with glory. Thereafter he was more in the midst of Trojans than his fellow Greeks. Like a winter torrent that has burst its barriers in full flood, he plunged through the Trojan phalanxes scouring the plain and sweeping the sons of Ilion, like debris, ahead and to either side of his path.

Into Astynoos's chest he drove his spear and, without a break in the rhythm, split open the collarbone of nearby Hypeiron with his sword. Next he slew Abas and Polyidos, both sons of dream-reader Eurydamas, who would never again have them sit at his feet to have him tell the meanings of their dreams. The two sons of Phainops he then killed and after them the sons of Priam, Echemmon and Chromios, who were together in a chariot. Pandaros stopped the bold son of Tydeus in his onslaught momentarily with an arrow to the shoulder, but Diomedes pulled it out and, his strength renewed by Athene, he stormed through the Trojan ranks, like a wounded lion, more ferocious than ever.

With Aineias now at this side, Pandaros moved in to cast his spear. His aim was true, but the son of Tydeus interposed his shield in the nick of time. The bronze point went through the middle of the shield and lodged in his breastplate just short of his skin. Pandaros, supposing him mortally wounded, closed for the quick kill. He stopped short when Diomedes' spear tore into his nose, severed the root of his tongue, and came out the back of his neck. His brightly polished armor clanged as he dropped to the earth.

Armed with shield and spear, Aineias took his stance over Pandaros's corpse. Diomedes lifted into the air a huge rock, so large that two men who live nowadays could not have lifted it, and heaved it at Aphrodite's mighty son, striking him high on the hip, shattering the joint and ripping open the flesh. Aineias, his head spinning, was overcome by darkness and slumped to the ground. He would surely have had his life ended there by a Grecian spear had not his golden mother hidden him with her mantle.

When she picked him up to take him from the field of battle, however, Diomedes saw her and gave pursuit. On the dead run he let go his spear at her, its point tearing through her ambrosial gown and penetrating the skin between her wrist and hand. Aphrodite screamed mightily to see the ichor from her immortal veins splash to the ground. Her cry brought strife-loving Ares, who lent her his chariot to flee to the sanctuary of Mount Olympos.

In spite of the heroics of Diomedes, however, and of great Ajax as well, who fought mighty Hector to a stand-off, the Greeks were unable to crush the spirits of the defenders and press on for the kill. At day's end the field was strewn with almost an equal number of Greeks and Trojans stretched out with faces downward upon the earth, who would never blink their eyes to another daybreak ever again.

As Dawn, decked in her saffron robes, began that next morning to spread her light out to all the corners of the earth, high atop Mount Olympos the great Lord of All the Immortals was calling his fellows gruffly into council. "Listen to me, every god and goddess of you," he said. "Do not cross me in that which I purpose, none of you, but do as I tell you. Should I catch any of you helping either the Greeks or Trojans hereafter, I will lash him mercilessly with thunderbolts or perhaps hurl him down into darkest Tartaros."

"As you say, my lord," responded Athene, speaking for them all.

"Cheer up, my child," said he. "In the end you will be pleased."

On the plain outside Troy, after the two armies had taken their morning meals, the battle of the previous day was resumed, but there were no rousing speeches this day from Agamemnon nor exuberant shouts from the ranks. The Greeks went spiritless onto the field, though not Hector and his Trojans. From the onset, with insults and arrows, the sons of Ilion lorded it over the invaders. Relentlessly they pushed them backward toward their own ramparts, great walls of earth, far down the shore next to their thousand ships.

Were it not for some few individuals, the Trojans might have penetrated deep enough to lay the torch to the closer of the Grecian galleys. At the moat's edge in front of the wall, bold Diomedes, almost as formidable as the day before, turned the attackers away with his thick-shafted spear. Nearby Teucros, son of Telamon, champion bowman of the Greeks, time and again bent double his bow and let fly his unerring arrows at briefly exposed Trojan throats and midriffs. No man that day struck down more of the enemy than he.

As the day wore on, however, the Greeks were forced back across the moat and behind the earthen rampart. Hera and Athene moaned in agony as champion after champion was cut down by raging Hector and his Trojan spearmen. The Greeks seemed beyond rallying, and both goddesses were afraid to enter the fighting themselves. Only nightfall kept the sons of Ilion from the Grecian ships.

At day's end both Hera and Athene plopped themselves angrily down upon their golden thrones in the midst of the other gods. "Why so wroth?" Zeus chided them. "You certainly were not tempted to join the fighting again I hope. Believe me, there was nothing you could have done. The battle went as I willed it."

"There is no need for you to impress us with your power," snapped Hera. "We are grieving the fine Grecian warriors who perished this day. Pray, have respect for our compassion if you have none yourself."

"Tomorrow's slaughter will be greater than today's," her immortal husband told her. "Fierce Hector will not be stayed in his fury till the son of Peleus is roused to new anger. That is my decree."

A thousand campfires blazed that night upon the Trojan shore, we are told, and by the glimmer of each fifty Greeks sat huddled, fearful of what the dawn might bring. The horses chomped their measures of oats and barley, dumb beasts, unconcerned, beside the chariots. Conversations among the men turned to abandoning their enterprise and pushing out to sea while darkness still staved off what might be the Trojan's final assault. Then it was that Diomedes rose up and asked the son of Atreus permission for the commanders to speak freely their minds. Agamemnon consented gladly to hear them.

Aged Nestor spoke for all. "Our woes began, illustrious king," he said, "the hour you offended Achilleus by taking the girl Briseis from his tent. With gifts and words you must now appease him, else we must accept our defeat and go empty-handed to our homes."

"I was wrong," the proud king admitted. "Seven tripods will I give him and ten talents of gold, twenty iron cauldrons, twelve prize-winning horses and seven maidens of unsurpassing beauty—all these and with them the girl Briseis whom I took from him. And when we return triumphant to Greece, he will have his choice of my daughters and a kingly dowry with her. Such will I give him and more, if he will leave off his fierce anger against me."

Delegates were then chosen to go to the tent of Achilleus and tell him all that Agamemnon had promised. Phoinix, dear to the son of Peleus, was selected for the mission and Odysseus and Ajax to go with him. When they came to Achilleus's tent, they found him playing on a silver lyre and singing songs of glory. He was alone except for Patroclos, who sat opposite him and listened to his sweet airs. The son of Peleus jumped up from his seat when he spied his old friends. "Welcome," he said, "you who of all the Greeks are dearest to me. Let us have wine, Patroclos. And spare the water, for these are very dear companions."

After they had toasted one another and eaten some bread and roasted meats, Odysseus began to explain why they had come. "The Trojans," he said, "are just beyond our rampart. Mighty Hector lords it over the battlefield like a raging god, convinced that Zeus is with him. He sits out there and prays for the dawn, when he will storm our walls and take the ax to our ships and lay the torch to their hulls. Only you, oh great Achilleus, can stand between us and certain disaster." Then he told the son of Peleus of Agamemnon's repentance and his offer of gifts and the fair Briseis herself if Achilleus would but leave off his anger and rejoin his erstwhile companions.

"If he were to offer me all the wealth of Egypt," Achilleus replied, "I would not lift one finger to help that man, so profound is my hatred of him. Horses and tripods and princesses will be available to me in Phthia, where by great Poseidon's goodness I shall be in three days' time. Long ago my mother told me that if I came here and fought, my name would live forever though early would I fill my grave; were I to stay at home, my name would die, but my days on earth, like the wild flowers in the vales of Mount Pelion, though seen by few, would be sweet and many. I have chosen to live."

When they were told Achilleus's response, the Greek commanders were much troubled; but after they had made drink offerings among themselves, they went each man to his own tent to lie down and try to sleep. While some rested, though most tossed sleeplessly upon their pallets, Agamemnon conferred with his brother Menelaos. One question was uppermost in both their minds: What if Hector, impatient for daybreak, should stage a raid that night while most of the men were asleep? Anxious for more counsel, Agamemnon went to the tent of aged Nestor, wisest of the Greeks, and then to Odysseus's and Diomedes'.

"Let me go behind the Trojan lines to discern their purpose," suggested the son of Tydeus. "It might be well, though, if someone went with me. On a night like tonight two would be able to pick up much more than one."

Several spoke at once, volunteering to accompany him, but it was Odysseus in the end who was chosen to do so. Prayers were offered up to Pallas Athene on their behalf, and then the two slipped out of a crude makeshift gate in the earthen rampart into the battle area of the day before. Like two lions on a nocturnal prowl, they moved silently amidst the scattered armor and the corpses of those who had fallen.

It was not long before they heard someone else not far away coming in their direction. Wily Odysseus beckoned to Diomedes, and the two lay down among the dead and did not stir until the lone man was well past them. Then, springing to their feet suddenly, they ran after him. The man's name was Dolon, and he had been dispatched by Hector to penetrate the Grecian lines to spy on them. At first he thought some of his fellow Trojans were running to join him; but when he saw by the faint moonlight the men were Greek, he took off. Cut off, though, from his own lines, he ran toward the camp of the enemy.

The two Greeks caught him just short of the moat in front of the earthen wall. He was trembling all over when they seized him each by an arm. His teeth were chattering and all the blood seemed drained from his face, so frightened was he. Weeping, he clutched the arms of his captors and said, "Let me live, for a huge ransom will I bring you. My father is rich and will pay dearly when he hears I am alive in the Grecian camp."

"You have no need to fear for your life," Odysseus told him. "We only want to know why you are out here. Was it to spy on us for some purpose or merely to plunder the dead?"

Still trembling, Dolon answered, "Hector sent me to find out if the ships are well guarded, or if perhaps, planning to flee, the Greeks are no longer keeping their watches as heretofore."

"And where is Hector?" asked the son of Laertes next.

"Well away from the battlefield, holding council near the monument of Ilos in the city."

"Are special sentries keeping watch over the Trojan camp?"

"No special sentries," Dolon told him. "At each campfire someone is supposed to stay awake. Our allies who have just arrived have no one at watch."

"These allies—who are they and where is their encampment?"

"Thracians," said Dolon, "a large contingent. They are at the far end of the camp. Rhesos, son of Eioneus, is their king, and their horses are the strongest and best I have ever seen. With these joining their forces with his, Hector is confident that final victory will at last be his and the Grecian ships by nightfall tomorrow will be in ashes. Now that I have said all, bind me and take me to your camp as your prisoner. You will both be rich hereafter for it."

Diomedes then spoke. "If we let you be ransomed, we might yet have you sneak upon us as a spy," he said. "Better to have it done with now."

The still trembling Trojan reached for the son of Tydeus's beard to beg him further for his life, but Diomedes brought his sword cleanly across Dolon's neck, slicing through bone and sinew, so that his head toppled to the ground and rolled a ways while his lips were still moving. After that Odysseus and Diomedes headed back across the battlefield, sidestepping bodies and armor, until they came to the Trojan encampment. Avoiding the watchfires, they were able to work their way undetected through the sleeping enemy to where the newly arrived Thracians slept with neither fires nor sentries to guard them.

While the son of Laertes quietly loosed the horses, which were indeed magnificent animals, Diomedes fell upon the sleeping men. As a prowling lion springs upon a flock of unprotected sheep or goats, savagely tearing into this one and that, thus did the son of Tydeus prey upon the unguarded Thracians. Twelve soldiers he slew and then, coming upon Rhesos, their king, killed him as well. He would have pressed on to slaughter more had not Odysseus, with the Thracian horses on a line, whistled to him to go.

Back through the Trojan camp they sped, each mounted, each with a line of horses trailing, past watchfires, past sentries and then across the blood-soaked battlefield toward the wall and the Grecian ships. The Greeks, less surprised than the Trojans, opened the gates for them to gallop through. When they related to their companions all that had happened, Diomedes and Odysseus tethered the horses next to their tents and made prayers and thank offerings to gray-eyed Athene for their safety and success. And after that the Greek camp slept. The exploits of the two were taken as a good omen for the morrow.

When Dawn, rising up from her couch beside Tithonos, parted the morning mists to bring light to a new day, both camps were equally eager for battle. Encouraged by the night's events, Agamemnon with loud battle cries stirred his troops to a fresh pitch of valor, giving them new heart to fight doggedly and with all their strength. Hector, though disheartened by the death of Rhesos, likewise rallied his men to high spirits.

And the two great armies descended on one another. Like opposing packs of wolves they fought, and the one would not yield to the other. Even as reapers mow through a field of thick barley, with sheaves falling now this way and now that, the Greeks and Trojans cut each other down, though neither line seemed to move. Both called upon the Son of Cronos, but he stayed aloft and aloof, peering equally down upon the ships of the Greeks and the marbled towers of Troy, equally upon the slain and their slayers.

Agamemnon, never mightier, never more grand, spurred his spearmen on. His fierce rage seemed to know no bounds. Wherever the Trojan ranks were the thickest the noble son of Atreus sped, his foot soldiers close behind. Whenever the Trojans showed their backs, Agamemnon bore the more fiercely down upon them, wielding his sharp two-edged sword more deftly than a seasoned farmer his sickle amid ripe, ear-heavy grain. As, when a vast dry forest is all aflame, the majestic pine crowns become charred and topple, thus fell the heads of the Trojans fleeing from the raging son of Atreus, and, we are told, many chariots raced empty across the battlefield, their drivers lying on the blood-slick plain, now more inviting to vultures than to their wives.

As long as the king of the Grecian kings stood dauntless and unwounded in the thick of the battle, his men prevailed over their enemies. If it be that into a single moment the true mettle of a man is sometimes compacted so that his greatest perfection, his highest glory is then achieved, as though it were for that moment and none other he had been born, such a moment had now come to the son of Atreus.

Brief, however, was the moment, for when he had slain Iphidamas, the son of Antenor, and was about to strip him of his armor, the noble Coon, the fallen man's older brother, rushed at Agamemnon from his blind side, driving his spear through the Argive lord's arm just below the elbow. Recoiling, the son of Atreus smote Coon through his shield with his bronze-headed spear. After that, as long as blood oozed from his wound, Agamemnon was able to continue fighting; but when the flow stopped and the arm became swollen, sending great shocks of pain throughout his body, he ordered his charioteer to take him back to the ships.

"Trojans, Lycians, Dardanians!" then shouted Hector, fresh on the scene from elsewhere on the battlefield. "Victory is within our grasp. Quit yourselves like the heroes I know you to be. Their best has been carried off. The battle is ours. On, my warriors, my friends! Turn your chariots and charge!" He himself thereupon plunged into where the Greeks were thickest and lashed out like a raging tempest that swoops down upon the sea. His men followed after him.

Were it not for Odysseus and fierce-shouting Diomedes, the Greeks would have been quickly driven all the way back to their ships by the invincible Hector. Prodding each other on by words and deeds, these, like two wild, white-tusked boars that turn on the hounds that pursue them and rend them without mercy, ripped into the ranks of the charging Trojans and slowed their advance. Soon, however, the son of Tydeus was taken from the field with an arrow through his foot, and before long Odysseus was likewise dragged by his companions to safety after a spear tore open his side.

In another sector Paris drew his bow on Machaon, most skilled of all the Greeks in the arts of healing, and let fly a triple-barbed shaft to the gentle physician's right shoulder. Idomeneus caught him as he fell and carried him to the chariot of Pylian Nestor. "Take him to the ships," he said, "and drive the horses as fast as you can. This man is worth a thousand other men, for the secrets of healing are his."

As aged Nestor lashed his powerful steeds into full speed to spirit Machaon to safety, Paris slipped a fresh arrow into his bowstring. Within his range Eurypylos, the brave son of Euaimon, was stripping the armor from Apisaon, whom he had just slain. The arrow caught him in the right thigh and broke off. He too, however, was dragged by his companions to safety in the nick of time and taken forthwith to the ships.

Ajax, his seven-layered shield bristling with arrows like the back of a slow-scrambling hedgehog, stood firm against the resurgent Trojans but in the end gave ground and was forced backward toward the moat. Nor could brave Meriones nor the Cretan chieftain Idomeneus for all their heroics stave off the Trojan advance. Hector, it seemed, was everywhere, urging his men closer and closer to the great wall of earth the Greeks had erected as a final barrier to protect their ships. Like a hound on scent of fresh blood, he pressed for the kill, his appetite for gore increasing all the while by what it fed on.

From the deck of his ship Achilleus watched as the wounded were brought back into the camp. When Nestor sped past with Machaon, the brooding champion called out to Patroclus, "Go see who that was. It looked like Machaon, son of Asclepios. Woe betide the Greeks if it were he."

Patroclos ran after the chariot and found that indeed the wounded man was Machaon. "If the sulking Achilleus is interested," snarled aged Nestor, "tell him brave Diomedes too is wounded as well as Odysseus and Agamemnon. Eurypylos was also hit just as I was leaving. If the son of Peleus wishes to see Trojan torches laid to our ships, he will not need to wait long."

Sadly Patroclos hurried back to the ships of the Myrmidons, though was delayed when en route he met Eurypylos, the broken arrow still in his thigh. "Tell me, noble Eurypylos," said Patroclos to him, "are we

Greeks doomed to be fed to the hounds of Troy, or is there yet some hope? Can mighty Hector be stayed?"

"There is no hope," Eurypylos replied. "Too many of our princes lie wounded. We shall surely perish with our ships, for the Trojans wax stronger and stronger."

Patroclos then took his companion to his own ship, where he removed the arrow and tended the wound, washing it and afterward rubbing into it powdered bitter herbs which numbed the pain and soon staunched the bleeding. All this Achilleus watched, his great heart torn asunder within him.

Through each of the crude makeshift gates the Greeks, for want of their foremost champions, were now being pressed. The great Ajax was among the last to seek the protection of the wall, but ere long he too discerned the folly of engaging the inspired Hector on the open battlefield and begrudgingly backed through the gates. From the ramparts the Greeks showered rocks and arrows down upon the attacking Trojans.

While Hector in one place dismounted from his chariot and pondered how best to penetrate the defense, at another point Glaucos and bold-spirited Sarpedon, king of Lycia, Zeus's own son, rushed headlong across the moat, holding their great bronze shields over their heads. With their bare hands they wrenched loose the timbers and tore down the breastwork. Menestheus, the defender at that point, called for the two Ajaxes and Teucros, who came on the run, but their best efforts could not turn away the two champions to whom glory was of greater value now than life. Glaucos fell to one of Teucros's arrows and had to be carried away, but Sarpedon with his powerful arms tugged at the battlement till it gave and a breach was made through which many could pass.

At that very moment before one of the main gates the mighty son of Priam raised a huge boulder. Six men as men are now could not have lifted the great rock that mighty Hector raised first shoulder-high and then above his shoulders. With every muscle in his body straining as one, he heaved the boulder into the barred gate, shattering it as though it were a gate of straw and its bolts bolts of wax. As swollen waters at springtime gush through weakened dikes, spreading out over rich farm lands, flattening young shoots, the raging Trojans burst now through the earthen wall, pouring out over the beach lined with Grecian galleys.

Horrified, Hera gazed down from Mount Olympos as the sons of Ilion swept in upon her beloved Greeks. With presence of mind she approached her lord on pretext of bidding him farewell before going to the ends of the earth to visit aged Oceanos. As she spoke, she batted her eyes flirtatiously and leaned just this way and that so as to show to advantage the charms that invariably excited his passions. She made it seem his idea to draw about them a curtain of clouds and take their pleasure on a bed of downy grass and clover hastily created by him for the purpose.

A brief while later, when the wily Queen of Olympos stole noiselessly from the lush, still soft bed which her lord had thoughtfully bordered with crocus and hyacinth, great Zeus was blissfully asleep. His dreams were as tranquil as his body, lissome, buoyant, and love-drained; his immortal mind transported from the battlefield to visions more gentle and sweet.

Quickly then with the assistance of earth-shaking Poseidon, Hera rallied the Greeks, now fighting in the shadows of their own mastheads. Though wounded, Agamemnon, at her urging, once more took charge. Diomedes and Odysseus too rose from their pallets and gingerly fitted their armor over their swollen and mutilated bodies. Their champions once more on the field, the rank and file found new courage and began to advance in vicious counter-attack against the cohorts of the mighty Hector.

# The Wrath
# Unleashed

I t was not until the Trojans had been driven back beyond the moat that the Father of Gods and Men stirred from his love-induced slumber. Rubbing the sleep from his eyes, he stood and looked Troyward. Everywhere the Trojans were in rout and the Greeks in hot pursuit, with wild-eyed Poseidon in their midst spurring them ever onward. Mighty Hector, felled by a rock heaved at him by Ajax, the son of Telamon, was being carried from the field under heavy guard. He was dazed and, even as they carried him, vomited up great torrents of blood.

"This is more of your mischief I perceive, my dear," he said sternly to Hera, now back at his side. "Do you never learn?"

" 'Tis the lord Poseidon who strides among the Greeks, not I," said she.

"Your Greeks will take Troy, my beloved trickster," he told her, "but today they must suffer humiliation such that shall redound to the glory of Achilleus. Behold, his hour is at hand. Do be patient now and not interfere."

So speaking, the Lord of Olympos called Iris to his side and golden-haired Apollo. The one he sent to order Poseidon, his unruly brother, off the battlefield; the other to bring quick healing to the mighty Hector so that he could rally the Trojans once more behind him. Forthwith the two deities set out to do as Zeus commanded them.

And so it was that the balance was tipped one more time in favor of the Trojans. With the ferocity of young lions the sons of Ilion, again behind their indomitable champion, turned on their pursuers. The fury of the revived Hector was that of strife-loving Ares or that of a fire raging through the bone-dry glades of a thick forest. Not with balms only had the Son of Leto anointed him but with venom and a potion derived from the blood of bulls as well. His head vibrated with such vehemence that his helmet shook against his temples. The Greeks panicked as does a herd of cattle when a rogue lion springs suddenly into their midst and tears at the throat of one of the heifers. The air trembled with the mighty son of Priam's bloodcurdling battle cries.

Once more to the shadows of their own ships the Grecian spearmen were driven. Under an avalanche of Trojan arrows Ajax, the son of Telamon, a mountain of a man, was forced to give ground, nor could Diomedes or Odysseus stand against the onslaught of the Zeus-inspired hordes of mighty Hector either. Like a flock of doves swooped down upon by eagles, the Greeks scattered every which way for protection that was not to be. At Hector's command his men darted in with blazing brands to set fire to the first row of ships beached along the shore.

From the deck of Achilleus's ship Patroclos looked upon all that was happening and turned to Achilleus and wept. Like the crystalline waters of a mountain spring cascading over the rocks of a lofty precipice, tears welled up in his eyes and flowed over his face.

"What grieves you, dearest of men to me?" asked Achilleus.

"It is for my friend Eurypylos I weep and for brave Diomedes and Odysseus who are also wounded," Patroclos answered him. "I weep over the disaster now being visited upon all my friends. Why, my lord Achilleus, are you so inexorable? Have you no heart? Did Thetis indeed bring you forth from Peleus's seed, or did the grim, gray sea conceive you by a jagged cliff and thus spawn a man with no soul?"

"You speak my heart, dear friend," said the son of Peleus, "but my dishonor at the hands of Agamemnon wars against it. Let him know I am not a common vagrant to be trampled upon. For want of my shield and spear let him be destroyed."

"Send me in your armor that I might fight in your stead," said then the man Achilleus loved most. "Let the Myrmidons rally behind me. If the Trojans mistake me for you, the day may yet be won and deliverance come to our comrades."

"Go," said Achilleus, "and when you have driven the Trojans from the ships, return to me quickly. Do not carry the battle elsewhere."

Quickly then Patroclos donned his friend's armor, each piece marvelously crafted and inlaid with gold and fine gems. Around his waist he fastened Achilleus's silver-studded bronze sword and last of all placed upon his head his lord's helmet with the familiar horse-hair plume dangling menacingly from its crest. Then, taking Achilleus's mighty shield, he called for the charioteer Automedon to drive him into battle. The Myrmidons cheered so mightily when Patroclos leaped onto the chariot that Greeks and Trojans paused for a moment in their fighting to look about and see whence came such an ear-shattering burst of thunder.

But more stunned were they when the Myrmidons, led by Patroclos in Achilleus's armor, suddenly appeared as if from nowhere. The Trojans, thinking it Achilleus, looked quickly this way and that for places to hide to escape certain death. Too late was it for Pyraichmes, prince of the Paionians, however, who was setting fire to a Grecian galley. Patroclos's spear hit him in the right shoulder, and he fell groaning to the dust; the last firebrand he would ever carry lay smouldering just beyond his fingertips.

The other Greeks, thinking Achilleus had somehow become reconciled to Agamemnon, split the heavens with their shouts and fell upon the panic-stricken Trojans. Men a moment ago defeated and awaiting death found fresh life. Patroclos was now everywhere, rallying his comrades onward and striking panic into the cohorts of Hector. Fearless and possessed of a strength not his own, he fought like the champion whose armor he wore. Pursuing the fleeing Trojans beyond the moat, he cut off one company after another, forcing them back into the spears of advancing Greeks. More than a dozen he slew in quick succession himself, thereby avenging many a fallen comrade.

When Sarpedon, the long-lived son of Zeus by Europa, came upon his companions in flight, he upbraided them for their cowardice and himself stood firm against the charging Patroclos. Patroclos, with a screech like an eagle-beaked vulture, leaped from his chariot and rushed toward him.

Zeus, with Hera at his side, looked on much aggrieved. "It is the lot of my dear son Sarpedon to perish now by the hand of the son of Menoitios. I am minded to snatch him up and spirit him safely home."

"Rescue a doomed mortal from his fate?" said Hera. "Suppose all the other gods did the same? Do as you wish, but you will only be inviting confusion."

"You are right. I cannot save him," said Zeus.

At that moment Patroclos struck down Thrasydemos, Sarpedon's squire, who blocked his way. Twice the son of Zeus threw spears at the onrushing Greek, but both times they went wide of their mark. Patroclos's spear, however, was not ill-aimed. It struck Sarpedon in the midriff just below his heart. Like a tall pine felled by woodsmen cutting timbers for ships, the great Lycian king dropped to the earth, his arms outstretched.

Nor did Patroclos, in his dauntlessness and folly, cease from his deeds until the Trojans were driven back to within their own walls. He

236

did not heed the words of Achilleus to return after he had chased them from the ships—a costly mistake, for mighty Hector did not stay for long within the city walls. He ordered the Scaian Gates opened and then sped straightway through them out onto the field. Standing his ground, Patroclos awaited the encounter from which he should have shrunk.

Never more bravely nor with greater strength had the son of Menoitios ever fought than he did now. Like a savage wild boar he parried the blows from Hector, any one of which would have killed a lesser man, and charged him in return, trading blow for blow. As though Apollo himself were constantly recharging him with strength and guiding his aim, however, mighty Hector in the end prevailed. It was not the lot of Patroclos that day to win the glory that Zeus had appointed to Achilleus. With the great son of Priam's bronze-tipped spear buried in his bowels, Achilleus's dearest comrade breathed his last. When Hector withdrew his spear, the soul of Patroclos slipped out with it.

Menelaos saw the son of Menoitios fall and quickly rallied his men to the spot to claim the body lest the Trojans drag it off as carrion for their dogs. Hector had, however, already stripped off Achilleus's armor from the corpse of Patroclos before the Greeks could move to stop him. From the city great waves of Trojans, seeing what had happened and regarding Patroclos's body as no mean trophy, now came surging onto the field. The fiercest fighting of the day ensued.

Ajax, the son of Telamon, stood astride Patroclos's body, protecting it like a huge savage lion guarding his freshly killed prey from young lions and marauding hyenas. The Trojans, however, proved as fully stubborn as the Greeks and would not easily give up the prize. As the sun moved ever closer to its setting in the westward Ocean Stream, the battle shifted increasingly toward the Grecian encampment. Suddenly, upon signal from Ajax, Menelaos and Meriones darted in and hoisted Patroclos's body to their shoulders, while the son of Telamon and his namesake gave cover. Back across the moat, however, the Greeks were driven, back once more to the lengthened shadows of their ships.

Antilochos was the bearer of the bad tidings. "I have terrible news, my lord," he said to Achilleus. "Patroclos is dead, and Hector, his slayer, has your armor."

Sorrow, like a dark cloud, settled over Achilleus. Scooping up dirt from the ground, he poured it over him until his tunic and countenance were black. Then he threw himself to the earth and tore at his clothes as he writhed in the dust and groaned mightily. The captive women aboard his ship groaned to hear him groan. Antilochos stood at his side and wept.

When she heard her son's piteous shrieks, Thetis from the depth of the sea where she was visiting with her aged father let out a loud moan, for she sensed wherefore he cried. Quickly she bade her father good-bye and hastened to Troy. On the beach next his ship she found her beloved Achilleus. She asked him why he wept, and he told her all that had come to pass. "And now I must slay the murderous Hector," he said.

"Death will stalk you once you have slain Hector," she told him.

"If I can kill him who killed my dearest comrade," he replied, "then will I abide my doom. Help me, my mother, for the villain whose blood I seek has my armor."

"Night now begins to fall," said Thetis. "Do nothing in my absence. At dawn's first light I will bring you a new armor." With that, she rushed out into the surf and dove beneath the waves and was gone.

Achilleus washed the grime and gore from the body of his friend and anointed it with oils. The wounds were closed with a balm that had seasoned over nine years. The Myrmidons after that placed the corpse on a bier and draped across the length of it a linen sheet. Over this they laid a rich white robe. Then they gathered round the bier and waited for the dawn.

Thetis, in the meantime, went to the palace of bandy-legged Hephaistos, the most splendid abode in all Olympos. No one was ever more welcome there than she, for she it was who centuries earlier had rescued Hephaistos when his own mother had cast him away as a baby. "Much am I honored," he said to her. "What can I do for you?"

Nereus's beautiful daughter, who had once drawn wayward glances from the lordly King of Olympos, told him of her son Achilleus's plight. "Could you make for him, whose end is near," she said, "a pair of greaves to protect his legs and a breastplate for his upper body and a helmet and shield as well? His own were lost when his friend was killed."

"The armor I shall make him will dazzle the eyes of all who behold it," said the kindly Smith God who quickly then limped back to his forge.

Into the fire he put tempered bronze and gold and silver. Grasping the metals in his tongs, he set them upon his great anvil and began to shape them with well-laid blows of his mighty hammer. First he fashioned the shield, massive and strong. Of five thicknesses of toughest oxhide he made the shield, overlaying them with three circles of hard metals. The straps were formed of purest silver. Many wondrous and intricate designs did his cunning hands emboss upon the outward surface of the shield.

After the shield he made a breastplate that glistened brighter than fire and then a helmet, close fitting and richly ornate, with a golden plume

238

on top. Then he fashioned greaves of beaten tin for Achilleus's legs. All these he made and gave to Thetis, Achilleus's mother, while the darkness of night yet covered the heavens and earth.

Just as Dawn in her saffron gown was hastening from the great Ocean Stream eastward to bring her first shafts of light to men and the undying gods, Thetis arrived at the Myrmidon ships with the armor wrought by Hephaistos out of love to her. She found Achilleus collapsed over the bier of Patroclos, still weeping bitterly. Those about him were also weeping.

When she presented him the armor, his eyes were suddenly ablaze as thoughts of fierce vengeance kindled his fury afresh. He then ran forthwith down the shore and with loud cries beckoned the Greek commanders to his tent. Wearied and wounded and uncertain of what the day might hold, they came running and hobbling from every direction. Nor did Agamemnon himself fail to answer the great son of Peleus's call.

Before the whole assembly the son of Atreus, commander-in-chief of all the Grecian hosts, made apology to Achilleus and offered again in retribution all that his emissaries had said when they went to his tent. But the king of the Myrmidons had no interest in such now. "Give me the gifts, son of Atreus, or keep them yourself," he said. "It matters little. We must not waste time on trivia while great deeds await us, for this day will I join my strength to yours against the Trojans. Let us lay low their ranks and bathe the battlefield with the blood of their murderous Hector!"

The indomitable son of Peleus then bent down to buckle about his ankles the greaves Hephaistos had made. Around his chest he next fastened the silver-studded breastplate and over his shoulders slung his great sword of tempered bronze. When he raised the stately helmet and set it on his head, the plume, of golden fibers wrought more delicate and fine than those of a feather, shimmered, catching the first rays of the morning sun so that it seemed to those looking from afar that the head of Achilleus glowed as if anointed with fire from above. He then took up the sturdy shield that gleamed with the brilliance of the moon and lastly grabbed his thick-shafted spear of Pelian ash, so heavy that only he of all the Greeks could lift it.

Thus armed, he sprang into his chariot and with a thunderous cry bade the rest of the Greeks follow him onto the field against the waiting Trojans. Shouting mightily so that their cheers could be heard across the strait in Thrace and even in Lemnos where Philoctetes still hobbled about cursing the sons of Atreus, this they did.

Then did Zeus, seated on Mount Olympos, give bold Poseidon, his brother, and Hera and gray-eyed Athene leave to move among the Greeks and kindle their fury, and likewise did he bid Ares and Apollo of the golden hair and Artemis, his sister, and laughter-loving Aphrodite mingle among the Trojans to bolster their courage and renew their strength. This he did lest the hosts of Ilion quake at the sight of the fierce, fleet son of Peleus, whom they always feared, and, making no stand, fly to the protection of their high walls.

His heart emboldened by far-shooting Apollo, Aineias, son of Aphrodite, was the first to rush forward to meet the attackers, brandishing his bronze-tipped spear defiantly as he came. Great Achilleus leaped down from his chariot to take him on. Like a monstrous, majestic lion, made furious by a young hunter's chance hit, the raging Myrmidon advanced, roaring mightily as he came, with foam gathered in the corners of his opened jaws, spilling down his chin, his eyes ablaze with the fire of his savage heart.

With all his might the stouthearted Trojan hurled his spear at the oncoming Achilleus, striking the magnificent shield dead center. Another shield the spear would have pierced, pinning its bearer, but against the shield made by Hephaistos it fared no better than if it had struck a sheet of granite. Achilleus's thick-shafted spear of Pelian ash in turn tore through the shield of Aineias as though it were parchment, whizzing past the Trojan, who was crouched aside, and lodging in the ground far behind him. To spare him certain death, for his time had not yet come, earth-shaking Poseidon intervened to snatch Aineias away in a cloud of darkness.

Achilleus quickly retrieved his spear and, shouting for the Greeks to follow him, charged into the thick of the Trojan ranks. He next cast his weapon at Demoleon, son of Antenor, who wore a tight-fitting helmet that came down across his cheeks. The thick bronze, however, did not stay the carefully honed tip of Achilleus's spear, which penetrated the bone as well, spraying Demoleon's brains every which way, thereby cooling his ardor for war. Yanking his shaft free, Achilleus then drove it into the midriff of Hippodamas, who was just leaping down from his chariot. He bellowed like a bull in his death throes. Next the son of Peleus ran the dripping spearhead through Polydoros's back and out his navel. The young man, apple of his father's eye, slumped to the dust holding his entrails in his hands.

Dryops fell also to Achilleus's spear and Demouchos, a huge mountain of a man, to his sword. Springing next into the chariot of Laogonos and Dardanos, the swift Myrmidon hurled the two brothers out onto the ground. One he cut down with his spear, the other with a quick blade in close combat. Tros, the son of Alastor, clasped Achilleus's knees when he was about to kill him. "Let me go," he implored, "for I perceive we are men of the same age." Achilleus plunged his sword into the man's chest so that his liver spilled out onto the ground followed by a rush of black blood. Then he wheeled around and drove his spear clean through the head of Mulios. Echelos next felt Achilleus's blade and after him Deucalion and Rhigmos, who had just arrived from Thrace and would never see its fertile vales again.

As fire rages at drought-time through a mountain glen dense with dry undergrowth, the swirling winds driving tongues of fire in every direction, even so did great Achilleus charge through the Trojan ranks, swinging his spear like an avenging god, his hands besmeared with gore, lunging now here and now there until the soft earth became muddied with the blood of those he slew.

Backward, ever backward, toward the full-flowing Scamandros the wrath-possessed son of Peleus now pressed the terror-stricken Trojans. Like creatures of the forest—swift deer and bears and curve-tusked boars— rousted from their homes by fast-spreading flames, they fled in panic from certain doom. When they reached the banks of the river, they leapt into its swift swirling eddies, confident of finding more mercy in its uncertain currents than in the fiery scourge that bore down upon them. They bobbed about in the water, men and horses, filling it from bank to bank, hoping Achilleus would pursue his vengeance in other quarters.

Such was not to be. Setting his spear against a tamarisk bush, the Grecian hero drew his sword and plunged into the river. The Trojans, like frightened fish fleeing from a huge dolphin, scurried in every direction but to no avail. The grandson of Nereus was as swift and agile in water as on land. Like a farmer flailing vermin in his grain bin, he lashed out wildly with his great silver-studded bronze sword until at last his arm was tired. Hideous groans rose up from the river, and the water ran red with Trojan blood.

At length the river itself rebelled over the great carnage Achilleus was perpetrating within its banks. "You fill my clear waters with blood and gore, oh, son of Peleus," it roared at him. "My channels to the sea are choked with corpses. Give me peace. If you must pursue your bloody enterprise, pray do it on the land." Then to make its point great Scamandros smote him with a wave that swept him off his feet. Grabbing the roots of a large elm that grew along the bank, Achilleus pulled himself ashore and continued his slaughter across the plain.

From the highest tower of the city wall aged Priam looked on as his Trojans fled in panic-rout before the great Achilleus. "Watch closely," he called down to the sentries. "Swing the gates wide open for our people. The son of Peleus is hot behind them. As soon as they are inside, slam them quickly shut again, for we will all be doomed if that man comes bursting through."

And so it was that the fleeing Trojans found safety at last in the city. Still trembling like frightened fawns, they huddled together inside the high walls, wiping the sweat from their brows and raising their cups to slake their thirst. Of all the sons of Ilion yet able to stand, only great Hector stayed outside the wall, waiting near the Scaian Gates for his fated rendezvous with blood-bedrabbled Achilleus.

Still in the tower, Priam watched the great son of Peleus, his matchless armor gleaming more brilliantly than Orion at harvest-time, as he hastened along the walls thirsting for further vengeance. "Hector," the aged king cried, imploring his son with outstretched arms, "do not face this man alone. This day he is mightier than you. Come inside, Hector, my son. Only if you live to fight another time will your wife, your child Astyanax, and I be safe from the fury of the unpitying Greeks."

"Better to fight him at once," replied the mighty Hector, "and find out to which of us Zeus is pleased to give the victory."

When presently the heroic Myrmidon descended upon him, however, Hector was overtaken by fear and quickly took to flight along the wall. Brandishing his great spear of Pelian ash, the relentless son of Peleus took chase. As a mountain falcon, swiftest of birds, bent on the kill, swoops down upon a cowering dove, thus did the great Achilleus make straight for the son of Priam, turned in flight and running as fast as his legs would carry him. Three times they ran at full speed around the city. Swift was the man who fled, his life the prize of the race, but swifter the one who pursued.

On the fourth circuit Hector turned and faced his adversary. "No longer will I run from you, son of Peleus," he called out. "Let us stand now against one another, to slay or be slain. Should great Zeus give me the victory, I will yield your body unviolated to your companions when I have stripped off the armor. I ask that you do likewise if you prove victor."

"Beasts make no promises," shot back Achilleus. "Summon up your strength, murderous son of Priam, for I am about to pay you full measure for the grief you caused my friends."

Saying this, he hurled his great thick-shafted spear at Hector's head, but the Trojan, seeing it coming, ducked in the nick of time and so the shaft flew harmlessly beyond him. Then, with truer aim, the mighty son of Priam let drive his spear. It struck the wondrously wrought shield of Achilleus in the center, but with a ring as if of a cymbal it glanced off, barely denting the tempered gold.

Deep dread overcame the heroic Trojan, for it seemed that the undying gods had conspired to make Achilleus invincible. Nonetheless, he drew his great sword and rushed his adversary, determined that if he were appointed then to die he would do so in a way that men would talk of for years to come. Holding the mighty Trojan at bay with his huge, impenetrable shield, Achilleus circled round until he was able to retrieve his great spear of Pelian ash. Then he studied Hector's armor to ascertain where the Trojan was most vulnerable, his eyes focusing at last on his throat just above the upper rim of his breast-plate. And this was where, suddenly springing forward, Achilleus drove the bronze head of his terrible thick-shafted spear. The mighty Hector stiffened in place and, dropping his sword, fell at Achilleus's feet.

"Did you think you could kill Patroclos and not reckon with me?" said Achilleus over him. "While he is honored with sacred funeral rites, dogs and vultures shall dine on you."

"By your parents I implore you," said Hector, the life quickly fleeing his body. "Let my father redeem my corpse with rich treasures of gold and bronze."

Pitilessly Achilleus looked down upon him and answered thus: "Though Priam were to give me your weight in gold—yea, or twenty times as much— I still will not yield up your corpse except to dogs, so much do I loathe you, whom men have called mighty."

"Heaven will curse you, stiff-necked son of Peleus," said then Hector, as his soul went out of him and flew down to the kingdom of Hades beneath the earth.

The Greeks now came running and crowded around. Men who the previous day had fled in mortal terror from the great son of Priam now darted in to bury their spearheads into his breathless corpse. "He's much tamer than when he was throwing firebrands onto our ships," they said to one another.

Nor was Achilleus himself loath to commit outrage on the body of the Trojan hero either; for when he had stripped him of his armor, he slit the flesh at the backs of both his ankles in from the tendons and into the holes thus made inserted thongs of thick rawhide. To the rawhide he tied ropes, which in turn he tied to his chariot. Then, loading the armor onto the chariot, he leaped aboard and cracked the whip above the heads of his horses.

Across the plain, even to the bier of Patroclos, Achilleus dragged the body of Hector. There he loosed it from his chariot and, in further dishonor to the noble Trojan, stretched out the corpse as if in obeisance to his dead companion, its face pressed downward into the dust. Then at the very moment Andromache within the city was being told of her husband's death, the great fear of her heart now come to pass, Achilleus called together his Myrmidons, and they mourned afresh for Patroclos.

Next day, when Dawn had stretched her rosy fingers across the skies, the son of Peleus gave orders that a pyre be built. Into all the nearby woods the Greeks went and cut down trees, pines and stately oaks, and split them and brought them to the place along the shore Achilleus had chosen for his friend's memorial. When the pyre was finished, they laid the corpse of Patroclos atop it, and then Achilleus and all his host cut locks from their hair and threw them over him. The pyre was a hundred feet in either direction.

After packing the body tightly with the fat of many sheep and cattle, Achilleus cut the throats of his dear friend's two favorite dogs and placed those beside him. Then he put twelve captive Trojans, young men all, to the sword and placed their bodies around him as well and after that brought on the torches. All night long winds from off the sea fanned the flames like a huge bellows so that the great fire roared and none could come near it for the heat.

In the morning the Myrmidons gathered the bones of Patroclos and laid them in a golden urn and built a barrow over them. Then throughout the day they celebrated funeral games in his honor. Until almost dusk the games continued, after which every man went to his own tent for supper and sweet sleep. Achilleus went to his tent also, but sleep did not take hold of him. Throughout the night he tossed upon his pallet and wept over the loss of his dearest of friends. When Dawn's first rays gave light to the sea and beach, he rose up and hitched his horses to his chariot and dragged the body of Hector three times around Patroclos's barrow.

For twelve days the son of Peleus continued to heap dishonor in this way upon the corpse of his greatest enemy. Each day after he had dragged the body around the barrow of Patroclos, he took it back to his tent and stretched it out with its face in the dust. The gods, however, forbade the dogs and vultures to come anywhere near it, nor would they suffer the body of Hector to be disfigured or to decay until Achilleus had surrendered it to Priam.

On the evening of the twelfth day old King Priam ordered a wagon to be filled with great treasures as a goodly ransom for his son and then a second wagon to be readied for himself. As soon as it was dark, the two wagons slipped out through the Scaian Gates. Idaios drove the first, Priam himself the other. Zeus, seeing them start off toward the Grecian camp, had pity on them and dispatched Hermes to escort them quietly and unseen to where Achilleus was.

When the wing-sandaled night-guide had brought Priam to the tent of Achilleus and had unbarred the door for him, he bade the aged king farewell and left him on his own. Alone the aged grief-wearied Trojan king entered the tent. Except for his charioteer Automedon and one other, Achilleus had no company. None of the three noticed Priam until he had come close to Achilleus and clutched his knees after the manner of a suppliant and began to kiss the hands that had bereft him of so many of his sons.

As a great lord looks in amazement at a dread manslayer who has fled to him for sanctuary, even so did the astonished son of Peleus stare down in loathing disbelief at the abject king of Troy. Nor could the other two believe their eyes either when they beheld the royal intruder.

Priam spoke quickly before Achilleus could react any further. "Think of your father Peleus, great Achilleus," he said, "who, like me, is wearied with old age. Greatly would he grieve had he the cause that I have. Fifty sons did I have before you Greeks came here. Most are dead, and now the bravest of all, my Hector, has been slain. I come with a great ransom for his body. Fear the gods, oh Achilleus, and think of your own father and have compassion on me. No man has ever been more humbled, for I have raised my lips to the hand that slew my son."

Tears once more clouded great Achilleus's eyes as he thought of his aged father in far-off Thessaly who he knew would go grief-broken to his grave without ever seeing him again. He took Priam's hands from his knees and gently moved them away. Both men then wept, Priam for his son and Achilleus for Patroclos and his father, until the tent itself seemed to join them in their lamentation.

At length, unburdened of his sorrow, Achilleus raised the aged kneeling king to his feet and bade him sit down. "Poor, wretched man," he said to him, "you have acted most daringly by coming here alone among your mortal enemies. Your courage amazes me. The gods give good gifts but evil ones as well. To my father Peleus they gave a kingdom and a goddess for wife; but only one son they gave him, who is doomed soon to die and whose face he will never look upon again. You too were once blessed greatly by the gods; but in the end, you see, they snatch back all they gave and grief is followed by more grief."

"Great prince," said Priam, "accept my ransom for my son. And, having shown compassion on me to let me live, may you return in safety to your father whom you love."

"I will yield to you the body of Hector, good Priam," replied Achilleus, "not because of your ransom, though I will take it, but because I know the gods are behind this. You would not have come through our lines or unbarred my door except that some god was with you." He then went outside with the other two and gave orders that Hector's corpse be washed and anointed and lifted onto Priam's wagon. While this was being done, under his breath he whispered, "Do not be angry, dear Patroclos. I can do no other."

He then went back into the tent. "Your son is now in your wagon, old man," he said to Priam. "Sup with me now and stay here until daybreak. And let us set our sorrows aside. You can weep again in the morning when you bear him back into Troy."

And so it was that the Trojan king ate with the son of Peleus and then slept the remainder of the night in his tent. Just before Dawn stretched out her rosy fingers to herald a new day, aged Priam took leave of Achilleus to go back to the city and prepare for Hector's funeral. "I will stay the fighting for eleven days while you mourn," the great Myrmidon prince said, as the grieved king mounted his wagon. "On the twelfth day we shall resume." The beauteous Briseis stood at his side but said nothing.

# The Fall of Troy

On the day that was appointed Achilleus to die, the far-shooting Son of Leto took the field and without disguise came upon Paris, who, his bow partially bent, was waiting for some Greek to drift within his range. "Why waste your valuable arrows on just anyone?" taunted Apollo. "Think of your fallen brother, and draw your bow on the greatest target of all—vain-glorious Achilleus."

He then led the son of Priam through the Trojan ranks and showed him where the great son of Peleus was laying low his countrymen with his thick-shafted spear, taking a dozen at a time. Paris's hands trembled as he fixed an arrow in his bowstring and bent double his bow. The deadly shaft sang as it whizzed through the air toward Achilleus, who was turned aside, and struck him in the heel. This was not where Paris aimed, but it was where Apollo directed the arrow, for he knew that Thetis had made her son invulnerable except for the heel when she dipped him as a baby in the River Styx.

The poison from the arrow took quick effect, and moments later the most honored Greek who ever lived was dead. Ajax saw him fall and fought valiantly through the thick to retrieve his corpse. The Trojans, inspired as the word was passed through the ranks, let loose a shower of arrows at the bold son of Telamon but did not deter him. He called for Odysseus to cover him and then lifted the body of Achilleus onto his huge shoulders and took him to the Grecian camp. For sixteen days the Greeks mourned their hero. On the seventeenth day they burned his corpse and placed his bones in the same golden urn that held the bones of Patroclos.

Neoptolemos, Achilleus's son by Deidamia, had not yet arrived at Troy; and so it was declared by Agamemnon that the matchless armor of Achilleus, fashioned for him by the lame smith-god Hephaistos, intricately wrought, would be given to the greatest champion among his comrades yet alive. The son of Telamon, to whom the honor rightly belonged, stepped forward to receive the armor, but Agamemnon for reasons of his own awarded it to Odysseus.

And so Ajax, the man who had once fearlessly faced mighty Hector in single combat, hung his head in humiliation and walked back to his tent. No one guessed that he had gone completely mad. The son of Telamon never was one of the world's wise, and now what little mind he had was taken from him. His only clear thoughts were those of the great hatred he bore Agamemnon and Odysseus, whom he blamed for his disgrace. Into the night he dwelt upon his hate and then, as if inspired, rose from his pallet and unsheathed his sword and stormed out of his tent.

In a pasture not far away some herdsmen watched over their cattle and sheep. Ajax heard the lowing and bleating and in his crazed state imagined the animals to be the armies of his now bitterest enemies. And so into the midst of the herds he charged, swinging his sword wildly, leaving in his wake the hacked and blood-bedrabbled bodies of men and animals. Two large, white-footed horned rams he bound with heavy cords and dragged back to his tent when he had finished his slaughter.

One of the rams he imagined to be Odysseus. He pried open the mouth of this animal and cut out its tongue; then, crying in triumph, he clove off its head. The other ram he thought was Agamemnon. This one he stood on its hind legs and lashed to a post. Taking a strip of harness, he next fashioned a two-thonged whip with which to flog the wretched beast. The terrible curses he screamed with each blow one would have thought he had learned, not from men, but from the foulest fiends of darkest Tartaros. At last he clove the horned head from this sheep as well.

Then, bolting from his tent, he ran out into the night laughing and screaming maniacally. "I've paid them!" he cried. "Smooth-tongued Odysseus and the cursed son of Atreus—oh, how I've paid them!"

When he came back into his tent, he sat down between the two slain sheep, their blood-splotched heads at his feet. For a long time he sat there, his head lowered, and did not move. Slowly, in agonizing stages, his sanity returned. When at long last he raised his head to look about, he did so almost laboriously as though he were finally forcing himself to look upon an unendurable reality that he wished were but a passing nightmare. He gazed in horror at the evidence of his madness near his feet and on either side and then beat his head with his fists and bellowed like a great bull in pain.

"Oh, how Odysseus, my enemy, will laugh at me now," he said, standing and walking about his tent. Then he took his sword from its sheath. "But I shall not hear it. This good sword is still mine, unless Odysseus has laid claim to that also. Stained with the blood of a hundred Trojans, its blade shall now take on more color—the richer, deeper stain of him who bears it. Only Ajax, alas, can draw the blood of Ajax." With that, he planted the hilt of the sword firmly in the dirt and the point against his chest and fell forward onto it.

Because of the shame Ajax had brought not only to himself but the army as well, Agamemnon was determined to treat him as an enemy and not allow his corpse to be either burned or buried. Teucros, Ajax's brother, was just as determined to give him normal funeral rites and bury him and would have spear-headed an insurrection to do so. "I shall lay him in his grave with honor and respect. Let Agamemnon frown all he wants to," he told Menelaos, who acted as his brother's courier.

For one of the few times in the war, however, Odysseus opposed his commander-in-chief. "No truer friend do you have in this whole army than I," he said to Agamemnon. "If you value me, then do not, I beg you, cast out this noble man's body unburied. Except for Achilleus, he was the bravest man of all who came to Troy."

"Are you siding then with Teucros against me?" asked Agamemnon.

"Yes, I am."

"Do with him as you wish," Agamemnon replied. "Make it clear, though, that it is your doing and not mine. I would make him a banquet for dogs and vultures."

And so it was that the great Ajax was buried, though not burned. Of all the Greeks buried at Troy, we are told, he was the only one to be laid in a coffin. His armor was buried with him.

The war itself was once more a stand-off. The Trojans were loath to venture far from their high-towered walls; the Greeks, with their two greatest champions now dead, became listless and yearned for their homes. Agamemnon, however, was not about to abandon the venture from which he expected so much glory and for which the price had already been too high. It was to the seer Calchas he now turned. "Tell me," he said. "What must I do to take the city?"

"Look to Lemnos," the seer answered him. "For without the bow of Heracles Troy cannot be taken."

Now the bow and arrows of Heracles were still in the possession of Philoctetes, son of Poias, whom Agamemnon had marooned on the island of Lemnos on their way to Troy because he screamed so mightily over his snake-bitten foot. "Surely that man cannot still be alive," said Agamemnon.

"Oh, but he does live," Calchas told him, "and unless he fights with you, your fighting will be in vain."

When he heard this, Agamemnon sent wily Odysseus and Neoptolemos, Achilleus's son, who had arrived that very day from Scyros, to Lemnos to fetch Philoctetes.

Anticipating the son of Poias's hatred of himself and the sons of Atreus, Odysseus convinced the guileless Neoptolemos that their best hope for achieving their ends lay in cunning rather than direct confrontation. "Play the rogue briefly now," he told the youth, "and repent of it your whole life hereafter. We must do what we have to do."

Although it was against his nature, the youthful son of Achilleus did as the crafty king of Ithaca instructed him. Once on the island, he went alone in search of Philoctetes and found him in a cave. In almost ten years the wretched man's foot had not healed, nor had his agony abated. Speaking the truth as much as possible, though at points not scrupulously, Neoptolemos gradually insinuated himself into the son of Poias's confidence. Indeed it was not long before Achilleus's son had in his own hands, freely given him, the bow and arrows for which he had been sent. He was at one time both pleased and ashamed.

Moments later, however, his natural forthrightness prevailing, Neoptolemos handed the weapons back to their owner. Odysseus, who had been waiting in hiding and just now burst into the cave, looked on aghast. Then in plain language the son of Achilleus described all that had happened at Troy and told Philoctetes exactly why it was he and Odysseus had come to Lemnos. "I ask you directly now as I should have at first," he finally said. "Will you, in the name of the gods whose will it is and for the sake of your own friends, go with us back to Troy?"

"Never," answered Philoctetes.

"Go!" suddenly boomed another voice. And there from behind the rocks rose the gigantic form of Heracles, dazzling like a god, which indeed he now was. "Do as I tell you, son of Poias, for the gods decree it. At Troy will you be healed of your wound and then will you slay Paris, the cause of all the grief, with this bow that was once mine. Out of your suffering you shall win a glory known only by a few. So go, I command you, with this noble youth."

And so it was that Philoctetes went back with Neoptolemos and Odysseus to Troy. Machaon, son of Asclepios, having recovered from his own wounds by that time, then drew on all of his healing skills in Philoctetes' behalf. He cut away the decayed flesh and cleansed the wound with strong wine and after that bound it with compresses of healing herbs and spices. The pain soon left Philoctetes, and before long his foot began to mend.

As soon as he was whole, Philoctetes walked from the Greek encampment out across the plain and on past the two fountains where Achilleus had slain the mighty Hector. Almost to the shadows cast by the high towers near the Scaian Gates he strode. And there he stood and called out for Paris, whose lucky arrow had killed the great Achilleus. He taunted and ridiculed the handsome son of Priam, saying that a god, not he, had shot the fatal shaft and that he would not be so lucky a second time.

Thus the bold son of Poias cast scorn at Paris until at last the Trojan prince donned his armor and, gathering up his bow and quiver, went out to meet him in single combat. Philoctetes quickly took advantage of his greater range. His first arrow whizzed past Paris's head. The second tore through the hand by which he was raising his own bow; and the third, before Paris could turn to run, grazed his right eye. Philoctetes' fourth arrow, catching the Trojan in flight, lodged deeply in his ankle.

Somehow, with the arrow in his ankle and the flesh about it already festering from its poison, the son of Priam managed to hop and hobble back to the safety of the walls. When they saw that he was dying, the Trojans sent a messenger to Oinone, who had been his wife before Helen and who was the most skilled of all the Phrygians in the art of healing, to tell her that Paris was at death's door. "Come quickly," the messenger said. "His life rests with you."

"No," said the woman whom Paris had once rejected for another.

After Paris died, his two brothers, Helenos and Deiphobos, contended with each other for the hand of Helen. Because he was the more valiant in battle, Priam sided with Deiphobos, and so it was he that the Spartan queen, quite unwillingly, took to herself as her third husband.

Helenos, angered by his father's decision, slipped out of the city and went to live in rustic solitude on Mount Ida. He was determined to have no more part with his family and their quarrels against the Greeks. His resolutions, however, were short lived, for the Greeks soon chanced upon him and brought him into their camp. It was he who told them about the Palladion.

"What is the Palladion?" they asked.

"It protects the city," he told them. " 'Tis a small image of Pallas, crafted in wood by Athene herself, with powers beyond belief. When Zeus cast it himself from the heavens, it landed near the tent of our forefather Ilos. Around it he built a temple and around the temple the city you now see. As long as the Palladion remains in Troy, the city is impregnable."

That night Odysseus and Diomedes sneaked up close to the walls. Posting Diomedes outside, Odysseus smudged himself with dirt and disheveled his hair and then, putting on rags, presented himself at one of the gates as a beggar, thereby gaining entrance into the city. As he was prowling about the streets, it so happened that he came upon Helen, who recognized him through his disguise at once. "And what brings the bold son of Laertes into our city this evening?" she said. "Maybe you had best come along with me."

At her mercy, Odysseus followed Helen as she led him into her own quarters. There she washed him and anointed him with aromatic oils and clothed him in silken garments. She was filled with questions about the Greeks, complaining of how she was a hostage of the Trojans, nothing less, and that she was continually trying to escape but could not. "All that keeps me from ending my misery with a noose or pointed dagger," she told him, "is the hope of being again with my only true husband and once more among my own people. Now why is it, son of Laertes, you risk your neck tonight clad in beggar's clothes."

"To steal the Palladion," he answered. "We cannot take the city as long as it's here."

"And if you have it," asked Helen, "what schemes then will you effect to gain passage through these gates? You can't disguise the whole army in beggars' rags."

"We'll find some way," was all that Odysseus would tell her.

Helen took him then to the temple where the Palladion was housed and, when he had seized it, guided him back through the city to the gate by which he had entered and stood by as he drew his blade across the watchman's throat. "Remember all this when you take Troy, son of Laertes," she said as they parted. "And let Menelaos, my husband, know of it too and all the Greeks." Soon joined by Diomedes, the wily Odysseus, with the wooden statue slung across his shoulders, made swift tracks for the Grecian camp.

What Odysseus did not tell Helen was that the Greeks had already contrived to get inside the city by means of a huge wooden horse. It was Odysseus himself who conceived the idea and Epeios, a skilled builder and designer, who oversaw the work. The horse was constructed so that there was room enough in its hollow belly for fifty men. Doors on either side were so carefully crafted that even those who knew where they were could not discern their seams. Odysseus instructed Epeios to inscribe in large letters on one of its flanks this dedication: FROM THE GREEKS TO THE GODDESS FOR A SAFE VOYAGE HOME.

Into the belly of the horse Odysseus placed the bravest of the Grecian warriors, including Menelaos, Diomedes, and the young Neoptolemos, whom he himself joined. Its doors shut, the gigantic wooden horse was then dragged across the plain and posited in front of the Scaian Gates. With great show the Greeks thereupon burned their tents and, boarding their ships, headed out across the sea in the direction of their homeland. When they came to the island of Tenedos, however, and had sailed round it to the side away from Troy, they cast anchor and waited for nightfall. Sinon, schooled in duplicity by Odysseus, stayed behind at Troy.

From their high towers the Trojans took note of the Greeks' departure and, when the ships were well out to sea, threw their gates wide open. Euphoria swept over them. Like foals at last let loose after being long penned in winter stables, they frisked and frolicked across the plain that had lately held so much grief for them. Then along the shore they scampered, pointing out to one another the place where Achilleus's tent had stood and Diomedes', now in charred ruins.

At the Scaian Gates others gathered and gawked at the huge wooden horse. They all marveled at the immense size of it, far too big to be drawn through even these gates, which were their largest. "Let us tear away part of the wall and bring it in," urged one man. "How handsome the Greeks' horse would look in front of the palace."

"No," said another. "We need no more Greek treasures in our city. Throw it in the sea rather, or get a good bonfire going under it."

And so the people were divided; nor did King Priam, who soon came upon the scene, know which side spoke more wisely. Striding then into their midst came the great soothsayer Laocoon. He stationed himself under the enormous belly of the horse and raised his arms for all to be quiet and listen as though he were speaking by inspiration of some god.

"Hear me, my simple-hearted countrymen," he cried out to them. "Are you suddenly trusting this enemy whose ways are full of deceit? Be sure this is a trap of some sort. Do not think we have seen the last of Agamemnon and his hosts. Beware the Greeks bearing gifts." Then with all his might the burly seer drove his spear into the planking of the horse's underside. The blow jarred the armor of those inside so that it rang like struck cymbals.

Had not a new commotion distracted the people, the prophet might have won his point, but it so happened at that moment that a band of

253

Trojan shepherds intruded excitedly onto the scene, dragging the young spearman Sinon. He was unkempt and in rags and visibly trembled as his captors cast him at the feet of Priam. "We found him in the marshes," their spokesman told the king. "He surrendered to us and threw himself upon our mercy."

The children round about began to poke at Sinon with sticks. Tears welled up in his eyes. Then with plaintive, almost sobbing voice he cried, "Alas, misery stalks me wherever I turn. The Greeks seek my life, and the Trojans would make me victim of their blood-sport. Will no one take me in?"

"Who are you, and why were you left?" asked Priam.

"I am a Greek, oh king," he answered. "I will not tell you otherwise, for never let is be said of Sinon that he was a liar. Early in the war Odysseus did in Palamedes, my dearest friend, and I made the mistake of cursing him for it in front of the whole army, for which I brought down his undying hatred upon myself as well. But why do I tell you? You should have killed me right away, for nothing would have pleased Odysseus more."

Snared now by curiosity, the elders about Priam pressed to know more of Odysseus's treachery. "What plots did he devise against you?" they asked.

"More than once," the still trembling trickster told them, "the Greeks grew weary of the war and decided to retreat from Troy, but each time untowards winds prevented us from sailing. Then was Eurypylos sent to the oracle and returned with these awful words: 'By innocent blood you bought the breeze to bring you here; thus, by more innocent blood must you pay for your return.' Calchas was appointed to choose the victim. Calchas, as you know, is Odysseus's friend. Few were surprised when his lot fell upon me. They tied my hands and feet and set about to prepare the altar, but before they got back I managed to loose my bonds and run for my very life to the marshlands, where I hid among the swamp grasses in the mud until they sailed."

"Which is where these herdsmen found you—is that right?"

Sinon told them yes, that was so. "I'll never see my home again or my dear children or the father whom I yearned to see," he continued, tears now rolling down both cheeks making gullies through the dirt. "If I know him, Odysseus will demand their innocent lives in retribution for my escape. Oh, you winds, gather yourselves against him that he may never reach Greece to visit his evil on those I love!"

Not a few of the Trojans around him were blinking back tears by the time Sinon finished. The son of Laertes could not have been more persuasive himself, for the play-actor's whole aspect so conformed to the temper of his much-practiced lines that nothing in his performance seemed other than natural and spontaneous. Those who had taunted him backed away in shame. Priam ordered him released.

"I am now no more bound by my country's laws," he said, in feigned gratitude, "but by yours."

"Tell us then," said Priam, "what is the meaning of this horse?"

"The horse," Sinon told them, "is to placate the goddess Athene, whose statue Odysseus and Diomedes stole out of its temple. When they brought it back to our camp, fire shot from its eyes, and its limbs were bathed with sweat. Three times it sprang up into the air. It was then Calchas advised us to take flight from this place, for, having enraged the goddess, we could no longer hope to take Troy; therefore, we must return to Greece and recruit a larger army and, in the meantime, to make our peace with Zeus's daughter. For that reason they built the horse as a gift to her."

"But why so large?" Priam wanted to know.

"So you could not bring it inside your city," Sinon said. "Calchas warned them that if you ever did give it a place of honor within your walls, you might soon lead an army against Mycenai, and the blessings of all the gods would be upon it."

Most who heard this implored their king to give orders at once that stones be pried loose to enlarge the gates so the horse could be dragged into the city, but some few still raised contrary voices. While they wrangled, two gigantic serpents skimmed shoreward across the crests of the waves from far out at sea, their blood-red hooded heads and throats towering high above the water's surface. The first to see them were struck dumb with fright and could but grab their companions and point. People scattered in every direction.

Straight toward Laocoon the serpents glided, as if some unseen hand were guiding them. The seer's two little sons were playing near him. Each monstrous snake seized hold of one of the children and, quickly wrapping its coils around him, opened its hideous jaws to swallow him whole. Laocoon, brandishing his spear, rushed in to save them, but in a flash the serpents entwined themselves around him as well. Twice about his midriff they coiled and twice about his throat. Then they struck him again and again so that black blood and venom covered his face. After killing Laocoon and his little boys, the twin serpents slithered through the gate and disappeared into the temple of Athene.

Immediately the men began tearing down part of the wall so they could bring the horse, now deemed sacred, into the city. Cassandra ran wildly from one workman to another. "Its hollow belly is filled with armed men!" she cried out to them. "If you bring it inside the walls, Troy will be in ashes by tomorrow and her women widows. Believe me! Somebody believe me!" But no one listened to her, even though they all heard the clang of Grecian armor within the horse as they carefully rolled it through the enlarged gates to a place of honor just opposite King Priam's palace.

Toward evening, when most of the citizens had joyously gathered in one place or another to feast and drink their deliverance, Helen strolled alone round and round the great horse. "Menelaos, my only true husband," she said, "this night will I await you in my chambers. Come to me soon, my dearest husband." Then to some of the other men in the horse she spoke also, imitating their own wives' voices and indeed so well that they almost answered her.

As soon as it was dark, the Greek ships, which throughout the day had been lying off the far side of Tenedos, weighed anchor and headed back to Troy. Noiselessly the oarsmen sliced into the still, black waters with their slender pine blades. No one spoke. A single beacon, a fire lit by Sinon atop Achilleus's tomb, guided them.

Not until the middle of the night when most of the reveling was over and the joy-wearied, wine-numbed city was at last asleep did the men within the great cavelike belly of the horse silently slip the bolts of their doors and slide down their ropes. While some stole up behind the sentries, whose senses were dulled by much celebration, and slit their throats, others, keeping in the shadows, worked their way toward the gates. Menelaos set out alone to search for Helen.

By this time Agamemnon and the army, having landed and moved with painstaking stealth across the plain, were crouched just beyond the wall. Then at once the gates were flung wide open, and the greatest expeditionary force until that time ever assembled slipped swiftly and furtively into the city without a spear's being thrown. Quickly they spread out to every quarter and broke down doors and dispatched the Trojans in their sleep. Screams, then smoke soon awakened the slumbering city.

Young Neoptolemos rushed toward Priam's great palace. Murderous fury raged in his heart. Onto the roof he threw blazing brands of fire and then attacked the heavy oaken door with his double-bladed battle-ax. The planks were soon shattered by his blows. Then from room to room he ran, smashing quickly through such doors as were barred against him. No man stood against him for long. Women clutched the railings and wept hysterically as though any moment might also be their last. Before long other Greeks had burst through the broken door and were overrunning the palace as well.

From his room above the courtyard Priam awoke to the screams within the palace and without. Fires were beginning to light up the sky outside, their orange tongues darting up everywhere as if to lick the dark, smoke-dense clouds overhead. Nor was the aged monarch slow to grasp the meaning. His pale arms shaking, he strapped on his armor, long stored, and took his spear in both hands. Down the steps he then strode, bearing himself like the king he was, and out into the courtyard.

In the middle of the courtyard was a broad altar to Olympian Zeus; already huddled around it were Queen Hecabe and her daughters. "Over here, my wretched husband," the queen called out to Priam. "Why the spear? Throw it down. Not even our mighty Hector could save us now. Seek mercy at great Zeus's altar, or here find death."

At that moment Polites, one of their sons, staggered into the court-yard and fell in front of the altar. The son of Achilleus was close behind him, his sword raised to finish the work his spear had begun, though not necessary, for Polites was then already dead. A stream of blood ran from his corpse toward his aged father's feet. "Infamous son of a great father!" cried Priam. "Take this for your outrage against my family!" And with that, he feebly cast his spear, which Neoptolemos easily deflected with his shield.

"Be now my messenger to my father," said the powerful youth. "Tell him of my deeds." Then seizing the aged king by the hair, he dragged him through his son's blood to the altar; and with Hecabe and her daughters looking on in horror, he drove his sword up to the hilt into Priam's side and, withdrawing it, clove off the old man's head.

Elsewhere in the city Menelaos, soon joined by Odysseus, had found the house of Deiphobos. Helen, having slipped from her Trojan husband's bed as soon as he was asleep, had unbarred the door and was awaiting them. It was she who pointed them to the bedchamber. What ensued was butchery, not battle.

The son of Priam, already stirred by noises, sprang from his bed when the two Greeks broke through the bedchamber door. Desperately he fumbled for the sword he kept under his pillow but which Helen had painstakingly confiscated before unbarring the door. Nor were his shield or spear in the room either. Menelaos advanced upon the defenseless man, for him his brother's surrogate, and sliced off both his ears. Then he slit wide both the Trojan's nostrils and with the sharp tip of his sword carved deep furrows down his face and arms. When at last his ghost left him, there was no part of the hapless Deiphobos that was not thoroughly mutilated.

Dawn brought no cheer to the Trojan women as she stretched out her rose-tipped fingers across land and sea that next morning. Though the slaughter was now over, or very nearly so, fires from the previous night still smouldered throughout the city. While the rank and file of the Greeks razed what had not burned and commenced to tear down the great high towered walls, having finished their looting, their princes met in council to decide the destinies and destinations of their principal captives.

Cassandra, whose long-guarded virginity had been violated by the son of Oileus the night before in the temple of Athene (causing her statue to blush, we are told, and her eyes to turn heavenward), became the war prize of Agamemnon. Odysseus was awarded Hecabe, and Andromache, mighty Hector's widow, went to Neoptolemos.

"But what of Achilleus?" asked someone.

Into several men's dreams, it seems, the great hero had recently intruded. "Our ships were out at sea," they each swore, "and from his tomb he rose, his armor flashing like the sun. His arm reached to hold us back. Then cried his voice, 'Do you sail, my Greeks, and leave my grave unhonored?' " Neoptolemos too said that he had had this dream.

"Did he not once say he wanted the fair Polyxena, Cassandra's own sister, for prize when Troy was ours?" said someone else.

Others also knew of this, and a concensus grew soon among them that the princess Polyxena should be taken to Achilleus's tomb and there be offered to the dead hero. Then Agamemnon rose up in their midst and said, "Are not our hands already red enough with gore? Need we stain them more with innocent blood? Let us incur the gods' blessing for our return home, not their curses."

"Is this our commander who speaks or Cassandra's new lover seeking a warmer bed?" shot back one of the Athenian princes.

Agamemnon did not give up easily, but in the end the will of the many prevailed and Odysseus was commissioned to fetch the girl and bring her to Achilleus's tomb. And for this occasion Neoptolemos was given the office of priest. He it was who drew the sacrificial knife across Polyxena's throat and held her so that her rich blood soaked the ground where the bones of Achilleus were buried.

The council also debated the fate of the child Astyanax, son of Hector, though not for long. It was of a mind to spare him until the seer Calchas rose up to speak. "Of a truth I tell you," he said, "the boy, if he should live, will be the avenger of his parents and his city. Look about you. He will make your cities even as this one." Although the princes shrank from killing a child in cold blood, they ordered that it be done, and so Astyanax was taken to the highest tower of Troy and flung to his death on the rocks below.

Menelaos was given full leave to dispose of Helen as he wished. More than once he had proclaimed his intention of "killing the harlot without mercy," although he had not done so the night before when he came upon her. She had seemed so pitiful then. Through her thin nightclothes he could see her trembling in fear of him. "No," he had told Odysseus, "there is no need to kill her right away. Morning will be soon enough."

And now that morning had come, he ordered her brought before him. He would grant her a few last words, he had decided, but that would be all. When the men who fetched her thrust her at him, she looked up as if half expecting his sword would already be drawn to receive her. Her eyes had tears, and her face bore that aspect of bewildered agony one often sees in a child struck without clear cause by his mother or a beloved nurse; her incomparable beauty, perhaps enhanced by the years rather than marred, nonetheless somehow shined through.

"Is there anything you wish to say before you die?" he said to her, his hand resting upon the hilt of his sword.

"Did you not know," she replied, "that the gods masterminded all this. And that I was as much the helpless victim of their machinations as anybody else? It was Aphrodite who bewitched me by her irresistible magic to come with Paris to Troy. Her power is awesome. I had no more choice than if the West Wind had grabbed me up in a gale and carried me hither."

"Aphrodite—nonsense!" called out Hecabe, who was standing nearby.

"It was she," shot back Helen. "When Paris first came to my house, she was at his side."

"Your lust got the best of you," said Hecabe. "My son was the most handsome man you ever saw. He dazzled you in his Asian splendor, his silken robes trimmed with gold. The sight of him stirred your juices to make them flow. Aphrodite is but a name for your own lust, my dear, nothing more."

Ignoring the queen's taunts, Helen went on. "As the goddess's spell left me," she said, "I tried to escape this, my prison. Oh, how many times I tried to escape and the watchmen, warned of my designs, prevented me! I would have ended it all with a noose around my neck, but I knew I would be of greater service to you alive. Ask Odysseus. Did I not help him steal the Palladion? Did I betray any of you in the horse? My dearest husband, you know where my loves and loyalties lie." With that, she fell to the ground before him and clutched his knees. Tears now rolled freely down her cheeks, and her breasts swelled as she heaved loud and plaintive sighs.

Menelaos raised his hand to push her away, then checked himself and said, "Better I take you with me back to Sparta and make an example of you there." He could not take his eyes from her lovely breasts.

Nearly insane by now was Priam's prophetic daughter Cassandra, for she alone of all the vanquished bore the double weight of the gloom that was and that which was to be. Only she was exempted from the greatest single gift ever bestowed upon mankind by the undying gods, that of blind hope. Both her own and her mother's futures were as vividly real to her as the spectacle of vultures now circling high in the gray sky above the smouldering ruins of the once invincible city or as the pungent scent of death beginning to sting her nostrils.

Polydoros, her youngest brother, she knew, was now dead, ruthlessly murdered by the Thracian king Polymestor, to whom Priam and Hecabe had entrusted him. Very soon, when the ships of Odysseus put ashore in Thrace, Hecabe would discover her child's mutilated corpse and in vengeance slay the two sons of Polymestor before the man's very eyes and then, howling with maniacal glee, with several twists of a dagger blind him. Thereupon she would be transformed into a cur, a bitch with blazing bloodshot eyes, her body becoming at one with her wretched soul.

But more than at her mother's fate, Cassandra drew back in terror at her own. Triumphantly with her at his side would Agamemnon, first of the Greeks to return, ride through the twin-lion gates of Mycenai. In his ceremonial bath, though, a net would await him and then the ax of Aigisthos, his wife Clytaimestra's lover and conspirator with her in his death. Thus would ten years of hate be brought to bloody climax, a daughter's death finally avenged. The murder having been accomplished, however, the weapons would then be turned against the pathetic girl brought home by the conquering hero to be his mistress. Slight consolation indeed was the knowledge that years later by the hand of Orestes, Agamemnon's son, would the slayers be slain.

All this the daughter of Priam cried out time and time again to her master and his men as they made ready to depart from Troy and many, many times en route to Greece, but no one believed her. Everything Cassandra ever prophesied invariably came to pass; this was no exception.

# The Wanderings of Odysseus

T he last great hero of the Trojan War to reach home was Odysseus. Had he been first and Agamemnon last, much grief might have been spared both their houses, but such was not to be. Agamemnon was long dead and indeed the faithless Clytaimestra also, and the wily son of Laertes had yet to step foot again on the soil of his beloved Ithaca. A virtual prisoner he was of the lovely nymph Calypso.

All things were available with her for his needs and pleasures, nor was there any food or drink sweet to his taste that was not daily set upon the table before him. Her island, adorned with lush foliage and a thousand different blooms, was a veritable paradise in which to stroll about, and the climate was ever as spring. Being marooned in such a place was many a sailor's fantasy, but for Odysseus it no longer held any charm.

By day the wily strategist of Priam's fall sat upon the rocks where the white-crested waves broke upon the shore and gazed tearfully out across the waters in the direction of what he thought, though did not know, was his home. Face cupped in his hands, he despaired of life itself, wondering if perhaps his shipmates, all perished at sea, might not have had the better fate. At night he crept into bed beside Calypso and dutifully performed his guestly service, reluctant man upon insatiable woman.

"Your thoughts were elsewhere again," the impassioned Daughter of Atlas was often wont to say. "Forget your homeland, my love, and stay forever here with me. I will make you as immortal as I. At least as fair as your beloved Penelope you must find me, and never less fair will I ever be."

"Sweet goddess," on such occasions he would answer, "Penelope's beauty is ugliness next to yours. That I know. But still it is she I pine for and my island home." Long it was then before the sorrowful wanderer could fall asleep, but Dawn's first fingers of light that next morning would find him once more upon the rocks staring intently seaward.

The misadventures that had brought the quick-witted son of Laertes to Calypso's flood-encircled realm began, we are told, when the Ithacans, greedy for additional trophies, went ashore at Ismaros and sacked the city of the Cicones, taking much booty in wine and sheep and women. Into the night they drank and feasted until their bellies bulged and their legs wavered. Back to their ships Odysseus ordered them, but, fools, they would not go.

With the first light of morning came the avenging Cicones and their allies, descending upon the unwary Greeks with horses and chariots not a few. Only by hasty retreat to their ships did Odysseus and his fellows escape complete disaster. As it was, each ship put out to sea six men lighter than it was the day before.

Winds now rose in the north, as if extensions of Thracian wrath, and swept down upon them. Nor was there a friendly port as far as they could see. Black clouds hung low over land and deep alike; the waves mounted, and then night bore down out of heaven and plunged them into utter darkness. The ships, at mercy of the unrelenting gales, were tossed like carrion fish upon the surface of the tumultuous sea and, masts broken, sails rent, were driven ever southward.

For two days and two nights the storm raged unabated, sweeping them past Cythera where they would, if they could, have veered westward toward home. Into broad, uncharted waters were they borne, hands helpless upon their tillers, their fates bound up in the winds. For nine days they drifted after the winds died down and on the tenth joyously set foot on what soon they discovered was the land of the Lotus-eaters.

Lotus was the honey-flavored fruit of a flowery plant which grew rank in the soil of that region. Over those who ate it it cast an enchanting spell so that they wanted to do nothing but remain where they were and continue to gorge themselves. All thoughts of home or noble purpose vanished from their minds; they were as the shades in Hades' dark kingdom beneath the earth, though content with their growthless state.

Out of hospitality the Lotus-eaters offered the first Greeks to come upon them the magic fruit of the lotus, which they took and ate. Immediately they forgot what had brought them there, their shipmates, their destination, everything; they became euphoric as in a sweet dream. Odysseus and the others soon happened upon them, however, and hauled them, protesting, back to the ships, where they bound them to the rowing bench until they were once more out to sea.

Their goodly oars brought them at length to a mountainous island of extraordinary fertility. The ground showed no signs of being tilled, but nonetheless wheat and barley grew as rank there as sedge-grass with heads the size of pine cones. Untended vines produced great clusters of plump, sun-drenched grapes. No villages ran down to the shoreline, however, nor was there so much as a shepherd's hut to be seen along a hillside anywhere.

"Let me and those of my ship go farther along this lush land to see what people might dwell here, whether they be civilized or savages," said Odysseus, after they had come ashore and eaten. "The rest of you wait our return here."

In among the crags overlooking the sea, high up one of the mountains was a great, high-vaulted cave, its mouth partially obscured by sprawling laurels. Nearby was a corral crudely fashioned of large rocks and untrimmed tree trunks, the gravelly surface of which was dotted with sheep and goat tracks, though there were no animals in it now.

When Odysseus came upon the place, he quickly ordered his men back to the shore. Then, admonishing most of the crew to remain ready at the ship, he took twelve men with him to discern what manner of man lived in the cave. He took also a skin of wine given him by Maron at Ismaros, so potent that when mixed with twenty parts water it put men more quickly under Dionysos's spell than any ordinary liquor.

Though the bleats of young lambs and kids greeted the Greeks from within as they stealthily entered the cave, there was still no sign of their keeper. Baskets of cheeses hung from natural pegs along the huge cave's walls. To one side, the young animals looked up from their pens as if in anticipation that their mothers, teats swollen by the day's grazing, might not be far behind. Pans filled with milk and whey sat about on ledges opposite them.

"Note the size of these pails and pans," said one of the men, "and how high some cheeses are hung. No ordinary man dwells here."

"Let us take all we can carry of cheese and lambs and then with swift oars fly from here," said another.

But Odysseus said, "Better to receive gifts as guests than steal as thieves. Let us wait here and greet our host."

And so it was, helping themselves to some of the cheeses, they awaited the master of the cave's return. They did not have to wait long; for very soon their host, if he could be called that, herding his ewes and she-goats into the cave ahead of himself, burst into view. Once inside, he rolled a great boulder across the entrance. Two and twenty horses could not have pulled the boulder aside.

The man was of gigantic size, towering above Odysseus and his men as they in turn towered above the smallest lamb in the pen. A Cyclops he could have been properly called; for, although he bore no kinship to that race sired on Gaia by overbearing Ouranos, nonetheless in the center of his huge, misshapen forehead he had but a single eye. The nymph Thoosa had borne him to Poseidon; his name, as Odysseus later learned, was Polyphemos. "Who are you?" he roared when he finally spied the Greeks. "What brings you, like pirates, to seize the goods of others?"

"Greeks we are," responded Odysseus. "We were on our way home from sacking Troy when it pleased Zeus to send winds to drive us hitherward."

"Where are your ships and the rest of your crew?" the Cyclops asked.

"At the bottom of the wine-dark sea," lied Odysseus. "Great Poseidon hurled them upon the rocks near your coast. Only we were spared the storm's fury. We claim your hospitality in the name of Zeus, protector of guests and suppliants."

The huge, single-eyed giant burst out into peals of laughter. "You're a fool, little man," he jeered, "if you suppose I care aught for Zeus. The only god I pay homage to is this belly of mine. To it I sacrifice roast lamb and venison and, as a drink offering, big pans of milk; then I take my ease beside my warm fire, and, as loud as your Zeus's thunder, I fart heavenward—a prayer, you might say, from my god to yours."

"Oh, Zeus and Pallas Athene," cried out Odysseus, "if you have ever helped us, do so now!"

But even as the son of Laertes spoke, Polyphemos reached out and took a man in either hand and dashed their heads against the cavern floor so that their brains spilled out. He tore them limb from limb and ate them after the manner of a jackal or mountain lion, devouring skin and entrails and cracking open their bones to suck out the sweet marrow. Then, drinking a vat of milk, he stretched himself out to rest.

The Ithacan king could then have crept close enough to plunge his sharply whetted sword into the giant's loathsome heart, and indeed was minded to had he not glanced over at the huge doorstone blocking their escape. Not even with levers could his men have ever hoped to dislodge it; they would be sealed in the cave forever. Putting back his sword, Odysseus sat down with his companions, as far from the giant as possible, to wait out the night.

Morning's first shafts of light beamed through the spaces about the boulder to stir the Cyclops from his slumber. For a time ignoring his guests, he went methodically about the chores of milking and feeding his animals. Then, as a housewife might crack eggs against her skillet for breakfast, he seized two more Greeks and broke open their skulls on the rocks. His meal over, he rolled aside the doorstone, drove out the sheep and goats, and then carefully rolled the boulder back into place behind him.

In one of the pens Polyphemos had left a staff of olive wood, long enough to be the mast for any Greek ship. Odysseus found the pole and cut off a length of it. Then he ordered his men to shave the end of it down to a sharp point, using their swords and fire. When it was finished, he hid it in the dung pile.

At day's end their host returned. As before, he routinely went about his afternoon chores, upon the completion of which he grabbed up two more of Odysseus's men and proceeded to make them his supper. Odysseus himself, holding out his wineskin, then stepped forward. "You have tasted our flesh, Cyclops," he said. "Now you might try our wine. If it delights you, perhaps you will find it in your heart to spare me and send me on my way home."

Polyphemos snatched the skin from Odysseus's hands and began to guzzle the powerful sweet drink. "We have wine from the grapes that grow untended on this isle," he said, "but nothing like this, little man. This is nectar by comparison. Tell me, what is your name? And in what land do you make such delicious wine?"

"Grant me the rights of guests, and I will tell you my name," Odysseus replied.

The Cyclops drank two more long draughts of Maron's miraculous wine, reeling as he did so. "Say your name, little man," he said, "and know what it is to be my guest."

"Noman," the wily Odysseus told him. "My name is Noman."

"And because you are my own little guest, Noman," said the Cyclops, quite tipsy now but raising the wineskin for another drink, "I will eat you last. That will be my guest gift to you." So saying, he staggered, belched thunderously, and, knees buckling, slumped to the floor, quite overcome by deep sleep before all parts of him hit the straw-strewn surface.

Taking the olive-wood pole from hiding, Odysseus and his men carefully turned its point in the fire until it was blazing hot. Then, as if courage had been breathed into them by some god, they raised the great shaft above the Cyclops' forehead and drove the sharp, burning point into his eye. Odysseus then twisted it like an auger. When, with an ear-rending shriek, Polyphemos stirred from his sleep, the Greeks scattered to the various nooks of the cave. He pulled the stake from his eye, with blood and gore following it in much abundance; and then, continuing to cry out with mighty screams, he groped in vain about the cave for his maimers.

His brother Cyclopes in their own caves miles away heard him and called out to him, "What's the matter, Polyphemos? Why do you awaken us with such cries on this peaceful night? Is someone murdering you or stealing your flocks?"

"Noman, my brothers," he shouted back, "is murdering me!"

"If no one is attacking you," they replied, "then 'tis but a pain you suffer sent by Zeus. Pray to our father Poseidon that it might pass." They then went back to their pallets and, turning deaf ears to his screams, soon fell back to sleep.

Nor did Odysseus's craft end there. Throughout the night he worked with sticks and fibers to make slings for his men, each to be supported by three sheep. In the morning, after rolling aside the doorstone to let his animals out to graze, Polyphemos squatted in the opening and felt the back of every creature that passed through lest the men escape; however, in the makeshift slings under the sheep the men were borne into the open air. Odysseus picked out the largest and shaggiest sheep in the flock and rode to freedom upside down tight against the animal's underbelly, his fingers clutching the coarse fleece.

Once outside, Odysseus gathered his six surviving men together and noiselessly made for the ship. Only when seated with their companions once more on the rowing benches did they dare give way to their long-pent emotions. As they churned the waters with their slim pine blades, the son of Laertes tauntingly called out to Polyphemos. "Cyclops," he cried, "we were not destined to fill your craw. You ate men who were guests in your habitation, and this is your punishment from Zeus."

The Cyclops broke off crags and angrily hurled them in the direction of Odysseus's voice, hitting the edge of the tiller and creating waves that carried the ship toward land. Barely did they escape shipwreck. Strong backs and quick oars soon took them well out to sea beyond the blinded giant's range.

Angered, Odysseus cried out again. "If anyone should ask you, Cyclops, who took your sight, tell him Odysseus of Ithaca, sacker of Troy."

"Hear you that, my father," shouted eyeless Polyphemos to the sea. "Prove me your son, oh, great earth-shaking Poseidon, and avenge me on this city-sacker Odysseus. Bear him away from his home, and in your murky depths bury his foul companions." The Greeks, ardent in their escape, heard the Cyclops' prayer only as a distant, muffled drone; however, the unruly god to whom it was addressed heard clearly all his son spoke.

Odysseus and his crew soon joined the men of the other ships, and for the rest of the day until the setting of the sun they celebrated their deliverance with mountains of roast meats and sweet wine. To Zeus they sacrificed the choicest animals of those they had. When night fell, they sank down in welcome sleep upon their decks, the stars shining brightly overhead.

They came next to Aiolia, the floating island where Aiolos, Keeper of the Winds, dwelt with his wife and twelve beautiful children. Six lovely daughters the ageless couple had and six equally handsome sons, who were married to each other. The children took their meals together each day with their doting mother and father, and at night each man slept in sweet repose beside his own wife.

For a whole month Aiolos and his family saw to the comforts of their Grecian guests. The Lord of the Winds seemed never to tire of Odysseus's tales about his and his comrades' exploits at Troy. When at last the Ithacans prepared to take their leave, Aiolos gave Odysseus the skin of a nine-year-old ox into which he had squeezed the winds the son of Laertes would need. With a silver cord he lashed the skin to the deck and showed Odysseus how to release the winds little by little as he had need. Then, giving his guests gentle westerly breezes to start them on their way, he bade them good-bye.

They were ten days at sea when their lookouts spotted the familiar shoreline of Ithaca. So close did they approach their destination that they could see men along the coast tending their fires, but no closer were they fated then to sail. Murmurs had arisen among the men, it seems, to the effect that the skin given their king by Aiolos contained rare and priceless treasures; and while Odysseus slept, wearied by his many tasks, they gave way to their curiosity.

"Is it right," said one, "that we, who have suffered all his hardships with him, should go away empty-handed? Quick, let us see what stores of gold and silver the Keeper of the Winds gave him."

And so they loosened the silver cord on the skin, and all the winds contained therein suddenly burst forth in unrelenting gales. Odysseus awoke, only to see his beloved country disappear in the distance as the storm swept them rapidly away from it. He leaned across the stern and wept. Great despair filled him, and he thought to cast himself into the sea to perish but in the end chose rather to persevere.

Back to Aiolia the fierce winds drove them, back to the island home of Aiolos and his family. "What brings you here again so soon, Odysseus?" asked the Keeper of the Winds. "What god opposes you?"

"My foolish comrades have destroyed me," he answered. "I throw myself once more upon your mercy, kind friend."

"You must go immediately," Aiolos commanded him. "I cannot help again a man the gods most certainly despise. Leave my island."

Silent, sorely grieved in their hearts, the Ithacans boarded their ships and rowed randomly they knew not where. For six days and nights they sailed upon the deep, and on the seventh they came to a rocky and precipitous coast. Beyond all civilization was this place, where days were long and nights but twilight interludes. Into a natural harbor they steered their twelve good ships and tied them fast to the jagged rocks. Odysseus then sent three men inland to see what people dwelt in that distant clime.

The men happened upon a maiden drawing water at a mountain spring. She was childish in aspect though of strapping size. They asked her where they might find the king who ruled over her people, and she pointed them to the path that led to her father's house. Taking the path, they came soon to the high-roofed dwelling and entered the huge hall. Too late they discovered they had wandered into the habitation of a race of giants called the Lestrygonians, for before them stood the maiden's mother, savage, unkempt, and as large as a mountain.

One of the Greeks was seized on the spot by the lord of the house and quickly eaten; the other two miraculously escaped and fled to the ships. Scarcely had they sounded the alarm, however, before the Lestrygonians, a thousand of them, poured down upon Odysseus and his men from all sides. Great boulders, such that ten ordinary men could not budge, they heaved from the high cliffs, crushing men and ships alike. Closing in, the monstrous barbarians skewered the fleeing Greeks, like fish, on their crude spears.

"To the ship!" the Ithacan king shouted to his own crew; and even as they leaped aboard, he brought his sharp sword blade down across the hawser that moored them. Swift oars took them beyond the harbor and out of harm's way, but little joy did Odysseus find in his escape. Of his twelve ships and the men who manned them, only this ship and a single crew were left.

When they next came to shore, not a little way from where these horrors befell them, they lay upon the beach for two days and nights, their bodies drained, their hearts overcome by grief. As Dawn stretched out her saffron fingers to pierce the half-light of morning on the third day, Odysseus rose up and, taking his spear and sword, climbed a nearby hillock in order to survey the land to which they had come.

Miles away he saw smoke curling up into the sky from an area densely wooded. Other than that there was no sign of any habitation. On his way back to the ship he chanced upon a handsome many-antlered stag come down to a brook for his morning drink. A single thrust of the son of Laertes' spear brought down the stately animal, and he bore him off triumphantly to his companions. Throughout the day they feasted on the roasted meat and drank their own sweet wine.

The next morning Odysseus sent Eurylochos and a party out to investigate the smoke he had seen, little suspecting that the island where they had landed was the domain of the enchantress Circe. To a thickly wooded glen Eurylochos and his comrades followed the curling column of smoke, and there it was they spied a modest mansion of polished stone. They could hear a woman's voice, melodic, sweet, singing within. Reluctant to trespass without invitation, they called out to announce their presence.

Immediately Circe came out and beckoned the men to step forth and be her guests. She was stunning to behold. Her dark eyes had a strange, irresistible sparkle to them; her carriage was that of a goddess. The men broke from their places and advanced toward her, with only Eurylochos himself staying back in hiding. Wild animals, great mountain wolves and lions, ambled about the grounds like household pets, but they did not charge the men; rather they approached them gently, their tails wagging, like doting dogs when their masters come in from the fields.

Into her house the dark Daughter of Helios led her guests, seating them on benches and in chairs with arms. Then she set about preparing a beverage for them of cheese and barley and fresh honey mixed with Pramnian wine, into which she also sprinkled magical drugs. This she gave them; and when they had drunk it, she tapped each with her wand and then chased them, now pigs, into a sty. Each had a swine's snout and the bristles and voice of a swine and walked on four cloven-hoofed feet. For the rest of their meal Circe tossed them acorns and coarse barley and such refuse as pigs like to eat.

Eurylochos, not seeing his men reappear from the house, waited a long time and then went back to report to Odysseus. The son of Laertes then girded on his silver-studded sword and picked up his bow and bade Eurylochos to lead him back to Circe's smooth-stoned dwelling. His companion, however, fearing the woman to be some malevolent goddess, begged Odysseus to flee the island with his remaining men at once.

The lord of Ithaca then elected to see to his men's rescue alone—a decision that would surely have spelled his doom too had not wing-sandaled Hermes, in guise as a youth in first beard, accosted him on his way. "You go you know not where," chided the god. "Your men are pigs now in Circe's sty, and you will join them ever to remain there, a swine yourself, if you think unaided you can save them. Here, take this herb. It will counteract the potion she will give you. When she reaches out her wand to touch you, draw your sword as if to slay her. She will then beseech you to lie with her. Do not reject her bed, but demand an oath of her first that she free your companions and succor you in your journey home."

Odysseus took from Maia's son the herb and then proceeded on his way to the wooded glen where Circe dwelt. When he came within sight of her house, he called out, and she heard him and opened her glistening doors and bade him come in. She sat him down in a cushioned chair, elegantly made, silver-studded, with arms. A footstool she placed beneath his weary feet and then, as before, busied herself with her evil concoction.

When the preparation was finished, she gave it to Odysseus and he drank. Then, not suspecting he had taken an antidote, she reached out her wand to touch him. "Now to my sty, fair stranger, to grovel with your companions," she said, but he did not change as had the others. Instead, he unsheathed his sword as if to kill her.

"What kind of man are you?" Circe screamed, falling before him and clutching his knees. "Why were you not charmed by my drug as all others are? Come to my bed and lie with me in love."

"Swear first an oath that you will restore my men and, when I am naked before you, you will not divest me of my courage or manliness," he answered, his sword's point at her throat. "And in my quest for my home lend me your assistance."

When she had sworn by the undying gods of Olympos all that he asked, Odysseus went with the bewitching goddess to her bed. Four maidens attended them. One draped blankets over a chair for his comfort, while another brought in a silver basket of ripe fruit and a third a bowl of honeyed wine. The fourth maiden prepared him a warm bath that brought relief to his fatigue-ridden limbs; when she had washed him, she anointed him with sweet-smelling oils.

All this, however, did not take the son of Laertes' mind off his men, still swine, still penned in Circe's sty. His anguish for them showed in his face. "Why so downcast, Odysseus?" asked his hostess. "You touch neither food nor drink."

"How can I," said he, "when my companions wallow in your sty?"

And so to her pig sty the beautiful enchantress led the despondent lord of Ithaca. Opening the gate, she drove out the swine before her, all huge animals of nine-year-old size. On each of their bristly backs she rubbed a restorative drug. The bristles immediately fell to the ground, the bodies became erect, and their features became once more human; but larger, more handsome were the men than before they were cast under Circe's spell.

Odysseus then returned to his ship and told Eurylochos and the men there all that had happened and brought them with him back to Circe's abode. They were astonished at the suppleness and splendor of their companions, whom the Daughter of Helios in the meantime had anointed with oils and provided luxuriant clothing.

"Men of Ithaca," their hostess addressed them all, "I know of your travails on the fish-filled deep and in savage foreign lands. Grieve no more. Eat, drink, and take your rest until your spirits are restored."

Odysseus took her at her word. Through twelve new moons he and his shipmates indulged themselves in dark Circe's hospitality, feasting daily upon meats without end and plenteous honeyed wine. Nor was Odysseus himself negligent of his hostess's needs.

At last his companions rose up and said, "Oh, foolish man, have you forgotten your own country? Were we not bound for Ithaca?"

Thus reprimanded, their king that very night at Circe's bedside grasped the goddess's knees. "The time has come, fair lady," he said, "for you to make good your promise to help me on my way home. My spirits are restored, and my men are beginning to complain."

"Leave if you must," she told him. "But go first into Hades' dark kingdom, and there inquire of blind Teiresias what your future holds."

When Odysseus replied that he did not know the route to Hades' kingdom, Circe told him how to set his sail and also what sacrifices he must make to appease the dead. "To reanimate the spirit of Teiresias so he can speak," she said, "slay a ram and a black ewe beside him, but let none of the dead come near their blood until he has told you all you need to know."

By dawn's first light the Greeks resumed their journey. Circe, clad in a gown that glistened with her father's splendor pulled about her waist with a finely spun golden girdle, saw them off and presented to Odysseus as a parting gift a handsome ram and a black ewe. Elpenor, one of his younger companions, did not sail with them, however; the foolish youth, drunk with sweet wine, had fallen off Circe's roof and broken his neck. Odysseus did not notice his absence until they were well out to sea.

Following Circe's instructions, they at length arrived at the place she described. There he ordered his men to dig a trench, into which they poured libations of honey and wine and then water. Over these he sprinkled white barley and, invoking the dead, slit the throats of the sheep. As their blood flowed into the pit, out of the shadows the souls of the dead began to venture forth. "Take the slain sheep," Odysseus quickly commanded his companions, "and burn them to the gods and pray." He himself, with drawn sword, stood over the trench to prevent the dead from falling down and lapping up the blood until Teiresias should come.

Shocked he was to see the soul of the missing Elpenor. "How came you here, my comrade?" he asked.

"Fate took me and strong wine," the sailor told him. "From Circe's roof I fell and broke my neck. Unburied on her island I still lie. Return there, I beseech you, to bury my corpse and tend my tomb with tears."

Odysseus promised to do as his comrade's shade requested. Next to appear whom he recognized was Anticleia, his own dear mother; but, though he wept when he saw her, he would not let her near the blood before Teiresias. When at last the great Theban seer's shade appeared, addressing Odysseus by name, the son of Laertes stepped aside and let him drink.

The blind prophet, when he had sated himself with the black blood, turned again to Odysseus. "You seek a sweet journey home, son of Laertes," he said. "But such is not to be, for you have raised the ire of the great earth-shaker Poseidon by blinding his beloved son Polyphemos. You may yet achieve your end, however, if you and your companions leave unharmed the cattle of Helios. Should you raise violent arms against them, your companions shall surely all perish; and, though you yourself may survive, only after long time and much anguish will you reach your homeland, by then given to lawlessness.

"By craft or daring you may win the day against your goddesslike wife's suitors. Should you do so, take an oar and venture inland to where men neither season their food with salt nor have ever seen a sea-going ship. Where a stranger asks whither you go with a winnowing fan, there plant the oar in firm soil and offer to Poseidon a ram, a bull, and a boar. Then, returning home, raise hecatombs to all the undying gods of Olympos. Far from the sea will death finally close your eyes, but only when you are ripe with years and by glad friends surrounded. This I tell you truly."

When Teiresias left off speaking, Odysseus allowed his mother to come near the pit and lap up the thick blood. She it was who told him of Penelope's steadfastness in the face of great trials and of his father Laertes' grief-prompted seclusion. As her voice grew faint, he thrice attempted to take into his arms the dear frame he had so many times in life held close; but each time, like a vapor, she eluded his embrace.

Others afterward came close to him also: Alcmene, Jocasta, Leda, Phaidra, the once beauteous Ariadne, then Agamemnon, Patroclos, Ajax, and the mighty Achilleus himself among them. Forlorn of hope and strengthless they all seemed, their former greatness now mattering nothing. Odysseus, heavy of heart, returned to the ship. Back to Circe's island he set the sails so that he could bury his companion Elpenor as he had promised.

When Circe saw them off a second time, she warned Odysseus of the honey-voiced Sirens who, with irresistible song, lured sailors onto the fatal rocks along their shore. Also she told him to eschew the Wandering Rocks in favor of the course that would take them past Scylla and Charybdis.

"Thrice each day the divine Charybdis sucks the dark waters under. If you are near the place, not even the earth-shaker Poseidon himself could save you," she said to him. "When you sail those narrows, therefore, favor the high cliff side where the monster Scylla dwells. Six great heads she has, and each will snatch up a man from off your deck. It is the price you must pay. Better six men than the whole ship."

Grieved by what she said, Odysseus bade her farewell and ordered his companions to begin rowing. In no time at all steady backs and goodly winds brought them close to the Isle of the Sirens. Odysseus then commanded his men to cut up a ball of wax into small pieces and knead them in their hands. The kneading plus the sun's heat quickly softened the wax so that Odysseus could stuff all their ears with it. He alone did not have his ears packed with the wax; but, following his orders, his companions lashed him to the mast so that he could not move.

Soon he heard the first strains of the enchanting honey-voiced sisters' song:

> Come hither, bold Odysseus!
> Sweet the delights men find with us!
> Come, mighty Greek, forsake your rue;
> Our hearts are true and set on you.
> Oh, come to us, Odysseus!

No more beautiful sound was ever heard. Hauntingly their voices drifted across the wine-dark waters—made the sweeter, if that were possible, by the passage—and filled the son of Laertes' heart with their magic.

"Cut me loose! Free me!" he shouted; and when he realized his men could not hear him either, he tried to make clear his will with arched brows and contorted jowls. The men rowed swiftly on.

Only when they were a great distance beyond the Isle of the Sirens did the men unplug their ears and undo the knots that bound their captain. Shortly thereafter they came to the straits of Scylla and Charybdis. To avoid the sure disaster of Charybdis, Odysseus defined a course close to the towering crags in which the six-headed Scylla lurked. He had not told his men what Circe had said of the monster.

Looking to the roiled waters where Charybdis dwelt, he did not see Scylla strike. Each foul head was at the end of a long reptilian neck; and it was indeed as a coiled snake strikes, suddenly, unperceived, that the heads of Scylla shot down to the deck of Odysseus's ship, each one grasping in its hideous triple jaws one of his most robust men. They cried out his name, but that was all. When he turned to look, they were already dangling, like fish on a line, high above the ship, their arms and legs thrashing violently, though not for long.

Soon it was that they came within view of the blessed Island of Helios. They could see on the green meadows the god's sleek, incomparable cattle and from the vales hear the bleating of his sheep. "Listen, my companions," said Odysseus. "Teiresias warned me of this place, that from it sure disaster might ensue. Let us, therefore, sail beyond it and not tempt our fate."

Eurylochos responded thus, speaking for all: "You are a man above men, Odysseus, with limbs of iron and strength to endure all things, but we are ordinary and right now bone weary and ready to drop. Have pity. Let us refresh ourselves here overnight."

Knowing he could not compel them all, Odysseus said, "Swear then a mighty oath that not one cow or sheep from the Sun God's herds will you slay but be content with what we brought from Circe's store."

Gladly they swore the oath. And so, against his better judgment, Odysseus directed the ship into a cove, and they went ashore. The men ate that night of Circe's provisions and afterward mourned their companions devoured by Scylla. Adverse winds came up, however, in the dead of the night, preventing their departure the next morning. For a whole month the untoward winds blew, and the Greeks were held as though prisoners on the Sun God's island.

What Circe had given them was soon used up, and the men set

snares for birds and tried to catch fish with bent hooks—all with little success. Hunger gnawed at their bellies. Odysseus, fearing what they might do, fought off sleep but could do so for only so long. When at last sweet sleep closed his eyelids, his companions in their desperation slaughtered several of the god's choicest cattle and gorged themselves upon them.

In horror Odysseus awakened to the aroma of roasting meat. There was nothing he could now do; the Sun God's sacred cattle had already been killed. As signs the gods caused the flayed hides to crawl along the ground and the meat upon the spits to bellow forth as cattle in pain. Odysseus refused to dine with his men.

On the seventh day after the slaughter of the cattle the winds abated, and they set sail. Soon a tempest rose, though, sent by the angry Son of Cronos, cracking the mast in two and whirling the ship wildly about on the raging flood. Thunder broke from the black clouds overhead, and a bolt of jagged lightning split the heavens and struck the deck, filling the ship with the fumes of brimstone. Men toppled into the sea. The planks from the keel tore loose.

By clinging to a piece of the mast, however, Odysseus managed to stay afloat after both the ship and his men had passed forever from his sight. Rowing with his hands, he tossed upon the surface of the deep for nine days and nine nights. On the tenth day the gods brought him to Ogygia, the island of Calypso.

# Home to Ithaca

The circling seasons passed and soon also the years, but the bright-eyed Daughter of Zeus did not forget the weeping, hapless, homesick son of Laertes, who for long had been her darling. "Son of Cronos," the goddess said to her father, "it has been above nine years since Troy's towering walls were razed and Priam was slain. All the Greeks, save only one, have returned to their homes. Stout-hearted Odysseus, long wracked by fate, yet pines for home and family, himself a slave to lusty Calypso. Hear you not his moans?"

"A favorite of mine is the man," replied her deep-thundering father. "It is earth-girdling Poseidon's rage that plagues him, not mine. The time has come, however, when we must lay schemes for his return."

And so to Ithaca, we are told, the Father of Gods and Men sent his bright-eyed daughter to bolster the spirits of Penelope, who was besieged daily now by her suitors' demands. To Calypso he dispatched swift-sandaled Hermes with orders that she help Odysseus build a raft for his departure from her island. The Daughter of Atlas complained but in the end agreed to do as the fleet messenger of Zeus commanded her.

When Odysseus came back to their cave quarters that evening, eyes red and cheeks streaked, the full-tressed nymph brought her face close to his and said, "Grieve no longer for your home, woe-plagued man, for I will help you construct a broad, seaworthy raft. Decks we will make to keep you dry and on them store food and water and sweet wine for your journey. Thus, winds and gods permitting, you will sail to your beloved country."

Odysseus, by this time no longer trusting appearances, said, "You are not plotting some means to my further undoing I hope."

"So full of tricks are you yourself," laughed Calypso, "that you suspect roguery in all others too. No, by the River Styx, I swear I am party to no plot except to help you after so long time on your way."

That night they ate sumptuously together, he of the tastiest of mortal foods and she of ambrosia, and then retired to the goddess's plush-quilted bed. In each other's arms they writhed in love's raptures, satisfying to both alike as when Odysseus first came there; and when dawn's first fingers of light penetrated the cave that next morning, both rose up refreshed and went to the woods to commence cutting timbers for the raft. Calypso supplied the son of Laertes with axes and adzes and augers, and, like a skilled craftsman, Odysseus exuberantly went about the work of cutting and fitting the timbers.

Aboard the raft, when it was finished, the goddess placed a skin of wine and another of water. Plenteous food of all sorts she also put there for Odysseus to enjoy. Then, when all was set, she bathed him, rubbing his skin with fragrant oils, and dressed him with kingly clothes and bade him farewell. She told him the stars by which to set his course, then stirred a gentle breeze to head him on his way.

Because he was partaking of sacrifices among the Aithiopians, remotest of all people, earth-girdling Poseidon did not know that his son's blinder was once more at sea. For seventeen days favorable winds swept the raft across the wine-dark waves; Odysseus, unable to sleep for excitement, held steady hand upon the tiller, navigating the craft by the stars in the cloudless heavens. On the eighteenth day he came into sight of the mountains of the Phaiacians, who, the Daughter of Atlas has told him, would take him on the last short leg of his journey to Ithaca.

It was on that day also that Poseidon, returning from Aithiopia, finally spied the son of Laertes and became exceedingly wroth. Waving his trident, the great unruly God of the Sea whipped up sudden gales and troubled the surface of the deep. He gathered black clouds quickly overhead. Though day, it was soon as night all about. Odysseus's knees became weak and his heart sank within him.

His vessel was now at the mercy of the raging, merciless sea; it spun round, its tiller was wrenched from his hands, the mast broke like a dead twig, sail and yardarm crashed into the churning waters, and ere long he too was carried down into their murky depths. Shedding the clothes that Calypso had given him, he fought his way to the surface and swam to what was left of his raft.

The storm did not abate for two days and two nights. Swimming, clinging to splintered timbers, Odysseus managed to survive its incomparable fury. When at last the winds subsided and the sea became calm, he sighted land not far off. With the relief of one passing the feverish crisis of a dread disease, he began with bold strokes to swim toward the shore. Nearer, he heard the surf crashing against the rocks, and once more despair filled his heart. Drained of strength, bereft of spirit, he cried out to the undying gods for mercy and swam in desperate hope of some protected haven.

Bright-eyed Athene guided him to the mouth of a river where no rocks were. He dragged himself upon the shore, kissed the firm ground, and, for shelter against the chill of approaching night, crawled under two bushes and covered himself with a thick blanket of leaves. The Daughter of Zeus then closed his eyelids and brought sweet sleep upon him to give him relief from his bone-weary fatigue. He did not know that he had found the land of the Phaiacians.

Shortly after dawn that next morning, Nausicaa, daughter to King Alcinoos, approached the place where Odysseus slept. Prompted by Athene, she had come to the river's mouth with her maidens to wash some of her dainty things in its clear, sparkling waters. Tasks accomplished, the girls gamboled along the river bank. It was their play that soon awakened the slumbering son of Laertes, who, rising and suddenly remembering his nakedness, quickly broke a leafy bough from one of the bushes to hide his manly parts before venturing out toward the maidens.

Only Nausicaa did not run at the sight of him. And so it was that, keeping his distance, he told her his plight and begged for clothing so that he might go into the city. In kindly tones she answered him and then called to her maidens. "Come back here, you silly girls," she said. "Bring food and drink for this stranger and a mantle to clothe him with, for such as he are in the care of Zeus."

The girls cautiously came out of their distant places of hiding and did as their mistress commanded them. When Odysseus had refreshed himself and donned the mantle, Nausicaa led him to the city and to her father Alcinoos's palace. There too he was received with such hospitality as befits a people dear to the hearts of the undying gods.

To King Alcinoos and his court the son of Laertes related all that had happened to him since he departed the smouldering ruins of Priam's city. His audience hung upon his every word. Wine flowed freely among the company, and Alcinoos gave commands that oxen be slaughtered and the tables be set with fruits and other good things to eat. In cordial turnabout, he had his singer, Demodocos by name, sing the tale of how slow-witted Hephaistos entrapped his wife Aphrodite and Ares in his great four-poster bed.

278

When the festivities in Odysseus's honor were over, King Alcinoos placed him aboard one of his own ships laden with such gifts, we are told, that his lost booty from Troy was meager by comparison. The Phaiacian king then said good-bye as if to a dear lifelong friend and bade his men commence rowing. Wearied, the godlike son of Laertes lay down upon a blanket in the stern and quickly fell asleep.

He did not awaken even when they beached the ship in one of the inlets of his beloved Ithaca. Without stirring him, the Phaiacian seamen lifted him carefully on the blanket out of the ship onto his home soil. Then, after heaping all the treasures Alcinoos had given him beside an olive tree next to him, they quietly headed back to their own country.

A much angered Poseidon, however, saw to it that they never reached their desired destination. In the very harbor from which they had embarked, with families and fellow countrymen looking on, the unruly earth-girdling god turned their vessel suddenly to stone, the tip of which juts up in the harbor to this day, stark reminder of offended deity.

When Odysseus woke up, he did not know the place was Ithaca, for mist obscured the landscape. It was Athene, coming upon him soon disguised as a shepherd, who told him where he was. Lest the shepherd prove loose-lipped and noise abroad his return prematurely, he did not identify himself but said rather that he was a stranger to the land, a refugee from Crete.

The gray-eyed Daughter of Zeus, gradually shedding her disguise, laughed at his guile. "You cunning rogue," she said to him. "It would take a god to out-perform you, but such you should have recognized now speaks to you."

"You gods have shape-changing powers. I have but my wits," replied Odysseus. "But I should have known you would not be far off."

"Nor have I ever been far off, son of Laertes," she told him.

"This is truly then Ithaca, my native land?"

With a stroke of her hand, the bright-eyed Daughter of Zeus brushed aside the mist to reveal to the king the familiar marks of his long-pined-for kingdom. "Take heed," she quickly cautioned him, however. "You must not run to see your wife. Hide your treasures in this cave over here, and let your presence be known only to those I say. So close to your goal, you can easily lose all."

When Odysseus had carried all the gifts the Phaiacians had given him into the cave, the goddess sat him down at the foot of the olive tree and told him about his wife's suitors who had turned his kingdom into an anarchy. For three years, it seems, the upstart lords of the region had camped in the royal palace as though it were their own. Above a hundred of them were there in all. No one dared send them on their way.

It was to court Penelope they had come, to vie for her husband's bed and throne, but like a pack of undisciplined ruffians they caroused long into the night, every night, swilling down Odysseus's best wines and stuffing their paunches with roasted meats and then boldly commanding the palace servants to fetch them more. Not a few of the maid servants had they taken for their mistresses, and now most recently they plotted to murder prince Telemachos, Odysseus's son, as soon as he should return from the mainland.

"And so, godlike son of Laertes, plan how to render these suitors their due before you barge through the doors of your own palace," Athene cautioned him. "You could as surely be cut down in your own halls as Agamemnon was in his."

She then gave him the clothes and aspect of a beggar and bade him go to the faithful swineherd Eumaios and abide with him until she could bring his son to him. This he did, though he did not reveal himself to the swineherd right away. In no way, however, did Eumaios withhold from him any of the generosity and courtesy civilized men have from time immemorial lavished upon strangers. In the meantime, the bright-eyed goddess sped off to Sparta to fetch stalwart Telemachos, who had gone to the mainland to inquire of Menelaos and Nestor what they might know of his father's whereabouts.

"Noble Telemachos," she said to him, when those about him were overcome by sleep, "it is time you were on your way. Your mother is being pressed now by her own father to choose one of the suitors. She cannot hold out much longer. Several of them plan to ambush you. Return, therefore, to your country by a different route and go to the hut of Eumaios, the swineherd. Then send him in secret to Penelope to tell her you are home."

Thus it was that the goddess who sprang from Zeus's head brought long-wandering Odysseus and his stalwart son at last together in the cottage of the swineherd Eumaios. Never in a thousand years, though, would Telemachos have guessed that the many-wrinkled old beggar in the hut was actually his father, nor did Odysseus disclose his identity until after the swineherd had left to bear to Penelope the news of her son's return. Then it was that the goddess touched him with her wand to give him the godlike stature and appearance of his true self.

Telemachos backed away in astonishment. "Surely I stand in the presence of a heavenly being," he said. "Be kind, and rich will be the gifts and sacrifices I will heap upon you."

"Not a god am I," said Odysseus, "but your father." Then he fell upon his son's shoulder and kissed him and wept uncontrollably.

When the young man was sure it was indeed his father, he embraced him mightily and wept as well. Odysseus and his son then sat down together; the father told of all that had come to pass with him, and Telemachos described the situation at the palace. They each rejoiced in the company of the other, father and dear son, and many more were the tears that fell from both their eyes. By the time Eumaios returned, however, the gray-eyed Daughter of Zeus had transformed Odysseus once more into the likeness of a beggar.

Telemachos left first for the palace; Odysseus and Eumaios shortly thereafter. While on their way, the son of Laertes and the swineherd encountered haughty Melanthios, royal goatherd and now traitor to his king, for he valued the suitors' praise above what was right. He was taking the choicest animals of his herds to the palace for the suitors' dinner.

"Disgusting swineherd," he jeered, "where are you leading this sickly wild pig? Means he to loiter at the suitors' tables? Stools, not morsels, will they throw at the sorry likes of him!"

Then to make his point the impious goatherd let drive the toe of his boot into Odysseus's mid-section. Odysseus was minded to crush the life from the insolent man right then and there, but he checked his impulses and continued passively toward the palace with Eumaios.

Near the dung piles not far from the palace gates lay Argos, an aged hound that Odysseus himself had raised from a pup. Time was when the young men from the court took him into the forests to hunt rabbits and wild goats and deer; now he was sprawled, emaciated and vermin-infested, next to the manure. When Odysseus came near, the dog perked his ears to the sound of his master's voice and struggled to get up but could not. Wagging his tail, he stretched out to lick the hand that years before had so often stroked his fur. The son of Laertes hastened past him and, turning his head aside, brushed a tear from his eye. Argos looked after his master, then was quickly overtaken by gentle death.

Inside the familiar palace walls, Odysseus went to all the suitors and begged bread of them. This he did to test who was worthy and who was not. "Who is this?" they asked among themselves. "And whence comes he?"

Melanthios, the goatherd, then rose up and said, "Eumaios over there, the swineherd, brought him here. I saw them on the way."

Antinoos, most brazen of the suitors, called out to Eumaios, "Have we not already enough beggars, foul swineherd, that you should have thought better than to bring yet another to devour your master's substance?"

"Strangers, noble Antinoos," said the swineherd in his own defense, "are always taken in by good men throughout the world."

When Odysseus came to Antinoos, however, to beg a loaf of bread, the arrogant suitor seized a footstool from under the table and with it struck him on the back of his right shoulder. "Shameless beggar!" he cried. "You'll not want to be making your rounds here again very soon I suspect." Odysseus gritted his teeth and like a rock stood there and did not kill the man on the spot as he was moved to do.

Penelope in her chambers was told of Antinoos's treatment of the stranger. "Bring the stranger here," she said. "In his wanderings he may have heard something of Odysseus."

Before the son of Laertes could be brought to his wife, however, he was accosted by a quarrelsome beggar whom the young men called Iros. More massive than the other beggars thereabouts, a brute with inexhaustible appetite, he lorded it over his fellows. "On your way, old man," he snarled at Odysseus. "They're nodding for me to throw you out. Can't you see? It'd be a pity if I had to thrash an old relic like you."

"There's enough here for both of us," replied Odysseus. "Do not anger me."

"Our wild pig has a sharp tongue," Iros said, glancing at the suitors. "We'll see how well he talks with his teeth on the ground."

"A roasted goat's paunch to the winner!" shouted Antinoos.

Iros swung first, landing a blow to Odysseus's shoulder. The son of Laertes could have at that moment sent the insolent wretch into the netherworld and indeed was tempted to do just that; but, loath to raise anyone's suspicions, he merely cuffed him with a much restrained blow across the jaw below his ear. Gore and blood shot from the beggar's mouth as he went sprawling to the ground. He made no move to get up but rather writhed where he lay and roared in pain and, after some moments, searched his mouth for his teeth.

Odysseus was then taken into the presence of his ever prudent wife. Only by great strength of will did he not cast off his beggar's garb and rise to full stature before her. As it was, lest a word or unguarded smile unwittingly give him away, he continued to play out the part of his disguise, though his heart seemed to burst.

"What is your city, stranger?" asked Penelope. "And who are your parents?"

"A man of many griefs am I," he answered. "Do not, I pray, dredge up painful memories by asking of my parents and home country."

"You are not the only one to suffer," she said next. "Life fled from me when my husband Odysseus boarded his ship for Troy; he has not returned. Then came all these noblemen from round about to court me against my will. They had no respect for anything, and soon I had to resort to subterfuges. 'Young men,' I told them, 'it is fit I should choose one of you to wed, but first I must weave a shroud for the great Laertes, whose days must now be few. It is my sacred duty.' And so I set up my loom and began to weave. Each day I wove and each night undid the day's work. For three years I thus kept them at bay, until one night, alerted by my serving girls, faithless bitches, they caught me unraveling the yarn. Both they and my parents have hounded me to make my decision ever since."

"Your husband Odysseus I once met," he told her. "He was on his way to Priam's Troy and took harbor on our island. I gave him gifts."

Tears formed in the lovely Penelope's eyes. "Oh, tell me of him. What was he wearing?"

Many-wiled Odysseus then described the purple mantle he had worn so long ago, clasped together with a brooch of gold. The intricate workmanship on the face of the brooch he also described and then spoke of his godlike appearance then.

"The purple mantle I gave him myself and also the brooch," said Penelope. "But, alas, I shall never see him again."

"Oh, you shall, good lady," he told her. "I have heard he is alive and not far hence. Ere long you will have him back home with you in Ithaca."

Whether or not in those moments Penelope guessed that the man before her was the one for whose return she had yearned for twenty years no one really knows. Every bit the woman that he was the man, his counterpart in every way, his complement, perfect mate, she well might have, though she gave no indication. When they had finished their conversation, she ordered her servants to wash his feet and tend to his needs.

It was Eurycleia, the nurse who had held Odysseus in her hands the day he was born and looked after him through his childhood, that came with basin and towels then to bathe his feet. Bent by years was she now. As she stooped to do her service, she studied him closely. "How like my master Odysseus you seem," she said.

"Men have told me so," he answered.

The old woman busied herself washing first one foot and lower leg, then the other. Just above the knee of one leg Odysseus had a scar, purple vestige of an encounter with a savage curve-tusked boar in his youth; aged Eurycleia ran her fingers over this place. Then of a sudden she let the foot drop into the basin so that water spilled on the floor. Her ancient eyes blurred by tears, she raised her hand and stroked his chin. "My dearest child," she said.

He grabbed her firmly. "Good mother, do not destroy me by giving me away," he said sternly. "Hold your peace!"

"Why this tone of voice with me, my child?" she answered him. "I am as resolute as you. Have no fear of betrayal. I will be your confederate and tell you who here has dishonored you and who has not."

When the old woman had finished washing his feet and rubbing into them aromatic oils, Odysseus moved close to the fire where Penelope was sitting. "Kind stranger, let me tell you something before I retire," she said to him. "Tomorrow may be for me the most evil of days, for I will announce a contest for which I myself am to be the winner's trophy. Twelve ax heads will be set up in a row in the great hall so that the handle holes will all be in a line. Whoever can string my husband's bow and shoot an arrow through all twelve axes, him will I marry."

"Before that happens, most honored lady," Odysseus told her, "the son of Laertes will surely appear."

"Gladly would I listen to you longer, good stranger, but men must sometimes sleep. The gods have made us so," she said. And thereupon she went to her own bedchamber and, as was her habit, wept for Odysseus until the bright-eyed Daughter of Zeus closed her eyes with sweet sleep.

The suitors had already gathered in the great hall that next morning and had for some time sported themselves by hurling jibes at Telemachos when the prudent Penelope came into the huge room with Odysseus's bow and quiver of arrows. A hush fell upon the place as she began to explain the contest with the axes. "You want to marry me," she told them. "This is your chance. Step forward and string the bow of the man whose place you would take. He always did it with strength to spare." She then ordered the swineherd Eumaios to set up the axes and hand his master's bow to the suitors.

"This handsome bow may not be so easily strung," said Antinoos. "As a child I once saw Odysseus. The likes of him is not among us."

"Let us not anticipate excuses. Get on with the contest," called out the lordly Telemachos, leaping forward and taking charge of the setting up of the axes so that all the holes were in a line. Then he took the bow and strove to string it himself, but Odysseus from the side with his eyes motioned for him to desist and pass it on to the suitors.

Leodes, despised by his fellow suitors as well as the whole household, was the first to try his hand with the bow. He strained mightily but to no avail. Each of the other suitors tried in turn to draw the string on the polished bow, but none approached the strength needed for the task. Antinoos himself and Eurymachos, chief among the suitors, waited till last.

As Eurymachos, that suitor who had counseled the others to lie in wait to kill Telemachos upon his return to Ithaca, advanced to test his strength with the bow, Odysseus, still in beggar's rags, edged close to Eumaios and his faithful cowherd Philoitios, who had come to the palace in the night. "Would you two fight for Odysseus, if suddenly he were to appear upon this scene?" he asked them.

"Were he to step into this place," answered the cowherd, "you would not believe the strength I could muster for his sake." Eumaios said the same. Then it was the son of Laertes revealed himself to the two servants, drawing the rags from the purple scar above his knee to give them proof. Both men by their emotions were rendered speechless.

"Take control of yourselves, and listen to what you must do," Odysseus told them. "Eumaios, bring me the bow when the last of the suitors has failed to string it. And you, good Philoitios, make sure the courtyard gates are firmly bolted. Both of you then come and take your places beside me. Telemachos and I have already locked up all the palace arms, and the worthy Eurycleia has shut up the faithless serving girls. Our moment is at hand."

Even as he spoke, Eurymachos strained with all his might to draw the bowstring; but, though he turned the bow near the fire to warm it, he could not bring the loop to the notches. Throwing it down in rage, he said, "It is bad enough to be rejected in marriage. What need have we for this humiliation on top of it?"

"Well said, Eurymachos," ventured Antinoos, afraid now himself to try the bow. "It is time now to raise our cups and bid the wine-pourer keep them filled. Another time, perhaps when we have curried Apollo's favor with sacrifices, we will continue this contest with the bow."

Then spoke Odysseus. "Wise words," he said. "Another time would be better. Pass then the handsome bow to me that I might test my strength and see how much or how little the years have left me."

"Be content with the food you're given, wretch!" snapped Antinoos. "Do not try the patience of younger men."

"Are you afraid he will win me, Antinoos?" chided Penelope.

"To let him try would be a disgrace to us all," Eurymachos answered her.

"If he strings it, I will but give him a sword and javelin and perhaps some sandals for his feet. I shan't marry him, if that's your worry," she replied. "Now pass him the bow."

Lordly Telemachos then said to Penelope, "Let the bow be my concern, dear mother. Why don't you go to your quarters and work at your loom or some such thing and let me tend to the manly matters hereabouts."

Penelope stood for an instant as if in disbelief of her son's words, then quickly left the hall. Eumaios picked up the bow and brought it to Odysseus. He and the cowherd then slipped out of the hall to secure the doors.

As a singer stretches a new string over the pegs of his lyre, even so Odysseus, seated upon a stool, drew the stout bowstring effortlessly over the notches of the magnificent bow. Having done so, he twanged the string to test it. The suitors, their mouths agape, turned crimson. Without standing, the son of Laertes next fitted an arrow into the bowstring and took careful aim. His shaft whizzed on a line through all twelve axes.

"The moment has come, Telemachos," he then said, "for these gentlemen to taste the bitter wine they so richly deserve. Let us get on with the music and dancing."

In an instant his lordly son was at his side, clad in glistening armor, with a two-edged sword about his waist and a bronze-tipped spear held firmly in his right hand. Casting off his rags, Odysseus sprang to the doorway and grabbed up the quiver of arrows.

Antinoos, not comprehending the situation, was raising a two-handled goblet of wine to his lips. The son of Laertes quickly drew back his bowstring again, this time leveling his arrow at this suitor he despised the most. His aim once more was true. The shaft passed cleanly through the soft part of Antinoos's throat. As he lurched to one side, his leg whipped out and knocked over the table. Blood spurted from his throat and nostrils, mixing with the spilled wine and spraying the bread and meat with gore.

The other suitors rose at once from their chairs and peered about at the walls for shields or spears, but all had been taken down. "You killed the most excellent man of all Ithaca," they shouted. "Now answer for it with your own life."

"You curs!" cried out Odysseus. "Did you not think I would return from Troy? How dared you lay waste my home and turn my serving girls into your whores and deviously court my wife while I yet lived?"

"Rush him, good comrades, or he will kill us all," said Eurymachos, unsheathing his sword. Odysseus's arrow, however, stayed his charge, striking him in the chest next to the nipple, penetrating deep into his liver. He fell across a table, scattering the bread and knocking several goblets of wine to the floor. Another also charged with drawn blade, but the spirited Telemachos drove his spear through the man's ribs.

Father and son stood beneath the broad lintel of the great hall's main entrance, blocking any escape by that route. All other doors had been barred save one, a small passageway at the far end of the hall. It was by this passage that the goatherd Melanthios slipped out to scour the palace for weapons. He was able to find several shields and spears and a like number of plume-topped helmets. These he brought back to the suitors, who quickly raised them in defiance of Odysseus; then he went back to search for more. He never returned, for Eumaios and Philoitios discovered him and bound him and left him suspended from a rope in a storeroom.

The swineherd and cowherd then went back to the hall to take their places at their master's side. Odysseus, seeing some of the suitors now armed, had no small misgivings as to their chances when all of his arrows were spent and the fighting became close. Four they were against more than a hundred. However, at that moment, disguised as his old friend Mentor, the bright-eyed Daughter of Zeus appeared beside him.

"Kill Odysseus, and the day is ours!" shouted one of the suitors. He and five others then cast their spears simultaneously at the son of Laertes. All six weapons went awry.

"Now it's our turn," said the king of Ithaca, and he and his companions hurled their spears into the thick of the suitors. Four men fell, never to rise again.

Another exchange of spears resulted in scratches for Telemachos and the swineherd but in death for another four suitors. It was as though the hands of some god and goddess were guiding the bronze-tipped shafts. Odysseus's arrows also sped true to their marks. No longer did any among the suitors call for his fellows to charge, but rather they all shrank back and sought protection from the shields procured by Melanthios. Darting into their midst, Odysseus and the other three wreaked havoc upon them. Their shields were, alas, no protection against the flashing swords and spears of the vengeance-bent men.

Only the minstrel Phemios, unwilling singer for the suitors, and the herald Medon of all those in the hall were spared the avenging fury of the foursome. Slicks of black blood were everywhere about on the floor; the walls were caked with gore as are the walls of a slaughterhouse. "Bring me Eurycleia," said Odysseus to his son.

When the old woman came into the hall, she was nonplussed with amazement. As a great lion fresh from the slaughter of some farmer's flock stands amidst his kill, the length of his body splattered with gore and filth, blood still dripping from his breast and out either side of his jaws, even so did Odysseus seem to his one-time nurse. Black slime lay thick upon his arms and legs.

"Do not gloat, old woman," he said to her. "I take no joy in this. They had no regard for the gods or any man and so have paid the price for their villainy. Now tell me this: Which of the serving girls have proven false, and which have you found loyal?"

"Of the fifty who card wool and serve our needs," she told him, "twelve have become insolent with my mistress and me and have disgraced themselves with the suitors."

"Send me those twelve. We have work for them," he said.

When the girls arrived, he set them to the task of cleaning the hall. Their faces aflood with tears, wailing loudly, they first helped Eumaios and the cowherd Philoitios carry the bodies of the suitors out into the courtyard. Next they washed the tables and chairs with sponges and water. Then, after Telemachos and the herdsmen had scraped the floor with shovels, Odysseus ordered the girls to gather up the scrapings and dump them outside.

His house once more set in order, the Ithacan king herded the unfaithful servants into the courtyard, where his son Telemachos had strung a thick rope taut between two columns. A noose was cast about each girl's neck and then drawn up over the taut rope until her feet no longer touched the ground. Like birds caught in snares, they dangled from the thick rope, finding death when all they wanted was endless diversion. The hated Melanthios was likewise dragged down to the courtyard and rendered a gruesome death for all the malice he had done.

Only after he had lighted fires and purged the house with the fumes of brimstone did godlike Odysseus allow the old nurse Eurycleia to awaken Penelope, over whose eyes Athene had cast deep sleep. No happier chore had the aged woman ever been given. "Wake up, dear child," she said, standing at the head of her mistress's bed. "Your beloved Odysseus has come home and already has dealt boldly with the suitors who devoured your substance."

"The gods have made you mad, sweet mother," replied Penelope. "Do not mock me. He will never return. Please leave."

"I do not mock anyone," Eurycleia protested. "The stranger in rags whom you met earlier—he and my master are one and the same."

Still Penelope dared not believe that Odysseus had come home to her, not even after the old nurse brought her downstairs and led her into the room where he was. From across the room she long studied him but said nothing. "Say something, dear mother," finally said Telemachos. "This, my father, has been twenty years gone from home and has at last returned, and you stand there like stone."

"Sheer amazement renders me speechless," she said. "I wince even to look at him closely lest it not be so. There are ways, though, whereby I can discover if it is really he."

"Permit me then to wash and change my clothes," said the wily son of Laertes. "Then you shall put me to whatever tests you desire." So saying, he withdrew to be bathed from head to foot by the housekeeper Eurynome and then to be anointed with scented olive oil. Over him the faithful woman placed a handsome mantle and atop that a beautiful tunic. Then upon his head the goddess Athene poured great comeliness, making him appear much larger to the eye and causing the locks to flow across his brow like an unfolding hyacinth. How like a god he looked.

When he returned to the room, however, Penelope continued to stare at him without speaking. "The heart in your bosom, woman, must be made of iron," he finally said in exasperation. "Good nurse, please prepare me a bed in the hallway, for it is certain I shall sleep alone."

"Yes, Eurycleia," said Penelope, "take that bed which Odysseus himself made into the hall and get it ready for this man." So saying, she studied his face for reaction.

"Aha," he retorted, "no man alive will soon be moving that bed. Its one bedpost is hewn from the trunk of an olive tree still rooted in the ground. Long did I toil to shape it just so and then to inlay it with silver and gold and ivory."

In an instant the lovely Penelope crossed the room to him and, weeping at last from joy rather than sorrow, threw her slender arms around her husband's neck and kissed his beloved face unceasingly. A great surge of emotion came also to Odysseus's breast. Holding his shapely wife almost as if to crush her, he too wept uncontrollably.

Neither would let the other go, and thus would they have passed the long night, entwined in one another's arms, until rosy-fingered Dawn dispelled the darkness had not Athene moved Odysseus finally to say, "I am weary with many labors, sweet wife, and more await me on the morrow. Let us go to bed." And so they did, but many were the hours yet before either of them fell asleep.

The bloody strife, however, was not at an end. Nor, had not the gods intervened, would it ever have been; for when the families of the slain suitors that next day learned of the slaughter in the great hall, they rose up against their newly returned king. Enraged, vengeance-bent, they advanced en masse against Odysseus and his allies. Old men mostly, friends of former times, not warriors at all, they nonetheless by reason of sheer numbers comprised a formidable force. Hardly had the battle begun, though, before Athene interposed herself between them. "Stop!" she shouted. "Ithacans, do not kill one another!" Then to reinforce the divine command, Zeus himself shot a smouldering thunderbolt that scorched the ground at their feet. The men quickly threw down their weapons.

Odysseus's final fate had already been prophesied by the seer Teiresias, who said that he would wander inland until he found a people who knew nothing of the sea and in their land would by sacrifices and prayers at last make his peace with Poseidon. His life thereafter would be rich and abundant and his death a gentle one. The blind Theban's prophecies, we know, always came to pass.

# After Heroes

With the passing of Neoptolemos and Telemachos and their generation (though not even these in daring and deeds approached their illustrious fathers) passed also the era of heroes. No longer did undying gods frequent the beds of mortals to sire babes fated to take on giants or become sackers of high-towered cities, nor were the sons of men inspired any longer to undertake feats of great moment. A glory had forever passed from the earth of which we today have only the faintest intimation; however, it fascinates us still, sometimes irresistibly so, haunting us with visions of what men once were, making us yearn for a time when they might be that again.

The age that followed this Second Bronze Age has been called by men the Age of Iron, which is the age in which we presently live. Neither have the men of this age found respite from a thousand sorrows by day, nor by night have they abandoned their destructive ways. When they have, at rare times, covered themselves with noble actions, they have been moved by infatuation merely rather than by patriotism or love of glory, and the deeds they have dared have seldom gone beyond the doorsteps of the women who inspired them.

It was in the early days of this age that Leandros lived and his beloved Hero. He dwelt in Abydos, not far from where proud Troy once stood; she across the Hellespont in Sestos, where she tended the altar in Aphrodite's shrine. It was at the feast of Adonis that the two first cast yearning glances the one at the other. Hero seemed to Leandros like her goddess's statue somehow come alive, and he to her like the legendary youth whose feast it was.

"Where is your home, dearest girl, that I might come there when

291

night, that patron of lovers, has cast her canopy over us?" asked the youth, after first declaring his heart.

"At cliffside by water's edge beyond the strait I dwell," she told him. "There in a tower a single servant attends me. But do not, sweet youth, imperil your life upon the pitch-black sea for my sake, for dearer than all else do you now seem to me."

"Light a lamp in your tower window," he replied. "And have no fear. Love's beacon will guide me safely to your side."

And so it was that next night that the lovely Hero, knowing her arguments useless to herself as well as to Leandros, lit a lamp and set it upon the ledge of a window overlooking the strait. On the other side of the Hellespont, Leandros saw it. Like an insect commanded by a candle's flicker, he plunged into the channel's dark waters and swam toward the light as though pulled there by its slender beams. Love gave him the strength of ten.

No less was the passion that burned within the breast of the lovely Hero. She had to restrain herself from diving into the sea so as to hasten their love by meeting him halfway. Thus, when he reached the tower, relieved, made drunk by love fancied and suddenly become imminent, the girl, like the nervous bride that in fact she was, first chattered without ceasing and then, as if catching herself, ceased her prattle altogether and busied herself with activity.

Matter-of-factly, innocently, as though it were no great thing, hospitality's routine and nothing more, she washed the brine from her beloved's stripped body, though, it must be admitted, with strokes far more carressing than she was wont to use on clay bowls. Then, with less innocence, she painstakingly anointed him from head to toe with oils of roses. All the while, he panted in short, quick breaths—whether because of his long swim or for some other reason we do not rightly know.

Preparations over, the dark-tressed maiden led Leandros to her bed, made soft with several layers of covers, and bade him rest from his labors there; then, kicking off her sandals, she slipped in beside him. Entwining her arms around him, she drew him close against her breast. "Poor foolish boy," she whispered into his ear, "banish from your mind the trials of your passage. You are here now, my brave, my sweet, and I shall reward you as I can."

No more was said nor needed to be. Nimbly, gently, he unloosed her thin shift, remaining vestige of modesty between them, her helping where he fumbled, and slid it from her shoulders. Willing worship then they rendered to Aphrodite. It was their wedding night, though, tech-

292

nically speaking, some of the customary amenities had been by their mutual consent adhered to more in spirit than letter. No marriage hymns had been sung nor bridal torches, save for the lamp in the window, lit. Hera, Goddess of Marriage, had not been invoked; nor had guests raised their cups in happy celebration. The love they shared in becoming one, however, was no less than that of couples more conventionally wed and, indeed, far greater than that of most.

And so throughout the summer their love, as most things, flourished. Each night, begun by Leandros's swim across the Hellespont, passed very much as the first. Ceremony strengthened their union; new discoveries enriched it. Nor did the strait prove to be as formidable and perilous an obstacle as it might seem to us, for the youth was a strong swimmer and the waters were invariably calm and always the lamp in the tower window guided him to the appointed place.

But winter came and with it blustery storms out of the north. Hero and Leandros ought to have given their love a holiday until spring brought calmer seas, but fate and the fires within would not have it so. Thus came the night when high waves tossed the lone swimmer randomly about and the gales extinguished the beacon in the tower. Through the long, stormy night Hero waited by her door, unaware that the lamp was out, but her beloved Leandros never knocked.

Dawn did not break brightly that next morning. Low gray clouds rather than saffron shafts of light stretched across the heavens. On the jagged cliff above the still roiling strait, the distraught, though yet lovely, Hero stood surveying the shore, the rocks, the troubled waters for some sign of her lover. Then, peering down, she saw Leandros's body on the rocks at the base of her tower. Its wounds had been washed pale clean, giving it a ghastly and spectral cast.

The girl ripped the mantle from her shoulders. "We shall not be separated, sweet love," she cried out, "no, not by death. Let the waves that bore you so oft to me now bear me to you." So saying, she cast herself in headlong plunge to the sea-lapped reef below.

Nor did love always go smoothly for the gods either in those days, for it was not too long after this that the now adult Eros, whose deadly darts had brought so much pleasure to others (and an almost equal measure of pain), himself fell in love. The story of what happened is, to say the least, an uncommon one.

It seems that in a certain city there lived a king who had three daughters. The oldest was fair to look upon and so also her next younger sister, though sufficient was the vocabulary of men to describe either one's pulchritude. But not so their sister's, the king's youngest daughter's, beauty. Neither words nor mortal comparison existed whereby one man could tell another of that maiden's extraordinary loveliness, nor could eyes comprehend such beauty, once beheld. "A second Aphrodite!" was how men spoke of her.

From far and near flocked the curious, the skeptical, the connoisseurs of comeliness to glimpse, perchance to gaze upon that far-famed beauty. And all agreed: It was as though indeed another Aphrodite had stepped upon the earth to invite their adoration. And adore her they did. Flowers were scattered at her feet wherever she went forth; with feasts and sacrifices the girl was feted. Called by Aphrodite's name, she was prayed to in the laughter-loving goddess's stead.

It was with no want of words that the real Aphrodite vented her rage over all this. "Must I, whose magic generates all life, give way to a mere mortal maiden?" she said. "Is it right that a girl should strut about in my likeness and usurp those honors due me alone? Ah, not so!"

Forthwith then did the fabled beauty of Olympos beckon her winged son to her side and led him to the city of Psyche (for that was the girl's name). Then, pointing out to him the object of her insensate fury, she said, "Riddle her with your darts, my child, and in her fire passion for mankind's sorriest soul, that one so bereft of looks and health and wealth and reputation as to have no one on earth his equal for wretchedness."

Thus speaking, the laughter-loving goddess with soft, full lips kissed her son long and generously and left him to his mischief. Eros, an arrow already in his bowstring, stealthfully advanced to scrutinize his prey more closely. Then, while he was yet a ways off, Psyche chanced to turn in his direction and face him fully. Apart from his mother, never had the youthful god beheld such beauty. His eyes widened, his divine jaw dropped, and likewise his arms; and then it was, we are told, his loin was grazed by the tip of his own dart.

For all her peerless beauty, it must be said, Psyche knew very little genuine happiness. To be sure, men gawked at her to the point of embarrassment, but only as they might also gawk at a rare butterfly or an exquisitely beautiful crown of jewels—a feast for the eyes, an exotic curio to marvel at but too unearthly to dare think of fondling. Thus, though kings and princes came from the corners of the earth to glimpse the maiden's incomparable loveliness, no one came to woo.

Great despair came over her, and the eyes that enchanted strangers by day were by night filled with tears. Sick at heart, the blessed and cursed princess soon also became sick in body. Grieved for her sake and wondering if perhaps his daughter was the object of heavenly wrath, her father betook himself to the ancient oracle at Miletos and there with gifts and sacrifices sought to know the girl's fate.

Heaping woe upon woe, these were the despised words Apollo's envoy spoke:

*On craggy cliff set your daughter down,*
*And, pray, make black, not white, her bridal gown,*
*For none of mortal seed will e'er she wed*
*But one in wild and distant regions bred:*
*A mighty, winged terror, rending hearts*
*With savage bow and fierce and fiery darts.*
*Before him quake the gods in realms sublime,*
*Brave men, and all the dead in Hades' clime.*

And so the king, his heart now nigh broken, returned home to prepare Psyche for the dreadful ceremony commanded by the god. He could not imagine what monster the oracle meant.

On the day appointed for the girl's wedding, great wailing and weeping could be heard throughout the kingdom. Torches burned low. Songs were begun as bridal hymns and ended as death laments, and heavy of heart was the train, black-clad, slow-gaited, that accompanied the doomed bride up the precipitous mountain path to a craggy ledge overlooking a wooded vale far below. Fresh torrents of tears burst forth from the girl's eyes as she came to her journey's end.

"Why I am damned I think I know," she said to her parents, after the wave of emotion had passed. "It is because men called me a second Aphrodite. Divine envy has passed sentence upon me, and so hopeless is my lot. My husband, whatever monstrosity he might be, awaits his bride. Farewell."

Thus the maiden, yet lovely in her tears, spoke and then walked to cliff's edge and calmly cast herself from it. All was over in a moment. So great was the weeping of those who watched, we are told, their torches were extinguished by the flood of their tears. Moaning uncontrollably, they started down the mountainside to their homes.

No one had peered over the cliff for the girl; but had someone done so a strange sight would have greeted his eyes, for the very moment Psyche began to fall, the West Wind caught her up, ballooning her gown with its gusts, and lowered her like an air-borne puff of cotton slowly and gently

295

into the verdant vale below. As a mother lays her new-born babe into its crib, even so the West Wind laid the beautiful princess on the soft, flowered grass beyond the base of the cliff. So wearied by her ordeal, so relieved to find herself whole, Psyche lay where she landed and soon fell asleep.

When she awoke, she felt strangely refreshed. Fears and apprehensions were replaced by curiosity and a spirit of adventure. Beyond the grassy clearing was a grove of trees, through which wound a sparkling, crystalline stream. The maiden followed the stream into the deepest part of the grove and soon came upon a palace. It was like no palace she had ever seen, resplendent and delicately designed, with ivory and sandalwood reliefs along the roof and scenes in silver on every wall, all expertly crafted as though by a god. The columns that supported the roof were of brightly burnished gold. Gems of all kinds glistened in the walkway that led to the exquisitely wrought gold-trimmed door.

Psyche, emboldened by all she saw, tripped briskly along the gem-strewn path and, trying the door and finding it unlocked, went inside. More elegantly fashioned were the walls and trim within than those without. "Who lives here?" she called out. "And whose is this palace that seems like a god's?"

"Sweet maiden, it is yours," came a voice out of nowhere. "Do not stare so in amazement. Go to your chamber and freshen yourself, and then come down for the banquet we're preparing for you. The voices you hear will be those of your servants, though none will be visible to your eyes."

Confident now that her fortunes had turned, the maiden did as the voice bade her; and when she entered the palatial dining room, she found a table spread with many meats and nectarlike wines. The dishes were served her, it seemed, of their own accord. She saw no one pass them, cover or uncover them, or, when she was finished, take them from the table; nonetheless, all these were done, as if by currents of wind within the room. When her repast was finished and the table cleared, the voices of her servants bade her remain seated on her satin-cushioned half-moon couch. Invisible fingers then struck the strings of an invisible lyre, and a thousand voices joined in the most beautiful singing ever to fall on her ears, though she still saw no one else about.

That night, as she lay in her bed pondering all that had happened, she heard a sound in the room as if someone were stirring about. Her first fear was of an intruder, but this was quickly superseded by another fear, not a fear of the natural but the supernatural. Someone was breathing near her head—whether visible or invisible she could not tell, for it was so dark she could not have seen her own hand before her face. The covers were raised, and whoever it was slipped into the bed beside her. He acted the part of her husband; and, concluding that this must certainly be who he was, she withheld nothing of herself from him but gave liberally. Shortly before dawn, however, he rose and left.

And thus did the next day also pass and the one after that and those that followed. All of her needs were promptly tended by her invisible staff, and she was free each day to gambol about the woods or explore the palace. Incomparable music followed each incomparable meal; and when all was still and dark, her husband came to her for a night of incomparable love, though invariably he left before daybreak.

Meanwhile, her mother and father grieved mightily for her, both showing age beyond their years because of their great grief. Psyche's sisters, though always secretly envious of her, also made a show of mourning and came from the foreign kingdoms where they were queens to console their parents.

"Your sisters will come mourning to the mountain," said Psyche's invisible husband one night as he held her in his arms. "Stay clear of them, lest much woe be visited upon us both."

The girl gave him her promise, but as the days wore on she could not help but think of her family and how they grieved in vain. And then too, although she had all she had ever dreamed about, she grew lonely for the sight of human faces, especially familiar ones. Her palace began to seem like a gilded prison. Soon she lost her appetite, then found no pleasure in exploring her enchanted environs; nor, lying down each night to weep, did she take delight in her husband's embrace.

"I know your heart, sweet wife," he said to her, "and the anguish that now rends it. Do as you wish, though ill may come of it."

"Only to soothe my sisters' sorrow and talk with them ever so briefly is what I want," she said.

"Give them both gifts too, as you will," he replied. "But one thing, for the sake of your happiness and mine, that you must not do is speak of me. Do that, and our love will vanish."

"A thousand deaths would I die rather than forfeit your sweet love, my husband," she answered him. "Loving you is like loving love itself."

The girl's unbridled gratitude quickly gave way to sweet passion, and so the two passed the night, neither much given to sleep, the one in the arms of the other. Before dawn's first light the young husband rose as usual and disappeared. And in mid morning Psyche excitedly greeted the new day, with her appetite and curiosities once more intact.

When she had eaten, she left her palace and went to the base of the cliff from which she had floated into her personal paradise. As she came close, she could hear her sisters' voices high above her. Both were carrying on with loud lamentation. "Oh, poor, poor Psyche!" they wailed. "What destruction your overrated beauty has brought down upon you! Poor hapless Psyche!"

"Stop crying!" Psyche called up to them. "Do not waste tears on someone alive and happy, dear sisters, but rather float hither and embrace her." She thereupon invoked the West Wind to gather them up and waft them gently down to her. Quickly the Wind complied. The sisters, not unpleased with their performance of sisterly grief, were taken back to find Psyche not only alive but, if it were possible, more radiantly beautiful than ever. More disappointment smote them when, delirious with joy, she took them to her palace and showed them all of its delicate splendors. At her insistence both bathed in her dainty baths; and, with the invisible celestial chorus providing them music, both sat at her table and tasted foods such as never had passed their lips before. Psyche told them how she was set down there by the West Wind but, remembering her promise, took care not to volunteer anything about her husband whatsoever.

When her sisters were about to leave, she gave them gifts of finely worked gold and necklaces heavy with rare jewels. Hot envy burned in both their breasts. "By the way, dear sister," said one of them, "tell us about your husband. What is he like?"

"He's a most handsome young man, tall with flaxen hair," said Psyche, thinking quickly. "The down of his first beard barely covers his chin. I wish you could meet him, but he's out hunting just now. Perhaps another time."

Accepting her answer, the sisters took their leave but, once beyond earshot, gave vent to the great pent-up malice within them. "Where is the justice of it?" snarled one. "We grew up in the same home, and look where it's got us. Both of us are married to kings with ordinary palaces, while she has all this and, by the looks, a god for husband."

"And have you ever seen anyone happier?" replied the other. "It's disgusting. She struts about as if she owned the place, getting and giving whatever she wants."

"My husband's old enough to be my father," complained the first, "bald as a gourd and feeble as a babe. Never lets me have a thing."

"And mine's an old gout-ridden goat whose idea of love-making is to have me rub his legs with smelly ointments. I'm his nurse, not his wife."

"Look at all she's got—and what measly little trinkets she gave us! Arrogant little bitch!"

"Never fear, my sister. Her day is coming. We'll see to that."

As the two conspired evil against their sister, Psyche's invisible husband, knowing of their hateful intent, did not cease from warning his young bride never to see them again, but trusting Psyche could neither comprehend nor believe what he said. "They mean to destroy you," he insisted. "If you speak with them again, they will insist you see my face. Should that happen, you will never see me again. And that would be sad, especially now."

"Why now?" asked Psyche.

"Because, my lovely wife, in your womb grows our child. Do as I say, and he will be a god; otherwise, mortal."

This news, meant to move Psyche to greater caution, had quite the opposite effect. Exhilarated by joy, she became impatient to pass word of her latest good fortune on to her family that they might rejoice with her. Weeks gave way to months; and as she felt robust life within her body, Psyche yearned all the more to talk with her two sisters one last time.

"Now is precisely the time not to see them," said her husband. "They are vile serpents; their venom is lethal. Sweet wife, take pity on yourself, the babe, and me. Do not insist on seeing them ever again."

"No evil came of it last time," she replied. "I proved then I could handle their questions. Trust me again, my dearest love. Since I cannot see your face, let me see theirs."

Thus she pled and at last, by tears and sweet entreaties, wore down her husband's resistance and won his consent to visit with her sisters one last time. When then her sisters, compelled by all the motives Psyche's husband had ascribed to them, came once more to the mountain, the overjoyed mother-to-be answered their shouts of greeting and, enjoining the services of the West Wind again, soon pressed them to her bosom with sisterly embraces. They seemed as thrilled to see her as she them, and both feigned such happiness over her pregnancy that she quite forgot her husband's warnings.

"We had hoped to meet your husband," said one of them, after they had bathed and dined.

"He's away on business," Psyche told them.

"Not hunting?" said the other sister. "Pray, describe him to us again. I forget what you said he was like."

Psyche, forgetting herself what she had told them, fumbled briefly, then said, "Oh, he's a great merchant—at the very prime of life, thick black hair just now graying at the temples, full beard. He's often away on business."

The two sisters arched their eyebrows simultaneously. "You poor, poor dear," said one, as if suddenly overcome by dark grief. "Share your hideous secret with us, for it is we who love you. The truth is that you have never laid eyes on your husband. Isn't that so?"

Psyche slowly nodded her head. "But he is a wonderful husband nonetheless," she feebly protested.

"He is the monster spoken of by Apollo's oracle," said the sister. "You are the bride, dear little sister, of a foul beast that means to use you to bear his unnatural child and then devour you. That is why he never shows his face."

"No, no!" said the innocent girl.

"We have heard of such monsters," said the other sister.

"Would we lie to you, sweet sister?" said the first. "We love you and seek only your safety."

"Whether he be beast or not I cannot say. Sweet is his embrace when he comes to me at night—that I know, but little else. What you say may be true. Both of you have always been more clever than I."

"Strike first or accept your wretched doom," the sisters said in unison.

And so it was they convinced the naive Psyche that her husband was her enemy and that she must, without delay, kill him while he slept. "Hide a dagger beneath your pillow," instructed one of them. "When he seems in deep sleep, light your lamp to show you his vile throat, then quickly with all of your strength thrust the blade to its mark. Then call to us, and we will help you bear your booty away."

That evening Psyche prepared to do as her sisters told her. Knife and lamp both in place, she waited for her husband. By reason of her anxiety he seemed longer in coming than usual; but at last, when all was dark, he crept into bed beside her and embraced her gently and kissed her and soon fell asleep. Psyche waited for what seemed half the night, though it was well under an hour, then slipped out to fetch her lamp and light it.

With lamp in one hand and dagger in the other, she stood over her husband and for the first time gazed upon his face. Of course, what she saw was the face of Eros, no monster at all but the fairest and sweetest person she had ever set eyes upon. Her hands trembled as if with palsy. The dagger slipped from the one; the lamp shook in the other so that a drop of oil from near the flame fell to the god's bared shoulder. The burning pain immediately awakened him. In a moment his deathless eyes comprehended all. Spreading his wings, he vaulted for the window, but Psyche clutched his legs and would not let go.

"Alas, dear Psyche," he said, "I betrayed my mother and now am myself betrayed in turn. Your sisters have poisoned your mind, turning you against me. Their punishment is nigh and yours too. Good-bye, my love." So saying, he wrenched himself free and flew off into the blackness of the night.

Her happiness destroyed, the girl wandered the forest for a number of days, at moments thinking to leap into a chasm or river to bring a quick end to her misery, pondering always her sisters' incredible malice toward her. Then it was that she sought out each of the sisters in turn and went to them and told them all that befell her right up to the point when Eros awakened.

"He glared at me fiercely," she told each, "and then said, 'Begone, faithless wretch! Out of my palace and out of my sight forever! In your place I will take your sister to wed in all due haste.' It was your name he spoke. Then he ordered the West Wind to wait again at the crag's edge to bear his new bride to him. My loss, dear sister, is your gain. Do not make the mistake that I made."

Each of the sisters, when she heard this, packed her belongings and hastened quickly to the lofty cliff that overlooked what had been Psyche's home. And each in turn, decked in her finest gown, called out to the wooded vale far below, "Receive, sweet Eros, a bride worthy of you. And you, great Wind of the West, bear your mistress to her domain." With that, each hurled herself from the crag and dropped like a sack of meal to the jagged rocks below, bursting upon impact.

Meanwhile, discovering her son's disobedience, a freshly enraged Aphrodite set about to visit other vengeance upon poor Psyche. The other goddesses of Olympos, taking Eros's part, tried in vain to dissuade her.

Psyche herself roamed the earth now in search of her husband. Since she was no more worthy to be called his wife, she had decided, she could at least cast herself at his feet and beg to be his loyal slave. To the temple of Demeter she went, seeking help, but the goddess out of fear of Aphrodite turned her out. Then she repaired to Hera's shrine but with the same result. And so she continued to search alone. It was not long, however, before one of the laughter-loving goddess's confederates spied Psyche going from door to door and seized her by the hair and dragged her into her mistress's presence.

When Aphrodite saw the pregnant girl, she burst into maniacal laughter. "So nice of you to drop in on your mother-in-law," she said sneeringly. "I see you thought you'd make me a grandmother. Well, forgive me, foul wench, if I don't gush with gratitude. You will not, however, go unrewarded." With that, the furious goddess fell fiercely upon her, ripping her clothes, tearing at her hair, and beating her mercilessly all over her head and body with closed fists.

Then, with the battered Psyche looking on, the goddess threw bushels of barley and millet and poppy seed and peas and lentils and beans all mixed together into a great heap in the middle of the floor. "Your famous beauty, vile creature, would scarcely now turn the head of a cowherd," said Aphrodite. "But maybe you can win one such by showing your domestic skills. Sort out those seeds and put each in a pile with its own kind. And have it all done by sundown!" The goddess then stalked out, locking the door behind her.

An ordinary humble ant, we are told, witnessed all and was moved with pity for the now nearly devastated girl. He scurried through the crack under the door to summon his fellow ants, thousands of them, to Psyche's aid. While she watched in amazement, the tiny six-legged creatures raced across the floor bearing burdens of seeds often larger than they. Well before Helios's great golden chariot disappeared beyond the mountains to the west, the grains were all separated into six piles throughout the room and Psyche's assistants had taken their leave.

Aphrodite was less than pleased when she came back, reeking with roses and tipsy from too much nectar, and found the impossible task so neatly performed. "You had help, and I know whose," she snapped, assuming that Eros had somehow come to Psyche's rescue (for indeed Eros was at that very moment in another chamber of his mother's palace). Tossing the girl a crust of bread, she retired to consider other chores and as a precaution doubled the guards at both Eros's and Psyche's doors.

Dawn's first rays had scarcely begun to penetrate the room when the laughter-loving goddess came once more to the quarters where she held her daughter-in-law prisoner. Taking the girl to the window, she said, "See the grove by the banks of yonder stream. Sheep feed there whose fleece is of purest gold. Fetch a wisp of that priceless wool, and do so without delay."

What Aphrodite did not tell Psyche was that the sheep with the golden fleeces were more savage than ravenous wolves and were wont to tear apart any and all intruders into their domain with spearlike horns and venomous fangs. Fortunately, however, as Psyche neared the grove, the reeds from the stream sang to her a timely warning: "Eschew the killer sheep and go near them not at all. The brambles along the stream where they drink have collected all the wool you'll need and will haply give the golden fibers up."

And so the girl, denied succor by two great goddesses and persecuted by a third, was once again rescued by one of the lowliest things on earth. She found where the sheep drank; and, sure enough, the thickets thereabouts sparkled with glistening strands of golden wool. In no time at all she gathered two handfuls of the precious wool.

Her immortal nemesis had not expected to see Psyche again, much less to see her back so soon and with the fruits of her errand in such measure. "So, my disgusting little trollop, he came to your rescue again, though I don't know how," said the goddess. "So be it. I have another test for your ingenuity and your courage. Follow yonder stream into that distant mountain where it begins, and you will come to a high falls, the waters of which are enchanted and icy cold. Fill this jar with the purest elixir from the middle of the falls and bring it back at once."

The falls Aphrodite spoke of were in a gorge with sheer, spray-slick granite walls on either side. Even if a skilled climber were able to scale the cliffs, certain death awaited him from the host of serpentine sentinels coiled in the rocks' crannies guarding the sacred waters, their curved fangs dripping of the deadliest venom. No mortal could have come within a half mile of the clear, sparkling cascade.

Psyche stood atop a crag overlooking the gorge, her spirits crushed utterly, her heart given up to total despair. Her climb in her condition had quite exhausted her. Should she, she wondered, make quick end to her wretched life by attempting the cliffs? Or should she go back to face the goddess's unbridled fury, of which she had had more than a goodly taste already? There was no place to run, none in which to hide.

While she thus pondered her doom, from his lofty heights in the heavens Zeus's eagle swooped down close to where Psyche was. "No chance have you, poor mortal, to capture so much as a drop from the falls below," he said to her, "for what you see is the source of the great River Styx. Even Zeus himself stays aloof from that. But, here, give me your urn and I will fill it for you." And so he did, and from the purest water in the very middle of the falls.

When Psyche returned before nightfall with the requested water, still icy cold, Aphrodite, who had made sure that Eros had stayed put throughout the day, was flabbergasted for want of explanation. "Surely you are a sorceress, you loathsome bitch, and draw your powers from realms below," she said. "So much the better for you, for I have one last favor to ask of you. Go to Persephone, who sits at grim Hades' side, and ask her to pour into this casket a day's worth of beauty, which I have recently lost from worrying over my wounded son."

Psyche took the casket from the goddess's hands, though she had no hope of being able to complete the mission. Neither did she know the way to the nether world nor how to appease its guardians to gain entrance nor, more important, to leave, once there. It was not on an errand the goddess was sending her but, as before, to her death, only this time making doubly certain of it. And so it was that the girl, bulging with life within, climbed a tower, thinking its heights would provide her the shortest route to the depths below.

As she poised herself, however, on the topmost parapet of the tower, ready to jump, a voice rang out as if from the tower itself. "Why slay yourself, foolish damsel," it said, "when your trials are almost over?"

"To Hades' dark kingdom beneath the earth am I commanded to go, and I know of no other way to get there," she replied.

At this, the tower responded by describing how Heracles had traveled to the underworld in the days of yore and before him Orpheus and Theseus. "But do not go emptyhanded into that gloom," it warned. "In each hand carry a barley cake and in your mouth two coins. At the river of the dead give the ferryman Charon one of the coins to bear you across. On the other side three-headed Cerberos guards death's portals. Throw him one of the cakes to abate his rage. Your errand achieved, appease the dog and ferryman with the remaining cake and coin to secure your safe return. Whatever you do, do not open the casket you bear hence."

Everything went as the tower had told her. Charon, totally grim and not much given to conversation, accepted her coin for the passage; and the barley cake sufficed to get her past the monstrous canine sentry. When she explained her mission, the Queen of the Underworld, Demeter's daughter, received her with astonishing cordiality, even offering her food, which she wisely refused. Taking the casket, Persephone went to her cupboard and filled it and sealed it and then handed it back. Psyche's exit from the underworld was as simple as her descent into it.

Her long journey back to Aphrodite's palace unfortunately, however, gave the unhappy Psyche time to ponder the powers of the cargo she carried. "All I need is but a drop of the celestial beauty in this casket, and my beloved will not be able to resist me," she thought.

Thereupon, within sight of her destination, she stopped and opened the sealed lid. It was not a beauty potion at all that Persephone had put in the casket but rather a death potion, for well had the Queen of the Underworld discerned her sister goddess's intent. A foul black cloud oozed

304

out of the box, enveloping the girl with its lethal Stygian fumes. She reeled in the path and fell.

Meanwhile, Eros had quite recovered from his burn and, discovering life without his sweet Psyche to be intolerable, had spread his pinions and flown out of his chamber window to look for her. His quick eye glimpsed her on the path at the very moment she opened the casket. Faster than he had ever flown before, the love-struck Son of Aphrodite sped to his fallen beloved's side. Driving the deadly clouds back into the casket with his wings and closing the lid upon them, he took his young wife into his arms and awakened her with a prick from one of his darts. "Dearest girl," he said, smiling, "when will you cease to court disaster with your curiosity? Go now and finish your errand."

Then, while Psyche proceeded to Aphrodite's palace to present her with the filled casket, Eros soared speedily to the highest pinnacle of Mount Olympos, even to the throne of great Zeus, the Father of Gods and Men himself. The Lord of Olympos greeted him by tweaking his cheek and kissing his hand. "Well, my roguish fellow, whose antics have always brought me much grief—and pleasure too, I must add—what brings you here?" said Zeus. "No great favor I trust."

Eros thereupon told him all and, with his no small powers of persuasion, implored the god whose dictates were now unquestioned law among the undying gods, speaking thus: "Let my sweet Psyche be as one of us and remain my wife, honored by all, throughout time without end."

"Your suit I will grant on one condition," the great Cloud-gatherer told him.

"And, pray, what is that?"

"That the next time you find a girl on earth of such extraordinary beauty you will save her for me," said Zeus, with a wink.

Then it was that the great Father sent wing-sandaled Hermes into every quarter of the heavens and earth to summon all of the undying gods and goddesses into council. And, dropping whatever they were doing, so they came. When all were assembled, he commanded Hermes next to bring the girl Psyche into their midst.

"Hardly one of you has not been stung at one time or another by Aphrodite's unruly son here," the wise Olympian king started. "It is time, I think you will agree, that he settle down and give us all a little peace. Impish youth ought not to last forever, even in a god. Now this girl is his choice. It is, therefore, my decree that he have her as wife forevermore and that they enjoy their love with no interference from anyone."

Beckoning Psyche to come forward, Zeus handed her a goblet filled to the brim with ambrosia. "Take this, my dear," he said, "and you shall become as deathless as we are. Your wedded bliss will never end." Then, as the girl partook of the ambrosia, he turned to Aphrodite. "There is now no more reason for your remorse. Your son is no longer stooping beneath his station. The girl is a goddess."

The council session thereupon turned into a great wedding celebration, more spirited than that of Thetis and Peleus. Bride and groom were toasted with goblets of nectar. Hephaistos cooked up a banquet; and Apollo and Pan played the sweetest of music on lyre and pipes, while the Muses in harmony sang and the mother of the bridegroom kicked up her heels in happy dance. A few weeks later, we are told, Psyche gave birth to a child, a daughter, whom they called Pleasure.

There were no more weddings that we know of at Olympos after that, nor do we know of any further instances of the gods intruding so personally into the lives of mortal men. This is not to say, however, that the gods were no longer concerned with the lots of humankind. No, by no means is it to say that.

To this day old Helios continues to make his daily trek across the sky, and great Zeus sends his fierce and gentle rains. Hera guards the hearth, though not always with consummate success, and Demeter covers the earth each spring with her incomparable greenery. And Eros, not entirely restrained by the shackles of wedlock, still ventures forth with his deadly darts. No, even in this Age of Iron, the gods of Mount Olympos have not forsaken us. They are ever moving mysteriously within, about, above, and beyond to remind us that we are only men and not gods and also that the glory of men is no small thing either.

# Index

Acastos, 86, 88, 132
Acheloos, 197–98
Achilleus, 89
  Agamemnon, 219–21
  Briseis, 226
  Hector, 242–43
  Patroclos, 237, 244
  Trojan War, 214–17
    armor, 238–39, 248
    battle, 240–41
    death, 247
    refusal to fight, 227, 231–32, 235
Acrisios, 71, 75–6, 84
Actaion, 62–4
Admete, 192–93
Adonis, 45–7
Adrastos, 167–69
Agamemnon, 206, 214
  Achilleus, 227, 239, 247–48
  Ajax, 249
  Briseis, 220, 226
  Chryseis, 218–19
  Trojan War:
    battles, 230–31, 233
    fall of Troy, 258, 260
    preparation, 216–17
    truce, 221–23
Agave, 62, 66–69
Agelaos, 207, 211–12
Aietes, 100, 117–18
  Jason, 102–06
  Plain of Ares, 110–14
Aigeus, 126, 137–39, 144
  death, 146
  Theseus, 141–42
Aigyptos, 54–7, 71
Aineias, 224, 240
Aiolos, 267

Aisacos, 206–07
Aison, 86–7, 122
Aithra, 138–39, 156, 172
Ajax (son of Oileus), 206, 216
Ajax (son of Telamon), 206, 216, 247
  battles, 226, 231, 234, 237
  madness, 248–49
Alcinoos, 278–79
Alcmene, 174–79
Althaia, 131–32, 135
Amazons, 74, 150–51, 192–93
Ambrosia, 9, 62, 306
Amphiareus, 168–69
Amphitryon, 174–80
Amycos, 94–5
Ancaios, 114–15, 133–34
Andromache, 244, 258
Andromeda, 78–84
Anticleia, 272–73
Antigone, 162, 170–72
Antilochos, 206, 237
Antinoos, 281–82, 285–86
Antiope, 150–51
Aphrodite, 5, 62, 97, 106
  Adonis, 44–7
  Alcmene, 177
  Ares, 23–6
  golden apple, 208–11
  Hephaistos, 16–17
  Jason, 101–02
  Phaidra, 153
  Psyche, 294–95, 301–06
  Trojan War, 223–25, 240
Apollo, 14, 18–21, 25, 41–2, 62, 203
  Cassandra, 213
  Chryses, 218–19
  Trojan War, 234, 240, 247
Apsyrtos, 115–18, 120

Arcadia, 2, 31, 38
Ares, 14, 24–5, 46–7, 60–2, 240
Arete, 88
Argo, 88–9
  Cyanean Rocks, 98–9
  escape, 115–18
  Lemnos, 89–91
  Phineus, 95–7
  Sirens, 120
  Talos, 121
Argonauts, 88
Argos, 52–3, 88, 91–2
Ariadne, 145–46
Artemis, 132
  Actaion, 63–4
  Agamemnon, 216–17
  Callisto, 38–40
  Heracles, 188
  Jason and Medea, 115–17
  Leto, 13–14
  Trojan War, 240
Astyanax, 258–59
Atalanta, 131–36
Athamas, 85, 99–100
Athene, 17, 22
  Argo, 88, 98–9, 119
  Bellerophon, 73
  Cadmos, 61
  Danaos, 55
  Giants, 203
  golden apples, 195, 208–10
  Jason and Medea, 101
  Odysseus, 276, 278, 281, 288, 290
  Palladion, 251
  Perseus, 77
  Trojan War, 224–26, 239, 255
Atlas, 6–7, 11, 194–95
Augeias, 102, 106, 189, 200
Autonoe, 62, 66

Bacchai, 66–9
Baucis, 47–9
Bebryces, 94–5, 117
Bellerophon, 72–5, 138
Belos, 54, 57
Briseis, 220, 226
Bronze Age, 21, 31

Cadmos, 59–62, 67, 69–70, 117, 159
Calais, 88, 96
Calchas, 217, 219, 249–50, 254–55, 259
Calliope, 88

Callisto, 38–40
Calypso, 261, 275–77
Capaneus, 167, 169
Cassandra, 212–13, 256, 258, 260
Cassiopeia, 79–80
Castor, 88, 106, 132–33, 157, 205
Celeus, 27–8
Centaurs, 87, 151–52, 199, 208, 215
Cepheus, 78–80
Cerberos, 128, 142, 157, 196–97, 304
Cerynitian hind, 187–88
Chalciope, 86, 100, 103, 106–07
Chaos, 1, 3
Charon, 128–29, 196, 304
Charybdis, 120, 273–74
Cheiron, 87–9, 123, 208, 215
Chimera, 73–4
Chryseis, 218–20
Chryses, 218–19
Circe, 119–20, 269–74
Clashing Rocks, 98–9
Clytaimestra, 205–06, 217, 219, 260
Cocalos, 148–49
Copreus, 186–90, 192–93, 195
Creon, 123–25, 161, 166, 168, 170–73,
  183
Cronos, 4–12, 21
Curetes, 7–8
Cyanean Rocks, 97–9
Cyclopes, 2–3, 5, 7, 9, 84, 263–66
Cyzicos, 91, 117

Daidalos, 143–49
Danae, 71, 75–7, 83–4
Danaos, 54–7, 71
Daphne, 41–2
Dawn, 18
Deianeira, 197–201
Deiphobos, 212, 251, 257
Delphi, 14, 51, 59, 85, 137, 159–60, 162
Demeter, 7–8, 12–13, 26–30, 301, 306
Demophoon, 28
Deucalion, 33–4, 150
Dictys, 76, 83–4
Diomedes, 191, 206, 214–16, 224–25
  battles, 230–31, 233
  spy mission, 227–28
Dionysos, 66–9, 130, 146, 203
Dolon, 228–29

Echo, 42–4
Eileithyia, 14, 178

Electryon, 84, 174–75
Eleusis, 27–8
Elpenor, 271–73
Epimetheus, 6, 11, 23, 33
Erginos, 182–83
Eris, 208
Eros, 41, 102–03, 203, 293–306
Eteocles, 162, 166–70
Eumaios, 280–82, 284–85, 287–88
Europa, 57–9
Eurycleia, 283–85, 287–89
Eurydice, 127–29, 156
Eurylochos, 269, 274
Eurymachos, 285–86
Eurynome, 13, 15
Eurypylos, 231, 235
Eurystheus, 184–86, 189–95, 197
Eurytos, 81, 152, 180, 200

Fates, 13, 131–32

Gaia, 1–5, 9, 16, 37, 194–95, 202–03
Ganymede, 208
Garden of the Hesperides, 194–95
Geryon, 193–94
Giants, 174, 180, 202–03
Glauce, 124–25
Glaucos, 94, 232
Golden Age, 6, 21
Golden Fleece, 85–8, 104–05, 112–14
Gorgons, 77–9, 82–3
Graces, 13

Hades, 7–10, 12, 46, 303–04
    Heracles, 195–96
    Odysseus, 271–72
    Orpheus, 128–29
    Peirithoos and Theseus, 156–57
    Persephone, 26–30
Haimon, 171–72
Harmonia, 62, 70
Harpies, 95–6
Hebe, 14, 203
Hecabe, 206–07, 212, 257–60
Hecate, 105, 107, 109–10
Hector, 212, 218, 222
    Achilleus, 242
    death, 243–46
    Patroclos, 237–38
    Trojan War, 225–31, 234–35
Helen, 156–57, 205–06, 211

Paris, 213, 222–23
    Trojan War, 251–52
Helios, 27, 35–7, 176, 193–94, 274–75
Helle, 85–6
Hephaistos, 15–17, 101–02
    Aphrodite, 24–6
    armor of Achilleus, 238–39
    Giants, 203
    Helios, 35–6
    Prometheus, 22, 163, 301
Hera, 7–8, 12–16
    Alcmene, 177–79
    Callisto, 40
    Echo, 42
    golden apples, 194–95
    Heracles, 183, 192, 202–03
    Io, 52, 54
    Jason, 101–03, 119
    Semele, 65–6
    Trojan War, 226, 232–33, 236, 239
Heracles, 178–80, 250, 304
    the Argo, 88–9, 91, 93–5
    death, 202–03
    Deianeira, 198–201
    madness and exile, 183–84
    Theseus, 139
    Thespios, 180–82
    Twelve labors, 157, 185–97
Hermes, 18–21, 57, 176
    Aphrodite, 25
    Argos, 53
    Baucis and Philemon, 47–8
    Deucalion and Pyrrha, 34
    Heracles, 196
    Odysseus, 270, 276
    Pandora, 23
    Paris, 209
    Persephone, 29
    Trojan War, 245
Hero, 291–93
Hesperides, 194–95
Hestia, 7–8, 12
Hippolyte, 192–93
Hippolytos, 150–51, 153–55
Hippomenes, 135–36
Hundred-handed Ones, 1–5. 7, 9–11
Hydra, 186–87
Hylas, 88, 93–4
Hyllos, 201–02
Hypermnestra, 56–7
Hypnos, 176
Hypsipyle, 89–91, 117

Iapetos, 6
Iasos, 131, 135
Icaros, 146–48
Idas, 106, 110
Idomeneus, 206, 216
Ino, 62, 66, 85
Io, 51–4
Iobates, 71–4
Iolaos, 186–87, 192, 197
Iphigeneia, 217
Iris, 234
Iron Age, 291, 306
Ismene, 162

Jason, 87–8, 101–03, 131
  Aietes, 104–06
  Apsyrtos, 115–18
  betrayal of Medea, 124–26
  Circe, 119–20
  Golden Fleece, 112–14
  Hypsipyle, 89–91
  Medea, 108–10
  Meleagros, 132, 134
  Phineus, 95–7
  Plain of Ares, 110–12
Jocasta, 159, 161–62, 164–65

Labyrinth, 144–46
Laertes, 132
Laios, 159, 161–65
Laocoon, 253, 255
Leandros, 291–93
Leda, 204–05
Lestrygonians, 268
Leto, 13–14
Libya, 54, 57
Lotus-eaters, 262
Lycaon, 31–2
Lycomedes, 158, 215
Lynceus, 56–7, 71

Machaon, 231, 250
Maia, 17–18, 40
Mainads, 130–31
Maron, 263, 265
Medea, 101–04, 107, 141–42
  Apsyrtos, 115–18
  betrayal, 124–26
  Circe, 119–20
  Golden Fleece, 112–14
  Jason, 108–10
  Pelias, 122–23

Talos, 121
Medusa, 77–9, 82–3, 196
Megara, 183–84, 197
Meleagros, 88, 106, 131–35, 196
Memphis, 54
Menelaos, 206, 211, 213–14, 216
  Helen, 256–57, 259–60
  Paris, 222–23
  Trojan War, 237
Menestheus, 157, 216, 232
Menoitios, 6, 10
Merope, 160–61
Metaneira, 27–8
Metis, 8–9, 16–17
Milky Way, 179
Minos, 59, 142–49, 190
Minotaur, 142–46, 190–91
Mnemosyne, 13
Mopsos, 88, 92, 106
Muses, 13, 62

Narcissos, 42–4
Nausicaa, 278
Nectar, 9, 62
Nemean lion, 185–86, 196
Neoptolemos, 247, 250, 256–58, 291
Nereids, 79
Nessos, 199–201
Nestor, 132–33, 216, 221, 226

Odysseus, 206, 214–16, 221
  Aiolos, 267
  Calypso, 261, 275–77
  Circe, 269–71
  Cyclops, 263–66
  Hades, 272
  Lestrygonians, 268
  Lotus-eaters, 262
  Penelope, 280–86
  Phaiacians, 278–79
  Scylla and Charybdis, 274
  Sirens, 273
  Trojan War, 226, 235
    Achilleus, 247
    Ajax, 248–49
    battles, 230–31, 233
    Heracles' bow, 250
    Palladion, 251
    spy mission, 227–28
    Trojan horse, 252–56
Oidipous, 160–66
Oineus, 131–32, 197–98

Oinone, 207, 213, 251
Olympos, Mount, 12, 75
Oracles, 14, 51, 55, 59, 85, 88, 135,
    137, 159–60, 162, 295
Orestes, 260
Orpheus, 88, 120, 127–31, 156, 304
Ouranos, 1–5, 7

Palladion, 251–52
Pallas (see Athene)
Pan, 147
Pandaros, 223–24
Pandora, 23, 82
Paris, 207, 231, 259
    Achilleus, 247
    death, 251
    golden apple, 208–11
    Helen, 212–13
    Menelaos, 222–23
    Philoctetes, 250
Parthenopaios, 168–69
Pasiphae, 143–44, 146, 190
Patroclos, 206, 220, 226–27
    armor of Achilleus, 235–36
    battle, 235–36
    death, 237, 243–44
Pegasos, 73–5
Peirithoos, 132, 150–52, 156–57, 196,
    205
Pelasgos, 55, 57
Peleus, 88–9, 100, 106, 132, 192, 207,
    214–15
Pelias, 86–8, 101, 119, 122–23
Penelope, 214, 261, 273, 276, 280,
    282–86
Pentheus, 67–9
Periboia, 144–45
Periphetes, 139–40
Persephone, 13, 26–30, 45–47, 128,
    156, 303–04
Perseus, 76–84, 174
Phaethon, 35–7
Phaiacians, 278–79
Phaidra, 150–51, 153–54
Philemon, 47–9
Philoctetes, 202, 206, 216–17, 239,
    249–51
Philoitios, 285, 287–88
Philonoe, 74–5
Phineus, 80–3
Phineus (the seer), 95–7, 99–100, 115
Phrixos, 85–6, 99–100

Pittheus, 137–40, 151
Polybos, 160–61
Polydectes, 76–7, 83
Polydeuces, 88, 94–5, 106, 132–33, 157,
    205–06
Polydoros, 62, 69, 260
Polyneices, 162, 166–70
Polyphemos, 263–66, 272
Poseidon, 7–12, 138
    Andromeda, 79
    Aphrodite, 25
    Giants, 203
    Io, 54
    Minotaur, 142
    Odysseus, 276–77, 279, 290
    Polyphemos, 272
    Theseus, 139, 145, 154
    Trojan War, 234, 239, 240
Priam, 206–07, 212, 222
    Achilleus, 241
    death, 257
    Hector's ransom, 243–46
    Sinon, 254–55
Procrustes, 141
Proitos, 71–2, 74–5
Prometheus, 11, 50, 100
    creation of man, 6
    Deucalion, 32–3
    freedom, 194, 207
    gift of fire, 21–3
Psyche, 294–306
Pyrrha, 33–4
Pythian Games, 14
Python, 13–14

Rhadamanthys, 59
Rhea, 5, 7–9
Rhesos, 228–29

Sarpedon, 59, 232, 236
Scylla, 120, 273–74
Seasons, 13
Second Bronze Age, 51, 291
Selene, 185
Semele, 62, 64–6, 69
Silver Age, 21
Sinis, 140
Sinon, 154–56
Sirens, 120, 273
Sisyphos, 128
Smyrna, 44–5
Sphinx, 161–62

Stheneboia, 71–2
Stygian Nymphs, 77–8
Styx, 21, 36, 128–29, 196, 214, 303

Talos, 121
Tantalos, 128
Tartaros, 2, 5, 7, 11–12, 127–28
Teiresias, 162–64, 171, 177, 179–80,
   271–72, 274, 290
Telamon, 88, 94, 102, 105–06, 110,
   132, 192
Telemachos, 214, 280–81, 284–89, 291
Terpsichore, 120
Teucros, 225, 232, 249
Thebes, 62, 66–9, 159
Themis, 13
Theseus, 132, 134, 139, 205
  Aigeus, 142
  Cercyon, 141
  Creon, 172–73
  Crete, 144
  exile, 153
  Hades, 156–58, 196, 304
  Hippolytos, 154–55
  King of Athens, 146, 149
  labyrinth, 145
  Peirithoos, 150–52
  Sinis, 140
Thespios, 180–82, 184
Thetis, 15–16, 207, 214–15, 220–21,
   238–39
Tiphys, 88, 91–4, 98–9
Titans, 3, 5–6, 7–12, 202
Triptolemos, 28–9
Trojan War:
  Achilleus, 240–42, 246–47
  battles, 225–26, 229–30
  fall of Troy, 257–60

Palladion, 252
Paris, 251
Patroclos, 235–37
  preparation for, 216–17
  spy missions, 227–29
  Trojan horse, 253–56
  truce, 221–23
Troy, 206, 212
Tydeus, 167–68, 206
Tyndareus, 156, 204–06, 213
Typhon, 185, 196

Wandering Rocks, 120, 273
Winds, 267–68, 295–96, 298, 301

Zetes, 88, 96
Zeus, 8–12, 136, 156, 163
  Alcmene, 174–77
  Baucis and Philemon, 47–50
  Callisto, 38–41
  Danae, 76
  Europa, 57–9
  Giants, 202–03
  Hera, 14–15
  Heracles, 178–80, 200
  Io, 51–4
  Leda, 204–05
  Leto, 13–14
  Lycaon, 31–2
  Maia, 17–18
  Metis, 16
  Minos, 145
  Odysseus, 276
  Prometheus, 21–3, 194
  Psyche, 303, 305–06
  Semele, 64–6
  Thetis and Peleus, 207–08, 220–21
  Trojan War, 225–26, 234, 236, 239